A HISTORY OF
AMERICAN HISTORY

A HISTORY OF
AMERICAN HISTORY

By

MICHAEL KRAUS, PH.D. *1901*

ASSISTANT PROFESSOR OF HISTORY
THE COLLEGE OF THE CITY OF NEW YORK

FARRAR & RINEHART, INC.
PUBLISHERS   NEW YORK

To the memory of Emile Edelstadt

ACKNOWLEDGMENTS

I wish to thank the following publishers for permission to quote from their volumes: G. P. Putnam's Sons, Moses Coit Tyler, *A History of American Literature*, *The Literary History of the American Revolution*; D. Appleton-Century Company, John B. McMaster, *History of the American People*; Henry Holt and Company, Frederick J. Turner, *The Frontier in American History*, *The Significance of Sections in American History*, *The United States, 1830-1850: The Nation and Its Sections*; Houghton Mifflin Company, John Fiske, *The American Revolution*, *The Beginnings of New England*, *The Discovery, Conquest and Colonization of America*, W. C. Ford, editor, *A Cycle of Adams Letters 1861-1865*, *Letters of Henry Adams 1858-1891*, Albert J. Beveridge, *Life of John Marshall*, *Abraham Lincoln 1809-1858*; Harcourt, Brace and Company, Vernon L. Parrington, *Main Currents in American Thought*; Yale University Press, Charles M. Andrews, *Colonial Background of the American Revolution*, *The Colonial Period of American History*; The Macmillan Company, Edward Channing, *History of the United States*, Charles A. and Mary R. Beard, *The Rise of American Civilization*, James Ford Rhodes, *History of the United States from the Compromise of 1850*, Herbert L. Osgood, *The American Colonies in the Seventeenth Century*.

PREFACE

At various times in the past the development of American historical writing has been treated in summary fashion in leading periodicals such as *The Monthly Anthology* and the *North American Review*. (George Bancroft wrote an article in the latter in 1838.) On later occasions critical essays on historians were printed in Henry B. Dawson's *Historical Magazine*. Moses Coit Tyler included historians in his study of American literature. It was not, however, until J. Franklin Jameson published his sketch of American historical writing, in 1891, that any satisfactory treatment of the subject appeared. Dr. Jameson's short study stopped before reaching the developments that occurred in the 1880's, after which time some of our most important contributions were made. John Spencer Bassett also turned his attention to the subject, and published, in 1917, *The Middle Group of American Historians,* which deals mainly with Sparks, Bancroft, and the archivist, Peter Force. Professor Marcus W. Jernegan's students at the University of Chicago have published a number of articles on historians in the *Mississippi Valley Historical Review*. Professor Arthur M. Schlesinger, in his stimulating *New Viewpoints in American History* (1922), dealt with some contributions of contemporary scholars in rewriting our history. But no survey of the whole field of American historical writing was available.

The need for such a volume became apparent to me when I was pursuing my graduate studies, and for more than a decade I kept the project before me—reading and sifting a great mass of materials. Finally I decided to include only those individuals who were influential in the creation of a tradition of historical scholarship and who have contributed most to the writing of American history in a comprehensive manner. Prescott, Motley, Lea, and other Americans who did not write on our history have been omitted. On the other hand, a few Europeans, because of their influence on the writing of our history, are discussed, for they unquestionably belong in a study of American historiography. Military, naval, constitutional, diplomatic, and religious histories are barely mentioned. I have omitted Alfred T. Mahan, who influenced international relations more than he did the writing of our history. Other historians have also been omitted because they did not fall properly within the scope of this book, but I hope I have included all those who fit into my design.

I am indebted to many of my colleagues in the History Department at the College of the City of New York who have aided me with their suggestions. Professor Nelson P. Mead and Professor Holland Thompson read portions of the material, and the entire manuscript benefited from the suggestions of Dr. Henry David. Professor Harry A. Carman of Columbia University also read a large section of the manuscript and his encouragement is deeply appreciated. I am especially indebted to Professor Allan Nevins, of Columbia University, who, despite his own busy schedule, always finds time to aid other scholars. He has been most generous and has made many valuable suggestions throughout the manuscript. I cannot easily express my gratitude for the patience and helpfulness of my wife, Vera Edelstadt, in bringing this book to completion.

M. K.

Stony Point, New York
August, 1937

CONTENTS

A HISTORY OF
AMERICAN HISTORY

I

INTRODUCTION

The writing of American history began before there were any Americans; it began in Europe long before John Smith wrote his first chronicle of events in the Jamestown colony. This historical writing depicted the exploration and settlement of a world that had outgrown its Mediterranean limitations, and it envisioned limitless fields to conquer. Sometimes it had the blustering quality of the successful Elizabethan adventurer, sometimes the pathos of quest defeated. Not until William Bradford wrote the *Plimoth Plantation* do we have a full-bodied narrative reciting the pleasures and pains of a transplanted people. To the end of the seventeenth century American historians were European emigrants or the sons of emigrants and were so near to the days of colonial foundation that they could not easily take the backward glance of the historian without also taking the forward view of the prophet. To them God had let His countenance shine upon the New World, and for decades to come historians continued to wonder at the marvel of divine intercession in the affairs of America.

With the appearance of Cotton Mather's work we

have American history by an American. Mather himself was one of the first to use the word "American." His contemporary, Robert Beverley, the Virginian, was an American historian with perhaps a more definite native stamp. This period of our historiography was almost exclusively regional in scope, and continued so down to the Revolution. Several of the colonies had matured sufficiently so that self-conscious provincials might gather the records of the earlier generations. Only a very few writers took a comprehensive view of all the colonies, and they were not provincial born. Some work of genuine merit, even when measured by later standards, was produced in this colonial period. Such writers as Thomas Prince, Thomas Hutchinson, and William Stith developed a method of historical research that was of great significance in establishing a scholarly tradition.

The War of Independence pervaded much of American historical writing in the last quarter of the eighteenth century and the first six decades of the nineteenth. Although the great struggle took shape as a glorious epic in the eyes of citizens of the young Republic, its poetry was not evident in the many prosaic treatments accorded it. Provincialism was still the hall mark of most historians; the histories of colonies had become the histories of states. Some individuals, however, such as Abiel Holmes and Timothy Pitkin, were now taking the whole of the American nation for their theme. Jared Sparks contributed the largest addition to the growing library of Revolutionary literature, but it was left for George Bancroft to transcend all other names in the popular imagination. Bancroft, like his contemporaries Prescott and Motley, belonged to the school of romantic historiography that flourished in America and Europe in mid-nineteenth century. With literary skill Bancroft captured the spirit of Jacksonian democracy and led it back to an earlier day to shed an unreal halo over the events of seventeenth- and eighteenth-century America. He was not alone in allowing a political bias to guide his pen. It should be remembered that the struggles between the Federalists and the anti-Federalists, Hamiltonians and Jeffersonians, were reflected for generations in the books of their spiritual descendants.

After the 1870's American historical writing ceased to consider itself only a branch of literature, and claimed the exalted position given to those subjects called "scientific." The influence of Von Ranke became paramount and the German seminar was transplanted to the University of Michigan, Harvard, and Johns Hopkins. As yet the teaching of history and the writing of history were, in the main, distinct crafts. Skilled amateurs with a broad humanistic culture continued to contribute the larger part of our historical narratives, as they had done before the Civil War. Within a short time this was no longer true. There were only eleven professors of history in the United States in 1880. Within two decades, however, their number greatly increased and they wrote history as well as taught it. The year 1884 was the *annus mirabilis* marking the birth of the American Historical Association and the publication of the first volume of Justin Winsor's "Narrative and Critical History of America," the open-sesame to American historical materials. The dazzling generalizations of Comte and Buckle on the unfolding of civilization stirred imaginative Americans to seek clues to their own country's development. Darwin and Spencer stimulated the intellectual world in all its phases, and American historical scholars quickly seized on so fruitful an insight as the theory of evolution.

A swarm of specialists now scoured the field and in limited surveys charted their small portions of American history. Some were courageous enough (and sufficiently long-lived) to take extended periods of our history, covering the whole of American territory. The tone of this writing was moderated and the content of the volumes was changed. The glamor of war and the intricacies of politics shared space with, or were even shunted aside by, details of institutional developments. Like their European colleagues, Americans turned to the history of civilization (*Kulturgeschichte*) and in John Bach McMaster's *History of the People of the United States,* whose first volume appeared in 1883, we have the real precursor of the social history school in America. The vastness of collected materials soon made it almost impossible for a single individual to cover the whole of American history, and so individual effort was supplemented by co-operative enterprise.

It is an old adage that we should study the past to understand the present. But we should also study the present to understand why contemporary historians interpret the past as they do. Our conception of the past has been molded by our historians whose personal tastes have chosen particular episodes around which to fashion their stories. Actually events do not live because of their occurrence; they live because writers have re-created them. Deeds themselves are short-lived, and the memory of them depends upon the skill of the narrator. Paul Revere's ride, for example, was quickly vanishing from the records in the first half of the nineteenth century when Longfellow snatched it from approaching oblivion and gave it a dramatic place in our history. The writer of prose was quick to catch the impulse communicated by the poet and Revere now rides on in spirited passages in our narratives. We may well consider the personalities as well as the works of those who have written our history, for it is often through our knowledge of the historian that we can understand the history he has written.

The Norse Voyages

In medieval lore there is mention of a lost continent in the West and of islands in the Atlantic that had disappeared beneath the sea, but the earliest authentic references to voyages of Europeans to America are found in the Icelandic Sagas. Two sagas have come down to us which have as their main theme the voyages to Vinland, but elsewhere in Icelandic literature are references to Vinland and its surroundings. The two sagas are the *Saga of Eric the Red,* considered the more dependable source for the Norse voyages, and the "Flatey Book," of the *Vinland History of the Flat Island Book (Flatey-jarbók).* These works, as written down, are later than Adam of Bremen's *Description of the Northerly Lands* (c. 1070). Adam, a writer on ecclesiastical history, had lived for a while at the court of the Danish king where he learned about Vinland, its grapevines and its wheatfields.[1] Adam of Bremen's manuscript is the first to use the name Vinland; the king of Denmark, Svend Estridson, "spoke of an island in that ocean discovered by many, which is called Vinland, for the reason that vines grow wild there, which yields the best of wine. Moreover that grain unsown grows there abundantly is not a fabulous fancy, but, from the accounts of the Danes, we know it be a fact."

The voyage of Leif, son of Eric, from Norway, and the discoveries that he made in 1000, are told in the *Saga of Eric the Red;* "Leif put to sea when his ship was ready for the voyage. For a long time he was tossed about upon the ocean, and came upon lands of which he had previously had no knowledge. There were self-sown wheat fields and vines growing there. There were also

[1] Matthias Thórdarson, *The Vinland Voyages* (N. Y., 1930), pp. 56, 57, note 64.

those trees there which are called mansur [maple] and of all these they took specimens. Some of the timbers were so large that they were used in building. Leif found men upon a wreck, and took them home with him, and procured quarters for them all during the winter. In this wise he showed his nobleness and goodness . . . and he was called Leif the Lucky ever after. Leif landed in Ericsforth, and then went home to Brattahlid (Greenland); he was well-received by everyone." [2] The *Flat Island Book* says of the return: "A cargo sufficient for the ship was cut and when the spring came, they made their ship ready, and sailed away; and from its products Leif gave the land a name, and called it Wineland." [3] It appears from the Eric saga that Leif did not name the country, but that it got its name of Vinland later, from the people of Greenland who seem to have spoken frequently of the new region.

In the Eric Saga we are told that "there began to be much talk at Brattahlid, to the effect that Wineland the Good should be explored, for, it was said, that country must be possessed of many goodly qualities. And so it came to pass, that Karlsefni and Snorri fitted out their ship, for the purpose of going in search of that country. . . ." This was in the spring of 1003. More of the narrative centers around the personality and accomplishments of Thorfinn Karlsefni than around Eric and his children, and hence the saga has sometimes been called after the name of Thorfinn. "They had in all one hundred and sixty men (and women) when they sailed to the Western Settlement, and thence to Bear Island. Thence they bore away to the southward. . . ." The Norsemen saw many wild beasts and a heavily wooded region which they called "Markland" (forest-land). Messengers were

[2] J. F. Jameson, ed., "Original Narratives of Early American History," *The Northmen, Columbus and Cabot* (N. Y., 1906), pp. 25, 26.
[3] *Ibid.*, p. 53.

sent to seek out the land, and when they returned "one of them carried a bunch of grapes, and the other an ear of new-sown wheat." [4]

These voyagers had arrived with livestock prepared for a permanent settlement, and "They remained there that winter. No snow came there, and all of their livestock lived by grazing." [5] The Norse engaged in trade with the natives, whom they called "Skrellings," exchanging bits of red cloth for furskins. "It so happened, that a bull, which belonged to Karlsefni and his people, ran out from the woods, bellowing loudly. This so terrified the Skrellings, that they sped out to their canoes, and then rowed away to the southward along the coast." When they came back, they were in a belligerent mood and a battle ensued between them and the Norse. "It now seemed clear to Karlsefni and his people, that although the country thereabouts was attractive, their life would be one of constant dread and turmoil by reason of the (hostility of the) inhabitants of the country, so they forthwith prepared to leave, and determined to return to their own country."

The consensus of modern opinion is that Leif Ericson and Thorfinn Karlsefni landed somewhere near the New England coast. The number of people who went with Thorfinn and their comparatively elaborate preparation indicate that they were planning to stay. Apparently the hostility of the natives was too much of a handicap. The unexpected bellowing of a Norse bull, it has been amusingly suggested, delayed the settlement of America for five hundred years.[6]

[4] *Ibid.*, p. 33.
[5] *Ibid.*, p. 37.
[6] G. M. Gathorne-Hardy, *The Norse Discoverers of America: The Wineland Sagas* (Oxford, 1920), Part II.

Early Histories of America

The Norse sagas contain the earliest historical narratives of settlement in America. Between these and the narratives of later centuries there is scarcely any continuity. Not until the works of Spanish historians appear do we have the beginning of a chain of narration which links up with our own day. Memories of adventure were still fresh when narrators wrote of the discovery and settlement of new lands. Their style had varying degrees of excellence but all their publications had a subject matter of novel interest.

It was fortunate, for American history, that printing had already been developed when Columbus announced his discovery. The manuscript records that disseminated the knowledge of earlier discoveries to a handful of scholars are scanty indeed when compared with the many printed accounts of voyages in the great era of exploration. A consciousness of the value of high achievement permeates the records of Peter Martyr and Hakluyt, and the literary discoveries made by Hakluyt are a fit counterpart to the far-flung geographical discoveries made by his heroes. Quite early, Spanish sovereigns realized the value of these documents relating to their overseas possessions. Charles V in 1543 established the archives at Simancas which were enriched by additions from various departmental organizations. Some twenty years later Philip II, adding many manuscripts to the collection, reorganized the Simancas archives so as to make them available for historical research. Apart from the letters and journals of Columbus himself, which hardly merit the classification of a sustained historical narrative although they furnished graphic materials for such a narrative, the work of Peter Martyr ranks him as the first historian of the newly discovered world.

Pietro Martire d'Anghera, better known as Peter Martyr, was born in Italy about 1457. Some thirty years later, after a career as student and teacher in Italy, he was established in Spain under favorable auspices, and there he was actively employed in diplomacy by the rulers of the vast empire. Martyr was, from the first, alive to the meaning of the great deeds achieved by Columbus and his fellow voyagers whom he knew and interviewed personally. To a friend, Count John Borromeo in Milan, he wrote on October 20, 1494, "I have begun to write a work concerning this great discovery. If I am suffered to live I shall omit nothing worthy of being recorded. . . . At all events I shall supply the learned world, in undertaking the history of great things, with a vast sea of new material." The letters that Martyr wrote to his friends about the discoveries were at length elaborated into the chapters that formed his history.[7] Martyr was appointed court historiographer in 1520, but the "first decade" of his *History of the New World* had appeared a number of years before, in an unauthorized version in Venice in 1504, and in an accredited issue in 1511. The whole work consisted of eight decades, but only four of these appeared in print before his death in 1526. Four years later the history appeared in its complete form. In addition to the information he received at first hand from the discoverers themselves, Martyr had access to official documents which enabled him to fill out important details in his narrative. His inclusion of fantastic items was no reflection on Martyr's worth as a historian, because for centuries after his death almost anything was believed of this "western hemisphere"—a phrase he originated.[8]

Of great significance in the historiography of the

[7] J. B. Thacher, *Christopher Columbus* (3 vols., N. Y., 1903-1904), Vol. I.

[8] See also F. A. MacNutt, *De Orbe Novo: The Eight Decades of Peter Martyr D'Anghera* (N. Y., 1912).

new world is the work of the Apostle to the Indies, Bartolomé de Las Casas, who went to Española (Haiti) in the first years of the sixteenth century. As a religious figure he performed a valuable missionary service to the Indians, for whose salvation he labored mightily. Devastatingly critical of Spanish cruelties to the natives, his *Short Relation of the Destruction of the Indies* was a highly colored disclosure of the brutalities that accompanied European expansion. Incidentally, Las Casas' booklet, reprinted frequently elsewhere in Europe, served as efficient propaganda against the Spaniards. The work that associates him more directly with historians of America is the *Historia de las Indias* begun in 1527 while Las Casas was still resident in Española. More than thirty years later, when he was approaching his ninetieth year, he was still at work on his history. The book remained in manuscript form for over three centuries, not appearing till the last quarter of the nineteenth century, but many scholars made use of it before its publication gave it wider circulation. The most intense period of Las Casas' literary life followed his return from America in 1549, when his writings gained in volume although primarily concerned with the same subject—defense of the Indians' welfare.[9] Despite the exaggerations that marked much of Las Casas' work, his history has continued to be of great value for the student. Personally acquainted with many of the early discoverers, he had in his possession Columbus' papers and other documents which have since disappeared. These made of his work a great storehouse where subsequent historians found the materials for their narratives; in the second volume of his history, for example, Las Casas included the journal of Columbus' third voyage.

Las Casas enjoined his executors from publishing his book until at least forty years after his death. Antonio de

[9] F. A. MacNutt, *Bartolomé de Las Casas* (N. Y., 1909).

Herrera saw it in manuscript, however, and made generous use of it, omitting the criticisms directed by Las Casas at colonists and explorers, in his *Historia General de los Castellanos en las Islas, y Tierra firme del mar oceano* (1601-1615). The *General History of the Indies,* as it is known, includes the story of the discovery to the year 1554. In his position as historiographer to the Indies there were available to Herrera innumerable sources of information (many of which have since been lost), and thus his work took on a comprehensiveness that gives it great importance.

It opens with the opinions of ancient peoples on the world outside of Europe and then proceeds to give the reasons why Columbus thought of finding a new world. This sort of opening is similar to that adopted by later historians who, like Herrera, wrote a chronological history. The first "decade," as each division is called, ends with 1514, and the second, which refers at length to Balboa, ends with 1520. The third, covering the period of Cortes, ends with 1526, and the fourth, five years later. In 1615 Herrera published the fifth part of the history which carries the narrative to 1536; the next decade, with material on Cabeca de Vaca, de Soto, Pizarro and others, ends with 1541. The seventh and eighth decades carry the story, respectively, to 1546 and 1554. A very large part of the work is on the discoveries and activities of the conquistadors; there is little on life in the new world, administration, or similar matters. This deficiency is to a degree compensated for by a short *Descripcion de las Indias Occidentales* which was published at the same time as the *General History.*

At the time that Las Casas was writing his history, another work was in progress under the authorship of Gonzalo Fernando de Oviedo y Valdes. As a young page at court, Oviedo had seen the reception accorded Columbus on his triumphant return in 1493, and his later career was largely associated with the new world. He held several important positions in the colonies, and was named chief chronicler of the Indies in 1532. Three years later a part of his *Historia General y Natural de las Indias* . . . was published. Complete publication awaited action by the Spanish Royal Academy of History in 1851, which issued it in four volumes with a biography and critical notes.

Oviedo wrote on the flora and fauna of the West Indies, and the natural resources of the continent, but a large proportion of political history was also included. The historian had royal authority to command the necessary documents from the governors of the colonial provinces, and, generally, he went about his task with judgment; his materials, however, appear rather to have mastered him. There is a lack of proportion in the narration of events that sometimes makes it difficult to follow him with interest. His learning was encyclopedic: "nothing was hidden to his penetrating view," observes his biographer and editor.[10] Washington Irving, however, thought that Oviedo was less to be depended upon for the history of Columbus' voyages than for those of lesser note.[11] Like other early works, Oviedo's was more valuable to the composers of later narratives, as a body of material, than as a finished product in itself.

Other historians celebrated more particularly the achievements of some of the better-known conquerors. The conquest of Mexico by Cortes is recorded by Francisco Lopez de Gomara in his *Chronicle of New Spain,* largely an elaborated biography of the conqueror. Gomara also wrote a *History of the Indies,* which is concerned chiefly with Columbus and the Peruvian conquest. The environment of his youth, Seville (where he was born in 1510), with all the richness of its associations stimu-

---

10 See edn. 1851-1855, p. lxxxiii.
11 Irving's *Christopher Columbus,* edn. 1850, III, 429.

lated him to write the history of the new world. Gomara's works were among the earliest written and had great contemporary fame, but his relationship to Cortes—he was the conqueror's secretary—and his uncritical acceptance of information, led him to make biased interpretations. An old companion in arms with Cortes, Bernal Diaz, sought to correct Gomara's inaccuracies. His work, *A True History of the Conquest of New Spain,* marked with a vigorous personal flavor, was issued in 1632 (3 vols.). Pizarro's adventure was chronicled at his order by Francisco de Xerez in the *True Narrative of the Conquest of Peru* in 1534, and at a later date, 1605, de Soto's story was published in Garcilasso's *History of Florida.*

Translations of Spanish works soon informed the rest of Europe of the stirring events across the seas, and within a short time collections of voyages were made so that the reader had easier access to these reports. The most famous of these collections in the sixteenth century was the work of the Italian, Giovanni Battista Ramusio, perhaps the greatest geographer of his day. He devoted a volume in his series, ''Delle Navigationi et Viaggi,'' to American voyages. Ramusio's publication, said Henry Harrisse, that close student of the literature of discovery, opened a new era in the literary history of voyages and navigation. Through Ramusio's efforts reports of some of the most illustrious of the voyages were preserved.[12] He was in correspondence with some of the Spanish historians, and in conjunction with Oviedo brought out in 1534, at Venice, a summary history of the Indies. Ramusio was the first man of mature judgment and wide scholarship to edit the narratives of the early voyages. The link between Ramusio and the English students of the history of discovery was direct and immediate.[13]

[12] *Bibliotheca Americana Vetustissima* (N. Y., 1866), p. 457.
[13] See pamphlet, A. C. Wilgus, ''The Histories of Hispanic America,'' Pan-American Union Bibliographical Series, No. 9 (1932).

Richard Hakluyt

English activity in colonial expansion had been slow in starting, but once interest was aroused in lands beyond the seas it was vigorous in its growth. A knowledge of important events was expected of the cultivated individual, for one of the marks of a well-read man was his familiarity with the facts of history. History also had a utilitarian value, for it was thought to produce the wise man. One of the significant aspects of culture in Elizabethan England was the emphasis on history, and the demand for historical literature was so great that summaries and condensations of larger works were published for the popular taste. The greatness of England and the spread of her power overseas were celebrated in numerous histories written in Tudor and Stuart days. The English bourgeoisie experienced a very rapid development in the sixteenth century, and to the need for broader economic opportunities perceived by a rising capitalist class was joined a swelling national confidence in England's imperial destiny.

Richard Eden was the first Englishman of importance to acquaint his countrymen with the new worlds in the East and West. In 1553 he published his *Treatise of the New India,* a translation of some material from Sebastian Muenster's *Cosmography.* A more elaborate work of Eden's appeared two years later, *The Decades of the New World.* This publication used the title of Peter Martyr's earlier work, of which it was a translation, and Eden took the first three of Martyr's decades which told the story of Spanish discoveries to 1521. To this material Eden added the account of Magellan's circumnavigation of the world, and the narratives of the new world from the later Spanish historians, Oviedo and Gomara. There is also an account, translated from the Italian, of the

Cabot voyages to America, as well as matter on Russia and Africa. Eden's work made available for the first time in England a considerable body of information on overseas territories, and it acquainted the English with the most important historians of new world discoveries. "With this book," says George B. Parks, "England woke to the new day." [14] Some years after this publication, Thomas Hariot, who was an adviser to Raleigh and had been with the latter's colony in the new world, wrote *A briefe and true report of the New found land of Virginia* (1588). But more important than all others in awakening Englishmen to the significance of overseas empire was Richard Hakluyt. The expansion of England was in large part, says his biographer, due in fact to the stimulus given it by his publications. Perhaps no historian again wielded so much power over a nation's destiny until the nineteenth century, when the German writers helped create Bismarck's empire, and Captain Alfred T. Mahan stimulated a naval race among the great powers.

It was from a cousin who was a lawyer and adviser to merchant companies that Richard Hakluyt received the guidance that directed his own interests to geography. Hakluyt was the adviser of Gilbert and Raleigh, and the history of his career is largely "the intellectual history of the beginnings of the British Empire." [15] As a young man at Oxford, where he prepared for the ministry, Hakluyt tells us that he read the narratives of voyages in several languages, and as he grew older he became acquainted with the leading merchants and mariners of England who valued greatly his geographical knowledge. When he was thirty years of age, in 1582, Hakluyt published his *Divers Voyages touching the discovery of America*. . . . Two years later Raleigh chose him to pre-

[14] G. B. Parks, *Richard Hakluyt and the English Voyages* (N. Y., 1928), p. 23.
[15] *Ibid.*, p. 2.

sent his case to the Queen, which he did in a paper called *The Discourse on the Western Planting*. About this time Hakluyt went to France to search for materials about explorations and trading expeditions to America so that he might better inform his own countrymen about conditions in the new world. In Paris he found the documents that related the story of French colonization in America, and in 1587 Hakluyt published a new Latin edition of the complete *Decades* of Peter Martyr, who was praised for "launching the history [of America] from its cradle." Hakluyt had already become in fact an organizer of geographical publishing, and his enthusiasm resulted in the publication of a number of works with which his name was not openly associated.

The work which established Hakluyt's fame is *The principall Navigations, Voiages and Discoveries of the English nation . . .* , published in 1589 and usually called *The English Voyages*. Gradually Hakluyt had evolved a plan to include in one work the whole record of English maritime activity from Arthur's day to the Armada. In this volume, however, actually only a tenth of the material was on the travels before Columbus, and most of that came from the imaginative Sir John Mandeville; the bulk of the book was on English enterprise in the sixteenth century. With the exception of the medieval travel accounts, Hakluyt's narratives were based on eyewitness accounts. As interesting as many of the narratives he printed was his own story of a two-hundred-mile trip he made to consult the last survivor of an early voyage to Newfoundland. In this work Hakluyt collected the documents that recorded the beginning of the expansion of the English people. It was a large volume of some seven hundred thousand words. While a small part of it was taken from material already printed, the major portion was published from manuscripts, an indication of the enormous labor Hakluyt performed in merely collecting his scattered materials. This book earned for Hakluyt a place with the Italian compiler Ramusio, whose work, the greatest of his age, had inspired the Englishman's collection.

Between 1598 and 1600, Hakluyt's last great work appeared. This was an enlargement of the *Voyages* with the title *The Principal Navigations, Voyages, Traffics, and Discoveries of the English Nation,* and was printed in three volumes. All his earlier publications were included in this comprehensive work, which had more than twice as much material as that in the book published in 1589. The greatly increased volume of matter in Hakluyt's masterpiece, especially on the regions westward, was a reflection of the expansion of English maritime activity in the decade between 1589 and 1598. The Englishman who in 1575 had access to a few scattered books of travel in his native tongue, by 1600 had a full library which made him a sharer in spirit of English imperial enterprise. For the most part Hakluyt did not include the records of the organizations at home; rather his volumes recorded the movements of English traders and discoverers overseas.

Hakluyt's *Principal Navigations* is unquestionably one of the most important works of the century, and it was the famous British historian Froude who once called it the "prose epic of the modern English nation." But Hakluyt, as has already been intimated, was more than merely the historian of English expansion overseas. The settlement of England's first colony in America owed much to his energy, and he was listed among the directors of the Virginia Company. Because he focused England's interest on the lands overseas, his place is high among her empire builders.

On the death of Hakluyt a large mass of his manuscripts passed into the hands of a fellow clergyman, Samuel Purchas, who seized the opportunity to carry on the work of the illustrious editor. Purchas had been an

unknown country curate until 1613, when he published his
historical compilation, *Purchas his Pilgrimage*. The book
brought him immediate preferment in the Church and
won him the acquaintance of Hakluyt. In 1625 Purchas
continued the great collection of his predecessor in a five-
volume work published with the title *Purchas his Pil-
grimes*. To Hakluyt's papers as a nucleus Purchas added
records of universal travel as well as of the latest English
voyages, and the large collection was brought out with a
dedication to the king. Unlike Hakluyt, who was not only a
historian but also a participant in the process of English
expansion, Purchas was essentially an antiquarian, with
little understanding of the chronicles he compiled. Although his work vastly enlarged Hakluyt's last publication of the *Voyages,* being more than twice as long, yet
with all his industry and sincerity, he had not Hakluyt's
ability and failed to make the best use of the materials bequeathed to him. Nevertheless his work, along with that of
Hakluyt, was of inestimable service for later historians of
the period who could not have written the volumes they
did without the compilations of the two clergymen. In
the nineteenth century the distinguished historian Jared
Sparks remarked that to Purchas and Hakluyt his generation was "still indebted as were our ancestors two
hundred years ago, for almost all the knowledge which
we possess respecting the early discoveries in America."[16]

[16] *North American Review* (October, 1829), p. 432. See in addition to
Parks's biography of Hakluyt, the spirited essay by Professor Walter
Raleigh in his *Early English Voyages* (Glasgow, 1910).

II

THE SEVENTEENTH CENTURY

With the names of John Smith, William Bradford, and John Winthrop we reach a period when the leaders of affairs in America write their own story of its early colonization and development. The new settlers brought with them the strong Elizabethan tradition that emphasized historical writing. As pioneers in a new land, however, they were less concerned with past events than with history in the making. Autobiographical to a great extent, their chronicles often have the flavor of freshness that comes from first discovery. Hidden away in a corner of the universe as so many of the early settlers felt themselves to be, they were often apologetic for detailing events that were big with meaning for them but which they felt would be thought trivial by the world outside. Cotton Mather once expressed this thought in his characteristic manner: "If a war between us and a handful of Indians do appear no more than a Batrachomyomachie [battle of frogs and mice] to the world abroad, yet unto us at home it hath been considerable enough to make a history."[1]

[1] *Magnalia Christi Americana*, II, 581.

The Argonauts were conscious of the importance of their work for posterity and they were fearful lest the record vanish. Their children's children must know of the dangers met and overcome in settling a new world in order that they might be proud of their forbears and draw courage from their courage. The need to render unto God a statement of actions done in His name, and the desire to thank Him for beneficent guidance also found an outlet in our earliest histories. The monastic chroniclers of medieval Europe had their successors in New England's long line of minister historians. That strain, however, was weak in Southern historical writing, for the religious element was of less significance in the settlement of the South. Virginia's historians had closer ties with Hakluyt, who savored more freely this mundane world.

John Smith

''Knight of the bounding main'' might be posterity's titular award to so undistinguished a name as John Smith. He was of the breed of Elizabethan adventurers whose exploits have been preserved by Hakluyt, and though he was a captain in the pursuit of gain, so glamorous an air of adventure surrounded his chase that we might consider him rather a contemporary of Don Quixote than a man of business.

As a young man Smith served in the armies of several European countries on different occasions, and for a short time was also slave to a Turkish pasha. The exciting experiences of his later Virginia days were the continuation of a life of hair-raising escapades begun in his youth. When Smith returned to England in 1604 he became interested in the proposals for a Virginia settlement. He served in an executive capacity in the young colony, but his temper was such that he was soon drawn into a bitter controversy over the management of Jamestown. After leaving the colony, Captain Smith was employed by the Plymouth Company, for whom he rendered services sufficiently distinguished to merit his inclusion among the founders of the Bay Colony. From 1615 to his death, in 1631, Smith lived in England, turning his restless hand to the composition of several works of literature.

His strictly historical works are two: *A True Relation of such occurrences and accidents of noate as hath happened in Virginia since the first planting of that Colony, which is now resident in the South part thereof, till the last return from thence* and, a more extensive book, *The Generall Historie of Virginia, New-england and the Summer Isles,* a brief continuation of which was printed as the second part of his *True Travels, Adventures, and Observation.* The other works of John Smith are of a descriptive character and though not historical writings they are of importance as historical material.

A True Relation, as the first of these works is known, was written in the Virginia wilderness in May, 1608, a year after the founding of the colony. Captain Nelson, in the ship "Phoenix," carried the manuscript to England, where it was published in London in August. It was a brief tract of some thirty pages, bearing none of the marks of literary polish, which its hasty preparation would have prevented even if there had been the intent. And yet with its crudities, it is a racy, virile English that bespeaks kinship with the picturesque language of Elizabethan adventurers. Smith tells of his personal experiences (the pronoun "I" is prominent in his writings), and the small space devoted to the events in Jamestown is colored with his strong bias against some fellow members on the Council. Smith's sharp censure of those whom he considered his opponents, and his glowing accounts of his own achievements render him suspect as a witness of unquestioned veracity. With simple clarity, however, he tells of the uncertainties of settlement, and of the dwindling food supply and how it was replenished: "Our provision being now within twentie dayes spent, the Indians brought us great store both of Corne and bread ready made; and also there came such aboundance of Fowles into the Rivers, as greatly refreshed our weake estates, whereuppon many of our weake men were presently able to goe abroad. As yet we had no houses to cover us, our Tents were rotten and our Cabbins worse then nought; our best commoditie was Yron which we made into little chissels. The president and Captaine Martins sicknes, constrayned me to be Cape Marchant, and yet to spare no paines in making houses for the company; who notwithstanding our misery, little ceased their mallice, grudging, and muttering."

Smith's encounters with the Indians fill most of the space, and although he was sometimes worsted, it was only great odds that overcame him; he was always a match for his opponents if there were not too many of them. Some Indians were in the habit of stealing things from the fort, and one day four of them arrived together with intent to steal. "I bade them depart," Smith writes, "but flourishing their swords, they seemed to defend what they could catch but out of our hands; his [i.e., the Indian leader's] pride urged me to turne him from amongst us, whereat he offred to strike me with his sword: which I prevented, striking him first. The rest offring to revenge the blow, received such an incounter, and fled. The better to affright them, I pursued them with five or six shot, and so chased them out of the Island."

Smith closes his *True Relation* on a note of optimism that subsequent events did not always justify: "We now remaining being in good health, all our men wel contented, free from mutinies, in love one with another and as we hope in a continuall peace with the Indians: where

we doubt not but by Gods gracious assistance, and the adventurers willing minds and speedie furtherance to so
honorable an action, in after times to see our Nation to
enjoy a Country, not onely exceeding pleasant for habitation, but also a very profitable for comerce in generall; no
doubt pleasing to almightie God, honourable to our gracious Soveraigne, and commodious generally to the whole
Kingdome.''

In 1612, at Oxford, appeared another publication
connected with Smith's name. It was *A Map of Virginia:
with a Description of the Countrey, . . . whereunto is
annexed the proceedings of those Colonies.* . . . Smith
wrote the ''Description'' while his friends combined to
write the ''proceedings.'' The men who had been opposed
to Captain Smith in the colony receive short shrift in the
narrative.

The description that Smith gave of Virginia did for
the southern colony what Wood's *New Englands Prospect* was to do for the northern colony twenty years later.
''The North Cape is called Cape Charles in honour of the
worthy Duke of Yorke,'' writes Smith. ''Within is a
country that may have the prerogative over the most
pleasant places of Europe, Asia, Africa, or America, for
large and pleasant navigable rivers: heaven and earth
never agreed better to frame a place for mans habitation
being of our constitutions, were it fully manured and inhabited by industrious people.'' Smith writes of a tribe
of giant Indians, the ''Sasquesahanocks'': ''Those are
the most strange people of all those Countries, both in
language and attire; for their language it may well be-
seeme their proportions, sounding from them, as it were
a great voice in a vault, or cave, as an Eccho.'' After
pointing out England's dependence on other countries for
various commodities, Smith strikes a true mercantilist
note in his plea for the colonization of Virginia: ''Then

how much hath Virginia the prerogative of all those flor-
ishing kingdomes for the benefit of our land, whenas
within one hundred miles all are to bee had, either ready
provided by nature, or else to bee prepared, were there
but industrious men to labour. Only of Copper wee may
doubt is wanting, but there is good probabilitie that both
copper and better minerals are there to be had for their
labor. Other countries have it. So then here is a place a
nurse for souldiers, a practise for marriners, a trade for
marchants, a reward for the good, and that which is most
of all, a businesse (most acceptable to God) to bring such
poore infidels to the true knowledge of God and his holy
Gospell.'' This description of the new colony reveals
Smith as a careful observer of nature, topography, and
Indian customs, although like others he ignored the difficulties of settlement.

While the *Generall Historie,* published in 1624, exhibited many of the animosities that characterized the
True Relation, it earned Smith a place among American
historians. This folio volume includes some maps and two
hundred and fifty pages, but of these only seventy-five
were written by Smith and nearly all were reprints from
three of his descriptive books. The remaining pages in
the *Generall Historie* were edited or compiled by Smith.

In Smith's last book, the *Advertisements for unex-
perienced Planters of New England, or anywhere,*[2] are
two chapters on the settlement of Salem and Charlton
(Charlestown), and a narrative of the condition of the
colony some months after the emigration of Winthrop.
Judged from a literary standard, this work is probably
his best.

*The Generall Historie of Virginia, New-england and
the Summer Isles* is divided into six books. The first tells
of the early voyages to America and of the attempts by

[2] London, 1631.

the English to settle there; the second is a reprint, with variations, of the *Map of Virginia,* first part; the third is a reprint of the second part of the *Map of Virginia* (1612); the fourth continues the history of the Virginia colony from the autumn of 1609 to the dissolution of the Virginia Company in 1624; the fifth includes the history of the Bermuda Islands from 1593 to 1624; and the last book is a history of New England made up of reprints of Smith's earlier writings, *A Description of New England* (1616) and *New England's Trials,* to which were added some other material.

The fourth book, the most interesting to the student of American historical writing, is but a compilation of other men's narratives, enlivened by the comments of Smith. L. G. Tyler, the editor of Smith's writings, stated that the Captain's work could not be called "history in the true sense for two reasons: first because the journals of the Virginia Company . . . were never consulted; and second, because of the extreme partisan character of the writers."

At the very beginning of this book is a graphic description of the "starving time," when the settlers were reduced to eating roots, nuts, berries, some even resorting to cannibalism. Here Smith told, rather simply, the story of his rescue by Pocahontas, which many modern students largely discredit, although recently Charles M. Andrews expressed faith in its likelihood. "After some six weeks fatting amongst those Salvage Courtiers, at the minute of my execution, she hazarded the beating out of her owne braines to save mine; and not onely that, but so prevailed with her father, that I was safely conducted to Jamestowne." The introduction of Negro slavery, so momentous for later America, is mentioned casually under date of 1619: "About the last of August came in a dutch man of warre that sold us twenty Negars." A number of pages vividly describe the terrible Indian massacre of 1622 which reduced the twelve hundred settlers of the colony by over three hundred. It seems amazing to the modern reader that the colony was still able to exist after so critical a loss.

As a kind of valedictory Smith penned these parting lines at the close of the fourth book: "Thus far I have travelled in this Wildernesse of Virginia, not being ignorant for all my paines this discourse will be wrested, tossed and turned as many waies as there is leaves; that I have writ too much of some, too little of others and many such like objections. To such I must answer, in the Companies name, I was requested to doe it, if any have concealed their approved experiences from my knowledge, they must excuse me; as for every fatherles or stolne relation, or whole volumes of sofisticated rehearsals, I leave them to the charge of them that desire them. I thanke God I never undertooke any thing yet (wherein) any could tax me of carelessnesse or dishonesty, and what is hee to whom I am indebted or troublesome? Ah were these my accusers but to change cases and places with me but 2 yeeres, or till they had done but so much as I, it may be they would judge more charitably of my imperfections. But here I must leave all to the triall of time, both my selfe, Virginia's preparations, proceedings and good events: praying to that great God the protector of all goodnesse to send them as good successe as the goodnesse of the action and Country deserveth, and my heart desireth."

It is the conclusion of Virginia's most recent and best-informed historian that Smith's works have much reliable information and that the captain was a man of real courage. A careful study of the sources now available has in the main substantiated Smith's judgment of conditions in the colony and the maladministration of the

Virginia Company.[3] The trial of time has left Smith high among those who have deserved well of posterity.[4]

EDWARD WINSLOW

Somewhat alike in spirit and purpose to the *True Relation* of John Smith was the small production from New England known as *Mourt's Relation*. There was a continuing demand at home for publications on the lands new found beyond the horizon, and leaders among the first settlers wrote their unfading narratives for eager English eyes. *Mourt's Relation,* or *Journal of the Plantation at Plymouth,* was first printed in 1622 in London and was used by Captain John Smith two years later in his own *Generall Historie.* William Bradford and Edward Winslow were the authors of this slim volume, which recorded the daily happenings of the first year in the newly planted colony. Winslow had joined the Pilgrim group at Leyden when he was about twenty-five years of age. He became an important character in Massachusetts, serving as governor of Plymouth, but his most valuable work was done in England as agent for the Bay Colony. Mourt, it is supposed, was a fellow Pilgrim in London who published the manuscript (against the will of Winslow) because he "thought it not a misse to make them [the journals] more generall." Written by the participants in the events they describe, *Mourt's Relation* is of the highest authority.

It refers to the famous Mayflower Compact in these words: "It was thought good there shoud be an association and agreement, that we should combine together in one body, and to submit to such government and gover-

[3] W. F. Craven, *Dissolution of the Virginia Company* (N. Y., 1932), p. 5.

[4] See Jarvis M. Morse, "John Smith and His Critics: A Chapter in Colonial Historiography," *Journal of Southern History,* Vol. I.

nours, as we should by common consent agree to make and choose. . . .'' The sense of wonder, the contact with phenomena of nature new to him, and the caution of man in unusual surroundings are vividly present in Winslow's *Journal*. With much delight the writer chronicles the recognition and discovery of familiar and unfamiliar trees ''and the best water that ever we drunke.'' Punctuating this narrative of the infant colony are the shots of muskets and the war whoops of unfriendly Indians.

When the time came for a more permanent habitation, says the *Journal,* ''we tooke notice how many Families they were, willing all single men that had no wives to joyne with some Familie, as they thought fit, that so we might build fewer houses, which was done . . . so Lots were cast where every man should lie [build his house] which was done, and staked out.'' Adventurous searches for persons lost in the wilderness give added excitement to a story of settlement sufficiently exciting in itself. Treaties and alliances with Indian neighbors were important steps in securing the safety of the colony. ''Wee have found the Indians very faithfull in their Covenant of Peace with us; very loving and ready to pleasure us; we often goe to them and they come to us,'' says the *Journal*. Far friendlier to the Indian was this narrative of the original settlers than the work of Cotton Mather eighty years removed.[5]

WILLIAM WOOD

Although Smith and Winslow wrote descriptions of the Indians and their environment, it is their history of white settlement which mainly holds our attention. Other writers, however, had far less interest in history than in arousing enthusiasm among prospective settlers

[5] Winslow was also the author of *Good News from New England* (1624), which was a continuation of *Mourt's Relation*.

or in furnishing vicarious adventure to the fireside reader. They were anxious to bring to the attention of Europeans a knowledge of conditions to be encountered in the new world, the novelties of nature and, the most fascinating novelty of all—the Indians. An interesting example of this type of literature was *New Englands Prospect,* which appeared in London in 1634.

William Wood, its author, after four years in the newly established settlement, returned to England in 1633. His small book provided answers to the questions that many prospective emigrants were asking, and the information he supplied included unfavorable as well as favorable comments on conditions in the new world.

The book is divided into two parts; the first treats of the topography of the region, the climate, the fauna and flora, and "what provision is to be made for a Journey at Sea, and what to carry with us for our use at hand." The second is a study of the Indians and their customs. In the section on Indians, "Of their Kings government, and Subjects obedience," Wood struck a note that was to interest the critics of royalty in eighteenth-century Europe: "For though hee [the king] hath no Kingly Robes, to make him glorious in the view of his Subjects, nor dayly Guardes to secure his person, or Court-like attendance, nor sumptuous Pallaces, yet doe they yeeld all submissive subjection to him, accounting him their Soveraigne." Wood was also thinking of conditions in England when he wrote of the Indians' punishment for thieving: "For theft, as they have nothing to steale worth the life of a man, therefore they have no law to execute for trivialls; a Subject being precious in the eye of his Prince, where men are so scarce."

The subordinate part of the title of Wood's book, "A true, lively, and experimentall description . . . ," is abundantly justified, for it is a sprightly composition, with all the vigor characteristic of Elizabethan English.

Within a few years the book went through several editions; its compactness and logical organization must have appealed to the inquiring voyager. Unlike many other writers who painted the colony either all dark or all bright, depending on their prejudices, Wood included a few pages "Of the evills, and such things as are hurtfull in the Plantation." Wolves were mentioned as a danger, and particular attention was called to the rattlesnake. The "Musketoe" (mosquito) was acknowledged to be a nuisance, although Wood said he had been troubled "as much with them or some like them, in the Fen country of England." He observed that many of the early difficulties of the settler were due to his own negligence: "The root of their want sprung up in England; for many hundreds hearing of the plenty of the Country, were so much their owne foes and Countries hindrance, as to come without provision; which made things both deare and scant; wherefore let none blame the Country so much as condemne the indiscreetnesse of such as will needs run themselves upon hardship." Wood assured the voyager of freedom from want and a comfortable home, if he carried provisions enough for a year and a half, and "if he either be industrious himselfe, or have industrious agents to mannage his estate and affaires."

America was a Utopia that could be won by the man willing to work, "for all New England must be workers in some kinde," writes Wood, in a spirit peculiarly American. "So little is the poverty of the Country," he continues, "that I am perswaded if many in England which are constrained to begge their bread were there, they would live better than many doe here, that have money to buy it." It was with a clear conscience that Wood wrote the final lines to the first part of his book: "As I have observed, so doe I desire to publish what I have written, desiring it may be beneficiall to posteritie; and if any man desire to fill himselfe at that fountaine, from whence this tasting cup was taken, his own experience shall tell him as much as I have here related.''

WILLIAM BRADFORD

It is the opinion of many students that the title of father of American history belongs to William Bradford. Bradford, who was the foremost man in Plymouth Colony during his lifetime, had been among the earlier fugitives to Holland and therefore knew the history of the Pilgrims at firsthand. The history of Bradford's manuscript is itself of unusual interest. After various wanderings it found a home in the palace of the Bishop of London. The Bishop presented it in 1896 to Massachusetts, whose leading historical society published it, in 1912, in an authoritative form under the editorship of Worthington C. Ford.[6]

Bradford began writing the *History of Plimoth Plantation* about 1630, and probably completed Book I, down to the landing at Plymouth, within a year or so. Book II, which carries the narrative through 1646, was written between that year and 1650. Soon after, a list of Mayflower passengers was appended to the manuscript. Although Bradford relied mainly upon his memory, he used a letter-book of correspondence, and he had some notes and a journal of the first year of settlement.

Bradford's work was used in manuscript by later historians for over two hundred years before it was printed. It remains today the prime source for the story of the colony from the time the Mayflower sailed, and even a little earlier, down to 1646. Thomas Prince, Hubbard, Cotton Mather, and Hutchinson used Bradford's work when writing their own histories.

It not only has permanent value for American his-

[6] An earlier edition had appeared long before this time.

tory, but it also possesses a singular charm as literature which is the result of conscious artistry. The writing is unpretentious and earnest, and bespeaks an intimate acquaintance with the English Bible. It is in the same tradition with Bunyan's *Pilgrim's Progress.*[7] The rhythm of his language paid musical tribute to the memory of the deceased William Brewster: "He had this blesing added by the Lord to all the rest, to dye in his bed, in peace, amongst the mids of his freinds, who mourned & wepte over him and ministered what help & comforte they could unto him, and he againe recomforted them whilst he could." Bradford's narrative reveals as clearly as words might the ideal Pilgrim, who, though not a learned man, was a thoughtful one with a rare degree of intelligence. Under his title Bradford begins: "And first of the occasion and indusments ther unto; the which that I may truly unfould, I must begine at the very roote & rise of the same. The which I shall endevor to manefest in a plaine stile, with singular regard unto the simple trueth in all things, at least as near as my slender judgments can attaine the same."

Like his contemporaries, Bradford was certain that it was God's intercession that kept Plymouth Colony alive, although he was grateful, too, for the aid that the natives, Squanto and Samoset, offered. Amidst the seventeenth-century atmosphere of bitter theological wrangling, it is refreshing to read Bradford's tender judgment on Roger Williams: "But he is to be pitied, and prayed for, and so I shall leave the matter, and desire the Lord to shew him his errors, and reduse him into the way of truth, and give him a setled judgment and constancie in the same; for I hope he belongs to the Lord and that he will shew him mercie." The forthright character of the historian is to be seen on many pages, and

---

[7] E. F. Bradford, "Conscious Art in Bradford's *History of Plymouth Plantation*," *New England Quarterly,* Vol. I.

his unaffected simplicity shines in contrast to the frequent pomp and splendor of John Smith's self-created circumstance. There is vividness also in his writing, as his description of a storm in 1635 attests: "It blew downe many hundred thousands of trees, turning up the stronger by the roots, and breaking the hiegher pine trees of in the midle, and ye tall yonge oaks & walnut trees of good biggnes were wound like a withe, very strang and fearfull to behould."

Bradford could write with anger, too, when he related the behavior of Thomas Morton of "Meriemounte," who was "lord of misrule." Morton and his rollicking companions "also set up a May-pole, drinking and dancing aboute it many days togeather, inviting the Indean women, for their consorts, dancing and frisking togither, (like so many fairies, or furies rather) and worse practises." Apart from his critical attitude toward the personal behavior of Morton, Bradford was incensed at him because of his profitable traffic in arms with the Indians. "O the horiblenes of this vilaine!" exclaimed the historian, "how many both Dutch & English have been latly slaine by those Indeans, thus furnished." Bradford went on to appeal to "princes & parlements . . . to prevente this mischeefe . . . by some exemplerie punishmente upon some of these gaine thirstie murderers" before the Indians might overthrow the white settlements.

Bradford had cause to fear the collapse of his colony that had been born in great travail. He clearly recalled the early days of the settlement in the Dutch provinces, and enumerated the reasons why the Pilgrims became dissatisfied with conditions in Holland. They had intended moving, "not out of any newfangledness," he carefully explains, "or other such like giddie humor, by which men are often times transported to their great hurt & danger, but for sundrie weightie & solid reasons."

Among other motives was the desire for a home where the struggle of life would be less hard: "As necessitie was a taskmaster over them, so they were forced to be such, not only to their servants, but in a sorte, to their dearest children; the which as it did not a litle wound the tender harts of many a loving father & mother, so it produced likwise sundrie sad & sorowful effects. For many of their children, that were of best dispositions and gracious inclinations, having lernde to bear ye yoake in their youth, and willing to bear parte of their parents burden, were, oftentimes, so oppressed with their hevie labours, that though their minds were free and willing, yet their bodies bowed under the weight of the same, and became decreped in their early youth; the vigor of nature consumed in the very budd as it were."

The place that held greatest promise for his small group, says Bradford, "was some of those vast & unpeopled countries of America, which are fruitfull & fitt for habitation" and which was "devoyd of all civill inhabitants," having "only salvage and brutish men, which range up and downe, litle other wise than the wild beasts of the same."

Objections had been raised against removal to the new world, where famine would be their portion, where the change of diet and drinking water would bring upon them "sore sickneses, and greevous diseases." There was also the likelihood that if they escaped illness, the savage lay in wait for them in the wilderness. To these and further objections, the brave answer was made, "that all great & honourable actions are accompanied with great difficulties, and must be both enterprised and overcome with answerable courages. It was granted the dangers were great, but not desperate; the difficulties were many, but not invincible."

Then followed delays while plans were made for the voyage overseas. Bradford explains why he writes at length about the preliminaries: ''I have bene the larger in these things, and so shall crave leave in some like passages following (thoug in other things I shal labour to be more contracte,) that their children may see with what difficulties their fathers wrastled in going throug these things in their first beginnings, and how God brought them along notwithstanding all their weaknesses & infirmities. As allso that some use may be made hereof in after times by others in such like weightie imployments. . . .''

Finally they got under way and ''after longe beating at sea they fell with that land which is called Cape Cod; the which being made & certainly knowne to be it, they were not a litle joyfull.'' After some deliberation the ship was turned southward ''to finde some place aboute Hudsons river for their habitation. But after they had sailed that course aboute halfe the day, they fell amongst deangerous shoulds and roring breakers, and they were so farr intangled ther with as they conceived them selves in great danger, & the wind shrieking upon them withall, they resolved to bear up againe for the Cape [Cod] and thought themselves hapy to gett out of those dangers before night overtooke them, as by Gods providence they did. And the next day they gott into the Cape-harbor wher they ridd in saftie.''

But from the safety of ocean storms they had been delivered only to face a friendless wilderness in late fall; ''the whole countrie, full of woods & thickets, represented a wild & savage heiw.'' The last days of November and the early days of December were spent in searching out a hospitable location, and ''the 25 day [of December] begane to erecte the first house for comone use to receive them and their goods.'' Thus ends the first book of Bradford's *Plimoth Plantation.* ''The rest of this History,'' he wrote in opening the second book, ''I shall, for brevitis sake, handle by way of annalls, noteing only the heads of principall things, and passages as they fell in order of time, and may seeme to be profitable to know, or to make use of.''

The tragedy of the first winter Bradford revealed in all its horror, but he remembered also the courage that it called forth. "Ther dyed sometimes 2. or 3. of a day" during those cruel months; "that of 100. & odd persons scarce 50. remained." And of these on various occasions, only six or seven were sufficiently strong to be about and attend to the needs of the other survivors. The surprise of meeting with the Indians, Samoset and Squanto, who could speak English and who were willing to help them reap the best fruits of the new land, lighted up the gloom of the dark first winter.

Difficulties continued to beset the Pilgrims. Under date of 1622, Bradford wrote: "Now the wellecome time of harvest aproached, in which all had their hungrie bellies filled." But the harvest was insufficient, and "also much was stolne both by night & day, before it became scarce eatable & much more afterward. And though many were well whipt (when they were taken) for a few ears of corne, yet hunger made others (whom conscience did not restraine) to venture." Soon after, Bradford wrote, "God fedd them out of the sea for the most part . . ." and thus early the cod became sacred in Massachusetts. An infrequent note of humor was struck in Bradford's answers to some objections made by prospective emigrants from England. One objection was that mosquitoes were an annoyance. Bradford answered, "They are too delicate and unfitte to begine new plantations and collonies, that cannot enduer the biting of a muskeeto; we would wish such to keepe at home till at least they be muskeeto proofe."

Slowly prospering despite its hardships, the colony sent for another pastor, Charles Chansey, to assist John Reinor. Bradford then mentioned a minor controversy that ensued which illustrates the influence of environment upon religion: ''Ther fell out some differance about baptising he [Chansey] holding it ought only to be by diping, and putting the whole body under water, and that sprinkling was unlawfull. The church yeelded that immersion, or dipping, was lawfull, but in this could countrie not so conveniente.''

The sadness of age Bradford expresses with a pathos that time has not made remote. He writes of the departure of some of the settlers to found newer settlements nearby (1644) : ''And thus was this poore church left, like an anciente mother, growne olde, and forsaken of her children, (though not in their affections), yett in regarde of their bodily presence and personall helpfullness. Her anciente members being most of them worne away by death; and these of later time being like children translated into other families, and she like a widow left only trust in God. Thus she that made many rich became her selfe poore.''

Although it was not intended for publication, Bradford's work, in manuscript and in print (since the middle of the nineteenth century), has been most effective in gaining for the Pilgrims and their settlement the distinctive place they hold in the history of America and in the folklore of her people. One of the finest legacies of the Plymouth settlement was the story told by Bradford, and his words have enriched the spirit of America. A grateful posterity has endowed the Pilgrims with a wealth of virtue and accomplishment, but the myths that were created about them are less interesting than the facts of their history.

JOHN WINTHROP

It is fortunate for historical students that the dominant figures in Virginia and Plymouth wrote their narratives of the early settlement. Since a third leader added his record of the transplantation of Englishmen to Massachusetts Bay, the student of history has at his hand the story of the first settlements by those best equipped to tell it. These men were not only in a position to know the "inside" story of their communities, but all three had good judgment and sufficient literary skill to re-create for the reader the life of their day, which, but for their efforts, might have gone unrecorded.

John Winthrop, lord of the manor of Groton, was one of the most important creators of the Massachusetts Bay Colony which he served, as governor and deputy governor, for nineteen years. With far more than the limited resources at the command of the Plymouth Colony, the Puritan group initiated one of the most important mass migrations of modern times. A good part of the record of the early years of that settlement is preserved for us in Winthrop's *Journal,* known also as *The History of New England from 1630 to 1649.* It remained in manuscript form and was used by several historians of New England until 1790, when part of it was printed under the auspices of Noah Webster. After the recovery of the missing section of the *Journal,* the whole, thoroughly edited, was issued under the direction of James Savage in 1825-1826.

The disconnected annals that are Winthrop's *Journal* are less interesting than is Bradford's history, whose greater unity and narrative charm make it a more distinguished performance. In justice to Winthrop it should be noted that his writing was done in the press of a very active life, more so perhaps than was Bradford's, and it is suggested that his *Journal* was to be the basis of a more carefully written account. In some ways, too, Winthrop's humanity was less generous than Bradford's.

The work begins on board the "Arbella," "Riding at the Cowes, near the Isle of Wight," on Easter Monday,

1630. The day before Winthrop had tenderly written to
his wife: "The winde hath been against us this weeke
and more; but this day it is come faire to the North, so as
we are preparinge (by Gods assistance) to sett sayle in
the morninge . . . and now (my sweet soule) I must once
againe take my last farewell of thee in old England. It
goeth verye neere to my heart to leave thee. . . ." After
a stormy voyage, which Winthrop notes with all the detail that gladdens the lover of the sea, the Puritans
finally made port, and after a monotonous fare on board
ship, were glad to go ashore and gather "a store of fine
strawberries." The frequent references to the entrance
and departure of ships, some of them with needed corn
from Virginia, others with passengers from England, the
transfer of livestock to the new community, the toll that
wolves levied on the cattle—all these are part of the narrative of the beginnings of settlement. Sometimes there
appear references of greater moment, as when Winthrop
remarked, under date of 1632, that "this government was
. . . in the nature of a parliament." The same year, it is
noted, the governor visited his Plymouth neighbor, William Bradford, whom Winthrop thought "a very discreet
and grave man." The process of expansion is briefly referred to in March, 1633: "The governor's son, John
Winthrop, went with twelve more, to begin a plantation
at Agawam, after called Ipswich."

Under date of 1635 the annalist wrote: "The depu-
ties having conceived great danger to our state, in regard
that our magistrates, for want of positive laws, in many
cases, might proceed according to their discretions, it was
agreed that some men should be appointed to frame a
body of grounds of laws, in resemblance to a Magna
Charta, which being allowed by some of the ministers,
and the general court, should be received for fundamental laws." Along with information of a political character, Winthrop writes about the costs of cattle, corn, and

wages paid to various types of workmen. ''The scarcity
of workmen had caused them to raise their wages to an
excessive rate,'' he says (1633), and because this resulted
in increased prices of commodities, ''sometime double to
that they cost in England,'' the court ordered that car-
penters, masons, and the like, should get only two shil-
lings per day, and laborers eighteen pence. No commodity
was to cost more than four pence in the shilling above
what it would sell for in England. A very prominent
merchant, Robert Keayne, was heavily fined for taking a
profit of above six and eight pence in the shilling.

Roger Williams and Anne Hutchinson often appear
in the pages of Winthrop, who was more lenient in his
judgments upon them than were many of his contemporaries. Mrs. Hutchinson is first presented as ''a woman
of a ready wit and bold spirit'' who had ''brought over
with her two dangerous [theological] errors.'' The long
struggle with Anne Hutchinson resulted in banishment,
''but, because it was winter, they committed her to a
private house, where she was well provided, and her
friends and the elders permitted to go to her, but none
else.'' In justification of his own share in the controversy,
Winthrop wrote that ''he saw, that those brethren, etc.
were so divided from the rest of the country in their
judgment and practice, as it could not stand with the public peace, that they should continue amongst us. So, by
the example of Lot in Abraham's family, and after Hagar
and Ishmael, he saw they must be sent away.''

The growth of the colony is clearly revealed in a
reference under 1638: ''There came over this summer
twenty ships, and at least three thousand persons, so as
they were forced to look out new plantations. One was begun at Merrimack, and another four or five miles above
Concord, and another at Winicowett.'' Winthrop makes
plain the constitutional problems that the youthful settlement had to meet: ''The people,'' he wrote in 1639,

"had long desired a body of laws, and thought their condition very unsafe, while so much power rested in the discretion of magistrates''; the ''Body of Liberties'' was the result of this agitation.

In the chronicle for 1640 there is an indication of a habit of mind that had profound influence in the law-making of the colonies in after years. Thomas Dudley was chosen governor, writes Winthrop, and ''some trouble there had been in making way for his election, and it was obtained with some difficulty; for many of the elders labored much in it, fearing lest the long continuance of one man in the place should bring it to be for life, and in time, hereditary.'' Winthrop, like his contemporary, Edward Johnson, was accustomed to note special providences in favor of the Puritans, but Johnson's assertiveness is far less agreeable than the gentle piety of Winthrop. ''It is useful to observe, as we go along,'' the latter said, ''such especial providences of God as were manifested for the good of these plantations.'' In Winthrop's *Journal* may be found an amusing example of the lengths to which an intelligent man would go in his will to believe. In a room of the house belonging to the younger Winthrop, where corn was stored along with many books, one volume was made up of the Greek Testament, the psalms and the common prayer bound together. The common prayer, which the Puritans heartily disliked, was found ''eaten with mice, every leaf of it, and not any of the two other touched, nor any other of his books, though there were above a thousand.'' This, wrote Winthrop the elder, was ''a thing worthy of observation.''

Far-off events in England had serious economic effects in the New England colony during the early 1640's and caused important changes in the distribution of population. ''The sudden fall of land and cattle, and the scarcity of foreign commodities, and money, etc., with the

thin access of people from England, put many into an unsettled frame of spirit, so as they concluded there would
be no subsisting here, and accordingly they began to
hasten away, some to the West Indies, others to the
Dutch, at Long Island, etc. (for the government there invited them by fair offers), and others back for England.''
Winthrop was very much concerned over this departure
of many settlers.

In the same year, 1642, he noticed the first commencement in an English American college: ''Nine bachelors
commenced at Cambridge; they were young men of good
hope, and performed their arts, so as gave good proof of
their proficiency in the tongues and arts.'' Three years
later Winthrop wrote that ''By agreement of the commissioners [of the New England Confederation] . . . every
family in each colony gave one peck of corn or twelve
pence to the college at Cambridge.''

In 1646 an occasion arose, says Winthrop, to consider
''in what relation we stood to the state of England.'' The
remarks that follow are of great interest to the student
of American political theory who would understand some
of the ideas that appear so prominently in the eighteenth-
century Revolutionary era. Although owing ''allegiance
and subjection'' to the mother country, some New Englanders maintained they ''might be still independent in
respect of government, as Normandy, Gascoyne, etc. were,
though they had dependence upon the crown of France,
and the kings of England did homage, etc., yet in point
of government they were not dependent upon France.''
The like was true of the Hanse towns in Germany, which
were dependent upon the Empire. Another item of significance for the history of the colony was the struggle
with the remonstrant Dr. Robert Child, which was given
the long space it deserves in the *Journal*. The *Journal*
ends in the early days of 1649, the year of Winthrop's

death, with an entry characteristically referring to the "righteous hand of God" raised against a man for profaning the Sabbath.

Winthrop's *History of New England* sometimes reads like a newspaper which features sensational news rather than routine affairs: fires, shipwrecks, and sex scandals. On the other hand there is much which tells of the building of a commonwealth in a not too friendly world, relations with the Indians, with the near-by Dutch, with the French and with an England in the turmoil of revolution. In the *Journal,* which is the most valuable chronicle of the Bay Colony, are the materials for the re-creation of a society that built itself homes, schools, ships, and taverns. Scattered through it are the details, which, when grouped together, tell of the construction of a social organization more enduring than houses or ships or taverns. In the *Journal,* too, are the materials to help us judge the author, wise beyond most of his colleagues, the aristocratic servant of his people. There can be only agreement with William Hubbard, another historian of Massachusetts, who wrote of Winthrop: "A worthy gentleman, who had done good in Israel, having spent not only his whole estate . . . but his bodily strength and life, in the service of the country; not sparing, but always as the burning torch, spending. . . ."

EDWARD JOHNSON

Edward Johnson came over to New England in 1630 with Winthrop, but shortly after returned to England. In 1636, however, he came back to America to stay. He was the leading figure in the founding of Woburn four years later, and down to his death in 1672 remained one of the important personalities in his town. He was town clerk and surveyor and served in the General Court of Massachusetts. In this legislative body he met representatives of other towns whose information, added to his own intimate knowledge, enabled him to reconstruct a large part of the history of the colony.

The Wonder-Working Providence of Sion's Savior in New England, which includes events from 1628 to 1651, was Johnson's contribution to American historiography. The volume was printed under another title and without the author's name, in London, 1654, but the work has become known by the quaint title which savors so much of the seventeenth-century Johnsonian mind. The volume was written mostly in 1650 and 1651. "The author," writes his descendant and editor, J. Franklin Jameson,[8] "was convinced . . . that there had been set up in New England an ecclesiastical and civil polity more closely according with the Word of God than any other which the world had seen, and that the Lord had manifested His approval by doing marvelous things in the wilderness for these His chosen people."

Adverse reports against the colony like those of Merrymount Morton were to be combated by writings like Johnson's. The latter's was the first published history of Massachusetts, and although it does not rank with the works of Bradford and Winthrop, it was an "honest attempt of a Puritan man of affairs to set forth to his fellow-Englishmen the first twenty-three years' history of the great Puritan colony." There are many challenges to the detractors of New England, and Johnson's was the language of a crusader.

The Wonder-Working Providence, as it is generally called, is difficult reading. It is burdened by frequent rhetorical and poetic flights, and is poorly arranged and contains many errors. Throughout it speaks "the dialect which the French wittily call the *patois de Canaan.*" In Johnson there is little of the gentleness of Bradford or

[8] "Original Narratives of Early American History," *Johnson's Wonder-Working Providence.*

the culture and comparative tolerance of Winthrop. He writes history from the standpoint of the rank and file. Thoroughly orthodox, he revealed an intense partisanship, and although personally a kindly individual, the zealousness and superstition that crowded his book with special divine favors, seem to place Johnson in an era much more remote than that which produced Bradford.

The volume is divided into three books, each having numerous short chapters. Book I, Chapter XIII, gives the financial cost of migration, or as Johnson put it, "of the charges expended by this poore People, to injoy Christ in his purity of his Ordinances." "The money is all Christs," adds Johnson, "and certainly hee will take it well that his have so disposed of it to his advantage." As one might expect from so orthodox a character, Johnson's words are bitter against Anne Hutchinson. In Chapter XLV of Book I, Johnson writes "Of the civill Government in N.England, and their nurture of the people upon their tender knees." "As their [the emigrants'] whole aime in their removall from their Native Country, was to injoy the liberties of the Gospell of Christ, so in serving up civill Government they daily direct their choice to make use of such men as mostly indeavour to keepe the truths of Christ pure and unspotted."

The Puritan was a militant Christian, and the references to the "Souldiers of Christ in New England" are plentiful. In Book II, Chapter VI, "Of the gratious goodnesse of the Lord Christ, in saving his New England people, from the hand of the barbarous Indians," is a cruel description of the slaughter of the Pequot Indians. In the same book, Chapter XXII, is the classic description "Of the manner of planting Towns and Churches in N.E. . . ." with particular emphasis upon Johnson's own town of Woburn. After describing how the officials laid out the town and distributed the land, Johnson goes on "to declare how this people proceeded in religious matters, and so consequently all the Churches of Christ planted in New England, when they came once to hopes of being such a competent number of people, as might be able to maintain a Minister, they then surely seated themselves, and not before, it being as unnatural for a right N.E. man to live without an able Ministery, as for a Smith to work his iron without a fire; therefore this people that went about placing down a Town, began the foundation stone, with earnest seeking of the Lords assistance, by humbling of their souls before him in daies of prayer, and imploring his aid in so weighty a work. . . ."

Book III, Chapter VI, "Of the Lords wonder-working Providence in fitting this people with all kinds of Manufactures, and the bringing of them into the order of a common-wealth," has interesting material for Massachusetts economic and social history. Johnson writes well in discussing the failure of a local iron works: "Experience hath outstript learning here," he observes, "and the most quick-sighted in the Theory of things, have been forced to pay prety roundly to Lady Experience for filling their heads with a little of her active after-wit." At the end of this chapter he concludes: "Thus hath the Lord been pleased to turn one of the most hideous, boundless, and unknown Wildernesses in the world in an instant, as 'twere (in comparison of other work) to a well-ordered Commonwealth, and all to serve his Churches. . . ." The work ends on a note of triumph for Christianity.

At the conclusion of his first book Johnson had written: "Yet let them [i.e., critics of New England] also know the Souldiers of Christ in N.E. are not of such a pusillanimous Spirit, but . . . resolved (the Lord willing) to keepe the government our God hath given us, and for witnesse hee hath so done, let this History manifest." This history manifested the tenaciousness of the Puritan

will and indicated, as Tyler observed, that Johnson
"handled the pen as he did the sword and the broad axe
—to accomplish something with it. Unlike the historians
Winthrop and Bradford, who were themselves leading
actors on the political stage and wrote with authority on
the whole development of their respective communities,
Johnson emphasized the founding of churches and the
routine life of the lower classes. In *The Wonder-Working Providence* the virtues as well as the limitations of
the middle-class Puritan mind are laid bare. The Puritan
had great courage and daring but to dissent of any kind
his hostility was unrelenting.

NATHANIEL MORTON

Nathaniel Morton, nephew of William Bradford, had
unusual opportunities to write a history; in addition to
his kinship with the leader of the Plymouth Colony (he
used Bradford's manuscript), he was himself a member
of the official family by reason of his long tenure as clerk
of the colony court. He had been brought as a child to the
colony, and in 1645 was elected clerk of the court, a position he held to his death forty years later. He was one of
Plymouth's most important men and was reputed to
know more of the colony's history than anyone else.

The short title of Morton's history, issued in 1669, is
New England's Memorial, and its publication, said the
author, was intended for the use of present as well as
future generations. His contemporary audience was
larger than might be supposed, for the reading of history
for recreation was general among the literate public.
New Englanders had a strong civic sense, and many of
them were people with a comparatively rich intellectual
background. The proportion of university men to the
whole population was very high; the ministers in particular made every sacrifice in order to send their sons

to Harvard. Almost all of New England's literary output before 1700—tracts, pamphlets, verse, and histories— were by the Harvard-trained clergy. Because of them a continuous tradition of intellectual vitality was maintained.

Two ministers, John Higginson and Thomas Thacher, sponsored Morton's volume, pointing out that a history was much needed. "It is much to be desired," they said, "there might be extant A Compleat History of the United Colonies of New England. . . . This being not attainable for the present, nor suddenly to be expected, it is very expedient, that (while sundry of the Eldest Planters are yet living) Records and Memorials of Remarkable Providences be preserved and published, that the true Originals of these Plantations may not be lost, that New England, in all times to come, may remember the day of her smallest things, and that there may be a furniture of Materials for a true and full History in after times." The sponsors of Morton's work hoped that it would stimulate similar compositions in other colonies, and that ultimately a comprehensive history of New England would be written.

In his dedication Morton acknowledged that most of his material came from his uncle, Bradford, but other sources of information, including Winslow's *Journal,* were also available to him. The author wrote that he would not speak of the natural history of the country nor of the civilization of the Indians, because these subjects had been treated at length by other authors. Morton's history is a chronology which takes the record of Pilgrim annals through 1668. Up to 1646 the work was almost entirely an abridgment of Governor Bradford's unpublished manuscript, and this part of Morton's volume was therefore extremely valuable. The remainder of the book was largely concerned with elections, the deaths of prominent individuals, and the blights of nature on

man, animals, and crops. Like the work of Edward Johnson, Morton's narrative is strewn with poetry, and it
ends with a sermon urging the rising generation to be as
worthy as the earliest generation of founders. With the
publication of Bradford's own manuscript in the nineteenth century, Morton's work became relatively valueless, but for a long time his volume and Johnson's were
New England's standard histories. Fortunately Morton
did more than *write* history. Early in the nineteenth century a grateful student pointed to Morton's care in preserving the historical materials of Massachusetts. "Had
it not been for this attention to manuscripts . . . the
present generation," he wrote, "would have very imperfect accounts of what was done . . . in New Plymouth in
New England, when they were only in the womb of their
existence." [9]

WILLIAM HUBBARD

To the list of New England clergymen who wrote
historical narratives must be added the name of William
Hubbard, who was graduated with Harvard's first class in
1642, and later served as president of his alma mater.
He was also a leader in the opposition to the Andros government in 1687 on the issue of tax collections. Hubbard
perhaps had personal reasons for resenting tax collections; he was, it seems, a difficult person to get money
from under other circumstances as well. John Hull, the
distinguished goldsmith in Boston, on one occasion
threatened to sue Hubbard for repayment of a loan, but
neither Hull nor his heirs were ever able to collect it.[10]
The clergyman seems to have been of an easygoing nature. He was not one to put himself out unduly, for in

[9] *The Monthly Anthology,* VII, 64.
[10] Samuel Eliot Morison, *Builders of the Bay Colony* (Boston, 1930),
p. 170.

writing his history he rarely acknowledged that he had appropriated whole passages from other writers.

In 1677, while others were also at work on histories of the Indian Wars, Hubbard published a *Narrative of the Troubles with the Indians in New England,* which was reissued in England with the title *The Present State of New England.* A more important work by Hubbard was *A General History of New England from the Discovery to MDCLXXX,* which remained unpublished until 1815, although Cotton Mather, Prince, Belknap, and others had used it in manuscript.

The General Court of Massachusetts in 1682 supported Hubbard with a grant of £50 toward the completion of his history, which was in celebration of the providential guidance given to New England. In his literary diary Ezra Stiles, noted president of Yale College in the eighteenth century, classed the works of Hubbard, Bradford, and Winthrop as "the three most considerable historical accounts of the first settlement of New England." Much of Hubbard's history is in the form of annals like Winthrop's *Journal;* in fact there was little of importance added, in the period before 1650, to the material he found in Winthrop and Bradford. Chapter headings like these are characteristic: "Memorable accidents in New England from 1641 to 1646"; "Ecclesiastical affairs in New England from the year 1646 to 1651." Although Hubbard was supposed to write a chronicle of some sixty years of New England's history, the major portion of his work was devoted to the first half of the period, on which his authorities were more complete. He hurried over the following three decades to 1680. Hubbard's short last chapter is a description of New Netherland, then recently added to British possessions, and he ends his history with the remark, "a true description of the country about New York was thought necessary to be published . . . for the encouragement of any that may have a mind to remove themselves thither."[11] Although prized by students in the eighteenth century, particularly by Thomas Hutchinson, Hubbard's history was neglected by later writers. However, in recent works by Professors Morison and Andrews (the latter quotes him several times in *The Colonial Period of American History*), Hubbard is somewhat re-established in esteem.[12]

INCREASE MATHER

Increase Mather, who has been called the foremost Puritan, belonged to one of New England's first families. He took a very active part in the life of Massachusetts as an official and as a minister, as well as president of Harvard, and, like other literary New Englanders, he sought to perpetuate the record of Puritan deeds. In 1676 he wrote the *Brief History of the War with the Indians* (King Philip's War) a day-by-day chronicle of the events reported orally and by letters when the news was fresh. Mather had an eye for the dramatic and his narrative vividly pictured the struggle. In this volume Mather writes: "I earnestly wish that some effectual Course may be taken (before it be too late) that a first *History of New England* be written and published to the World. That is a thing that hath been often spoken of but was never done to this day, and yet the longer it is deferred, the more difficulty will there be in effecting of it." (Mather apparently had no high opinion of the works of Johnson and Morton, which were the only histories of New England that had been published up to that time.) It was reserved for his son Cotton to make the attempt twenty years later.

In 1677 Increase Mather made another contribution

[11] P. 676.

[12] Hubbard's history is printed in the Massachusetts Historical Society *Collections,* second series, Vols. V-VI.

to historiography with his *Relation of the Troubles which have happened in New England, By reason of the Indians there: From the Year 1614 to the Year 1675*. In this volume Mather again revealed his capacity to narrate the picturesque and significant, but on the other hand it has been pointed out that important elements were omitted from the narrative. Nothing was said of the effort of Roger Williams to prevent a union between the Pequots and Narragansetts to destroy the English; nothing was mentioned about Plymouth's dislike of the war, nor about the complaint of Connecticut that Massachusetts had unnecessarily brought it on.[13] As a moral lesson Mather took occasion to draw a distinction between those who, he said, had come to America for reasons of trade ''and worldly Interests, by whom the Indians have been scandalized,'' and other settlers who had come because of religious motives ''having in their Eye the Conversion of the Heathen.'' The first type, the traders, says Mather, ''have been attended with blasting ruining Providences,'' while the others ''have been signally owned by the Lord Jesus, for the like hath been rarely known in the World, that a Plantation should be raised out of nothing.'' To which the nineteenth-century editor of Mather, S. G. Drake, answers: ''That any Settlement was, or could have been made independent of Trade is preposterous.''[14]

In composing his history of King Philip's War, Mather was conscious of a rivalry with other New England historians, particularly Hubbard, who was likewise writing on this theme. But Mather was never one to doubt his own intellectual superiority. He felt that his own work was superior to that of Hubbard, whose book, in the eyes of one Puritan leader, had more mistakes than

---

[13] See S. G. Drake's edition of Mather's work under the title *Early History of New England* . . . (Boston, 1864).
[14] Drake's edn., p. 238.

truths.[15] However, Mather's outlook was generally broad
enough to welcome other workers in a common cause—
the composition of New England's history. He corresponded with them on the subject, and Nathaniel Morton
wrote to Mather asking him "to sett on foot and put forward a Generall History of New England." By communicating to his son Cotton a desire to write history,
the father may be said to have put well forward the
project of a history of New England.

HISTORIES OF THE INDIAN WARS

Hubbard and the Mathers, father and son, were not
the only historians of the Indian Wars. The struggles
between the whites and the natives were of absorbing
interest; the narrow escapes from Indian capture and the
sudden raids on lonely farms were the very essence of
thrilling narrative. Most of the narrators, however, were
too near the scene of the conflicts to think and write of
them in thrilling tones (in King Philip's War, one in ten
of the men of military age was killed). The accents were
generally sober as befitted a people who acknowledged
with heartfelt thanks God's favor in crushing the enemy.

New England, in this type of history as in more general narratives, supplied the greatest number of writers.
Although several contemporaries left accounts of the
Pequot War, Captain John Mason wrote the one best
known. His *History of the Pequot War* (1677) was a cal-
lous account of the struggle.[16] The exploits of another
noted Indian fighter, Colonel Benjamin Church, one of
the best soldiers New England produced, were commemorated in the volume by his son Thomas, *Entertaining
Passages Relating to Philip's War . . . as also of Ex-*

---

[15] K. B. Murdock, *Increase Mather* (Cambridge, 1925), pp. 110-111.
[16] Charles Orr, ed., *History of the Pequot War* (Cleveland, 1897), contains four contemporary accounts.

*peditions . . . against the . . . Indian Rebels in the
Eastern Parts of New England* (1716). This volume, full
of the nervous tension of Indian warfare, remained a
great favorite with readers long after its original publication. Stories of cruelty and heroism similarly fill the
pages of Samuel Penhallow's *History of the Wars of
New England with the Eastern Indians 1703-1725,* which
was published in the year of the author's death, 1726.
Penhallow, who was chief justice of New Hampshire,
belonged in the tradition of Bradford, Winthrop, and
Morton—community leaders who wrote the history of
their times.

Daniel Gookin also wrote of the Indians but his was
a gentler spirit that sought to understand them and promote a friendlier relation between them and the whites.
With the exception of John Eliot he was perhaps the
most distinguished friend the Indians had. Gookin had
known persecution in Virginia under Governor Berkeley
and had moved to Massachusetts, where he became super-
intendent of Indians. He wrote two books; one, *Historical
Collections of the Indians in New England,* remained unpublished until 1792, and the other, *An Historical Account of the Doings and Sufferings of the Christian
Indians,* was also published long after it was written
(1836). In the second book Gookin sought to protect from
the fury of the whites the Christian Indians who had not
joined with King Philip. Gookin's position was of course
opposed to popular opinion, and his protests were dis-
regarded.

Similar in theme but different in narrative construction were the hair-raising accounts of men and women
captured by the Indians and later restored to white civilization. Their stories, generally referred to as the "Indian captivities," have held enthralled generations of
readers, who first marveled at the tale of Mrs. Mary

Rowlandson captured during King Philip's War. "Now away we must go with those Barbarous Creatures, with our bodies wounded and bleeding, and our hearts no less than our bodies. . . . Oh the roaring, and singing, and dancing, and yelling of those black creatures in the night, which made the place a lively resemblance of hell. . . . All was gone, my Husband gone . . . my Children gone, my Relations and Friends gone. . . . There remained nothing to me but one poor wounded Babe, and it seemed at present worse than death . . . and I had no refreshing for it, nor suitable things to revive it." In the eighteenth century and later, other narratives of captivity were published for an awed but unsated audience. In 1854, Samuel G. Drake, an antiquarian interested in Indian lore, gathered in one volume a number of the most famous of these "captivities," some thirty in all, and many thousands of copies were sold to a still eager public. Americans today, who know Indians only as museum pieces, are still thrilled by new editions of these old "captivities."

COTTON MATHER

Cotton Mather was colonial New England's "literary behemoth"; a bibliography of over four hundred titles justifies the description. A rich intellectual heritage had helped to endow him with a capacious memory that filed away references in all fields of knowledge which, appropriately and inappropriately, his pedantic mind would later parade across the pages of his numerous works. Cotton Mather naturally enough went to Harvard. But for him student days were not pleasant, largely because of his own shortcomings and his priggish ways. Mather, who could not understand college boys when he was one of them, grew more shortsighted in after years. For him it was scandalous behavior for college boys to read in private the seductive Epistles of Ovid.[17] But although Mather seemed to have little knowledge of human nature, he had vast erudition, and on his death in 1728 an obituary in a Boston paper said of him: "He was perhaps the principal ornament of this Country, the greatest scholar that ever was bred in it."

Like many other educated New Englanders, Cotton Mather turned to writing on history as well as on other subjects. The influence of his father's historical interests served to spur on a pen that needed no urging, and about 1693 the son determined to write a general church history of New England. It was finished four years later, sent to London to be published and, after many delays that caused heartaches in the Mather household, appeared in 1702. In his diary, on October 30 of that year he wrote, "Yesterday I first saw my Church-History, since the Publication of it." [18]

The *Magnalia Christi Americana; or the Ecclesiastical History of New England* contains seven books. In the first book Mather writes of the planting of the New England colonies; the following two books treat of the lives of the governors, magistrates, and the most famous divines. Book IV is concerned with the history of Harvard College, and an account of some of its eminent graduates; Book V is ecclesiastical history, "Acts and Monuments of the faith and order in the Churches of New England"; the next book includes a record of "remarkable providences"; and the seventh is "A Book of the Wars of the Lord."

In his General Introduction the author says: "I write the Wonders of the Christian Religion, flying from the deprivations of Europe, to the American Strand; and . . . report the wonderful displays of His infinite Power,

[17] S. E. Morison, *Harvard College in the Seventeenth Century* (Cambridge, 1936), Part I, p. 177.

[18] "The Diary of Cotton Mather," Mass. Hist. Soc. *Colls.*, 7th ser., I, 166.

Wisdom, Goodness, and Faithfulness, wherewith His Divine Providence hath irradiated an Indian Wilderness.'' Then, after enumerating the divisions of his work, Mather adds: ''Let my readers expect all that I have promised them, in this Bill of Fare; and it may be they will find themselves entertained with yet many other passages, above and beyond their expectation, deserving likewise a room in History.'' ''Of all History it must be confessed,'' Mather asserts, ''that the palm is to be given unto Church History, wherein the dignity, the suavity, and the utility of the subject is transcendent.'' [19] He writes that he has ''endeavoured, with all good conscience, to decline this writing meerly for a party,'' but he asks that readers be lenient toward historians, who are not expected to be infallible in everything. In defense he quotes Polybius that ''it is not the work of an historian to commemorate the vices and villanies of men, so much as their just, their fair, their honest actions: and the readers of History get more good by the objects of their emulation, than of their indignation.''

He strikes boldly at the criticisms he expects: ''I observe that learned men have been so terrified by the reproaches of pedantry, which little smatterers at reading and learning have, by their quoting humours, brought upon themselves, that for to avoid all approaches towards that which those feeble creatures have gone to imitate, the best way of writing has been most injuriously deserted.'' To those who would say that his style was ''embellished with too much of ornament,'' Mather quotes in Latin, ''As a little salt seasons food, and increases its relish, so a spice of antiquity heightens the charm of style.''

New England was settled solely to plant the Gospel, writes the seventeenth-century historian who ignored the economic motives of many Puritans. The section dealing·

[19] 1855 edn., I, 28.

with the Plymouth colonists, whom Mather called "Ply-motheans," is a well-written, straightforward account which evidently gained much from an acquaintance with Bradford's manuscript. "About an hundred and ninety-eight ships were employed in passing the perils of the seas, in the accomplishment of this renowned settlement [of New England] whereof, by the way, but one miscarried in those perils." "Briefly," said the voluble Mather, "the God of Heaven served as it were a summons upon the spirits of his people in the English nation; stirring up the spirits of thousands, . . . with a most unanimous inclination to leave all the pleasant accommodations of their native country, and go over a terrible ocean, into a more terrible desert, for the pure enjoyment of all his ordinances." Mather never could resist penning what were to pass for witty conceits: "The persecutors of those Puritans, as they were called, who were now retiring into that cold country from the heat of their persecution, did all that was possible to hinder as many as was possible from enjoying of that retirement."

Mather found more than a score of ministers who, because of their "erroneous" principles or "scandalous" practices, he could not "croud . . . into the company of [his] worthies." "I had rather my Church History should speak nothing," he says, "than speak not well of them that might else be mentioned in it." He did think, however, that some Anabaptist and Episcopalian ministers deserved inclusion because of their piety. The historian agreed with his father, Increase Mather, that "of all historical narratives, those which give a faithful account of the lives of eminent saints, must needs be the most edifying." There is a note of beauty in the reference to John Eliot, the apostle to the Indians. "He was one who lived in heaven while he was on earth," says Mather, "and there is no more than pure justice in our endeavours that he should live on earth after he is in heaven.'' ''He that will write of Eliot, must write of charity, or say nothing.'' There was a barb for readers in his remarks about Eliot's generous nature. ''He did not put off his charity to be put in his last will, as many who therein shew that their charity is against their will; but he was his own administrator; he made his own hands his executors, and his own eyes his overseers.''

Mather reveals the usual contempt of the settler for the Indian who uselessly cluttered up the land. ''These abject creatures live in a country full of mines; we have already made entrance upon our iron,'' he noted. ''Our shiftless Indians were never owners of so much as a knife till we come among them; their name for an English man was a knife-man.'' ''They [Indians] live in a country where we now have all the conveniencies of human life; but as for them, their housing is nothing but a few mats tyed about poles fastened in the earth, where a good fire is their bedclothes in the coldest seasons.'' ''They live in a country full of the best ship-timber under heaven; but never saw a ship till some came from Europe hither.'' European settlers were therefore justified in taking over so fair a portion of God's territory from infidels who knew not how to use it.

To indicate the advanced state of learning at his alma mater, Harvard, Mather writes: ''I am sure, they do not show [there] such a veneration for Aristotle as is express'd at Queen's Colledge in Oxford; where they read Aristotle on their knees, and those who take degrees are sworn to defend his philosophy.'' He was very proud of his college, among whose names ''it will be found that, besides a supply of ministers for our churches from this happy seminary, we have hence had a supply of magistrates, as well as physicians, and other gentlemen, to serve the commonwealth with their capacities.'' ''Europe, as well as America,'' he declares, ''has from this learned seminary been enriched with some worthy men.'' Although Mather promised much information on the Harvard graduates, a large part of the space devoted to them was taken up with a description (once before printed) of his brother Nathaniel, who had died at the age of nineteen.

In his "Remarkable Providences," which composes the sixth book, Mather attempted to carry out a plan proposed by his father years before. Increase Mather had published an essay "as a specimen of a larger volume, in hopes that this work, being so set on foot, posterity would go on with it." The son, Cotton, expresses regret for his delay in carrying out this proposal, but he declares his "Church History is [now] become able to entertain the world with a collection of remarkable providences that have occurr'd among the inhabitants of New-England." "Having received sufficient attestations, I shall now invite the reader to consider them." They include unusual rescues from disaster at sea or at the hands of Indians. Mather also narrates the cases of criminals who paid for their capital crimes. In the section "Of the Indians' Government when Christians," Mather reveals an unexpected degree of toleration: "During the late unhappy war between the English and the Indians in New-England, about nineteen years since [King Philip's War], an evil spirit possess'd too many of our English, whereby they suffer'd themselves to be unreasonably exasperated against all Indians. . . ."

It is partly because of Chapter VII in this book, "Relating the Wonders of the Invisible World," that Mather's reputation has severely suffered. But in this he indicates that he was not above the superstitions of his day, in which he was joined by others in America and Europe who were perhaps equally learned. "Molestations from evil spirits," he asserts, "have so abounded in this country, that I question whether any one town has been free from sad examples of them."

The Salem witchcraft episode, of which the author had previously given a long account in the life of Sir William Phips, again appears in a transcription by Mather of an account by John Hales. Mather mentions that the "increasing number and quality of the persons accus'd" of witchcraft, "amaz'd" the officials. "And at last it was evidently seen that there must be a stop put, or the generation of the children of God would fall under that condemnation. Henceforth, therefore, the juries generally acquitted such as were tried, fearing they had gone too far," and Governor Phips reprieved the condemned. Mather adds that "it was thought safer to under-do, especially in matters capital, where what is once compleated cannot be retrieved." His conscience was somewhat soothed by noting "the like mistakes in other places [England and France] so that New England is not the only place circumvented by the 'wiles of the wicked and wily serpent' in this kind."

In the introduction to the last book on "the Wars of the Lord" against heretics and Indians, Mather complains of the lack of aid in writing his volume. "I believe such a work as this," he says, "was never done with so little assistance from the communications of inquisitive and intelligent friends." He does acknowledge, however, the assistance of John Higginson, William Hubbard, his own father, and a few others. Mather named some who shared in the expense of publication, or as he expressed it, "Mecenated these my labours." Making a verb out of Maecenas was but one of Mather's many literary oddities.

Mather sarcastically comments upon the niggardly maintenance of ministers. "The people . . . have many times been content," he writes, "that their pastors be accounted rather the stars than the lamps of the churches, provided, like the stars, they would shine without the supply of any earthly contribution unto them."

He was comparatively lenient toward Roger Williams, whom "many judicious persons judged . . . to have had the 'root of the matter' in him, during the long winter of [his] retirement." "There was always a good correspondence held between him and many worthy and pious people in the colony from whence he had been banish'd." Mather is not so gentle toward Anne Hutchinson, "the prime seducer of the whole faction which now began to threaten the country," but he leaves her unnamed, because he wished to avoid hurting "so many worthy and useful persons" related to her.

The Quakers are the object of his bitter invective: "I know not whether the sect which hath appeared in our days under the name of Quakers be not upon many accounts the worst of hereticks, but this I know, they have been the most venomous of all to the churches of America." However, he distinguishes between "the old Foxian Quakerism . . . the grossest collection of blasphemies and confusions that ever was heard of," and "the new turn that such ingenious men as Mr. Penn have given to it" so that it had "become quite a new thing." On a later page Mather asserts that the Quakers would have amounted to nothing "if the civil magistrate had not inflicted any civil penalty upon them; nor do I look upon haereticide as an evangelical way for the extinguishing of heresies." No magistrate should "take the life of an offender solely for the crime of heresy," Mather maintains, "but only, when to heresy is added some horrible and insufferable blasphemy against God, or open sedition against the state."

Mather felt the need of drawing attention to some extreme Quaker writings "against all earthly powers, parliaments, laws, charters, magistrates and princes," and believed himself justified in asking "whether the infant colonies of New-England had not cause to guard themselves against these dangerous villains." "It was also thought," he adds, "that the very Quakers themselves would say, that if they had got into a corner of the world, and with an immense toyl and charge made a wilderness habitable, on purpose there to be undisturbed in the exercises of their worship, they would never bear to have New-Englanders come among them, and interrupt their public worship, and endeavour to seduce their children from it, yea, and repeat such endeavours after mild entreaties first, and just banishments, to oblige their departure." Mather thus concludes Chapter IV of Book VII: "Well, the enemy of the New-English churches is hitherto disappointed; he has not succeeded here, let him try elsewhere."

Mather's work ends with a doleful note: "It must, after all, be confessed, that we have had one enemy more pernicious to us than all the rest, and that is 'our own backsliding heart,' which has plunged the whole country into so wonderful a degeneracy, that I have sometimes been discouraged from writing the church-history of the country. . . . And since this degeneracy has obtained so much among us, the wrath of Heaven has raised up against us a succession of other adversaries and calamities, which have cast the land into great confusions; to rescue us from which the jealous kindness of Heaven has not made such quick descents as in former times. . . . For which cause I now conclude our church-history, leaving to the churches of New-England, for their admonition, an observation which the renowned Commenius has made upon the famous churches of Bohemia, 'that they were nearer to the sanctuary than other churches, by reason of a more pure discipline professed and embraced among them; and therefore, when they came to be depraved with apostasies, the Lord poured out his righteous displeasure upon them, and quickly made them sad examples to the other churches of the Reformation.'

"God knows what will be the End."

Cotton Mather's *Magnalia,* one of the most influential books in American historiography, has been variously appraised. Barrett Wendell, in his biography of *The Puritan Priest,* rates it among the great works of English literature in the seventeenth century, while bitter critics of Puritanism have execrated it. Professor Samuel Eliot Morison, who made considerable use of Mather's work in his recent *Builders of the Bay Colony,* indicates that he has a higher opinion of it than have most historians. Despite Mather's pedantry and inaccuracy and the fact that he "was not above *suppressio veri,*" he "does succeed in giving a living picture of the persons he writes about, and he was near enough to the first generation to catch the spirit and flavor of the times."[20] In justice to Mather, it should be mentioned that neither he nor any other qualified person was ever allowed to correct the proof of the history, which was being printed three thousand miles away in London. Had he corrected it himself he might have caught some of the errors which are today charged against him.

The book has no form and seems to have been literally thrown together. "All the time I have had for my Church-History," Mather said, "hath been . . . chiefly, that which I might have taken else for less profitable recreations; and it hath all been done by snatches." Jumbled together with much new material, were reprints of many of his earlier writings and the history was of such bulk as to make it the largest work which had been produced in the British colonies.

In his *Manuductio ad Ministerium,* 1726, Mather laid down a plan for a scholar's preparation for the ministry. History was to "be read with constant reflection upon God's power as revealed in past events"; but in studying history, the reader was always to "believe with Dis-

[20] See also interesting remarks on Mather in *North American Review,* VI, 255-272.

cretion.'' He criticized histories which he felt were hardly more than romances. ''What I write,'' he said in the *Magnalia*,[21] ''shall be written with all Christian veracity and fidelity.'' On one occasion, when referring to Indian folklore, Mather had written, ''There is very little in any Tradition of our Savages, to be rely'd upon.'' It is a pity that the skepticism he showed toward the tales of ''red devils'' was absent when he wrote of the devilish spirits in white man's society.

[21] I, 354.

III

THE FIRST HALF OF THE EIGHTEENTH CENTURY

In the eighteenth century, American historical writing continues the spirit of treating reverently the founders of the colonies, and the narratives still have a note of awesome wonderment. But there is also present in the works of some of the later colonial historians a secular approach which locates the causes of events in a mundane and not in a supernatural plane. Ministers continue to write history, but even in New England they no longer monopolize the field. European letters deeply influenced American life, which went through profound changes in its economic and intellectual phases during the half century following King Philip's War.[1] Doctors, lawyers, merchants, and planters became historians, and their broad interests are reflected in the volumes they wrote. A critical temper is clearly evident in much of their work, and a skepticism characteristic of more recent scholarship is revealed in their volumes.

From annals of conflicts with nature and malignant

[1] C. K. Shipton, "Provincial Literary Leaven," *New England Quarterly* (June, 1936).

spirits, writers turned to narratives of conflicts with governors and imperial administrators; the Indian, however, still played a dominant part in the lives of the colonists and therefore merited the space given him in histories. The task of gathering materials was tremendous, and the limited library facilities were a serious handicap, but at their best these provincial writers compare favorably with most of their English contemporaries. With the passing of the century there had emerged a society fairly well stabilized, proud of its past, and confident of the future. Historians were quite conscious of the necessity of correcting English misconceptions of America, and there is evidence in their writing of a nascent pride in the evolution of a distinctive colonial society diverging from that of the homeland.

ROBERT BEVERLEY

Robert Beverley was the type of Virginia aristocrat who easily combined politics and literature. Many of the landed gentry, who were at the same time officeholders, were interested in the early history of America and some of them recorded it. Like many other Virginians, Beverley, who married the sister of William Byrd II, spent much time in England. It was while he was abroad that he determined to write the history of his colony. The publisher of Oldmixon's *British Empire in America* had asked Beverley to read the pages on Virginia, and the many mistakes he found therein prompted him to write his own version.

The History of Virginia in four Parts appeared in 1705 and in an enlarged edition in 1722.[2] Part I contains "The History of the First Settlement of Virginia, and the Government thereof, to the Year 1706." In the next part Beverley writes on "The Natural Productions and

2 I use the second edition.

Conveniencies of the Country suited to Trade and Improvement." Part III treats of "The Native Indians, their Religion, Laws and Customs in War and Peace." The concluding section deals with "The Present State of the Country, as to the Polity of the Government, and of the Improvements of the Land."

In his preface the historian explains his early attachment to his subject and the special circumstances that brought his own work into being. "My first business in the World being among the public Records of my Country," Beverley writes, "the active Thoughts of my Youth put me upon taking Notes of the general Administration of the Government: but with no other Design, than the Gratification of my own inquisitive Mind; these lay by me for many Years afterwards obscure and secret, and would forever have done so, had not the following Accident produced them"; then follows the reference to Oldmixon's manuscript. The Virginian adds that he had undertaken his task "in Justice to so fine a Country because it has been so misrepresented to the common People of England. . . ." Beverley writes of Oldmixon's work in disgust: "It would take a Book larger than his own to expose his errors."

The purely historical narrative is of less general interest than are the other parts of the *History of Virginia*. This first section is largely in the form of annals, and Beverley's feelings toward the colonial governors are rather obvious. Here, as elsewhere in the volume, John Smith is quoted at length. Beverley's interpretation of the dissolution of the Virginia Company was nearer the truth than were the narratives of many later historians. The material on the Indians must have proved very interesting to contemporary readers who learned, from the pictures and accompanying explanatory remarks, a great deal about Indian care of children, their homes, dress, and so on. While taking a dig at Hennepin and Lahontan, whom he considered inaccurate in their observations on Indians, Beverley said: "I don't pretend to have div'd [divined] into all the Mysteries of the Indian Religion . . . and because my Rule is to say nothing, but what I know to be Truth, I shall be very brief upon this Head."

In the chapter "Of the Laws, and authority of the Indians among one another," the author supplied ammunition for critics of eighteenth-century society, who, in their idealization of aborigines, made of them "noble" savages. "They claim no Property in Lands," said Beverley, "but they are in Common to a whole Nation." "They seem as possessing nothing, and yet enjoying all Things . . . without toiling and perplexing their Minds for Riches."

The historian painted a picture of his colony that would attract the prospective emigrant who had been frightened by exaggerations of burdensome work. In the chapter "Of the Servants and Slaves in Virginia," Beverley writes: "Because I have heard how strangely cruel, and severe, the Service of this Country is represented in some Parts of England, I can't forbear affirming, that the Work of their Servants and Slaves is no other than what every common Freeman does." "And I can assure you with great Truth, that generally their Slaves are not worked near so hard nor so many Hours in a Day as the Husbandmen, and Day-labourers in England." The pride in his colonial home, coupled with a promoter's zeal, led Beverley to say: "This may in Truth be term'd the best poor Man's Country in the World. But as they have no body that is poor to beggary, so they have few that are rich; their Estates being regulated by the Merchants in England, who it seems know best what is Profit enough for them in the Sale of their Tobacco, and other Trade." (This resentment of the Virginia planters against their London factors was to grow with increasing strength in the next sixty years.) Even Paradise had no more to offer than Virginia, whose climate must indeed be a "happy" one, "since it is very near of the same Latitude with the Land of Promise."

Beverley's writing is fresh and his comments often shrewd. His style has a noticeably lighter touch than most of contemporary New England historical literature which often appears labored by contrast.

John Oldmixon

John Oldmixon's history was familiar to American writers, who usually quoted it only to contemn it. It has already been remarked that Beverley was so strongly affected by its errors that he was led to compose his own history in refutation. Oldmixon was as much of a pamphleteer as he was a historian, and, in common with the other pamphleteers, he knew no restraint when speaking of his political opponents.

In 1708 he published his two-volume work on *The British Empire in America, containing the History of the Discovery, Settlement, Progress and present State of all the British Colonies, on the Continent and Islands of America.* The first volume deals with the continental colonies, the second with the West Indies. Oldmixon tells us he had never been in America and admits the probability of inaccuracies in his work, but he hopes "there are fewer than will be expected." He mentions his authorities: Cotton Mather for New England's history, and Cox and Penn for New Jersey and Pennsylvania. For the history of Hudson's Bay he used original papers, and on America generally he secured his information from people who had been to the colonies. Because his materials on New England and Virginia were fuller, the historian's sections on these regions were larger.

Oldmixon's main desire in writing his history was

to emphasize the value of the colonies for the mother country. Thus his function was that of a pamphleteer doing an expanded job. But while his work was held in disrepute by Americans, who frequently had access to the original authorities from whom Oldmixon drew, the latter's history is important in at least one respect: it serves to remind the student that the English, when referring to the colonies, usually thought of the West Indies and the continental group together and as something of a unit. American historians, concentrating their attention on the continental colonies, forgot that more comprehensive viewpoint and thus largely missed the proper perspective of colonial history. Not until the twentieth century, particularly in the work of Charles M. Andrews, did American writers recapture that perspective.

JOHN LAWSON

In 1709 a historical publication with the usual lengthy title appeared in London. It was written by John Lawson, "Gent. Surveyor General of North Carolina," who called his book *A New Voyage to Carolina containing the Exact Description and Natural History of that Country: To-gether with the Present State thereof.* An account of a thousand-mile journey among the Indians was included in the volume. Slightly different issues of the same book were published afterwards. Lawson, who had gone to America in 1700, was slain by the Indians twelve years later, when they began to suspect him of threatening their lands. Most of the time he lived in Carolina was spent in traveling and in making his surveys.

In his preface Lawson wrote, " 'Tis a great Misfortune, that most of our Travellers, who go to . . . America are Persons . . . of a very slender Education, who being hir'd by the Merchants to trade amongst the Indians, in which Voyages they often spend several Years, are yet, at their Return, uncapable of giving any reasonable Account'' of their experiences. Lawson thought the French were superior in this regard.

The book was dedicated to the proprietors of Carolina, and it was to be expected that the advantages of settlement in this region would be glowingly pictured. After a description of edible products, Lawson writes on ''the Present State of Carolina,'' whose inhabitants, he says, ''thro' the Richness of the Soil, live an easy and pleasant Life.'' They are, he adds, '' a straight, clean-limb'd People; the Children being seldom or never troubled with Rickets, or those other Distempers, that the Europeans are visited withal.'' Like the Indians, the whites have no bodily deformities. Women, who had been sterile elsewhere, ''have remov'd to Carolina, and become joyful Mothers.'' In his pages on the animals of this region, Lawson was careful to note their utilitarian value. He was anxious also to point out to the prospective emigrant that Carolina offered more advantages than any of the other English colonies. Half the book is a detailed examination of Indian customs—not an unusual division of space in works on America in the eighteenth century. European interest in Indians was insatiable, and Lawson gave the public what it wanted. So well, too, did he perform his task of giving a natural history of the colony that, long after, ethnologists and historians continued to use his work, sometimes without acknowledgment.

WILLIAM BYRD

William Byrd II, author of the sprightly *History of the Dividing Line betwixt Virginia and North Carolina*, belonged to one of Virginia's leading families who were rulers of a princely domain. A large part of his life was spent in England, as a student in his younger years, and as a colonial politician in later life. Through his efforts the landed possessions of the family increased from some 26,000 to almost 180,000 acres.

Although a sophisticated gentleman who had been very much at home with the wits in London coffee houses, Byrd had a great love for his native province and his hospitable Westover mansion. There he indulged his taste for letters among his 4000 volumes, the largest library in the colonies. His wide correspondence reveals that he was a gifted writer. He was also a member of the Royal Society, a rare honor for a colonial.

Not until he was nearly sixty did he attempt any comprehensive literary work; then during the next twelve years, to his death in 1744, he wrote the *Progress to the Mines, Journey to the Land of Eden,* and the two *Dividing Line* histories. Byrd, along with some other individuals, was instructed to settle the long-standing boundary controversy between the two provinces, and his *Dividing Line* histories were the narratives of his experiences on this survey in 1728. The two books were written within the next ten years, but the *History of the Dividing Line* was not published until 1841. In fact, not until the recent publication by the North Carolina Historical Commission of *The Secret History of the Line,* under the editorship of Professor William K. Boyd, did a wider group of students know of the existence of this second book which throws a new light on the work of the boundary commission. Generally speaking, the *History of the Dividing Line* is a fairly faithful picture of the frontier, but its selection of incidents leaves in the mind of the reader misconceptions regarding life in North Carolina.

The *History of the Dividing Line* is twice as long as the *Secret History* and contains a great deal of information which the latter lacks. It includes a short introduction on general colonial history, a description of the fauna and flora in the surveyed region, Indian and pioneer life. The tart comments on North Carolinians, which are so characteristic of the *History of the Dividing Line* are, with one exception, completely absent in the *Secret History*. The original Jamestown colony, writes Byrd, consisted of "about an Hundred men, most of them Reprobates of good Familys"; "like true Englishmen, they built a Church that cost no more than Fifty Pounds, and a Tavern that cost Five hundred."

The *Secret History* may be more dependable than its companion volume, but the latter is amusing reading. Where the survey began, he writes, "dwelt a Marooner, that Modestly call'd himself a Hermit, tho' he forfeited that Name by Suffering a wanton Female to cohabit with Him." ". . . as for raiment, he depended mostly upon his Length of Beard, and She upon her Length of Hair. . . ."

Present in the *History of the Dividing Line* but absent in the other is this characterization of North Carolina: "One thing may be said for Inhabitants of that Province that they are not troubled with any Religious Fumes, and have the least Superstition of any People living. They do not know Sunday from any other day, any more than Robinson Crusoe did, which would give them a great Advantage were they given to be industrious. But they keep so many Sabbaths every week, that their disregard of the Seventh Day has no manner of cruelty in it, either to Servants or Cattle." On a later page Byrd returns to the same subject: "Surely there is no place in the World where the Inhabitants live with less Labour than in N. Carolina. It approaches nearer to the Description of Lubberland than any other, by the great felicity of the Climate, the easiness of raising Provisions, and the Slothfulness of the People." The lawlessness, considered so typical of frontier life, Byrd found nearly everywhere in North Carolina, "where they pay no Tribute, either to God or to Caesar.'' These and similar observations when published were very influential in creating a distorted picture of North Carolina civilization which was adopted as authentic by later historians, including Parkman.

The man who added extensively to the Byrd family acreage could also think more generally in imperial terms: ''Our country has now been inhabited more than 130 years by the English, and still we hardly know any thing of the Appallachian Mountains, that are no where above 250 miles from the sea. Whereas the French, who are later comers, have rang'd from Quebec Southward as far as the Mouth of Mississippi, in the bay of Mexico, and to the West almost as far as California, which is either way above 2000 miles. And the reason the French know the resources of the Country is because they have traversed it on foot. So long as Woodsmen continue to range on Horseback,'' says this lover of the forest, ''we shall be strangers to our own Country, and a few or no valuable Discoveries will ever be made.'' At the conclusion of his *History of the Dividing Line,* Byrd writes: ''We had now . . . been out Sixteen Weeks, including going and returning and had travell'd at least Six Hundred Miles, and no Small part of that Distance on foot.''

Byrd was fond of the frontier, but he was not so careful a student of the psychology of the frontiersman as was a writer of the next generation, de Crèvecœur, author of the *Letters from an American Farmer.* Byrd represents a cosmopolitanism none too common in the America of his day. One of the finest of Virginia's aristocracy, he was the most brilliant forerunner of the imaginative group that dominated American life in the Revolutionary era.[3]

[3] J. S. Bassett, ed., *Writings of Wm. Byrd of Westover* (N. Y., 1901); Richmond C. Beatty, *William Byrd of Westover* (Boston, 1932).

Cadwallader Colden

Indians were more than mere biological novelties to the colonists. They were aids to commerce and threats to peace. They were also determining factors in the diplomatic game played by the English and French for a continent. As political makeweights and as subjects of scientific inquiry, Indians attracted the attention of the versatile Cadwallader Colden. Like William Byrd, Colden had something of that imperial vision so lacking in many other officials in the colonies as well as in the mother country.

Cadwallader Colden was one of New York's most illustrious citizens. In his public life, during many years in office, he made his impress on colonial policy; in his life as a doctor, student, and writer his achievements merit him high rank. He died at the age of eighty-seven, and the end of his life coincided with the passing of English rule in 1776, a rule he had done so much to uphold during his career as lieutenant governor.

Colden wrote *The History of the Five Indian Nations depending on the Province of New York* largely because he wished to convince the public in America and England of the importance of the Iroquois to the colony as a bulwark against the French and as a means of holding the West. He was anxious also to draw the attention of English officials to the "interest of North America in respect to the Fur Trade." He wished as well to preserve the materials relating to Indian life. Colden had little time for historical or anthropological research, and he depended largely on the reports of the Indian commissioners and of the French authors, de la Potherie and La Hontan. William Bradford, pioneer printer, published this first New York history in 1727, and it was later reprinted in England with additions and alterations.

An English correspondent, Peter Collinson, who was the intellectual godfather of many Americans, urged Colden to continue with his work, saying that dependable books of the type of Colden's were much in demand in London. He suggested, however, that Colden should omit any material that might prove helpful to the French, "who are Ever on the Watch." Colden acceded to the request and, under great difficulties, worked on the continuation of the history. Pressure of public and private affairs took up nearly all his time; he was further handicapped by the distance of his home from Albany and New York, where were the materials he needed for his book.

By 1742 he had finished the second part of his narrative, which carried the history from the Revolution of 1689 down to the Peace of Ryswick. In a letter to Collinson, Colden says: "I now send you the greatest part the Indian History continued to the Peace of Reswick which I presume to put under your tutelage because I may truly say that it is owing to you that ever it had a Birth, by your giving me your approbation of the first part, & desining it to be continued as a work which you thought may be useful for I had for several years laid aside all thoughts of it." In fact, as early as 1725 Colden had gathered together most of the materials which he put into the second part. He promised to continue his history further into the eighteenth century if "life and Health be preserved" but for the present he did not wish to trouble his readers "with too much at once." No more of his proposed history appeared, but he did leave a continuation in manuscript.

In his dedication of the original work to William Burnet, governor of New York, Colden accuses the whites of exercising a degrading influence upon the Iroquois. He says that if the vicious practices of the English continued to be "winked at," the Five Nations would "joyn

with every Enemy that can give them the hopes of
Plunder.'' Colden justifies an English interpretation of
the history of the Iroquois because up to the time of
his publication the French alone had written on this subject. In fact, English writings were mainly translations
from the French. His many references to the military
adventures of small groups are excused on the ground
that the Indian art of war was so expressed. Speeches
were frequently inserted by the author, who thought that
he might thus show to better advantage the genius of
the Indians. His inclusion of treaties with accounts of
their signing was justified on the ground of their extreme
interest to contemporaries.

With a regard for authenticity that was characteristic
of other historians of his own day Colden remarks: ''He
that first writes the History of matters which are not generally known ought to avoid, as much as possible, to make
the Evidence of the Truth depend entirely on his own
Veracity and Judgment; For this reason I have often
related several Transactions in the Words of the Regis-
ters. When this is once done, he that shall write afterwards need not act with so much Caution.'' The New
Yorker's disparagement of unsubstantial work has a peculiar propriety in our own day. ''I have sometimes
thought,'' he said, ''that the Histories wrote with all the
Delicacy of a fine Romance, are like French dishes, more
agreeable to the Pallat than the Stomach, and less whol-
som than more common and courser Dyet.''

Part I, ''From the first Knowledge the Christians
had of the Five Nations, to the Time of the Happy Revolution in Great Britain'' is preceded by a short sketch of
the government of the Indians. A good share of the space
is allotted to the relations of the Five Nations with the
English colonies. Colden blames the Jesuits for alienating the Iroquois, but he cannot refrain from lauding the
bravery of the missionaries who lived among the Indians

"at War with their Nation." Like so many other histories written in this period, Colden's few narrative passages only serve as threads to connect the lengthy selections of documentary materials. In the second part of his history Colden's narrative passages are more frequent and lengthy. The historian's work was widely read in his own day, and its observations on Indian character make it still worthy of consultation. It was one of the few books in English that gave significant details about the history and social and political institutions of the Indians who occupied so strategic a place in the life of the colonists.[4]

In the continuation of Colden's history of the Indian nations, recently rescued by the New York Historical Society from a mass of forgotten papers, may be seen the author's constant preoccupation with the need of winning the Iroquois to the English side. Colden also left a history of New York during the administrations of Governor Cosby and Lieutenant Governor Clark, which included a section on Zenger's trial. The author, whose friend James Alexander was one of Zenger's counsel, was friendly to the printer charged with libel.[5]

Colden was always rather sensitive to criticism, but he held it a man's duty to his country to "patiently submit to Scoffs & Jests & revilings when he thinks he cannot avoid them by being usefull." He hoped that in writing his history he had been "in some degree usefull" to his country; "If it be so," he said, "I shall truely gain my end without any further view. . . ." The testimony of his contemporaries and of later generations is that Colden did indeed write a "usefull" book.

[4] Lawrence C. Wroth, *An American Bookshelf 1755* (Phila., 1934), p. 92. See article on Colden's history in *Historical Magazine* (January, 1865), probably written by the editor, John G. Shea.

[5] N. Y. Hist. Soc. *Colls.*, "Cadwallader Colden Papers," IX (1935), 283-355, 359-434.

DANIEL NEAL

The ministerial tradition was comparatively absent in Southern historiography, although William Stith, a Virginia churchman, did contribute a notable work during the eighteenth century. In New England, on the other hand, it was the clergy who, for the most part, continued to conserve historical records and to cast into a characteristic mold their interpretation of the past.

Daniel Neal was a dissenting minister in England who was very much interested in the life of New England. Apart from his history of that region, he also co-operated with its leading clergymen, who were anxious to introduce into England the practice of inoculation against smallpox. Neal was in correspondence with New Englanders who, in the pursuit of their own historical interests, made frequent reference to the contributions of their colleague in the mother country. Harvard recognized his work with the highest honor it could grant—the M.A. degree.

The History of New England . . . to . . . 1700 was published in two volumes in 1720. The new world region was praised as a "Retreat for oppressed Protestants in all Parts of the World"; and, for a better understanding of the settlement of New England, Neal included an account of the sufferings of the Puritans in old England. His authorities were, for the most part, those familiar to the learned of his day—Winslow, Nathaniel Morton, Wood, Increase Mather, Hubbard, and especially Cotton Mather. Neal writes, he says, with "Freedom and Impartiality, tho' I can't help declaring myself sometimes on the Side of Liberty, and an Enemy to Oppression in all its Forms and Colours. Accordingly I have taken the Liberty to censure such a Conduct in all Parties of Christians, wherever I have found it." [6]

[6] Preface, III.

The early chapters of the first volume are on the discovery of America, with a description of native civilization and a narrative of the Puritans in the old world. Neal thought very highly of the clergy who went to New England. Though not all learned, they had a better share of learning "than most of their neighboring Clergy at that Time." [7] The historian writes profusely on missionary activities among the Indians, using materials composed by John Eliot. Neal devoted a large amount of space to the Quakers, and his treatment was in the nature of an apologia for New England's attitude toward this sect. However, in much the same manner that Samuel E. Morison adopted in his *Builders of the Bay Colony,* Neal argued that disturbing elements might rightfully be curbed: "If turbulent and seditious Persons, who disquiet the Minds of People, disturb the Peace of the Government, and refuse Obedience to their Superiors ought to be punished, I leave all Mankind to judge whether the Behaviour of the Quakers . . . did not absolutely require the Interposure of the Civil Magistrate in this way, for the Preservation of the publick Peace." [8] Neal himself was opposed to depriving a man of his civil rights because of his religious doctrines; such deprivation should be visited only on the disturbers of the public peace. Writing a half century or more after the events he describes, Neal expresses his pleasure that New England's attitude had changed toward the Quakers.

The second volume, which continues the account after the year 1661, devotes many of its pages to the wars with the Indians, and, in particular, to King Philip's War. The activities of Sir William Phips are chronicled at length, and so, of course, is the witchcraft episode. On these incidents and characters in New England's history Neal had fuller authorities, but in the main he tran-

[7] P. 197.
[8] P. 328. See also Winthrop and Cotton Mather.

scribed much of what he found in Cotton Mather. He was hostile to the Mathers in his treatment of the witchcraft hysteria. "All the Confessions that were made, seem to me," says Neal, "either the effects of a distemper'd Brain, or extorted from Persons to save their Lives." [9] For his chapter on "The Present State of New England," [10] Neal used John Josselyn's account of his voyages, as well as some material in the Philosophical Transactions, when he wrote on the natural history and geography of the region. Like so many other writers in the eighteenth century he referred to the absence of poverty and illiteracy in these colonies.[11] With others, Neal weighed the possibility of a revolt against the mother country. He found such a possibility remote, however, and New England disinclined to attempt revolution. For, he maintains, in order to live New England must trade with Europe; "so that if we could suppose them to rebel against England" they would only fall into the hands of another power "who would protect them no longer than he could sell them to advantage." Because it was New England's interest to remain subject to England, she was likely to do so, concludes Neal.[12]

A second edition of the history of New England was issued in 1747, and although it claimed changes and additions, it was practically the same as the first. Another large-scale work by Neal was a four-volume history of the Puritans (1732-1738), revised by Joshua Toulmin and published in five volumes (1816-1817). This work had little material on the Puritans of New England, and most of that was interwoven with the history of their coreligionists in England. Although much criticized by Thomas Hutchinson and others as scarcely more than an adaptation of Mather's *Magnalia*, Neal's history of New England continued to be quoted by historians for many years. It contained the "medulla" of the *Magnalia,* said one writer, but it was superior in style, "with such sentiments and observations as Mather had not language to describe nor a head and heart to conceive." [13]

Thomas Prince

Neal was an observer living in the homeland who recorded New England's history with sympathy. Better known and more valuable in the establishment of a continuous historical tradition was the work of a native New Englander, Thomas Prince. Prince, one of the many eighteenth-century historians from Massachusetts, was born in 1687. Some years after study at Harvard, he entered upon a pastorate in the South Church, Boston, that he held to his death in 1758. He had traveled widely abroad, and conscientious study fitted him for a career of distinction. He enjoyed an intercolonial reputation as a scholar, but on at least one occasion he crossed pens with too strong an adversary. The lecture of Professor John Winthrop, of Harvard, on an earthquake that had occurred in 1755 explained it on natural grounds. To the minister such an interpretation was harmful to religion, for he thought these phenomena were exhibitions of God's displeasure. Denying that such philosophic discussion was impious or irreverent, Winthrop was supported in his stand by leading intellectuals in other colonies, including Ezra Stiles. In fact, a Connecticut clergyman wrote that "Mr. Winthrop has laid Mr. Prince flat on his back," and added, since "an Error in Philosophy is neither Heresy nor Treason it would have been most for Mr. Prince's honour to have acknowledged the mistake." [14]

[13] *The Monthly Anthology,* Vol. VII, an article on Neal's history.

[14] *Itineraries of Ezra Stiles,* Devotion to Stiles, March 24, 1756; Winthrop to Stiles, April 17, 1756; see, however, a more favorable view of Prince's scientific knowledge in Theodore Hornberger's "The Science of Thomas Prince," *New England Quarterly* (March, 1936).

Prince's interest in history was aroused at an early date. When he was but a freshman he began collecting the books for his New England library, gathering many that had belonged to earlier generations of Harvard students. In the preface to his *Chronological History,* he says: "I was from my early youth instructed in the history of this country." After naming the author's works whose acquaintance he had made while still young—Morton, Edward Johnson, Hubbard, the two Mathers (his friend, Cotton Mather, was a stimulus to historical writing)— Prince confesses: "I longed to see all things disposed in the order of time wherein they happened, together with the rise and progress of the several towns, churches, counties, colonies, and provinces throughout this country." "In my foreign travels, I found the want of a regular history of this country everywhere complained of." While he was in England Prince had gathered books on our early history and thought that, on his return to America in 1717, he would have sufficient leisure to "attempt a brief account of facts at least in the form of annals." But the cares of his pastorate allowed him time only to collect materials and not to digest them. Active in social and political affairs, he was able to acquire a fund of learning vast enough to rank him second only to Cotton Mather.

In 1728, ten years after he had begun his work as pastor, Prince was able to get back to his historical task, and in 1736 appeared the first volume of his *The Chronological History of New England in the form of Annals . . . with an Introduction containing a brief Epitome of the most considerable Transactions and Events abroad. From the Creation . . . to the Discovery of New England.* The *Annals* of Archbishop Usher was Prince's model—brief statements of events as they had occurred in the order of sequence, with no literary ornamentation.

Prince invited ministers everywhere in the country to send in accounts of their communities. In his preface

he referred to the large mass of manuscripts at his disposal—Bradford's history of Plymouth, the records of
the colony, Hubbard's *General History of New England,*
and so on—and his history was in part an effort to preserve valuable materials, some of which had already been
destroyed by fire. Prince wrote that Bradford's grandson, Major John Bradford, had given him permission to
use the Plymouth history "& take out of it what [he]
thought proper for [his] New England chronology."
Prince added the old Bradford manuscript to his New
England library, where it remained until the time of the
Revolution.

His standard of scholarship was unusually high,
guided as it was by a healthy skepticism. "I would not
take the least iota upon trust; if possible, I examined
the original authors I could meet with." "I cite my
vouchers to every passage; and I have done my utmost,
first to find out the truth, and then to relate it in the
clearest order. I have labored after accuracy, and yet I
dare not say, that I am without mistake; nor do I desire
the reader to conceal any he may possibly find." After
paying his critical respects to writers who protest their
impartiality, Prince states his credo: "I own I am on
the side of pure Christianity; as also of civil and religious liberty, and this for the low as well as high, for the
laity as well as the clergy, I am for leaving everyone to
the freedom of worshipping according to the light of his
conscience; and for extending charity to everyone who
receives the gospel as the rule of his faith and life; I am
on the side of meekness, patience, gentleness and innocence. And I hope my inclination to these great principles
will not bias me to a misrecital of facts, but rather to
state them as I really find them for the public benefit."

As an editor, Prince was not much in advance of the
best contemporary practice: "I know not that I have ever
changed any words or phrases," he writes, "unless they

were very uncouth, or obsolete; and then I have taken
special care to answer them with others of the same exact
importance; only in some very few instances I have used
a softer term for a severer.'' Like the medieval historians he feels it necessary to start his history with
man's beginning, from Adam ''Year one, first month,
sixth day.'' His chronology goes on to the birth of Christ,
then to Columbus's discovery of the new world, and the
''Introduction'' closes with the ''discovery of New England by Captain Gosnold.'' After this very lengthy introduction, Prince begins with the chronology of New England. Part I includes the annals down to the Plymouth
settlement; Part II contains the events to August, 1633.
His history, which appeared in one volume, stops with
the events of 1630; the annals for the following three
years, which were to be part of Volume II, were published in three separate numbers, long after the first
volume was issued, and publication then ceased. Nowhere
in the American colonies of that period was there a public demand for so detailed a history. In a letter referring
to Prince's work John Callender, a contemporary historian in Rhode Island, expresses sorrow that the *Chronology* was so ill received. ''I look on it as an honor to
the country, as well as to the author,'' he wrote, adding
prophetically, ''and doubt not but posterity will do him
justice.'' [15]

With but few exceptions Prince adheres to his intention to give the unadorned facts. Some notable events
draw from him unexpected comment, as does the discovery of America: ''We are now to turn our eyes to the
west, and see a new world appearing in the Atlantic
Ocean to the great surprise and entertainment of the
other. Christopher Columbus or Colonus, a Genoese, is
the first discoverer. . . . Ferdinand and Isabella, . . .
after five years' urging, are at last prevailed upon to fur-

[15] R. I. Hist. Soc. *Colls.*, IV, 178.

nish him with three ships and ninety men for this great
enterprise; which . . . he at length accomplishes, to his
own animated fame and the infinite advantage of innumerable others.''

The settlement of New England moves him to speak
a more vibrant language than the author of a dry chronology ordinarily utters: ''Divers attempts are made to
settle this rough and northern country; first by the
French . . . and then by the English, and both from
mere secular views. But such a train of crosses accom-
pany [sic] these designs of both nations, that they seem
to give it over as not worth the planting; till a pious
people of England, not there allowed to worship their
Maker according to his institutions only . . . are spirited to attempt the settlement.'' ''So there were just one
hundred and one who sailed from Plymouth in England
. . . and this is the solitary number who for an undefiled
conscience and the love of a pure Christianity, first left
their native and pleasant land, and encountered all the
toils and hazards of the tumultuous ocean, in search of
some uncultivated region in North Virginia, where they
might quietly enjoy their religious liberties, and transmit
them to posterity, in hopes none would follow to disturb
or vex them.''

A reader of *The Chronological History of New England* experiences no elation. Instead one feels that he has
been handling old bones. And yet it was the orderly arrangement and classification of those bones, and the tests
to which he submitted them before their inclusion in his
catalogue, that have given Prince his reputation as an
American pioneer in scientific historical writing. Prince's
history, wrote Tyler, ''was the most meritorious piece of
historical work published in America up to that date.''
It is true that the volume marked a great improvement
in research over previously published histories, but an
examination of the works of the best of Prince's contem-

poraries reveals them to be equally scholarly. Probably as important as any inheritance we possess from Thomas Prince is the extremely valuable collection of Americana he spent so many years in gathering, and which, though diminished, forms the Prince Library now in the Boston Public Library.

The prophecy of Prince's contemporary that posterity would do him honor was abundantly fulfilled, and the long list of historians who later paid their tributes to him included Jeremy Belknap, Ebenezer Hazard, and Abiel Holmes. His *Chronology* inspired similar attempts and, as late as 1791, a keen student of history, John Pintard of New York, who was compiling an American chronology, wrote to Belknap, "I shall do pretty well as long as Prince holds out. But shall be at a loss after I part with him." [16] Many historians, it might be added, clung to Prince to avoid getting lost.[17]

JOHN CALLENDER

Though many of the writers we have mentioned called their works histories of New England, their books were mainly histories of Massachusetts. Other New England colonies, however, had their historians of greater or lesser merit. Among them was the author of a history of Rhode Island, John Callender. Callender was a Baptist clergyman who had been graduated from Harvard, that mother of many ministers and historians. Most of his ministerial labors were performed in Newport, Rhode Island, where a rich intellectual environment was conducive to his fruitful avocation—collecting historical materials. Some of these documents, it is interesting to note, were used more than half a century later by Isaac Backus

[16] Mass. Hist. Soc. *Colls.*, 6th ser., IV, 489-491.
[17] See W. H. Whitmore, "Life and Labors of Thomas Prince," *N. A. Rev.*, XCI, 354-375.

in his history of the Baptists. Callender contributed to historians more than the bare raw materials; his own composition, which was likewise useful to later writers, was *An Historical Discourse on the Civil and Religious Affairs of the Colony of Rhode Island and Providence Plantations in New England in America.* (1739.)

In the spirit of his two contemporaries, Prince and William Stith, Callender said that he had sought to prevent mistakes by carefully reviewing "the publick Records, and my other Materials." Like others before and after him, he apologized for the portions that "will be tho't too minute or personal by Strangers," but he was sure the present inhabitants of the colony and their descendants would pardon him. Callender asked that a group of individuals be formed to collect the documents and private papers before they were all dispersed. His own *Discourse* was no substitute for such a plan, added Callender, but he hoped it would be a stimulus to such a collection on which a comprehensive history could be based; Prince's *Chronology* was also mentioned as an additional incentive for Rhode Island students to record their history.[18]

Callender's kindly outlook is more that of the rationalist spirit of the eighteenth century than of any narrow sectarianism. For example, in speaking of the religious differences among the Puritans that prompted the settlement of Rhode Island he writes: "In Reality the true Grounds of Liberty of Conscience, were not then known, or embraced by any Sect or Party of Christians; all Parties seemed to think, that as they only were in the Possession of the Truth, so they alone had a Right to restrain and crush all other Opinions. . . ."[19] Nearly a quarter of Callender's one hundred and twenty pages are taken up with the religious disputes that led to the colony's

---

[18] See "Dedication."
[19] P. 15.

founding. When he came to write of those things with which he assumed his readers to be familiar, Callender hurriedly passes them by: "As every one knows the Form of Government . . . I need say but little about it." [20] As the member of a persecuted sect, libeled by other historians of New England, it was natural that Callender justified the ways of the Baptists, but he went beyond a mere partisan plea: "It must be a mean, contracted way of thinking," he writes, "to confine the Favour of God . . . to one Set of speculative Opinions, or any particular external Forms of Worship." [21]

Too much of Callender's *Discourse* is a sermon in praise of liberty of conscience, and too little is connected with the history of the colony. It is true that it reads much easier than many similar writings of this period, but his own statement appears sufficiently descriptive: "I confess the Account I have been able to collect is very lame and imperfect." [22] But it was the most important survey of the colony's history for more than a hundred years.[23]

WILLIAM STITH

At the time that Thomas Prince was writing his *Chronological History of New England,* another minister was writing with equal care the story of Virginia. William Stith, who had been educated at Oxford, was rector of the parish of Henrico and a governor of William and Mary College. In 1747 he published *The History of the First Discovery and Settlement of Virginia: being an Essay Towards a General History of this Colony.* Like his New England contemporaries Stith was afraid that

[20] P. 46.
[21] P. 54.
[22] P. 2.
[23] Callender's *Discourse* has been reprinted in the Rhode Island Historical Society *Collections,* IV.

historical materials then available might be lost to future historians if not immediately made use of.

Stith begins his history in a rather sophisticated tone: "Every Country," he writes, "hath it's Fables concerning it's Original, which give great Scope to light and fanciful Historians, but are usually passed over with a slight Mention by the solid and judicious. The late Discovery of America, in historical and well-known Times, might, one would think, have exempted it from this common Fate of Nations. Yet such is the Pride of some Men to seem of deep Reach and Insight . . . and such their preposterous Delight in groping after Truth in the Dark, and yet neglecting her in the clear and meridian Brightness of Day, that even this new World hath been endowed with it's fabulous Age." He expresses "Contempt and Aversion for all such learned Trumpery" and writes that he will apply himself "To give a plain and exact History of our Country, ever regarding Truth as the first requisite and principal Virtue in an Historian, and relating nothing without a sufficient Warrant and Authority." In his preface, Stith tells the reader of his sources, and critically estimates the worth of John Smith's publications. Through William Byrd the historian had access to the London Company's records and in other ways was indebted to Byrd. An appendix containing charters was added to this volume.[24]

Book I brings the history to about 1605; Books II and III continue the narrative to 1620. The next two books, the last, conclude with the events of 1624. It is strange to read references of a Virginian to tobacco as a "stinking, nauseous, and unpalatable Weed, . . . certainly an odd Commodity, to make the Staple and Riches of a Country." [25] Stith goes into great detail on the

[24] A valuable index to Stith's history was published by Morgan P. Robinson in the *Bulletin* of the Virginia State Library in 1912.

[25] P. 182.

squabbles within the London Company. Aware of the difficulties of making such history interesting, he points to the failure of even the best writers to attract the reader when writing of such matters. But he clings to his procedure doggedly, saying that "as these publick Papers contain the most authentic Reason and Account of things, and as they are the surest and most indubitable Materials, for an Historian to proceed upon, I shall not be turned from my Course, by the accidental Dislike of some Readers." [26]

The earlier part of Stith's *History,* beginning with Book II, is mainly based upon Smith; for the latter part the "Records" of the London Company are the important source. Stith characterizes John Smith as an honest and reliable writer for the events with which he was connected in America, but he considers him somewhat confused. With respect to the quarrels between the Company and the King, Stith's sympathies lie with the former.

Although he wrote with the consciousness of America's growing strength and challenged English historians to take account of her history, his narrative is temperate and written with unusual regard for scholarly standards. His errors of interpretation, which favored the company, were the result of too great a faith in the court records, which were partisan in character, presenting as they did the point of view of Sir Edwin Sandys. But in behalf of Stith it should be added that since his day most historians who have also taken these records at their face value have misunderstood much of Virginia's early history. [27]

The historian had promised that he would add more to this *Essay Towards a General History of Virginia,* but despite his own interest in the subject and the leisurely eight years of life that remained to him, he never went on with the work. It is supposed that so detailed a

[26] Pp. 283-284.
[27] W. F. Craven, *op. cit.,* pp. 5-7.

narrative was not to the taste of Virginia gentry, and this lack of public support discouraged Stith. In point of scholarship, Stith's history ranks with the very best produced in the colonial period, and has long been one of the standard works in early Virginia history.[28]

WILLIAM SMITH

The middle colonies also had their historians. Their volumes incorporate valuable descriptions of contemporary society and reflect the bitter controversies that marked the history of political developments in these provinces. William Smith, the historian of New York, was born in that colony in 1728. His father was a person of importance, holding several high offices in the province. Smith was educated at Yale and then returned to his native city to study law. Very shortly he gained a large practice, becoming a leading member of the bar, and like other lawyers of his day, entered politics.[29] Named a member of the council at the time when revolutionary discussions were alienating friends of long standing, Smith drew up a plan of colonial union that would prevent dismemberment of the British Empire. The historian became more conservative as the radical temper of the colonists increased, and when the war broke out Smith remained in New York as a Loyalist. He left for England when the British troops evacuated the city and remained abroad until his appointment as chief justice of Canada in 1786. He held this post until his death in 1793.

Because of the stigma of Toryism, Smith's history was long in disrepute, but it scarcely deserved such a fate. *The History of the late Province of New York from*

---

[28] A valuable essay, bibliographical in character, on Stith's history, appeared in *The Southern Literary Messenger* (September, 1863), XXXVII, 554.

[29] He and William Livingston published a digest of the laws of New York (2 vols., 1752, 1762).

its discovery, to the appointment of Governor Colden, in 1762 was the title of the two volumes when the New York Historical Society published the completed work in 1829. The original history, which closed with the events in 1732, appeared in 1757, but the historian's son later added a "Continuation" down to 1762, which his father had left in manuscript. Finally, the whole work came out under the auspices of the New York Historical Society.

When he closes his history with the year 1732, Smith writes: "The history of our public transactions, from this period to the present time c. 1756 is full of important and entertaining events, which I leave others to relate. A very near relation [father] to the author had so great a concern in the public controversies with Colonel Cosby, that the history of those times will be better received from a more disinterested pen. To suppress truth on the one hand, or exaggerate it on the other, are both inexcusable faults, and perhaps it would be difficult for me to avoid those extremes. Besides, a writer who exposed the conduct of the living will inevitably meet with their fury and resentment. The prudent historian of his own times will always be a coward, and never give fire till death protects him from the malice and stroke of his enemy."

Although Smith did not write with a disinterested pen, he managed to avoid the extremes of falsity that often come from suppression or exaggeration. Smith, one of the leading dissenters in the colony, engaged in a number of serious religious controversies, and it was hardly possible for him entirely to avoid partisanship. He had no direct acquaintance with the Dutch documents and therefore understood little of the early history of the colony. In fact, only some thirty out of the total of over six hundred and fifty pages of the historical narrative are devoted to the story of New Netherland. The larger portion of the two volumes is concerned with the eighteenth century. Because of favored family associations the historian knew many of the actors in the later part of his story; the second volume thus has much of the value of a contemporary account. His writing, though good, did not escape that moralizing which was characteristic of most historians then and which was transmitted to some in the following generations. He often wrote with an editorial pen that asked support for a cause in which he was interested. Some sentences he neatly turned, as when writing of missionary activities among the Iroquois Indians he remarks: "The French priests boast indeed of their converts, but they have made more proselytes to politics than religion."

Most of Smith's pages are devoted to strictly political history; thus one chapter heading runs, "From the year 1720 to the commencement of the administration of Colonel Cosby." Appended to Volume I, however, are nearly a hundred pages of descriptive material: "A geographical description of the Country"; "Of the Inhabitants"; "Of our Trade"; "Of our Religious State"; "The Political State"; "Of our Laws and Courts." To the modern reader these pages are probably the most interesting, and especially so are the references to such subjects as the laws and courts of which Smith had personal knowledge. His education and wealth prompted him to write from the standpoint of an aristocrat, but he did supply some interesting information about the life of the poorer classes. Smith was proud of the place of his birth: "With respect to riches, there is not so great an inequality amongst us as is common in Boston, and some other places." But he could also see the flaws in his colony: "Our schools are in the lowest order—the instructors want instruction; and, through a long shameful neglect of all the arts and sciences, our common speech is extremely corrupt, and the evidences of a bad taste, both as to thought and language, are visible in all our proceed-

ings, public and private.'' ''In matters of religion we are
not so intelligent, in general, as the inhabitants of the
New England colonies; but both in this respect and good
morals, we certainly have the advantage of the southern
provinces.''

Smith on various occasions quotes long extracts from
the *Independent Reflector,* a paper that he and William
Livingston edited in the interest of dissenters, and
throughout his work appears his sensitiveness against
real and fancied Episcopal oppression. When Lord Cornbury caused two Presbyterian ministers to be brought
before him on charges of preaching without a license,
Smith says of them: ''They appeared before his lordship
with an undaunted courage, and had a conference with
him, in which it is difficult to determine whether my Lord
excelled in the character of a savage bigot or an unman-
nerly tyrant.'' A native New Yorker, Smith disliked many
of the governors sent over from England, but he was very
complimentary to William Burnet. His narrative was
severely handled by Cadwallader Colden, who, in the
course of writing his own memoirs of public transactions,
made caustic reference to Smith's misinformation. ''It is
not fit,'' wrote Colden to his son, ''that Mr. Smith's history should pass for a chronicle of the Province of New
York.'' [30]

Smith understood that much of his narrative was
unimportant. ''The history of an infant country,'' he
wrote once, ''must consist of many events comparatively
trivial.'' Modern historians are frequently pleased that
trivialities were included by older writers, because today
they may borrow these bits of local color.

[30] See Colden's letters on Smith's history, 1759-1760, in N. Y. Hist.
Soc. *Colls.,* Vol. VIII (1868).

Samuel Smith

A contemporary of the New York Smith was the author of *The History of the Colony or Nova-Caesaria, of New Jersey . . . to the Year 1721, with Some Particulars Since; and a Short View of the Present State.* This volume by Samuel Smith appeared in 1765 under the imprint of James Parker, one of the most famous of colonial printers. The work was found sufficiently serviceable to be issued in a second edition more than a century later (1877). Samuel Smith, who was born in 1720 and lived for fifty-six years, came of a Quaker merchant family. He held several important public offices, and was the author of other works besides his *History.*

In his preface Smith says that he is anxious to present the "plain state of facts" of New Jersey's history, because so little had "appeared abroad of what the settlers here have been doing." Unlike Rev. Thomas Prince, who went back to Adam for a beginning to his history of New England, Smith went no further back than Columbus for his account of New Jersey. Two hundred out of his five hundred pages of chronological narrative describe the events of the seventeenth century. Interesting materials on immigration are included, along with the text of many documents not easily accessible to the eighteenth-century reader and which today are the joy of the genealogist. Much of the volume is of the nature of a chronicle. For example, Smith writes: "We are now come to the year 1701; a memorable era in New Jersey, on account of the disturbances and confusions that violently agitated several parties and the change of government that followed in consequence of them."

In the pages on Lord Cornbury's administration, Smith writes from the standpoint of a patriotic colonial. "Tho things were carried to arbitrary lengths," he writes, "there was not wanting in the province, men of discernment to see and lament the unhappy situation of their country, and of spirit to oppose its greatest enemies." One quarter of the volume is on the struggles during the few years of Governor Cornbury's administration. The historian's favorable judgment on Governor Hunter's appointments and assent "to most of the laws the people wanted," is tempered by the reflection that Hunter "had a ready art at procuring money, few loved it more; this foible 'tis said drew him into schemes, gaming, and considerable losses."

When Smith reaches the year 1721, and the end of his detailed narrative, he writes: "What follows are partly matters incidental; the rest tho' not a regular course of events, nor perhaps more important than others omitted may nevertheless assist in a future volume, and in the meantime possibly be of some historical service here." In various portions of his work the New Jersey Smith made use of the history of his New York namesake and drew slightly upon Beverley's *History of Virginia*.

As in most of the histories written in colonial America, a great deal of space is devoted to Indian customs and to the relations between the colonists and the various tribes. Smith's observations on the Indians are free from rancor; his Quaker background led him rather to emphasize their peaceful qualities. The last pages are on the animals native to the province, and also include several appendices of documents.

There is nothing exciting about Smith's narrative, and it must be admitted that he adhered strictly to his intention of presenting his facts plainly. There appears to be less of his own writing in his book than that of the authors of various public and private papers whom he quotes at great length. When describing the political state of the province in 1765, he says that "harmony

reigns in a considerable degree in all branches of the legislature; the public business is consequently dispatched
with ease, and at a small expence." One gathers that
these words are an index to Samuel Smith's character;
he disliked any disturbance and expended little of himself
emotionally.

WILLIAM DOUGLASS

The historians of the eighteenth century continued to
write on their own colonies, but there was in much of
their work a consciousness of a broader field of historical
inquiry. The dawning realization of a certain unity
among the colonies is already apparent. At least one
colonial historian viewed the provinces as a whole, and
although his work was inadequate, it was indicative of
the American mind in transition. William Douglass was
by profession a physician, but his varied interests included the study and writing of a history whose fame
was enhanced when Adam Smith referred to it in his
Wealth of Nations. Douglass had settled in Boston, in
1718, to practice medicine after a student career that began in Scotland and included apprenticeship in Leyden
and Paris. He was quick to take offense and was frequently engaged in controversies with his colleagues and
the clergy of Massachusetts. Elsewhere in the American
colonies, Douglass was held in high esteem, particularly
by Cadwallader Colden in New York, with whom he often
exchanged letters.

*Summary, Historical and Political, of the First Plant-
ing, Progressive Improvements, and Present State of the
British Settlements in North America* was the title of the
publication brought out by Douglass in separate releases
beginning in 1747. Two volumes were ultimately bound
together and issued before he died in 1752. In the arrangement of the 1755 edition, Part I of the first volume
contained "general affairs," a short survey of ancient

and modern colonies, the settlement of the North American colonies, "with remarks of various natures." Part II of the same volume dealt with Canada and Massachusetts. Volume II, said Douglass, was concerned with "the sundry other British provinces . . . of North America." "Throughout is interspersed several miscellaneous affairs, such as the natural history, the distempers at times epidemical, and the endemical diseases in these various climates, with their paper currencies." The materials on the colonies outside of New England are comparatively scanty.

In view of the strong animosities that lent acid to his pen, it is rather amusing to read of his protestations of fairness: "I have no personal disregard or malice," writes Douglass in one instance, "and do write of the present times as if these things had been transacted a hundred years since." In the introduction to the second volume he says: "As the writer is independent, being in no public office, no ringleader of any party, or faction; what he writes may be deemed impartial. If facts related in truth offend any . . . he will not renounce impartiality and become sycophant." Such protestations, however, will deceive no reader, for the partisanship of Douglass was so obvious that it hardly offends today. The offenses of Douglass against historical scholarship and composition were many. Apart from his temperamental frailty, his work was badly organized, and appeared to be more like a mass of ill-digested notes, rather than a finished history. "He is essentially a journalist and pamphleteer," is Tyler's opinion. "He is hot, personal, caustic, capricious; and his history is only a congeries of pungent and racy editorial paragraphs."

Douglass had written that because of the dryness "of descriptions and bare relations . . . a little seasoning is used." The flavor of his contentious personality was "seasoning" enough for this historical potpourri.

The digressions in which Douglass indulged often took him far afield. In his closing chapter on Virginia, for no intelligible reason he injected a discussion of smallpox, and in the studies of other colonies, Douglass sometimes included digressions on medicine. In the many footnotes that weigh down his pages, Douglass finds an additional vent for his private prejudices. He definitely denies the necessity of studying original sources in the preparation of his history. "This is a laborious affair, being obliged to consult manuscript records." He sneers at New England historians: "The printed accounts in all respects are, beyond all excuse, intolerably erroneous."

Despite the mass of misinformation that Douglass supplies, the volumes do possess some value. "A Digression concerning the settling of colonies in general; with an Utopian amusement, or loose proposals towards regulating the British colonies in the north continent of America" [31] contains some interesting regulations of an imperial nature. Douglass's work includes far more economic and social history than do the volumes of historians who were his contemporaries, but it requires a deep knowledge of colonial affairs to find the information that is trustworthy in his book. Douglass's statements on currency matters, evidencing strong dislike of anything tending toward inflation, have gained the approbation of modern economists but contemporaries were more impressed by Douglass's history than posterity has been. The *Monthly Review* in England, for example, thought it contained "a fuller and more circumstantial account of North America, than is anywhere else to be met with." [32]

Although he had been a tireless opponent of Cotton Mather and the Boston physicians who had urged the adoption of inoculation in the prevention of smallpox in

[31] 1755 edn., I, 234.
[32] October, 1755, quoted in L. C. Wroth, *An American Bookshelf 1755*, pp. 88-89.

the 1720's, thirty years later Douglass proved sufficiently broad-minded to write, "The novel practise of procuring the small-pox by inoculation, is a very considerable and most beneficial improvement in that Article of medical practice." "The first promoters of it were too extravagant, and therefore suspected in their recommendations of it." So small an olive branch could not bridge the gap that parted Douglass from many of his bitter foes.

IV

HISTORIOGRAPHY 1750-1800, AND THE GROWING NATIONAL SPIRIT

The growing self-consciousness of Americans which the revolutionary years evoked fostered the study and writing of history and was itself nurtured by historical compositions. Many histories of provinces and states now appeared, and historians also began to transcend local boundaries. The argument that state histories would "lay a good foundation for some future compiler in writing a general history of the country" encouraged Jeremy Belknap to write his history of New Hampshire. Minute treatments of each state were urged on the ground that the history of no people "admits of being written with greater certainty than our own."[1]

Over a period of many years Ezra Stiles corresponded with individuals in diverse places, collecting materials for an *Ecclesiastical History of New England & British America*. According to Stiles, an Englishman offered to secure five thousand subscriptions for his history.[2] Other Englishmen showed an active interest in

[1] A. Wibird to Belknap, April 14, 1779, Mass. Hist. Soc. *Colls.*, 6th ser., IV, 139.
[2] Stiles, *Diary*, February 11, 1770.

American history: Dr. John Fothergill, a Quaker physician who was closely attached to America, hoped that an American historian would describe contemporary civilization in the new world, and he suggested that a fresh description be made every twenty years. "If the history of the actions of men in civil life are of any use to posterity," wrote Fothergill to William Bartram, the naturalist, "what advantages might not be gained by thus taking time by the forelock?"[3] Stiles, in an exchange of letters apropos of Hutchinson's *History,* wrote to the historian of Massachusetts that a European could not "do justice to the history of the American provinces." He was glad that Hutchinson was of New England descent, and urged him to include all of the four New England colonies in his survey. "You would thus write a complete history of an intire people," he said, "or of one intire emigration and settlement." Stiles said that his own plan was to write on "British American History"; at first he would write the history of New England "as of one intire emigration, people and settlement, to deduce it through the civil, military, commercial, moral and ecclesiastical changes and revolutions to the late . . . war" (Seven Years' War). But he added his doubts of ever completing it; perhaps he might do an Ecclesistical History.[4] Although his work was never published, Stiles left to his son-in-law, Abiel Holmes, many volumes of manuscripts which were of service in preparing the latter's *American Annals.*[5]

Baptist historians like John Comer, Morgan Edwards, and, later, Isaac Backus, ranged over all the colonies in search of materials. Edwards made large collections on church history in planning his twelve-volume work, and he impelled others to preserve their ecclesias-

[3] September 10, 1766, Port. 38 (86), Friends House, London.
[4] *New Eng. Hist. and Genea. Reg.* (1872), pp. 159 ff., May 7, 1764.
[5] The ms. of Stiles's "History" is in the Yale Library.

tical records; parts of Edwards's materials were eventually published. The three volumes published by Backus, *A History of New England with Particular Reference to the . . . Baptists* (1777, 1784, 1796), were the result of a wide search for materials. Following in the footsteps of Roger Williams, Backus was perhaps the leading champion of religious liberty in his day, and his history was an argument in support of his position. In accord with the best practice of his time, he sought out documentary sources and "named his principle vouchers on purpose to have his performance thoroughly examined, and every material mistake corrected."[6] Backus objected to most of the existing histories as biased, particularly in their treatment of minority religious groups. When he reached the Revolution Backus broadened his work to include a discussion of the causes of the war and also its progress, but on the whole it remained an ecclesiastical history.[7]

Shortly after the middle of the century, newspapers, magazines, and almanacs began to reflect a rising interest in history. A writer in a New York paper proposed to publish by subscription a work dealing with most of the American provinces.[8] The next year, Nathaniel Ames included in his almanac "An Account of the several Provinces in North America," which was copied and expanded by a New York almanac. Another editor, Samuel Nevill, began a history of North America in his *New American Magazine*. Nevill's history, which began with Columbus and ran through to the second half of the eighteenth century, was compiled, he tells us, from the works of Hakluyt, Purchas, Mather, Neal, Stith, Beverley, Colden, Douglass, and others. To prepare a large body of citizens

[6] Preface to Vol. I.

[7] See Alvah Hovey, *A Memoir of the Life and Times of the Rev. Isaac Backus* (Boston, 1858).

[8] N. Y. *Post-Boy,* May 5, 1755.

for participation in politics to the end that popular control might be insured, Ames recommended the study of geography and history, adding the true note of nationalism, "it is proper to begin with the history of your own nation." [9] During this period the magazines devoted hundreds of pages to history of one kind or another, and in the 1780's, with the problems facing the young Republic demanding solution, there was a special interest in ancient history.[10]

The Revolution, of course, was a strong impetus to history. A "History of the Late War in America," a serial copied from the *Annual Register,* was run in *The Worcester Magazine* (1786-1788). *The Columbian Magazine* in 1789 also levied on the *Annual Register,* giving its readers a historical digest of the late war. *The Boston Magazine,* 1783, seemed to specialize in history; some of its original backers became members of the Massachusetts Historical Society when it was formed a few years later. *The American Magazine,* edited by Noah Webster, awakened interest and discussion in American history. Some of the articles that Belknap included in his *American Biography* were first published in a series in *The Columbian Magazine,* 1788, under the title of *The American Plutarch or a Biographical Account of the Heroic and Virtuous Men . . . of the United States.* Belknap's intimate friend and literary adviser, Ebenezer Hazard, published his *Historical Collections; consisting of State Papers . . . intended as materials for an History of the United States of America.*[11] Hazard stated in his preface that his aim was to "lay the Foundation of a good American History." Belknap told Hazard that people wanted to know why he did not write history in-

[9] S. Briggs, *The Essays . . . of Nathaniel Ames, Father and Son . . . from Their Almanacks* (Cleveland, 1891), pp. 269-270, 381-383.

[10] Cf. Lyon N. Richardson, *A History of Early American Magazines 1741-1789* (N. Y., 1931).

[11] 2 vols., Phila., 1792-1794.

stead of publishing historical materials. He thought that a "regular history of the United States would be a more popular and profitable work than such a collection," but warned that "it would cost you years of labor." [12] To assist him in his work Hazard drew up a list of over fifty titles (some of which were more theological than historical in nature), which he called "Histories of America." Belknap and Hazard were part of a circle that assisted one another in historical pursuits; other members included William Gordon, David Ramsay, and, later, Jedidiah Morse.[13]

In the warm glow of an exuberant independence, plans were formulated in the 1780's for national education, and, naturally, to history was assigned a special place. "Above all," wrote Dr. Benjamin Rush, who was especially prominent in this movement, "let our youth be instructed in the history of the ancient republics, and the progress of liberty and tyranny in the different states of Europe." The young student was also to familiarize himself with American history, especially with the years just ended.[14] Another writer of the day, Nathaniel Chipman, pointed to the need for a more careful investigation of the laws determining national development. Earlier historians, he maintained, had been too largely concerned with "battles and sieges only, the intrigues of statesmen, and the revolution of empires." For a deeper understanding of civilization, Chipman urged the study of the "history of man in society," and of "the development of the human mind." [15] Still another contemporary writer, Samuel H. Smith, in his "Remarks on Education," speak-

[12] Mass. Hist. Soc. *Colls.*, "Belknap Papers," 5th ser., III, 258; May 16, 1791.
[13] See Mass. Hist. Soc. *Colls.*, 6th ser., IV, 151; September 13, 1779; also Hazard mss. in Library of Congress.
[14] A. O. Hansen, *Liberalism and American Education in the Eighteenth Century* (N. Y., 1926), pp. 56-57.
[15] *Ibid.*, p. 99.

ing in the accents of the eighteenth-century philosophes, stressed the educative value of history in liberating man from "fanaticism and superstition"; history, too, would teach the student to look upon war as the instrument "of vice and folly." A knowledge of the causes of mankind's progress or retrogression, said Smith, would enable man to view his own society more intelligently.[16] A leading publicist of the period, Noah Webster, had written in 1787 that "a selection of essays, respecting the settlement and geography of America, the history of the late revolution and of the most remarkable characters and events that distinguish it, and a compendium of the principles of the federal and provincial government, should be the principal school book in the United States.[17] Even before the Revolution, the New York lawyer, William Smith, in recommending studies for prospective members of his profession, strongly urged the reading of history. He understood also that history was distinguished from chronology and required the student to "take a larger scope." [18]

During the years of military hostilities, Americans had little time for historical interests. Encouragement was given to William Gordon and some others, but, as Ebenezer Hazard found to his dismay, "the war and the numerous avocations consequent upon it, have thrown every man's mind into such an unsettled and confused state that but few can think steadily upon any subject." [19] During the war, however, the *Annual Register,* appearing under Whig auspices in London, published serially a history of the struggle which interpreted favorably the American side of the controversy.

Other European observers were interested in the

[16] *Ibid.,* p. 153.
[17] *Ibid.,* p. 239.
[18] William Smith's *Common Place Book,* N.Y.P.L.
[19] Mass. Hist. Soc. *Colls.,* "Belknap Papers," 5th ser., II, 11-13; Auust 31, 1779.

Revolution and sought information from leading Americans for proposed histories. To the Abbé de Mably, John Adams communicated his thoughts in 1782 on the writing of America's revolutionary history. After stating that "it is yet too soon to undertake a complete history of that great event" and that no one had the necessary materials for writing it, Adams explained that a writer should divide the history of America into several periods. The first was up to 1761, when the disputes began; the second up to 1775, fourteen years of "a war of the quill"; thence to 1778, when the "war was exclusively between Great Britain and the United States"; and finally the last period to the peace. Adams spoke of the necessity of consulting colonial history for an understanding of later events, searching manuscript records in all the colonies, and reading the various provincial histories. "The whole of a long life, to begin at the age of twenty years," said Adams, "will be necessary to assemble from all nations, and from all parts of the world in which they are deposited, the documents proper to form a complete history of the American Revolution, because it is indeed the history of mankind during that epoch. The histories of France, Spain, Holland, England, and the neutral powers, must be united with that of America." Adams suggested a study of the four New England institutions—the towns, congregations, schools, and militia—to learn how the Revolutionary spirit was fostered.[20]

With peace came the histories of the war, and it was from the *Annual Register* that their authors secured their material. Such was their debt to this English publication, that Orin G. Libby, writing on "Some Pseudo-Histories of the American Revolution," referred to seven works appearing in these years that plagiarized in lesser or

[20] Adams, *Works*, V, 491-496.

greater degree from the same source.[21] Historians of a
more original quality were not absent, and, with the
words of Benjamin Trumbull as guide, we can read the
mind of many Americans. "After the revolutionary
war," he tells us, "it was the desire of many pious men,
that the remarkable deliverances, which the United
States of America had experienced might be fully exhibited to the public, as a tribute of praise to their Great
Deliverer, and for the instruction of posterity." Such
writing would bring the people of the country "into a
more general acquaintance with each other," he said,
"awaken their mutual sympathies, promote their union
and general welfare." [22]

The phrases of Trumbull indicate that the historian
was still tracing the finger of God in history, and that the
past was to be studied for a guide to social behavior.
With respect to the latter point, Trumbull and all the
proponents of national education were in accord with one
of the greatest historians of their century—Voltaire.
Voltaire, like other men of the Enlightenment, looked
upon the study of history as a training valuable in creating a virtuous citizenry. The historian was to describe the
progress of society to his own day, presumably the highest goal yet achieved, and he was to suggest as well the
lines of future conduct. Voltaire's writings were read
overseas in whole volumes or in extracts printed in periodicals. That alert Boston clergyman, Jonathan Mayhew,
wrote to Harvard's benefactor, Thomas Hollis, in thanks
for the gift of Voltaire's *The Philosophy of History* and
the *Philosophical Dictionary*. He disagreed with their
religious ideas but added: "I cannot but think, these, as
compositions, to be very fine performances. I have read
them with delight, as containing much useful learning,

[21] *Trans.* Wisconsin Academy of Sciences, Arts, and Letters, XIII, 419.
[22] Preface to *A General History of the United States of America* . . .
(Boston, 1810).

many fine observations on antiquity, & written throughout in a most spirited, entertaining & masterly way; so
that I would not be long without them for twice their
value." [23]

Where earlier historians saw the working of God's
will, the later writers saw the working of natural laws.
The historians who followed Trumbull, with some notable
exceptions, were less interested in observing providential
interference in history. But throughout the nineteenth
century and to our own day, despite the development of
"scientific" history, there has been a strong tendency to
make history a lay sermon instructing the reader to enlightened social conduct. Even recent histories of utmost
"impartiality" are not free of some "lessons," and although the lessons may be somewhat different and their
didactic quality less repellent than those contained in the
volumes of colonial American historians, in spirit they
are less widely separated than may superficially appear.

THOMAS HUTCHINSON

Thomas Hutchinson, historian, was but one aspect of
a personality that devoted itself to a long life of public
service which was cut off by the outbreak of the War of
Independence. A good part of the history of Massachusetts was the story of Hutchinson's forbears who had
played roles of varying significance in the one hundred
and fifty years of the colony's existence. Hutchinson was
born in Boston, 1711, and sixteen years later, after graduation from Harvard, entered his father's business. As a
young man he was interested in politics, and in 1737 entered the legislature. There he became an expert on the
subject of public finance, and for more than thirty-five
years held such offices as chief justice, lieutenant governor, and governor, gaining with each step the increasing

[23] Bancroft *Transcripts,* January 7, 1766, N.Y.P.L.

confidence of a larger number of voters. The British government, too, had learned to place a similar confidence in Hutchinson. It was his fate to attempt the part of a moderator between two antagonists who had passed beyond the stage of reasoning. Radical Americans would not listen to his words of loyalism, while British ministers scorned his advice.

He left Massachusetts in 1774, never to return, although his spirit, spent in futility in London, sought anchorage in his native home. "I am not able to subdue a natural attachment to the very soil and air, as well as to the people, of New England," he wrote in his exile. "I assure you I had rather die in a little country farm house in New England, than in the best nobleman's seat in Old England." For only a brief moment, when his property was confiscated in America, did Hutchinson become vindictive toward his former neighbors. In these last bitter years of frustration, the historian found solace in the completion of his history. In his diary for October, 1778, Hutchinson writes: "I finished the revisal of my History, to the end of my Administration, and laid it by." The last volume remained in manuscript for fifty years, when his grandson published it in London, in 1828.

From boyhood, Hutchinson tells us, history was his favorite study. "Before he went to college," he writes in his diary, in the third person, "he chose rather to spend an evening in reading Morton's *New England Memorial,* Church's *History of the Indian War,* Dr. Mather's *Lives of the New England Governors, etc.* than to be at play with boys in the street. And he had made some advances in the 'England History.' " At another time Hutchinson wrote: "The history of Great Britain and of its dominions was of all others the most delightful to me; and a thorough knowledge of the nature and constitution of the supreme and of the subordinate governments thereof, I considered as what would be peculiarly beneficial to me in the line of life upon which I was entering; and the public employments to which I was early called, and sustained for near thirty years together, gave me many advantages for the acquisition of this knowledge.'' As this quotation suggests, Hutchinson's approach to the study of history is mainly that of the student of institutional history. Hutchinson, like others in the eighteenth century, knew the great value of primary documents, and his favored position made it possible to gather a great many manuscripts relating to New England history. The library of Samuel Mather, son of the historian, Cotton Mather, which had a rich collection of materials, was open to Hutchinson. He was fond of reading old records, and, in the true spirit of the historian, he explained that men were interested in the past because of the need to prolong their lives ''to the utmost length.''

In the last days of 1764 appeared the first volume of *The History of the Colony of Massachusetts Bay from the First Settlement thereof in 1628, until . . . 1691*. Hutchinson was unfamiliar with the Winthrop manuscripts, but he did use Bradford's materials and the well-known New England histories published at the time. His critical eye saw nothing more ''than an abridgement of Mather's *Magnalia*'' in Neal's *History of New England;* Hutchinson was also distrustful of Douglass's work. He could on occasion be critical of his native province as he was in recording the persecution of the Quakers. In a reflective passage the historian writes that ''after forty years, the greatest part of our first emigrants had finished their pilgrimage, and were arrived at the place of their everlasting abode. Some of them lamented their being born too soon to see New England in its most flourishing state. This will be the case,'' Hutchinson prophesies, ''with their posterity for many generations to come.''[24] The

[24] I, 222.

first three chapters of Volume I are straight political narrative; the fourth is on the religious life of Massachusetts; the fifth on the laws, and the sixth, and last, on the Indians and the geographical conditions of settlement. Hutchinson makes an apology for his inadequate treatment of the natural history of the country, and adds the hope that someone with greater leisure would write such a book. On the proud note that history could offer no parallel to the speed of American material development, Hutchinson closes.

The welcome reception accorded to this volume, which was rather annalistic in form, stimulated Hutchinson to continue his history, and he had made considerable progress on it, carrying his story to 1730, when the political storm broke. In the summer of 1765 Stamp Act rioters broke into Lieutenant Governor Hutchinson's home and scattered his possessions in the muddy streets. "But the loss to be most lamented," wrote a contemporary observer, "is that there was in one room, kept for that purpose, a large and valuable collection of manuscripts and original papers which he had been gathering all his lifetime, and to which all persons who had been in possession of valuable papers of a public kind had been contributing, as to a public museum. As these related to the history and policy of the country, from the time of its settlement to the present, and was the only collection of its kind, the loss to the public is great and irretrievable—as it is to himself the loss of the papers of a family which had made a figure in this province for a hundred and thirty years." With the help of a generous friend, Hutchinson recovered the manuscript of the second volume of his *History* which had been tossed about with other papers, and it bears to this day the mud stains of Boston's riotous streets of '65. After bringing the story of the province down to 1750, he published it in 1767. It has been pointed out by Lawrence S. Mayo that the criticisms made of the first volume were helpful in making the second one better. In answer to a request for criticisms, Ezra Stiles said, among other things, that much of the material in the notes might better have gone into the text.[25]

The calm and moderate tone of the first volume is also characteristic of the second, despite the savage events that marked its progress; with much dignity he writes in the preface to Volume II: "We shall never be all of one mind in our political principles." Hutchinson rarely permitted his personal feelings to intrude, believing that the historian's function was to tell a disinterested story. A good account of the witchcraft episode is in these pages, and Hutchinson's words have bite in them when he writes: "In all ages of the world superstitious credulity has produced greater cruelty than is practised among the Hottentots, or other nations, whose belief of a deity is called in question." [26] With his strong belief in the system of English parliamentary government, he was moved to remark, "in a well constituted government it is of importance to the people that the share even of the popular part of the constitution should not be unduly raised to the suppression of the monarchical or aristocratical parts." [27] Chapter IV contains a long narrative of the controversy between the advocates of paper money and the defenders of "hard money," among whom was numbered Hutchinson himself.

Not until 1828 did the third volume covering the period 1750-1774 appear, and this contains much on the author and his contemporaries, who were active in the Revolutionary controversies. Even in this last volume, finished amid alien surroundings, in which he writes of events that burned deep in his soul, no hard flame shines through; for example, there is a very straightforward

[25] Am. Antiq. Soc. *Proc.* (October, 1931).
[26] II, 45.
[27] II, 175.

account of the Stamp Act riots. In the sadness of exile he knew the costs of civil war, and he writes movingly on its evils.[28] The judicial temper of Hutchinson's mind, to which Charles Deane ascribed so much of the value of his *History*, remained unruffled, and although his portraits of some of his political adversaries are unflattering, they are largely true. A few months before the first volume had come off the press, Hutchinson told Stiles that he might write a volume on his own period, and remarked not ill-naturedly, "I threaten Mr. Otis sometimes that I will be revenged of him after I am dead."[29]

Although he was sincere in his aim to write the truth, being mortal Hutchinson failed at various points. Despite his great industry, his public life exacted so much of his energy that he had not sufficient time to examine many pamphlets, newspapers, and legislative documents that might have served as a corrective to some of his judgments. Hutchinson was aware of his deficiencies as a stylist. He once wrote to a friend, in explanation, that his work was unpolished because the constant calls of public business never gave him time "to write two sheets at a sitting."[30] "I am sensible," he writes in the preface to Volume I, "that whoever appears in print should be able to dispose his matter in such order, and clothe it with such style and language, as shall not only inform but delight the reader. Therefore, I would willingly have delivered over everything I here collected to a person of genius for such a work. But seeing no prospect of its being done by any other, I engaged in it myself, being very loth that what had cost me some pains to bring together, should be again scattered and utterly lost." In a letter to his confidant, Ezra Stiles, Hutchinson wrote that he had "no talent at painting, or describing characters,"

[28] III, 255.
[29] July 4, 1764, *New Eng. Hist. and Genea. Reg.* (1872).
[30] James K. Hosmer's *Life of Hutchinson* (Boston, 1896), pp. 85-86.

adding that "it requires great delicacy." Perhaps the historian was too modest, for his literary skill increased the more he wrote; it is true, however, that he did not speak the language touched with magic. The writing has the vigor of the author's personality, and, in the portraits he draws of characters of his own and earlier days, Hutchinson often writes very well. In fact the modern reader usually finds these character sketches the most interesting portions of the *History of Massachusetts Bay*. As the number of his pages lengthened, the note of political conservatism strengthened—a natural consequence of the stand Hutchinson took in the Revolutionary controversies. Volume III was mainly a defense of the administrations of Governor Bernard and of Governor Hutchinson.

Hutchinson's book was the first general history of that province which produced so many historians. Among the motives that prompted Hutchinson to write the history of the colony was a desire to preserve its records, many of which he had seen burned in Boston fires. One authority, William Frederick Poole, said that Hutchinson's three volumes on the *History of Massachusetts Bay* and his one-volume *Collection of Original Papers relative to the History of the colony of Massachusetts Bay* (1769) were "the four most precious books" relating to that period of American history. The severest modern critic of Hutchinson, A. C. Goodell, has charged that the historian did not make the best use of the materials at his disposal. The basis of his work, the legislative journals of governor and council was inadequate, says Goodell, who further criticized Hutchinson for omitting a survey of the advance of civilization in New England in the eighteenth century.[31] While this criticism is, in some respects, justifiable, Hutchinson's work, nevertheless, ranks

[31] *Am. Hist. Rev.,* Vol. II.

above all other colonial historians. His organization of
materials and his historical sense were far beyond most
of his contemporaries. His analysis of the Revolutionary
controversy showed greater objectivity and was nearer
the truth than that of any succeeding historian for almost
a century. Some of the generation that had reviled the
chief loyalist of Massachusetts lived to witness, a half
century later, the successful effort of leading citizens of
the state to get Hutchinson's last volume published. The
cooling ardor of controversial spirits permitted then a
clearer reading of the events that had torn apart an
empire.[32]

ROBERT PROUD

Hutchinson was not the only historian whose work,
written during the war years, awaited quieter days for
publication. *The History of Pennsylvania in North
America* . . . is but a short part of the long title of
Robert Proud's two volumes, published in 1797 and 1798.
These volumes were written between 1776 and 1780, the
historian tells us, "but the great change in this country,
which ensued and was then forming," prevented their
publication. In the spirit of Thomas Prince he answers
for the authenticity of his materials. In origin, Proud's
history was an enlargement of the work of Samuel Smith
on New Jersey. In the view of Proud, Pennsylvania's
golden age lay in the past, before the Revolutionary years
had tarnished its glory.

Proud had personal reasons for placing Pennsylvania's golden age in the past, for he was a loyalist in
sympathy. He was in his early thirties when he landed in
Philadelphia from England in 1759. In London he had
been a protégé of the distinguished Quaker, Dr. John
Fothergill; in his new home he became an instructor in a

---

[32] Lawrence Shaw Mayo, ed., Hutchinson's *The History of the Colony
and Province of Massachusetts Bay* (3 vols., Cambridge, 1936).

school conducted by fellow Quakers, where he remained until the outbreak of the Revolution. His loyalist associations during the war soured him against his rebellious neighbors. During the war he wrote to his brother in England that he "lived in a very private and retired Way, even like a Person dead amidst the Confusions, and conversing more with my Books than with Persons. . . ." [33]

A long introduction, divided into two parts, precedes the narrative proper of Proud's history. The first part of the introduction contains the memoirs of William Penn and "a general and comprehensive view of the rise, principles, religious system and practice . . . of the people called Quakers." The second part relates the early settlements of Europeans, with especial reference to West New Jersey. Smith's *History* was useful to Proud in these pages.

Proud's first chapter describes Penn's effort to obtain the grant, and it gives an account of the province together with complete versions of important documents and letters. In the manner of so many other histories of that century, Proud's sentences appear to be threads connecting pages of documents in a chronological sequence. The second volume continues from the year 1709 to 1771, but after 1725 the narrative is very thin and the selections from documents much fewer; more than five hundred pages chronicle the first forty years of the colony, while some thirty pages suffice for the next fifty years. Proud concludes the history proper with some characteristic remarks: "Thus far appears the manner of the rise, colonization, increase and happy establishment of the flourishing province of Pennsylvania, which, by means of the very remarkable industry, honesty, moderation, and good policy of the first and early colonists and their successors, from a wilderness, became as a

[33] See Proud's letters in *Pa. Mag. Hist. and Biog.*, Vol. XXXIV.

fruitful field. . . ." "But all things have their time; and both kingdoms and empires, as well as smaller states, and particular persons, must die. . . ."

Although the historical narrative is inadequate for the later years of the colony's history, the hundred pages or more that describe the province in the ten years between 1760 and 1770 offer some compensation. This descriptive section was a feature of other eighteenth-century histories; William Smith's of New York is an illustration in point. The historian of Pennsylvania took great pride in the number of eleemosynary institutions in his province. As in other histories of the time, Proud includes many details on the Indians, but his critical sense is much sharper than that of other writers on the subject. He made use of the works of two New York historians, Colden and Smith, in his pages on the Indians. With justice, Proud makes much of the religious toleration that prevailed in Pennsylvania.

In an appendix of over a hundred pages Proud gathered together some documents that he could not fit into the text. At a time when these documents were scattered in various places, if in print at all, Proud's diligence in grouping them together was of great value. The comment on his history made by a Pennsylvanian over a hundred years ago is even more applicable today: "It is exactly that stately old fashioned article that its author himself was." [34]

ALEXANDER HEWAT

Historians of the South were few compared with their contemporaries in the North in the colonial period. Apart from Virginia, historical literature emanating from the southern part of America was indeed rare, and continued to be so for many years. During the Revolu-

[34] Biographical sketch by C. W. Thomson, *Memoirs* of Hist. Soc. of Penn., Vol. I.

tionary era, however, when the English were eager for information on all parts of their empire, there began to appear historical material on the lesser-known colonies. In 1779 a two-volume work was published in London by Alexander Hewat, *An Historical Account of the Rise and Progress of the Colonies of South Carolina and Georgia.* Hewat had migrated from Scotland to Charleston, South Carolina, where, as a Presbyterian minister, he was in a position to learn much of the character of American society. Although he sided with the loyalist position when the war broke out, returning to England, his friendly relations with some of his neighbors in Charleston were maintained to the end of his life.

In his modest preface Hewat refers to his work as "only a rough draught" intended to acquaint England with the commercial possibilities of the Southern colonies. During his residence of several years in Charleston he had collected historical materials, and in his book he gave in entirety long extracts which he might have abridged but did not, because they were his principal authorities. Like others writing on Southern history, with an implied sense of superiority, Hewat could not resist a criticism of New England: "We may challenge the annals of any nation," he says, "to produce a code of laws more intolerant than that of the first settlers in New England." [35]

The first volume ends with the change from the proprietary form of government in South Carolina to a royal province in 1728. A good deal of social history, as well as some natural history, is interspersed in this political narrative, but it is rarely related to the theme of politics. On the first page of his second volume, Hewat speaks of a new era in the government of South Carolina when it became a royal province—an era of freedom, security, and happiness. The settlement of Georgia constitutes a large part of the early chapters in the second volume. A good

[35] I, 34.

firsthand description of life in South Carolina—manners, the state of learning among the people, and the like—is to be found near the close of the work,[36] which carries the story to the outbreak of the Revolution. Although he promised to write further on the subject, Hewat does not appear to have published anything additional. In naming the causes for the disputes with the mother country Hewat makes some interesting observations on the development of the colonial consciousness of power, and the gradual rise in disaffection toward the mother country among the second and third generations of colonists.

Hewat's work was the first history of South Carolina and as such deserves the praise that any pioneering work merits. David Ramsay, a contemporary historian, in recommending the work to Belknap, said it was unsafe on the background of the war because of Hewat's Tory sentiments, but on other matters, "you may rely on his accounts." [37] Historians, including Bancroft, years afterward turned to the pages of Hewat for material not readily available elsewhere.

WILLIAM GORDON

The historians who lived in the Revolutionary era, even when writing on earlier periods, reflected the heightened pulse of the body public. The nearer the writers approached the Revolution, the greater was the acceleration of the pulse beat, although some authors maintained a fairly even temper in the course of writing their narratives. These historians were familiar with many of the events and personalities they described, and their volumes were thus credited with veracity. But in the case of at least two, Gordon and Ramsay, that confidence seems to have been misplaced. For a hundred years Wil-

[36] II, 289-307.
[37] Mass. Hist. Soc. *Colls.*, 6th ser., IV, 568-569; March 13, 1794.

liam Gordon received respectful attention from students of American history because of the contribution he was supposed to have made to its records. And then an inquisitive scholar discovered it was all a mistake, that Gordon's history was not his own.

Gordon had come to America from England in 1770, when he was middle-aged, because of his attachment to the colonial cause. For some fourteen years before 1786, when he left for England, he served as pastor of the Third Congregational Church in Roxbury, Massachusetts. He was an ardent participant in colonial politics, although many American leaders were scarcely friendly to him. John Adams, for one, wrote in 1775: "I fear his indiscreet prate will do harm in this city. He is an eternal talker and somewhat vain, and not accurate nor judicious." Gordon appreciated the significance of the events that were then transpiring and he determined to collect information from the leading actors in America. He traveled widely in search of manuscript records and gathered his needed sources given orally or in writing. He wrote to John Adams in March, 1777: "I am collecting materials for an history of the rise, progress, and successful issue of the American revolution." Gordon asked for his assistance and mentioned that others had already helped him; Washington gave him access to his papers. "I am more and more sensible," Gordon said in April, 1778, "that to make my proposed history as complete as possible I must travel thro' most of the continent."

When the war was over Gordon thought that it would be safer to write his history in England, at which distance his intended impartial remarks on the colonies would prove less dangerous to his person. To Horatio Gates he wrote in 1782: "Should Great Britain mend its constitution by the shock it has rec'd . . . life liberty property and character will be safer there than on this side the Atlantic; and an Historian may use the impartial

pen there with less danger than here." [38] Unfortunately
for Gordon, he found that England also objected to an
impartial history. John Adams, then in London as American representative, described, in a letter written years
later, what had happened to Gordon's history. "His object was profit. He was told that his book would not sell
if printed according to his manuscript. It was accordingly
thrown into a new form of letters between a gentleman in
England and one in America . . . the style and spirit
was altered and accomodated more to the British taste
and feelings. . . . Had the original manuscript been
printed the work would have appeared very differently."

In February of 1789, Gordon wrote to Washington
that he was sending him the four volumes of his history,
which had been published toward the close of the previous
year. Its title was *The History of the Rise, Progress and
Establishment of the Independence of the United States
of America; Including an Account of the late War, and of
the Thirteen Colonies from their Origin to that Period.*
An American edition in three volumes appeared in 1789.
In his letter to Washington, Gordon revealed his standard of scholarship: "I apprehended it to be often necessary to introduce sentiments and information, while I
suppressed the names of the writers from whose letters
they were taken, and at times inserted them as though
they were originally my own."

A modern student, Orin G. Libby, has shown that
Gordon inserted far more than he admitted to. [39] In the
preface to his history, Gordon wrote: "The Americans
remarked that Dodsley's *Annual Register* to which Edmund Burke was a leading contributor contained the best
foreign printed summary account of their affairs. . . .
That *Register* and other publications have been of service

---

[38] Mass. Hist. Soc. *Proc.,* "Letters of William Gordon" (June, 1930).

[39] "A critical examination of Gordon's 'History of the American Revolution,' " *Ann. Rep.* of the Amer. Hist. Assn. for year 1899, I, p. 365.

to the compiler of the present work, who has frequently quoted from them, without varying the language except for method and conciseness." This statement scarcely tells the truth, for, as Professor Libby has shown by deadly parallel readings, Gordon's history copied the *Annual Register* "wholesale," so that it is "one of the most complete plagiarisms on record." Nearly all the material available to him in America had been collected to no purpose—the *Annual Register* was evidently a more convenient source. Gordon was also heavily indebted to Ramsay's *History of the Revolution in South Carolina*.

The history, which was published in the form of letters, contained thirty-two from Massachusetts and eighteen dated from three leading European cities. Only one-tenth of the material in the foreign letters, Libby estimated, was Gordon's: "Of the first part of the first volume, Letters I and II, he may be the author, or at least the compiler." The remainder of the work was on the whole "a sorry patchwork in which selections or adaptations from Burke and Ramsay are raggedly joined to material of quite another kind." Only in his first letter did Gordon give his authorities with any fullness, and shortly thereafter he refrained from referring to a bibliography. Ramsay had been kind enough to send to Gordon his history while still in manuscript, but Gordon was sufficiently unkind to use it frequently with no acknowledgment. The work that was once prized by Edward Channing as "the most valuable history of the Revolution from a British pen" in more recent years has been entirely rejected as a source for this period.

DAVID RAMSAY

For more than a century the work of David Ramsay, physician and distinguished political figure in South Carolina, had been looked upon with favor as historical literature of a high order written by a contemporary of the American Revolution. But the same deflation of a well-established reputation that befell William Gordon has occurred in the case of Ramsay.

The History of the Revolution of South Carolina from a British Province to an Independent State was published in two volumes in 1785. Four years later Ramsay brought out *The History of the American Revolution,* also in two volumes. Both works were republished in Europe, the second appearing in several English editions and in translations on the Continent.

In the preface to *The History of the American Revolution,* Ramsay states that he had collected materials between 1782-1786, during which years, with the exception of 1784, he was a member of Congress and "had access to all the official papers of the United States." "Every letter written to Congress by General Washington," he says, "was carefully perused and its contents noted." He claims to have done the same with the letters of other important officials.

Despite the opportunities for gathering materials that Ramsay had, and that he tells us he made use of, his protestations will no longer impress the reader. Orin G. Libby, who had done a similar disservice for Gordon, proved beyond question that Ramsay plagiarized many of his pages from that fertile source of many histories— the *Annual Register.* It is evident also that in some instances Ramsay used Gordon's book as well.

Instead of utilizing the documents that were near at hand, Ramsay copied them as they were printed in the *Register.* He and Gordon, in many cases, had copied identical passages from the *Register.* Ramsay's account of events in the South, where he was presumably on familiar ground, also shows plagiarisms from the same periodical, and for his narrative of occurrences outside of colonial boundaries he continued to copy from the

Register. To a lesser degree *The History of the Revolution of South Carolina* is also in part plagiarized from this English publication. The *History of the American Revolution,* says Professor Libby, is guilty of so much plagiarism "as to condemn it as well nigh worthless"; and in his book on the Revolution in his own state, Ramsay "has plagiarized sufficiently to raise in our minds a reasonable suspicion as to his absolute trustworthiness in any portion of his published work." Gordon and Ramsay changed indirect discourse to direct discourse in using the *Register.* "Each copied from the other," concludes Professor Libby, "and the fault was shared mutually." The fault, it might also be said, was shared by publishers, who knew the public appeal of such literature and stimulated the issuance of such spurious works.

In 1809 another publication by Ramsay appeared in two volumes, *The History of South Carolina from its first settlement in 1670, to the Year 1808.* In his preface he says that the history of the United States as a whole is so vast that it could not "be done to purpose otherwise than by local histories of particular provinces or states." The first volume is divided into two parts, the civil and military history of the colony and the state, with much the larger share for the military events of the Revolution. For this section Ramsay made use of his earlier work on the Revolution. In his second volume he deals with special phases of South Carolina's history, ecclesiastical, medical, legal and constitutional, and with biographical sketches, and so on. It is very likely that many of the pages of this later work will escape the charges of plagiarism that have nullified the value of his volumes on the Revolution.

George Chalmers

Far more substantial work than that of Gordon or Ramsay was contributed by the loyalist George Chalmers. In the early years of the troublous 1760's he had gone from Edinburgh to the city of Baltimore, where he practiced law. When the War of Independence broke out, he sailed for England, to settle in London, where he was appointed to an important government post. His official connection gave him access to state papers which he used intelligently in discussing many historical problems.

The relations between Great Britain and the colonies from their earliest settlements interested Chalmers, who believed that an examination of the development of those relations would show that the constitutional position maintained by the rebellious colonies was wrong. With this thesis in mind, he published in 1780 his *Political Annals of the Present United Colonies, from their Settlement to the Peace of 1763.* . . . In his preface he notes that although much attention had been given to the history of Great Britain and Ireland, "the annals of that considerable part of the empire, the British colonies have been hitherto resigned to neglect as unworthy of notice." The difficulty of getting materials and the comparative obscurity of the colonies until 1763 explained the lack of attention bestowed upon them by historians. "But the confederated provinces have lately demanded the notice of the world with uncommon success," writes Chalmers, "because what is boldly asked is seldom refused."

Chalmers wished to examine the exact legal status of the colonies and the logic of their demands. The *Political Annals* was to be divided into two books: the annals of the colonies from their settlement to the revolution of 1688, and colonial history to the peace of 1763. Chalmers stated that he was issuing the first book in 1780 "because the author thought that it might at this time possibly do some good." His sources include the acts of assemblies, the printed collections of state papers, and the journals of the Board of Trade and Plantations. "He hath always cited minutely the various authorities on which he relied," writes Chalmers in the third person, "partly in order to authenticate his own assertions, but more to enable succeeding writers . . . to pursue his track with greater ease to themselves and advantage to the world."

Chalmers was very critical of Massachusetts and of the Northern colonies generally. He writes of the actions of the colonies when William and Mary came to the throne: "In the colonists of the south we see a just regard to their liberties as Englishmen, and to the laws of the state; but in the proceedings of those of the north, we behold their characteristic principles breaking out; and their expressions of 'dependence upon England, and relationship to it,' were at that time what they have always been mere words. For the essence of subordination is obedience." [40] Elsewhere Chalmers revealed his animosity to the Northern colonies. "Of New England," he writes again, "it is a remarkable characteristic, that she has at all times found delight amid scenes of turbulence." [41]

At the close of his volume the author described what privileges emigrants really could claim as subjects of the crown of England in 1689: "The various plantations formed no more than the dependencies of a great kingdom which directed their affairs. And they enjoyed no portion of sovereignty. . . ." But the colonists, Chalmers adds, "enjoyed perfect freedom" though their legislatures were restrained. Colonists were not inferior to Englishmen because both were equally subject to the king. "Colonial legislatures were only subordinate because they were neither coordinate nor supreme." Where the

[40] P. 342.
[41] P. 593.

colonies invoked doctrines of natural rights to establish their claims, Chalmers traces the historical development of the colonies to prove those claims unwarranted.

Although he had intended to continue his *Annals,* the success of the colonial revolt caused Chalmers to change his plans. At his death, however, in 1825, he left a continuation of the *Political Annals* in manuscript. This work, which ends with the seventeenth century, was eventually published by the New York Historical Society.

In 1782, Chalmers brought out privately his *Introduction to the History of the Revolt of the American Colonies.* The first section gives the story from James I to the close of Queen Anne's reign, while the second section, printed many years later, ends with the opening of the reign of George III. In this book Chalmers intended to prove that from an early date the colonists had aimed at independence, and secondly, that the government under successive administrations had exhibited tragic negligence when it permitted the colonial assemblies to increase their authority. Although he failed to substantiate his first thesis, Chalmers was successful in proving the second. The correspondence of governors and other crown officers in the colonies formed the basis for much of the material found in this work of Chalmers. Obviously this meant that only the British official point of view was presented. "Yet we are enabled to ascertain from these volumes, better than from any others," writes the editor of the Boston edition printed in 1845, "the kind of intelligence which the ministers received from their agents in America, and to arrive at a clearer understanding of the grounds of their public acts."

His assertions of the early colonial desire for independence may be found in passages like the following, which show also the same partiality to the Southern colonies that he had exhibited in the *Political Annals.* "The Original Virginians," wrote Chalmers, "who, long subjected to martial law, derived a kind of emancipation when placed under the domination of prerogative, transmitted habits of respect for the constitution of England, which long engaged their obedience to her rules. . . . The enthusiasts, who planted New England derided the authority of their native land and neglected the jurisprudence of their fathers, the moment wherein they no longer felt the coercion from which they had fled; and forming systems on congenial principles, they acted during sixty years rather as the allies than subjects of the state." Chalmers further charges that the "contagion" of the New England spirit of independence even before the end of the seventeenth century, "soon overspread the southern colonies, because predisposition of habit naturally attracts infection." [42]

Although the works of Chalmers were thought to be unfair by many Americans, they were of value in stimulating them to a fresh study of their own history. The American editor of the *Introduction to the History of the Revolt of the American Colonies* writes of the earlier book of Chalmers: "Notwithstanding the time and object of Chalmers's *Annals,* the work has ever been quoted by American writers with entire confidence and respect, and this circumstance speaks clearly in favor of the author's candor and honesty. Judging from the free use which has constantly been made of this work, as well as from the matter it contains, we may justly regard it as holding an important place in our historical literature. The author was a lawyer, and he has discussed the subject before him in the spirit of his profession, adhering strictly to legal interpretations and distinctions." The fault of Chalmers, the student of today can readily see, was the fault of many of the most eminent Englishmen of his day in their attitude toward the American colonies. He placed too great an emphasis on the legalistic approach to the prob-

[42] 1845 edn., pp. 220-221, 222.

lems that confronted the mother country and her rebellious provinces. But the historian was reported as saying, long after, that the mother country should have yielded to expediency and not insisted on her legal rights in her relations with the colonies.[43] For many years American historians, even when they disagreed with details in Chalmers's work, looked to it as a standard by which to gauge the merit of their own achievements.

JEREMY BELKNAP

Jeremy Belknap belongs in the very front rank of historians who wrote in the revolutionary period. So close in spirit to the modern historian was his approach that his work has been of lasting value. He was born in Boston in 1744 and received his education at Harvard. When he was twenty-two years of age he was ministering to the religious needs of the community of Dover, New Hampshire, remaining there until 1786. After difficulties with his congregation he accepted a call to a Boston church the next year, and from then on to the end of his life Belknap was satisfied with an arrangement that left him some time for his literary pursuits.

Belknap had from his youth been interested in history, an inclination no doubt strongly fostered by Thomas Prince, who had been one of his teachers. In the preface to his history of New Hampshire, Belknap tells us that very early he had been "impelled by his natural curiosity to inquire into the original settlement, progress, and improvement of the country which gave him birth." He was still a college student when he indicated his conception of the high achievement of historical composition: "There are required so many qualifications and accomplishments in an Historian, and so much care and nice-

    [43] H. B. Adams, *Life and Writings of Jared Sparks* (Boston, 1893), II, 383-384.

ness in writing an history that some have reckoned it one
of the most difficult labors human nature is capable of.'' [44]

Belknap had access to Prince's historical library in
the Old South Church before 1775, and, during his pastorate at Dover, Governor Wentworth of New Hampshire
opened his collection to him. Writing to a friend in 1772,
Belknap said that the ''principal amusement'' of his leisure hours was to learn what he could ''from printed books
and manuscripts, and the information of aged and intelligent persons, of the former state and affairs of this town
and province'' (New Hampshire). In his dependence on
tradition, Belknap was very cautious, and, as he says in
his preface, made allowance for ''the imperfection of human memory.'' During the feverish days before military
hostilities had begun, Belknap stirred up enthusiasm for
the patriot cause, and in the pages of his history describing the Revolution his feeling was too strong to be bound
by the canons of impartiality. In his letters to Ebenezer
Hazard we learn of Belknap's high degree of self-criticism, and also of his many difficulties in historical research. To his correspondent he wrote of hunting in ''gar-
rets and ratholes of old houses'' for private papers when
not one paper in a hundred ''would repay him for the
trouble.'' [45]

In 1784, the first volume of Belknap's *History of
New Hampshire* was published in Philadelphia, under
the supervision of his friend Hazard; its subtitle is
''Comprehending the Events of one Complete Century
from the Discovery of the River Pascataqua.'' Belknap
points to the need for such a work, saying, ''The few
publications concerning New Hampshire are fugitive
pieces dictated by party or interest. No regular historical

---

[44] J. S. Bassett, *The Middle Group of American Historians* (N. Y.,
1917), p. 28.
[45] Mass. Hist. Soc. *Colls.*, ''Belknap Papers,'' 5th ser., II, 293-298; January 13, 1784.

deduction has ever appeared." In keeping with the highest standards of his day, he notes his authorities. He intends, so he informs his readers, "not barely to relate facts, but to delineate the characters, the passions, the interests and tempers of the persons . . . and to describe the most striking features of the times in which they lived."

From the vantage point of New Hampshire it was easier for him to be critical of Puritan intolerance, and he writes: "Impartiality will not suffer a veil to be drawn over these disgraceful transactions." And from the height of a rationalist's seat in the late eighteenth century, Belknap looks back with disdain to the seventeenth century. Speaking of King Philip's War, he says: "Our gravest historians have recorded many omens, predictions, and other alarming circumstances during this and the Pequod war, which in a more philosophical and less credulous age would not be worthy of notice." [46] To his dear friend Hazard, Belknap once uttered the wish that they could be together to laugh at Mather's *Wonders of the Invisible World*.[47]

Although this first volume met with a discouraging reception from the general public, Belknap went on with his history and brought out a second volume in 1791, followed by a third the next year. When, on the appearance of the first volume, Hazard urged him to hurry along the second, Belknap replied that it would take a few years. The first took him "off and on, nine or ten years," he said, and then he added, "I know that it might be run through in a much shorter time by a Grub Street Gazetteer, who would take everything on trust and had materials ready prepared." [48] In writing this second volume "Comprehending the Events of Seventy-five Years, from

[46] P. 162.
[47] Mass. Hist. Soc. *Colls.*, "Belknap Papers," 5th ser., III, 198; October 22, 1789.
[48] Bassett, *op. cit.*, pp. 40-41.

MDCCXV to MDCCXC," Belknap takes issue with
Chalmers's description of the people of New Hampshire,
and, on other matters also, he differs with that well-known
authority. A very interesting sentence near the close of
the second volume illustrates Belknap's historical per-
spicacity. "By the funding of the Continental debt, and
the assumption of the debts of the individual states, into
one general mass," he says, "a foundation is laid for the
support of public credit; by which means the American
revolution appears to be completed." The narrative was
finished with Volume II.

The third volume has a geographical description of
the State, its natural history, the condition of its society
and manners and its laws and government. The list of
subscribers at the close of Volume III indicates that many
of the leading citizens of the country had begun to show
an interest in Belknap's work. The many technical difficulties in publishing the history made it impossible to
produce as finished a piece of work as Belknap would
have wished; for example, it missed the benefit that his
proofreading might have given it.[49] More than two score
years later, de Tocqueville, in speaking of Belknap, said
that he had "more general ideas and more strength of
thought, than are to be met with in other American historians, even to the present day."

While working on his history, Belknap broached the
idea of collecting the lives of noted Americans in an
"American Biographical Dictionary." He had already
gathered materials for it, and asked Hazard to undertake
its publication.[50] In the spirit of mutual encouragement
that animated them both, Hazard offered to aid Belknap
with the Biographical Dictionary. He brought it to the

[49] See L. S. Mayo, "Jeremy Belknap and Ebenezer Hazard 1782-1784,"
New Eng. Quart. (April, 1929).
[50] Jane B. Marcou, *Life of Jeremy Belknap,* p. 214; see letter of
May 12, 1779.

attention of others, but with the wisdom born of sad experience Hazard supposed that the gentlemen who had promised their assistance would be likely to forget it.[51] The matter rested for some time until Belknap returned to it about fourteen years later. In the preface to the third volume of his *History,* he said that in the course of his researches he had found materials for an American biography and was contemplating the publication of such a work. It would contain statesmen, literary personages, warriors, inventors, navigators, and travelers. In 1794 the first volume of the "American Biography" was published, in 1798, the second. Considering the time and the limited materials available, the whole was a very creditable performance. This work was the forerunner of similar collections in the century following, and of our own contemporary *Dictionary of American Biography.* Before Belknap's death, collections for a third volume had been begun, and to complete it Hazard proposed a coöperative work, each contributor writing one life.[52]

From the fertile minds of Belknap and Hazard came fruitful ideas and developments, sometimes a century in advance of their day. It was a long time before historians in the nineteenth century adopted the view Hazard asserted in a letter to Belknap: "British emissaries," he said, "have diligently propagated an idea that the Colonies were disaffected to the royal government, and thirsted after independence; and I think it a duty incumbent on every American historian to use his endeavours to wipe off so unjust an aspersion."[53] At one time Hazard proposed an "American Chronology" on the model of Prince's work for New England.[54] He actually

[51] Mass. Hist. Soc. *Colls.,* "Belknap Papers," 5th ser., II, 7-8; August 4, 1779.
[52] Mass. Hist. Soc. *Colls.,* 5th ser., Vol. III; October 28, 1803.
[53] "Belknap Papers," *loc. cit.,* 5th ser., II, 119-126; March 20, 1782; April 10, 1782.
[54] *Ibid.,* p. 37; March 11, 1780.

began the work, abridging Prince by leaving out the "Creation, Adam, Noah and some other things which did not peculiarly belong to America." He also added other materials so that his collection was of a respectable size, and he asked Belknap's aid in the pursuit of his studies.[55] But he did not complete the chronology, and twenty-five years passed before the project was finally consummated in the work of Abiel Holmes.

To Belknap most of the credit is given for the formation of the Massachusetts Historical Society; he was its leading member in its early years. John Pintard, one of New York's most useful citizens, who was then collecting materials on the American Revolution, had written to Belknap in 1789 to urge the formation of a Society of Antiquaries. Less than two years had passed when Belknap wrote to Hazard that an "Historical Society" had been organized.[56] In an earlier communication, Pintard asked that Hubbard's manuscript history of New England be printed. "I am extremely anxious," he said, "to multiply copies of our original historians." [57] The long and valuable series of publications of the Massachusetts Historical Society date from 1792, when the first volume of its *Collections* was published, largely through Belknap's efforts.

Belknap's work as a historian is of the first importance, but perhaps of equal significance was the enthusiasm for historical study that he evoked in others. He assiduously hunted down manuscripts to be added to the collections of the Historical Society, not waiting for the donors to seek him out. The high standard of scholarship maintained by Belknap is clearly revealed in a reply to Matthew Carey, the Philadelphia publisher, who had asked him to write the historical section of a projected

[55] See Hazard mss., "American Chronology," in Library of Congress.
[56] Mass. Hist. Soc. *Colls.*, 5th ser., III, 157, 165, 244-245.
[57] *Loc. cit.*, 6th ser., IV, 446-448; August 26, 1788.

Annual Register. Among other things, Belknap said that it was almost impossible to write contemporary history.[58] The death of so illustrious a scholar was a deep blow to New England. Writing to an American correspondent, Christophe D. Ebeling, the noted German historian of America, said of Belknap, "He died, alas, too early for your literature and history." [59] The small circle of historically minded people with whom he gathered in the 1790's widened steadily in the following years, and the standards of Belknap's scholarship were a guide to excellence.

GEORGE MINOT

The uncertainties of the critical period drove some students to a search for political wisdom among the ancient Greeks and Romans. But some writers—among them, George Minot—drew a lesson from the events of their own day, and stressed the value of strong government. Shays' Rebellion caused shivers to run up and down the spines of conservatives, and Minot clearly revealed the Federalist hostility to the rebels. His volume, *The History of the Insurrections in Massachusetts in the year 1786 . . .* (1788), giving only one side of the controversy, failed to explain why the debt-burdened farmers flouted authority.

Minot belonged to the Boston group which recalled with mingled feelings the history that Hutchinson had left unfinished when he departed for England in 1774. Although the portrait of Hutchinson was maliciously etched in the mind of Mercy Otis Warren by her acid recollections, other historians felt no strong enmity against the governor who had died an exile in London. Rather there seemed to be disappointment that the his-

[58] Mass. Hist. Soc. *Colls.*, 6th ser., IV, 335-338; May 18, 1787.
[59] "Letters of C. D. Ebeling," W. C. Lane, ed., Amer. Antiq. Soc. *Proc.* (October, 1925), 306, to Rev. Wm. Bentley, September 16, 1798.

tory of Massachusetts, begun by Hutchinson, remained incomplete. Minot set himself the task of picking up the narrative where Hutchinson had left off in his second volume. In 1798 he published the *Continuation of the History of the Province of Massachusetts Bay from the year 1748,* with an introduction of four chapters summarizing the history of the colony to that date. Like John Adams, Minot was aware that the records in England would be necessary for a more complete history. This volume, which brought the story down to 1756, is to a large extent concerned with the first stages of the Seven Years' War. Minot was at work on a second volume when he died in 1802, and it was brought out, unfinished, the next year. It ends with the Stamp Act riots of 1765, occurrences which elicited the condemnation of the historian who had treated in similar fashion Daniel Shays; the mob that destroyed Hutchinson's home is referred to as a "triumphant demonocracy" [60]

Minot, who had had a thorough legal training and held a judicial position, gave a good account of the constitutional questions at issue between Massachusetts and England. His sources were few, but among them were the manuscripts of Jasper Mauduit, the colony's agent in England. Hutchinson, it will be remembered, did add a third volume to his own history, and with its publication in 1828, Minot's work was entirely eclipsed. His volume on Shays' Rebellion was, however, used by a number of historians and for a long time helped perpetuate the conservative interpretation of those troubled times.

HANNAH ADAMS

In the Revolutionary era, plans were made for histories of all the New England States and even for the whole United States. Benjamin Rush, for example, asked

[60] P. 216.

Belknap to write the history of the establishment of the Federal government.[61] There was, however, more talk than action, and not much of great significance was accomplished. One reason for this was the fact that on Massachusetts was concentrated most of the attention, to the exclusion of the other states; another reason was the paucity of genuine scholarship. A volume that attempted to fill the need for an inclusive survey was *A Summary History of New England* . . . (1799) by Hannah Adams. Miss Adams, who was a distant cousin of John Adams, inherited a love of books from her father, and it is supposed that she was the first American woman to earn her livelihood by writing. "It was poverty . . . that first induced me to become an author, or rather a compiler." [62] Her life spanned the period of the Revolution and the first thirty years of the nineteenth century, and her intellectual achievements made her a member of the New England literati. Toward the latter part of her life her friends settled an annuity upon her and the timid, absent-minded old lady spent part of her last years poring over ancient tomes in the Boston Athenaeum.

Miss Adams followed the procedure of most of the other historians—she compiled her book on New England from the few volumes of history that had been written up to that time. In addition she utilized some manuscript materials, particularly on the colony of Rhode Island, which, especially in the earlier chapters, is apportioned a fair amount of space. She also quotes from Ezra Stiles's manuscript lectures on ecclesiastical history,[63] which supplied much of the material in her pages on the state of learning in New England.[64] In keeping with the spirit of her day, Miss Adams is critical of the intolerance of the

---

[61] Mass. Hist. Soc. *Colls.*, 6th ser., IV, 473; January 5, 1791.
[62] *A Memoir of Miss Hannah Adams, Written by Herself* (1832), p. 22.
[63] Pp. 158, 179.
[64] Chap. XIV.

early settlers,[65] and when her narrative approaches the Revolution she mentions the opposition that had been aroused by the proposed establishment of the Anglican episcopacy.[66] Almost half of her volume of over five hundred pages is on the Revolution, and she drew much from Ramsay and Gordon, who were considered the leading historians of the war. Miss Adams also used the *Annual Register,* and some of her material came from conversations with men who had fought in the war. From the pages of George Minot, the historian extracted a Federalist interpretation of Shays' Rebellion,[67] and in Morse's *Geography* Miss Adams found the materials for her last section on the condition of literature and learning.[68] An abridgment of the *Summary History* for the use of school children was published in 1807 and this, too, was accorded a welcome in New England. While Miss Adams's history was inadequate, there were few alternatives to her work at the beginning of the nineteenth century.

MERCY OTIS WARREN

Hannah Adams was not the only woman historian of New England. A lady with an illustrious name, Mercy Otis Warren, set down her record of the Revolutionary era, her relationship with many of the leading figures of the day having given her a peculiar insight into some of the events of these years. The sister of James Otis and the wife of James Warren, she shared their intensely patriotic view of the struggle. It was in the home of Thomas Hutchinson, bought by the Warrens, that she wrote much of the history that singled out the exiled governor for her bitter scorn. In 1805 Mrs. Warren brought out her three-volume *History of the Rise, Progress and Termination of the American Revolution interspersed*

65 Pp. 102-103.   67 Pp. 487-491.
66 Pp. 211-212.   68 Pp. 500-510.

with Biographical, Political and Moral Reflections. Although published more than a score of years after the
treaty of peace, Mrs. Warren said that she had been collecting materials "many years antecedent to any history
since published," and it is probable that much of her
work was written contemporaneously with the events they
describe. During the Revolution Abigail Adams, wife of
John Adams, had written to Mrs. Warren that "many
very memorable events which ought to be handed down to
posterity will be buried in oblivion merely for want of a
proper Hand to record them." Mrs. Adams reminded her
friend, who had stopped writing, that she should continue
lest future historians miss many things that might go
unrecorded.[69] John Adams gave Mrs. Warren firsthand
information regarding his negotiations with the Dutch;
and a few years later another noted figure in Massachusetts politics, Benjamin Lincoln, offered the use of
his papers to the historian.[70]

After some introductory remarks, Mrs. Warren begins her history with the Stamp Act. Halfway through
her first volume she reaches the period of military hostilities, where the Warren bias is immediately apparent. A
special object of vituperation is, of course, Thomas
Hutchinson. In the eyes of the historian, Hutchinson was
"dark, intriguing, insinuating, haughty and ambitious,
while the extreme of avarice marked each feature of his
character"; and his was a Machiavellian attitude toward
government.[71] In her second volume Mrs. Warren broad-
ens her view of the war period to include references to
discontent in Ireland and internal politics in England,
which she relates, rather lamely, to the American Revolution.[72] Some eighty pages in the third volume [73] reveal the

[69] Mass. Hist. Soc. *Colls.,* "Warren-Adams Letters," Vol. LXXII; August 14, 1777.
[70] *Loc. cit.,* Vol. LXXIII; October 24, 1782; March 25, 1790.
[71] I, 79.   [73] Chaps. XXIV, XXV.
[72] II, 211-223.

broader scope of the history of the Revolution, which now includes the naval history of these years—Rodney in the West Indies, events in Minorca, Gibraltar, and elsewhere. The following chapter refers to the war's repercussions in Great Britain and in Ireland. In thus making more comprehensive her history Mrs. Warren was in accord with John Adams, who held that to write on the American Revolution one must write the history of mankind during that period. After her description of the war, said the author, her mind was ''now at leisure for more general observations on the subsequent consequences, without confining it to time or place.'' [74] The remarks that follow on the later history of the United States are practically valueless as historical writing. As honest John Adams bluntly wrote to Mrs. Warren: ''After the termination of the Revolutionary war your subject was completed.'' [75]

A long correspondence with Mrs. Warren initiated by John Adams, who felt himself aspersed by the historian, makes a valuable addition to the work because of the inclusion of many interesting items on our diplomatic history. The Warren family's leaning to Jeffersonianism was a cause of friction with Adams, although friendly relations between the families were maintained to the end. Adams remarked ungallantly that history was ''not the Province of the Ladies.'' ''It is my opinion . . . ,'' said Adams to Mrs. Warren, ''that your History has been written to the taste of the nineteenth century, and accommodated to gratify the passions, prejudices, and feelings of the party who are now predominant.'' To which she replied by saying that her history had been under consideration long before the nineteenth century and had received encouragement from John Adams himself.[76] The

[74] III, 338.
[75] Mass. Hist. Soc. *Colls.*, 5th ser., IV, 432; August 8, 1807.
[76] *Ibid.*, pp. 463, 489-490.

writing of Mrs. Warren was often diffuse and her rhetorical passages, especially on the Declaration of Independence, were of the stuff that makes typical patriotic orations. To read Mrs. Warren's history, however, is to get
a vivid glimpse of the thoughts and feelings of the leaders during this period.

JOHN DALY BURK

The spirit of Jefferson that hovered over Mrs. Warren's history completely suffused Burk's history of the
Old Dominion. John Daly Burk was born in Ireland and
came to America as one of the many political refugees
that were leaving Ireland at the end of the eighteenth
century. From New York he eventually found his way to
Virginia, where his law practice was too little to keep him
busy, and, to exercise his literary talents, he turned to
writing a history of his adopted state. (Burk was also a
well-known dramatist.) The first three volumes of his
history were published in 1804 and 1805, but he did not
live to complete the work. He was killed in a duel, 1808,
and the fourth volume, the last published, was completed
by two other writers, Skelton Jones and Louis Hue Girardin. Ill fate dogged this work, for after writing but a
short part of the last volume, Jones also was killed in a
duel. Nearly the whole of this volume, therefore, was
written by Girardin.

The *History of Virginia from its first Settlement
to the Present Day* is dedicated to Jefferson, who permitted Burk, an ardent Jeffersonian, the use of his library. The author refers briefly to his predecessors in the
field; Smith was a "faithful guide" as far as he went,
which was only twenty years; Beverley was a "mere
annalist of petty incidents" and an "apologist of
power"; John Smith's narrative was a "sort of epic history or romance, where the author like Ossian, recounts

his achievements in the spirit with which he fought";
but Smith, said Burk, was the groundwork for succeeding
histories. In addition to these authorities, Burk claims
to have used the minutes of the London Company and the
proceedings of the Virginia legislature. We are told also,
that Burk had access to Byrd's manuscripts.[77]

The first volume goes only to 1624, but the author,
in a statement to the public, says that he could not com-
press his materials any more than he had. The next volume extends to about 1710, and in order to "preserve
unity and compactness," says Burk, he left out the details of revenue and finance, the organization of courts of
justice, the state of arts and manners; these were to be
examined in the appendix. Despite his disparagement of
Beverley, Burk used his volume freely for these materials. The third volume, which brings Burk's narrative to
the outbreak of the Revolution, presented opportunities
for the free display of the author's rhetoric; with this
volume, however, he did something to raise Virginia's
history out of its provincial setting to a place in relationship with the whole colonial world. The last volume, on
the war, ends with 1781. Although Burk spoke of his
acquaintance with valuable sources, he made scarcely
any use of the records in the Secretary's office. In general, Virginians have not been very favorably impressed
with his work.[78]

BENJAMIN TRUMBULL

Among the historians of the late eighteenth and early
nineteenth centuries who labored to preserve the memorials of an earlier day, none worked harder than Benjamin
Trumbull. Practically all his life was associated with his

[77] Charles Campbell, ed., *Some Materials to serve for a brief memoir
of John Daly Burk* . . . (1868), p. 33.
[78] *Virginia Historical Register*, I, 48.

native province, Connecticut, whose history he narrated. Trumbull died in 1820, when he was eighty-five years old; for sixty years he had been pastor of the North Haven Congregational Church. Although his historical publications did not appear until late in life, Trumbull had been collecting materials over a period of many years.

In 1801 he published *A Century Sermon, or Sketches of the History of the Eighteenth Century . . ."* This was "a sketch of the works of God in the century past," he tells us, "in Europe and other parts of the old world, and especially His dispensations towards America, the United States, New England, and this town" (North Haven). The publication was in the nature of a preliminary survey for Trumbull's larger work on the United States.

In 1810 there appeared *A General History of the United States of America from the discovery in 1492, to 1792. . . .* Three volumes were promised, of which this was the first; it took the narrative to the year 1765. The other two never were published, although Jedidiah Morse was supposed to carry the work to completion. The second volume was to cover the next thirteen years or so to the capture of Burgoyne, and the last to 1792, thus completing a narrative of four centuries of American history. Trumbull's remaining materials were given to Morse, who was busy on his own historical projects. In his preface Trumbull speaks of his work as a thank offering for divine aid granted to America in the Revolutionary years; his history, he hoped too, would promote a national feeling. His difficulties in research were multiplied, he says, because of the interconnection of colonial and British history, "which rendered a constant study of the history of [England] as well as of America necessary to authenticate and elucidate the work." Trumbull does not pay much attention to ecclesiastical history in this volume, because that was to be the subject of another work. At the beginning of his history there is a large amount of material on Indian civilization. Though the period 1700-1750 is hastily skimmed over, and more than a quarter of the book is on the wars from 1748 to 1763, measured by contemporary standards, Trumbull's volume was not badly proportioned.

A few years ago a manuscript, written by Trumbull in 1767, was published. It was *A Compendium of the Indian Wars in New England* [79] with special reference to Connecticut. Trumbull had made an attempt to collect all available authorities and compare them carefully: Increase Mather, Hubbard, Hutchinson, Callender, Mason (or Allen), Church, and Prince. This material is mainly on the war with the Pequots. The manuscript shows Trumbull's conscientiousness and his ability to evaluate critically his sources. This material he later used in the history of his native state.

The work for which Trumbull is best known is *A Complete History of Connecticut: Civil and Ecclesiastical from the Emigration of its First Planters, from England in the Year 1630, to the Year 1764; and to the Close of the Indian Wars.*[80] In his preface Trumbull gives the reasons that so many others had given for studying and writing history, especially that of New England: ''The pious man views a divine hand conducting the whole, gives thanks, adores and loves.'' Trumbull saw Prince's collection of historical materials and made use of those bearing on Connecticut. His history had been planned before the Revolution, but the war postponed publication for many years. Meanwhile he had been asked by the General Association of Connecticut to prepare a history of the United States to 1792. In collecting and compiling

[79] 1926, F. B. Hartranft, ed.

[80] Vol. I in 1797; 2 vols., edn. in 1818; another edition was published in 1898.

his materials for the latter work, says Trumbull, he stole hours from the dawn and followed a strict routine (he had his ministerial labors to perform as well) for some ten years. Then, at length, he turned back to his history of Connecticut.

"As this is the first history of the colony . . . ," says Trumbull, "the compiler judged it expedient to make it more full and particular, than otherwise might have been necessary or proper." He wished to assist future historians and was anxious that nothing of importance relating to the church or state should be lost. The historian says that he had avoided the "florid and pompous style," which he thinks "unnatural and improper in historic writings," and that he attempts the "easy and familiar." He gives his sources and follows a soundly established precedent when he writes, "very little has been taken upon tradition." Remembering the experiences of Ebenezer Hazard and others in those days, we can well believe Trumbull's statement that "the labor of collecting the materials for the history . . . has been almost incredible." [81]

The first volume of the edition of 1898 goes to about 1710, and contains an appendix of documents. In accordance with his promise Trumbull gives us a very detailed and plainly written text. The ecclesiastical portion of the history is treated separately. The work contains economic and social history, and materials of value on the history of various towns; it touches incidentally on regions outside Connecticut borders as well. Trumbull thinks that New England was settled "purely for the purposes of Religion"; [82] he believes also that New England's treatment of the Pequots after the war was very unfair. [83] In his work which, like other writings that belonged to the

[81] P. xvii, 1898 edn.   [83] P. 88.
[82] P. 1.

eighteenth century, was more of a chronicle than a history, Trumbull was encyclopedic in his inclusiveness; he "got Connecticut by heart before he began writing its history," said Bancroft. "He could tell the name, birthplace, and career of every minister that had preached a good sermon, and every militiaman that had done a notable thing. Not a savage was overcome, not a backslider censured by the church, but he knew it all." [84] Not only did he know it all, but he felt the necessity to *tell* all, and the details were spun out to tedious length. He was Connecticut's first historian and proudly treasured her facts, observing conscientiously the New England injunction, "Despise not the day of small things."

J E D I D I A H   M O R S E

Trumbull's younger contemporary, Jedidiah Morse, grew up in the Revolutionary era when the self-consciousness of Americans sought an expression in all fields of life. He was born in 1761, and attended Yale with Abiel Holmes, who also became a historian. Morse taught for a short time, then entered the ministry in 1785. A member of the Society for the Propagation of the Gospel, he took a leading part in the Unitarian controversy that rocked New England. His career as geographer and historian lasted for over forty years to his death in 1826.

It was when he was teaching in New Haven, in 1783, that Morse became seriously interested in geography. Guthrie's *English Geography* was the one then generally used in American schools, and it was very poor on American material. The next year Morse put his lectures into a book, *Geography made Easy,* which was the first on the subject published in America. He was constantly gathering information from wide sources, and on his travels he noted additional materials to be included in

[84] *N. A. Rev.* (April, 1838).

an enlarged edition of his geography. Belknap wrote to him in 1784 that "to be a true geographer it is necessary to be a Traveller," and he urged Morse to see things for himself and not get information from authors at secondhand. "As water passing through various strata of earth acquires different tinctures," said Belknap, "so a story told by a succession of writers, partakes of the humours, inattention and prejudices of them all." [85] Dr. Ramsay, the historian, also helped Morse to gather materials.

To Belknap, who went over the section on New Hampshire, Morse wrote in 1788: [86] "The nature of the work does not admit of much originality. The book must derive its merit—if it have any—from the accuracy and good judgment with which it is compiled, rather than the genius with which it is composed. To save me from the odious character of a Plagiarist, general credit will be given in the preface for all selections inserted in the work."

In March, 1789, the geography was published. Of its more than five hundred pages, some seven-eighths are on the United States, and in addition to the geographical material, there is much historical matter. Some of his friends thought Morse should have restricted the geography to America exclusively, but he designed it in part to compete with English geographies then used in American schools. In a later edition he gave even more space to non-American areas. The geography was an immediate success and was adopted at Yale as a textbook. European editions of the book were published also, but in that day of pirating publishers Morse received no royalties. Christophe D. Ebeling, the greatest European student of American history and geography, testified to the contribution of Morse "as the first who has cut a road through

[85] W. B. Sprague, *The Life of Jedidiah Morse* (N. Y., 1874), p. 193.
[86] *Ibid.*, p. 196.

a vast wilderness."[87] A second edition, called *The American Universal Geography,* was published in two volumes, of which the first was mainly on America.

In 1794, writing to Ebeling, Morse said that since his "first juvenile essay" was published ten years before, over twenty thousand copies of his geography had been printed in America. His financial success was a topic of gossip among his contemporaries. Ebenezer Hazard, writing to the third member of the group, Jeremy Belknap, referred to Morse as the "only successful author in the triumvirate," and added with mild regret, "What a pity it is that *we* had not been geographers instead of *historians.*"[88] Morse was more or less continually at work on geographical research and, along with other New England intellectuals, he was in correspondence with Ebeling for their mutual benefit. Eventually, however, Ebeling became annoyed with Morse, saying that since the American would not learn German he could not help him.[89]

Morse did not restrict himself to geography. He was, in fact, planning a gazetteer of the United States to acquaint the world with the new nation. Although other writers had also thought of such a work, they abandoned their projects in favor of Morse. *The American Gazetteer,* with seven thousand separate articles in it, came out in 1797. In his preface to *The American Geography* (1789) Morse had written that Europeans had been the sole writers of American geography and were often inaccurate. "But since the United States have become an independent nation . . . ," he continues, "the rest of the world have a right now to expect authentic information." The author had worked on his gazetteer for four years,

[87] *Ibid.,* p. 205; 1793.
[88] Mass. Hist. Soc. *Colls.,* 5th ser., III, 361; January 14, 1796.
[89] Amer. Antiq. Soc. *Proc.,* October, 1925; To William Bentley, March 25, 1816.

and was greatly in debt to Ebenezer Hazard's collection
of papers for his historical information. Hazard's collection, said Morse, "is the most complete deposition of
facts relating to the history of America . . . that is to
be found in the United States."

Morse was also engaged in the writing and compilation of purely historical works. He wrote the article
"New England" in the supplement of the American edition of the *Encyclopaedia Britannica,* 1801. With the
aid of Rev. Elijah Parish, the article was revised and
enlarged into a history of New England that went
through several editions. It is interesting to note that
Morse and Parish began their history of New England,
in the introduction, with the Reformation, not with
Columbus or some earlier figure; the next step of the historians, who in this respect approached more nearly the
modern point of view, was to continue the narrative with
the Pilgrims in Holland. One hundred years before James
Truslow Adams spoke critically of New England's part
in the Pequot War, Morse had written: "This is a dis-
mal section of our history. The time has been, when pious
Christians had so lost sight of their Saviour's precepts
and example as to engage in unnecessary war." [90] It is
supposed that Morse's disapproval of New England's
wars with the Indians, of whom he was fond, came from
his experience as a missionary to them. There is also a
fair statement of the witchcraft episode to be found in
this history.[91] On the whole this is a well-written and
well-proportioned piece of work. Although in an earlier
volume Morse had taken precautions to avoid "the odious
character of a Plagiarist," his history of New England
was the cause of a bitter controversy between him and

[90] *A Compendious History of New England* . . . (3rd edn., 1820), p.
158.
[91] Pp. 254-261.

Hannah Adams, who alleged that he had plagiarized her materials.

In 1824 Morse brought out his *Annals of the American Revolution* . . . , which includes, in its varied features, biographies of the war heroes. Morse was a tired man by this time and had little interest in the book. He said it was "professedly a compilation" the plan of which was drawn up by the publishers, who timed its issue to coincide with Lafayette's visit to America. Section VI, "Causes of the Revolution, assigned by Dr. Franklin, and the late President Adams," is perhaps the most interesting part of the volume. Adams's letters, printed here, had been written some years earlier in answer to Morse's inquiries. This was a poorly arranged work, of which Morse was not particularly proud, but Americans had nothing better for many years to come.

JOHN MARSHALL

The Revolution was the major interest of the next generation of writers, but the deeds of some of the war heroes were commemorated even earlier by grateful contemporaries. No one so dominated the American consciousness as did Washington. The First President was the subject of a lengthy work by Chief Justice John Marshall, and it was officially classed as a biography. It has long been recognized, however, that these volumes are more a political history of America during the life of the first president. The first volume, of the five which appeared between 1804 and 1807, is expressly a history of the colonies; the title of the miscalled biography is *The Life of George Washington . . . to which is prefixed an Introduction containing a Compendious View of the Colonies Planted by the English in the Continent of North America*. Marshall's public and private associations gained him access to materials that few people of

that day could have secured. Bushrod Washington permitted the use of his collection of the President's papers;
not until twenty years later did Jared Sparks get a similar privilege. Bushrod Washington, indeed, urged Marshall to write the biography, and the latter's need for
money at the time was one of the impelling causes for
undertaking it.[92]

Marshall tells the reader that he had used materials
from other publications, and in the custom of his day
ran together separate quotations without distinguishing
marks. Because the history of Washington was the history of the country during that period, said Marshall, it
was necessary to write the history of America; it was
particularly important to have a survey of the colonies,
because "that period of our history is but little known
to ourselves." Although there were several histories of
the provinces, the desideratum, said Marshall, a year before Holmes's *American Annals* appeared, "is a composition which shall present, in one connected view, the
transactions of all those colonies which now form the
United States." [93]

This first volume, which covers the period to the
Stamp Act, was compiled from the few standard authors
used by most historians; the writer covering the years
to the reign of William and Mary, said Marshall, needed
little in addition to George Chalmers.[94] In justice to the
historian (whose work, by the way, was praised by
Herbert L. Osgood), it should be pointed out that
Marshall himself appreciated the inconclusive character
of his first volume, but realized that there was a place
for it in the absence of any other. A reviewer in the Boston *Monthly Anthology,* although criticizing the inclusion

[92] A. J. Beveridge, *John Marshall* (N. Y., 1916-1919), Vol. III, Chap. V.
[93] P. xviii.
[94] P. xx.

of an early history of the country in a biography, noted that it was the ''first attempt to give a connected history of the various states.'' [95]

Some of the observations made by Marshall antici-pated, by many years, later studies of the colonial period. He refers, for example, to the resolutions of the New York Assembly, in 1711, against taxation without con-sent: ''This strong assertion of a principle, the contro-versy concerning which afterwards dismembered the British empire, passed away without notice. It was prob-ably understood to be directed only against the assump-tion of that power by the governor.[96] In speaking later [97] of another legal problem, Marshall points out that no ac-curate definition had ever been made of the degree of authority exercisable by the mother country over the colonies: ''In Britain, it had always been asserted, that Parliament possessed the power of binding them in all cases whatsoever. In America, at different times, and in different colonies, different opinions had been enter-tained on this subject.'' In the following pages [98] Mar-shall presents a very good discussion of this question, and in somewhat the temper of the modern student he also writes of the rise of animosity against new taxation. His sentiment on England's retention of the tax on tea has since been echoed many times: ''Never perhaps did a great and wise nation adopt a more ill-judged measure than this.'' [99]

The first eighty pages or so of the second volume deal with Washington's early years, and at the halfway point in the volume Marshall again picks up the biogra-phy of Washington with his appointment as commander in chief. There is a good statement of the adoption by

[95] V, 267.
[96] I, 249; see Channing, *History of the United States,* II, 310.
[97] II, 82.   [99] II, 146.
[98] II, 82-89.

the states of the republican form of government.[100] In his remarks on the Declaration of Independence Marshall is much more moderate and restrained than were Bancroft and James Grahame later.[101] The third volume goes to 1778, and the fourth finishes with the conclusion of the war and Washington's retirement to Mt. Vernon.

The subject of the biography is lost in a general history of the war and is only picked up again at the very end. What the reviewer in the *Monthly Anthology* complained of was "not that there is too much history, but that there is too little biography."[102] Marshall's service as a soldier in the Revolution was useful to him when he came to write on military operations. In the last volume Marshall has an excellent chapter on the causes that led to a change in the government of the United States and the adoption of a stronger central power, and he emphasizes the influence and prestige of Washington in promoting sentiment for a vigorous national government.[103] In a discussion of the rise of parties, Marshall notes the antagonism between creditors and debtors,[104] and he also indicates the influence of Shays' Rebellion in driving the States toward a stronger union.[105] Naturally this whole critical period of adjustment is presented from the Federalist standpoint. The biography then becomes a history of national politics and of the diplomatic relations of the United States, but at the conclusion of his work is an estimate of Washington's character so sound that Jared Sparks, the distinguished historian, could later add little to it.

The political associations of Marshall had an adverse effect on the sale of the work. Only eight thousand of the anticipated thirty thousand subscriptions materialized. The price was high, and Republicans spread the

[100] Pp. 399-401.
[101] P. 408.
[102] V, 261.

[103] Pp. 27-55.
[104] Pp. 72-77.
[105] Pp. 94-95.

report that Marshall's work was a Federalist history of the United States and was being written as propaganda for use in the election of 1804. Jefferson, in a letter urging Joel Barlow to write a history of the United States, expressed himself vigorously on the partisan purpose of Marshall's biography, to which he referred as "that five-volumed libel." [106]

Marshall's *Washington* was an acceptable piece of work, Madison once told Sparks, but the fifth volume, he thought, was inaccurate. That staunch Federalist, Chancellor Kent, however, thought the fifth volume was "worth all the rest," and said of the work as a whole that it was "an excellent History of the Government and Parties in this country from vol. 3 to the death of the general." [107] Madison's personal knowledge of the events of those years gave him the vantage point of criticism. It was also his opinion that Marshall "would write differently at the present day [1827] and with his present impressions." [108]

The Chief Justice was conscious of his haste in bringing out the biography and always hoped to issue a better, revised edition. He was able to do so in 1832, and the first volume was published separately as a *History of the American Colonies*. Granting the faults of disproportion and frequent dependence on secondary authorities, Marshall's work filled a distinct need, and his first volume, in particular, was a notable achievement for his day.

PARSON WEEMS

The Revolutionary era and its leading figures were memorialized in rather sober histories, some of which

[106] McMaster, *History of the People of the U. S.*, V, 294; Beveridge, *John Marshall*, III, 267.

[107] Beveridge, *John Marshall*, III, 265.

[108] Adams, *Jared Sparks*, II, 37.

were very well known among the literati. These volumes created for the serious reader a more or less realistic pattern of our past, but a construction of different design was sketched for a general audience by the famous Parson Weems. The books of Weems were a particularly colorful culmination of the literature of the Revolutionary period and from them countless Americans have received an indelible impression of those stirring years. "For thirty years there was no more familiar figure on the roads of the Southern States than this book peddler and author who, . . . gipsy-like . . . travelled his long route year after year, sleeping in wayside inn, farmhouse or forest, fiddling, writing [and] selling books." [109] He spent almost thirty-five years on the road before his death in 1825. So successful was Mason Locke Weems that his publications in the first half of the nineteenth century were better known than those of any other American.

Weems was born in Maryland in 1759 and at an early age, tradition tells us, he was in an atmosphere conducive to the glorification of Washington's name. Weems studied medicine abroad, but it appears that he practiced little. His healing was of the soul rather than of the body, for Dr. Weems became Parson Weems of the Anglican Church in 1784. Within eight years he had given up the ministry as a regular profession for the more irregular livelihood of writer and bookseller. Before the end of the century he was the Southern agent of the famous Philadelphia book publisher, Matthew Carey.

With the publication of the *Life of Washington* in 1800, Weems came into his own as an author. For more than two decades thereafter he reaped the rewards of being the foremost writer in a field little touched before in America—juvenile literature. But adults as well as

[109] L. C. Wroth, *Parson Weems* (Baltimore, 1911).

boys and girls read his books, which inculcated the prized virtues of industry, temperance, and frugality. The biography of Washington, Weems's most successful work, is supposed to have reached between forty and seventy editions. These thousands of volumes made the story of Washington and the cherry tree (which first appeared in the fifth edition) part of the national folklore. Despite the fact that Weems is generally recognized as an inaccurate historian and careless biographer, his simple writing was so warm with enthusiasm that it brought to life figures already grown austere and remote.

" 'George,' said his father, 'do you know who killed that beautiful little cherry-tree yonder in the garden?' This was a tough question; and George staggered under it for a moment. . . . 'I can't tell a lie, Pa, you know I can't tell a lie. I did cut it with my hatchet.' 'Run to my arms, you dearest boy,' cried his father in transports . . . ; 'glad am I, George, that you killed my tree; for you have paid for it a thousand fold. Such an act of heroism in my son is more worth than a thousand trees, though blossomed with silver, and their fruits of purest gold.' " The style of the preacher was the style of the biographer, and in an age which admired oratory Weems waxed eloquent indeed.

In his *Life of General Francis Marion,* Weems produced a historical romance that later received the praise of so good a writer as William Gilmore Simms. His accounts of military events associated with the careers of Washington and Marion, even though described with intense partisanship, are fairly dependable. In other respects his biographies drew more from his imagination than from the lives of his subjects. The spontaneity that characterized the biographies of Washington and Marion is absent in Weems's life of Franklin, a large part of which was borrowed from Franklin's autobiography and from his other writings. Weems's fondness for the

Franklinian virtues was not enough to color the work richly; perhaps it is not always easy to write gloriously of industry, temperance, and frugality.

In his books Weems not only crusaded in behalf of temperance reform, but he also attacked gambling. The moralist was consistently true to himself, whether in publishing biographies or moral tracts—he was first and last an uplifter. It has been estimated that over a million copies of his books have appeared. Two of the outstanding books in all of American history, the *Federalist* and Franklin's *Autobiography,* have had no longer life than the *Washington* of Weems. "As a 'Maker' of history," remarks Channing, "Mason L. Weems vies with the household poets." Long stretches of Bancroft's work on the United States, Longfellow's "The Courtship of Miles Standish," or Whittier's "Barbara Frietchie" were no nearer the facts of history than was the *Washington* of Weems; and the latter, says Channing, "has had equal or greater influence on succeeding generations of Americans than any of these." It might not be too much to say that generations of historical scholars since his time have been unable to modify seriously the popular picture Weems created of our Revolutionary heroes.[110]

[110] See Wroth, *Parson Weems.*

V

HISTORIOGRAPHY IN THE FIRST HALF OF THE NINETEENTH CENTURY

The stirring events of the two score years which followed 1760 were a stimulus to historical composition and the collection of documentary materials. It is therefore surprising that so little was done on a comprehensive scale. Old John Adams complained to his fellow revolutionist, Thomas McKean: "Can you account for the apathy, the antipathy of this nation to their own history? Is there not a repugnance to the thought of looking back? While thousands of frivolous novels are read with eagerness and got by heart, the history of our own native country is not only neglected, but despised and abhorred."[1] To Elbridge Gerry he also complained of the "total ignorance and oblivion of the revolution" among the younger generation.[2] Mercy Otis Warren likewise thought the younger generation too negligent in seeking information about the Revolutionary era.[3] Conditions were not quite so bad as John Adams declared. He him-

[1] *Works,* X, 62; August 31, 1813.
[2] *Ibid.,* p. 37; April 14, 1813.
[3] Mass. Hist. Soc. *Colls.,* "Warren-Adams Letters," LXXIII, 73; July 10, 1814.

self, in the midst of the war years, had written to Mrs. Warren of a plan to retire and spend his leisure hours in writing a history of the revolution, "and with a hand as severe as Tacitus, I wish to God it was as eloquent, draw the portrait of every character that has figured in the business. But when it is done, I will dig a vault, and bury the manuscript . . . not to be opened till a hundred years after my death." [4]

Adams never wrote the manuscript, but he carried on a correspondence for years with a number of individuals whose interest in the Revolution was whetted by his memories. John Jay in 1787, then Secretary for Foreign Affairs, told Adams that he was collecting the latter's public letters and dispatches. "It is common, you know," he wrote, "in the course of time for loose and detached papers to be lost, or mislaid, or misplaced. It is to papers in this office that future historians must recur for accurate accounts of many interesting affairs respecting the late revolution. . . ." He expected the work to take much time and labor, but he intended to persevere. [5]

While the war was still in progress Elbridge Gerry had moved, in Congress, that each State should designate an official to collect memorials of the Revolution. Had the motion been adopted, said John Adams in 1813, "we should now possess a Monument of more inestimable Value than all the Histories and Orations that have been written." To Gerry's suggestion that he write a narrative, Adams answered: "You talk to me at seventy-seven Years of Age of writing History. If I was only thirty, I would not undertake an History of the Revolution in less than twenty years." [6] In recalling old times McKean told Adams that he, too, had often been asked to write a history of the American Revolution, Benjamin Rush

[4] *Works,* X, 475-476; December 15, 1778.
[5] *Ibid.,* VIII, 446; July 25, 1787.
[6] "Warren-Adams Letters," *loc. cit.;* April 26, 1813.

having been especially insistent.[7] Rush himself had contemplated writing such a history and had gathered materials for it while the war was in progress.[8] Joel Barlow,
too, had prepared documents to write a history of the
Revolution, and in his collection were the papers of General Gates.[9]

Jedidiah Morse wrote to some of the participants in
the Revolution for eyewitness accounts to be included in
a prospective narrative of the struggle. John Jay, like
John Adams, emphasized the need for consulting a large
mass of materials in the preparation of such a history.
He suggested that a colonial background might be properly included. The colonial history section, he said, should
be divided into three parts, the first to 1689, the second
to 1763 and the last to 1774.[10] Almost twenty years later,
when Morse was still seeking original materials on the
Revolution, he turned to John Adams and received long
and revealing letters from him which were appended
to Morse's *Annals of the American Revolution* . . .
(1824). "A history of military operations from April 19,
1775, to the 3d of September, 1783, is not a history of
the American Revolution," said Adams.[11] "The revolution," he said to Morse and to others, "was in the minds
and hearts of the people, and in the union of the colonies;
both of which were substantially effected before hostilities commenced"; the Writs of Assistance in 1761
marked the beginning of the Revolution. Pamphlets,
newspapers, handbills from 1761-1774, the letters of the
committees of correspondence—a study of all these was
necessary to understand the growth of union. "Here
sir," said Adams, "opens an extensive field of investi-

[7] *Works*, X, 17; January, 1814.
[8] H. B. Adams, *Jared Sparks*, II, 49.
[9] *Ibid.*, I, 499.
[10] H. P. Johnston, *John Jay: Correspondence and Public Papers* (4
vols., N. Y., 1890-1893), IV, 224-225; February 28, 1797.
[11] November 29, 1815.

gation, even for a young historian, who might be disposed to undertake so laborious an enterprize.'' The real American Revolution, Adams reiterated, was the ''radical change in the principles, opinions, sentiments and affections of the people'' toward Great Britain. He suggested that young men of letters in all the States, especially in the original thirteen, should collect the historical materials bearing on the Revolutionary period.[12] To Hezekiah Niles, who later compiled a useful volume of documents, Adams was writing in the same vein, although he was doubtful that ''the true history of the American Revolution'' could be recovered.[13]

The Italian Botta's history of the American Revolution with its invented speeches placed in the mouths of the leading actors, called forth questions from various quarters. ''Who shall write the history of the American Revolution?'' Adams asked McKean. ''Who can write it? Who will ever be able to write it? The most essential documents, the debates and deliberations in Congress, from 1774 to 1783, were all in secret, and are now lost forever.'' [14] In replying to Adams, McKean said that Major General James Wilkinson had written the history of the Revolution, but Adams retorted in the words he had recently written to Jedidiah Morse—the history of the war is very different from a history of the American Revolution.[15] At this same time Jefferson and Adams were also discussing these issues, and Jefferson likewise questioned whether anyone could write the history of the Revolution. He felt that the task could not be performed adequately because only its external facts were known, ''all its councils, designs and discussions having been conducted by Congress with closed doors, and no mem-

[12] December 22, 1815.
[13] *Works*, X, 274; January 14, 1818; February 13, 1818.
[14] *Ibid.*, p. 17; July 30, 1815.
[15] *Ibid.*, pp. 176, 180; November 20 and 26, 1815.

bers, as far as I know, having ever made notes of them. These, which are the life and soul of history, must forever be unknown." [16] Allowing for his invented speeches and his "fancying motives of action which we never felt," Jefferson thought Botta's history better than any yet written.[17] Wiser than Adams, who insisted that the Revolution began about 1761 with the Writs of Assistance, Jefferson said that it would be as difficult to name the moment when the "embryo becomes an animal, or the act which gives him a beginning" as to say when the Revolution began "and what incident set it in motion." [18]

In his more acid moments Adams doubted the truth of any historical account, modern or ancient. "Our American history for the last fifty years," he said to Morse, "is already as much corrupted as any half century of ecclesiastical history, from the Council of Nice to the restoration of the Inquisition in 1814." [19] A quarter of a century earlier Adams had written in similar vein to Jeremy Belknap, asserting that important facts are often concealed, false ones accepted, leading personalities little known, while "many empty characters [are] displayed in great pomp." "All this," said Adams, "I am sure, will happen in our American history." [20] As for the American histories already published, McKean agreed with Adams that they were not popular because their authors were little known, and it was understood that "they had not an opportunity of personal knowledge of the facts they related, and in several of them were mistaken.[21]

The elder statesmen were busy in their last years

[16] Paul Wilstach, *Correspondence of John Adams and Thomas Jefferson 1812-1826* (Indianapolis, 1925), p. 114; August 10, 1815.

[17] *Ibid.,* pp. 159-160; May 5, 1817.

[18] *Ibid.,* p. 161; May 17, 1818.

[19] *Works,* X, 133; March 4, 1815.

[20] Mass. Hist. Soc. *Colls.,* 6th ser., IV, 438; July 24, 1789.

[21] *Works,* X, 81; November 15, 1813.

looking over old papers and answering all sorts of questions. About a rumor that he was writing a political history of the country, Madison wrote to Edward Everett
that he knew nothing of its origin. He did say that he and
others had papers worthy of preservation, that, in fact,
he was then putting together his notes on the Convention.
"It has been the misfortune of history," wrote Madison,
"that a personal knowledge and an impartial judgment
of things rarely meet in the historian. The best history
of our Country therefore must be the fruit of contributions bequeathed by contemporary actors & witnesses to
successors who will make an unbiassed use of them." If
the materials of America's history should fall into proper
hands, he added, "the American History may be expected
to contain more truth, and lessons, certainly not less valuable, than those of any Country or Age." [22] Jared Sparks,
J. K. Paulding, and others, wrote to Madison for biographical and historical materials relating to figures and
events of the Revolutionary period.[23]

To William Tudor, then editor of the newly established *North American Review,* John Adams wrote of
various incidents in the Revolution, and in these and
other retrospective letters, Adams suggested so wide a
scope of inquiry that historians a century later have not
yet filled in his outline.[24] Although he was more than
eighty, his energy never flagged, and his dimming eyes
visioned broad areas for research. To younger men was
communicated the enthusiasm of Revolutionaries still
alive, and to the expansive national spirit that came after
the War of 1812, Jefferson, Adams, Madison, and others
contributed their reminiscences of the founding of the
nation.

[22] Gaillard Hunt, ed., *The Writings of James Madison* (9 vols., N. Y.,
1900-1910), IX, 128; March 19, 1823.
[23] *Ibid., passim.*
[24] *Works,* X, 230, *passim,* especially letter of November 16, 1816.

William Tudor was one of those who came under their influence, and through the pages of the *Review* he popularized among the elite an eagerness for historical research. In the *Review* he included extracts from books on American history, combined with his own critical comment. The scholarly maturity of Tudor is seen in his urbane attitude toward early Puritan historians, particularly Cotton Mather, which might well be copied in our day.[25] Tudor's historical interests were of long standing, for in *The Monthly Anthology,* a predecessor of the *North American Review,* he had included articles on colonial historians.[26] More than any other force the *Review* stirred the slow stream of intellectual life to a swift-flowing current whose sparkling waters refreshed spirits long laden with dust.

Biographies of Revolutionary heroes were read carefully by the old guard, who conserved jealously the reputations of their dead comrades. "American History," wrote Adams to a friend, Dr. Benjamin Waterhouse, "whether in Fable, Allegory, Painting, Sculpture, Architecture, Statuary, Poetry, Oratory, or Romance: which forgets to acknowledge James Otis to have been the Father of the American Revolution, will be nothing but a Lie."[27] Tudor published a biography of James Otis (1823), and in recommending it highly to a friend, George Ticknor wrote: "There is nothing like it in print —that I have ever seen—among our materials for future history, nor could such a book be made twenty years hence for then all the traditions will have perished with the old men from whose graves he has just rescued them. It takes prodigiously here [Boston] and will, I think, do much good, by promoting an inquiry into the most in-

[25] *N. A. Rev.,* VI, 257.
[26] Vols. V, VII.
[27] W. C. Ford, ed., *Statesman and Friend* (Boston, 1927), p. 137; August 17, 1817.

teresting and important part of our history." [28] William Wirt drew from Jefferson his remembrance of Patrick Henry, and when Wirt's biography of Henry appeared, letters praising and censuring the work were exchanged among the Revolutionary leaders.

The survivors among the signers of the Declaration of Independence and of the Constitution were conscious of a certain unity among themselves; Jefferson once spoke of the "Declaration-men." [29] They were aware also of their unique position in American life. A few months before he died Jefferson wrote to Adams, introducing his grandson, Thomas Jefferson Randolph: "Like other young people, he wishes to be able in the winter nights of old age, to recount to those around him what he has heard and learnt of the heroic age preceding his birth, and which of the Argonauts individually he was in time to have seen." [30] In the summer and in the winter nights of their own old age these Argonauts spun tales of their heroic era and bemoaned the fact that no one had written its history. But the time was near at hand when materials for it would be systematically gathered. McKean admitted that the United States possessed no Thucydides, Tacitus, Hume, Robertson, or Gibbon, yet, he said, "we have gentlemen of great talents, and capable of writing the history of our Revolution with at least as much regard to truth as any of them has exhibited." [31] There may have been some who were then capable of writing the history of the American Revolution, but many years were yet to pass before the task was seriously attacked.

[28] *Life, Letters and Journals of George Ticknor* (2 vols., Boston, 1876), I, 338; February, 1823.
[29] P. L. Ford, ed., Thomas Jefferson, *Writings,* X, 191, to Henry Dearborn; August 17, 1821.
[30] Wilstach, p. 195; March 25, 1826.
[31] *Works,* McKean to Adams, X, 177; November 20, 1815.

Gathering the Records

Before any large-scale history could be written, the materials had to be gathered. There was no lack of materials, for New Englanders, as George Bancroft pointed out, "have always been a documentary people." [32] In fact, an overwhelming number of authors who wrote history or biography or gathered annals came from New England.[33] In an essay on "Materials for American History," in 1826, Jared Sparks said that "no work approaching to the character of a complete history of America, of the United States or of the American Revolution, has yet appeared." He noted that good histories of single states had been published, but they were "rather of the narrative than the philosophical kind, telling much of events, but little of causes and consequences. . . ." These, he thought, were "valuable chiefly as materials, and indexes to materials, for future use, in composing a perfect colonial history." Sparks wrote of the scattered materials for American history and praised the work of historical societies in preserving them. But he wished the societies to do more than merely preserve materials and he laid out a generous program of publication for them. Sparks, who was soon to go abroad to search for historical materials, said that "the colonial history of America is shut up in the office of the Board of Trade and Plantations in England." Half a century before Sparks, John Adams had written of the need for consulting "the records of the board of trade and plantations . . . as also the files in the offices of some of the Secretaries of State." [34] Thomas Hutchinson, too, had

[32] *N. A. Rev.* (April, 1838).
[33] Edwin L. Clarke, *American Men of Letters: Their Nature and Nurture* (N. Y., 1916).
[34] *Works*, V, 491-496.

once told some friends that no complete history of the colonies could be written until access was had to papers in the Plantation Office where George Chalmers had gotten materials.[35]

Sparks wrote also of the poor library facilities for the historical student; he could number but seven libraries "in which a whole stock of books relating to America may not be ranged in the corner of a single case."[36] George Ticknor measured the influence of his education in Europe by the different perspective it gave him upon the resources of the Harvard Library. "When I went away," he said, "I thought it was a large library; when I came back, it seemed a closetful of books."[37]

At the time that Sparks was complaining of the difficulties that beset the American historian they were beginning to be overcome. Hezekiah Niles published the *Principles and Acts of the Revolution . . .* in 1822, "dedicated to the young men of the United States." In his preface he made it clear that he was presenting documentary evidence "to show the *feelings* that prevailed in the revolution not to give a *history* of *events*." Between 1827 and 1830 Jonathan Elliot brought out four volumes of documents (a fifth was added later), *Debates, Resolutions and other Proceedings in Convention on the Adoption of the Federal Constitution*. Although he published other historical materials, the compiler is best remembered for this collection, usually referred to as Elliot's *Debates*. Publication of the *American State Papers, Documents, Legislative and Executive of the Congress of the United States* came not long afterward. The introductory note to the first volume [38] said that "in this compilation the future historian may find a body of authentic materials ready prepared for his hand."

[35] *The Monthly Anthology,* 1806, III, 373.
[36] *N. A. Rev.,* XXIII, 276-292.
[37] *Life . . . of George Ticknor,* I, 72.
[38] 1833, p. xi.

Extensive work by Sparks and others in behalf of American history had been in progress for some time. Historical literature promised greater financial, as well as spiritual, rewards than any other branch of writing. America's past had been glorious, and her future promised to be more brilliant. With the zeal of the missionary, the new generation fused memories of the hallowed past with glowing expectations for the coming age. In a survey of historical writing published in the *North American Review,* April, 1838, Bancroft referred to the diligent exploration of "every form of ancient records, gleaning hints from minutes of trials, extracting a fact from the registry of a will, tracing measures to their primary sources in the journals of our towns, or collecting the inscriptions in grave-yards." The same year *The Journals of each Provincial Congress of Massachusetts in 1774 and 1775 . . . and other Documents* was edited by William Lincoln. The primary object of the publication was "to *perpetuate materials* for the history of a glorious era in our national existence." Francis L. Hawks, lawyer, clergyman, and historian at various stages of his career, was commissioned by the Episcopal Church to collect materials on its history in the colonial period. He went to England and brought back a mass of material which he used in his *Ecclesiastical History of the United States: Virginia* (1836) and in a volume on Maryland (1839). Similar activity further South was represented by Bartholomew R. Carroll's compilation, the *Historical Collections of South Carolina* in two volumes.[39]

A very notable effort to collect historical materials on the Revolution was begun in 1822 by Peter Force, a journalist and printer. In partnership with Matthew St. Clair Clarke, clerk of the House of Representatives, Force began his work of collecting materials, and in a

[39] N. Y., 1836.

report made some years later said they had made a
large collection of documents, correspondence, speeches,
legislative proceedings, and the like. As their plan developed it became far more comprehensive in scope, embracing in six series of volumes materials on the origins
of the colonies to the adoption of the Federal Constitution. After many delays, the first volume was published
in 1837 with the title *American Archives . . . A Documentary History of the Origin and Progress of the North
American Colonies; of the Causes and Accomplishment
of the American Revolution; and of the Constitution of
Government for the United States to the Final Ratifica-
tion thereof*. This volume, the first in the fourth series,
running from March 7, 1774, to the Declaration of Independence, was introduced with a preface explaining the
enterprise: "The undertaking in which we have embarked is emphatically, a National one; National in its
scope and object, its end and aim." "The tendency of
the present age has been justly and philosophically designated as historick." They noticed that governmental aid
had been granted for the publication of national records
in England and France, and suggested the value of similar support in the United States. Force and Clarke wrote
that they had examined records in each of the thirteen
original States. Their investigations, they said, had rescued many papers from destruction, and at the same time
had awakened "a feeling of interest in the memorials of
our past history." Between 1837 and 1853, six volumes
were published in the fourth series and three volumes in
the fifth series (1776-1783), and then publication, which
had been accomplished with government support to the
amount of $228,000, ceased. Force also brought out four
volumes of *Tracts and other Papers relating to the
Origin, Settlement, and Progress of the Colonies in North
America*. In a review of the *American Archives*, Bancroft writes of Force's endeavor "to sweep the land for

every document of a public nature, that tended to prepare the revolution." "Here are the clay and the straw," he says, "everything necessary but the forming hand" for historical composition.[40]

In addition to preserving many materials for the use of historians, Peter Force, in his role as editor and collector, was a focus of the historical interests of the country. He found time to participate in the activities of a short-lived American Historical Society and was, in fact, its most vital spirit. Collectors and authors wrote to him seeking information and encouragement. Lyman C. Draper, then making his great collection of the sources for Western history, wrote to Force: "Limited and unimportant as they are, compared with your great researches and achievements, I yet hope, in my humble way, to effect something for the biographical literature of our country." [41] When Bancroft wanted information on the attitude of American newspapers toward the Stamp Act he sought it from Force.[42] A list of the latter's correspondents would almost exhaust the names of Americans who were then interested in the writing of history. In 1867 Force's remarkable library of some fifty thousand titles, perhaps the best collection of Americana in existence, was bought for the Library of Congress.[43]

At the very time that Sparks was complaining of the poor library facilities in the States a decided improvement was getting under way. New life was infused for a time into the older historical societies, and additional ones were being formed. Philip Hone, a famous figure in New York, boasted, perhaps incorrectly, that the library of the New York Historical Society was the "most valuable in this country in books and manuscripts relating to

[40] *N. A. Rev.* (April, 1838).
[41] Bassett, *The Middle Group of American Historians*, p. 278; 1847.
[42] *Force Papers,* Library of Congress, Vol. XXI; January 4, 1847.
[43] On Force, see Bassett, *op. cit.,* Chap. V, and *Historical Magazine* (November, 1865), p. 337.

the history of the United States particularly the State of New York,'' and added that it was now more accessible to its members.[44] Thirty-five historical societies were founded between 1830 and 1850, but few of them functioned actively.

Public and private libraries were being developed on a grand scale. A great addition was made to the Harvard Library with the purchase of the American collection formed by the German historian, Christophe D. Ebeling. The Library of Congress was founded in 1800 and, after a slow start, grew very rapidly in importance, especially after the acquisition of collections like the libraries and papers of Jefferson and Madison. As early as 1829 Sparks was urging that a ''copy of every book and manuscript in existence relating to America'' be secured for the library.[45] Booksellers like John R. Bartlett in New York, improvident Obadiah Rich, a transplanted American in Europe, and especially Henry Stevens, Jr., performed valuable services for the libraries and scholars in uncovering rare Americana. According to Sparks, who should have known, Stevens had ''made the British Museum one of the best places in the world for American historical research.[46] Bartlett's headquarters in New York became a center for the city's literary and historical scholars. The collections of John Carter Brown of Providence, Rhode Island, and James Lenox of New York were of surpassing excellence. Bartlett went back to his native Rhode Island in later years and was associated with Brown in the formation of the latter's library. Having over five thousand titles dealing with America's history before 1800, the library was a valuable aid to research. It was made accessible to scholars some time before 1865, when the first volume of the catalogue

[44] *Diary*, I, 271; September 28, 1837.
[45] *N. A. Rev.* (October, 1829), p. 432, note 1.
[46] Adams, *Jared Sparks*, II, 522, note 1.

was published; thereafter the riches of the library were made known to all.

Through the efforts of some of the earliest American scholars who had studied in Germany—Joseph G. Cogswell, George Ticknor, and Edward Everett—and who had brought back to America a love of learning, historical scholarship was greatly advanced. It was Cogswell who helped Harvard get the Ebeling collection, and at a later date he became the adviser to John Jacob Astor when the latter was building up his library.[47] Ticknor, the historian of Spanish literature, was an inspiration to Prescott. There was sharp competition among bibliophiles for choice rarities, and Ticknor was not one to be outdone. His famous Spanish collection—the best in the world, he thought—was enshrined in a palatial home, and above the mantel in the library hung the portrait of Sir Walter Scott, whose spirit hovered over Ticknor's whole generation. Here was a favorite meeting place for Boston's intellectual elite. Ticknor's friend, Everett, was always interested in the advancement of American scholarship, and that frequently meant historical study. One of the most indefatigable bibliographers of the period was a German, Herman E. Ludewig, who had recently emigrated to New York. Among his publications was *The Literature of American Local History: a Bibliographical Essay* (1846), dedicated to Peter Force.[48]

Through the efforts of some enthusiasts a movement apparent in several of the States eventually resulted in the publication of vast quantities of materials. No one individual was responsible for it, but the movement had its distant origins in the work of Ebenezer Hazard, in the stimulus of the correspondence of the Fathers, and, more immediately, in the impulse to search for and pre-

[47] A. E. Ticknor, *Life of Joseph Green Cogswell* (Cambridge, 1874), Chaps. XXI-XXVI.
[48] *Historical Magazine* (February, 1857; September, 1867).

serve the historical records of the nation of whose wax-
ing power Americans were now strongly conscious. Judge
Archibald D. Murphey, of North Carolina, proposed in
1819 a very comprehensive history of the State, and he
suggested also the necessity of consulting documents in
London; but little of immediate importance followed.
Georgia and South Carolina took some inconclusive steps
to get copies of documents in England relating to their
history. Rhode Island and Massachusetts, in this same
decade of the 1820's, made similar slight efforts to get
copies of historical materials in British repositories.[49]

New York, however, was far more successful in her
attempt to gather the materials of her history. The work
was initiated in 1814, with a memorial to the State legislature by Governor DeWitt Clinton, then vice-president
of the New York Historical Society. Clinton mentioned
the need of setting the State records in order and of copy-
ing from the archives in England and France those materials that would shed light on relations with the Indians in the colonial period. He pointed out how lightly
William Smith had passed over the Dutch period in his
history of New York, and said that to obtain the records
for those years "we must have recourse to the papers
of the Dutch West India Company, and to the archives
of the then government of that nation." Chalmers's
Political Annals referred to manuscripts on New York
that were in the Plantation Office, and the British Museum also had papers and books on America which the
student of her history must consult. In asking public support, even in the midst of war, for these researches,
Clinton wrote with great dignity: "Genuine greatness
never appears in a more resplendent light, or in a more
sublime attitude, than in that buoyancy of character
which rises superior to danger and difficulty; in that mag-

[49] Bassett, pp. 240-243.

nanimity of soul which cultivates the arts and sciences amidst the horrors of war; and in that comprehension of mind which cherishes all the cardinal interests of a country, without being distracted or diverted by the most appalling considerations.''

The State legislature supported the plea, and in the following years many volumes of Dutch records in the State's archives were translated by Dr. Francis A. Van Der Kemp. This memorial of 1814, which resulted in the organization and exploration of the New York State archives, was followed by another in 1839, having reference solely to legislative support for an investigation of documents in Europe relating to the colonial history of New York. It stated that permission had been granted by England to other states to copy records: "An Agent appointed for that purpose by the State of Georgia is now in London, receiving every facility from the Departments of the English government." In recommending the memorial to the legislature, Governor William H. Seward pointed to the example of Georgia and Massachusetts; the latter had published the Journals of her Colonial Congress. After passage of an act defraying the expenses for the collection of materials from archives in England, Holland, and France, John Romeyn Brodhead was named agent. After a stay of three years in Europe, Brodhead returned in 1844 with eighty volumes of documents. His homecoming was an event of the first importance to historical societies in New England and the Middle Atlantic States, who sent representatives to a dinner at which Brodhead was an honored guest.[50] In his characteristic style Bancroft said that Brodhead's ship "was more richly freighted with new materials for American history than any that ever crossed the Atlantic." [51]

[50] Philip Hone's *Diary*, Bayard Tuckerman, ed. (2 vols., N. Y., 1889). II, 236-237.
[51] E. A. and G. L. Duyckinck, *Cyclopedia of American Literature* (2 vols., N. Y., 1856), II, 595.

While still in manuscript Brodhead's collection of materials was of immediate service to historians in New York and in other States. Many of the documents dealt with the history of New York's neighboring colonies. George Bancroft, then working on his history, consulted the collection for the period after 1748; the "Paris Documents" were of value to students in the Northwestern States and in Canada; materials from England were of general interest to all students; the "Holland Documents" contained much of value to the historian of New England and of the middle colonies. Part of Brodhead's material was published a few years later in *The Documentary History of the State of New York* (four volumes), and the remainder in *Documents relative to the Colonial History of the State of New York* (fifteen volumes). Other States published more of their records at this time, and some of them acknowledged the impulse communicated by New York. The editorial preface to the first volume of the *Documents and Records relating to the Province of New Hampshire* (1867) said that valuable papers for the history of the colony had been taken from the New York colonial documents. Samuel Hazard in his *Annals of Pennsylvania* (1850) acknowledged his gratitude to New York for permission to see the recently collected manuscript materials. In his *Pennsylvania Archives* (1852), the same compiler observed generally that "the States of New York, Massachusetts, New Jersey, Maryland, Virginia and other members of the Union have commenced the publication of their Colonial and Revolutionary history."

Under the caption "A Great Historical Enterprise," one writer proposed that historical societies in the United States undertake the publication of a general index to all documents in English archives referring to the American colonies, thus anticipating by forty years the series issued by the Carnegie Institution of Washington. A volume in the New Jersey series contained an index to the English documents on her colonial history.[52] Sparks had long been urging that transcripts be made of materials in English libraries for deposit in Washington, where they would be accessible to American historians.[53]

Thus the amassing of materials went on apace, but the historian who had been eagerly awaited did not make his appearance until 1834. It was then that George Bancroft published his first volume. Wholly apart from his proper mixture of rhetoric and fact, so necessary to the success of a historian in that day, the acclaim that rewarded him was in large measure due to the intense need of Americans for a national historian. "A matured work of genius," on the settlement and progress of the colonies to the Declaration of Independence "would be of incalculable value," said a writer in the *American Quarterly Review,* a few years before Bancroft presented his work.[54] In welcoming Bancroft's history, Prescott expressed the common feeling when he said that Americans had to go to the work of the Italian, Botta, for "the best history of the Revolution" and to the Scotsman, James Grahame, "for the best history of the Colonies. Happily the work before us," he said, "bids fair, when completed, to supply this deficiency." Although he conceded the meritorious quality of these histories written by foreigners, still, Prescott insisted, they were written by men who could not enter into the sympathies nor comprehend "all the minute feelings, prejudices, and peculiar ways of thinking which form the idiosyncrasy of the nation." [55]

Shortly before Bancroft's history appeared, William Ellery Channing, in discussing national literature, said: "We think that the history of the human race is to be re-

[52] *Historical Magazine* (October, 1860).
[53] Roger Wolcott, *Correspondence of William Hickling Prescott;* Sparks to Prescott, October 19, 1840.
[54] 1827, I, 25-26.
[55] W. H. Prescott, *Biographical and Critical Miscellanies,* pp. 308-310.

written. Men imbued with the prejudices which thrive under aristocracies and state religions, cannot understand it. Past ages, with their great events, and great men are to undergo, we think, a new trial, and to yield new results. It is plain, that history is already viewed under new aspects, and we believe that the true principles for studying and writing it are to be unfolded here, at least as rapidly as in other countries.'' With these sentiments Bancroft's spirit was in perfect harmony. In the year in which his first volume appeared, he wrote to Sparks that Americans had a history worth knowing, and that, ''a vein of public feeling, of democratic independence, of popular liberty, ought to be infused into our literature.'' [56]

Bancroft lived so long that he became a tradition before he died. For half a century he dominated historical scholarship. His narrative mood, which celebrated the triumphs of democracy, touched a prideful people and was welcomed by the great majority. In a more restrained mood a small minority established a tradition of a critical approach, but it was not until a later generation that this tradition found firm support. Charles Francis Adams wrote in the *North American Review,* 1831: ''In this country, and more particularly in this section of it, we are fond of celebrating the virtues of our forefathers . . . by festive anniversaries and eloquent panegyric.'' ''Yet it is much to be feared, that this is not the right way to come at that real history, and those cool and rational conclusions which can alone be supposed likely to confer permanent benefit.'' Adams was critical of oratory because he believed that its exciting stimulus made it difficult for people to accept ''more natural food.'' He observed, too, that ''the modern fashion of what is called philosophical history is attended with one great disadvantage, in the ease with which it admits of the perversion of facts, to

[56] Adams, *Jared Sparks,* II, 192, note 1.

suit the prejudices of each particular writer.[57] Despite the criticism of Adams, who was ahead of his time and against the tide of contemporary historical writing, "philosophical" history was to be written and read for some time to come. The *American Review* [58] reported that "the great English historians are to be found in our huts and farmhouses, and editions of them are multiplied without number." [59] Twenty thousand copies of Macaulay's history are said to have been sold in the United States in 1849.[60] It was an exultant reviewer who acclaimed Bancroft as "our Western Macaulay." [61] The volumes that Bancroft, Prescott, and Motley wrote were well suited to the public taste; historians had not yet begun to write largely for one another.

ABIEL HOLMES

The transition from the historians of the colonial and Revolutionary years to the writers of the full-flowering national period was effected by Abiel Holmes. His was the first important attempt to comprehend American history in its entirety. Ezra Stiles and others in the eighteenth century had talked of such a project, but its fulfillment was delayed until Holmes took up the task.

Abiel Holmes, father of Oliver Wendell Holmes, was one of the many New England divines who wrote history. His particular contribution was *American Annals; or a Chronological History of America from the Discovery in MCCCCXCII to MDCCCVI,* published in two volumes in 1805. A second edition under a slightly different title appeared in 1829. The author was not only the son-in-law

---

[57] P. 177.
[58] January, 1811.
[59] Quoted in F. L. Mott, *The History of American Magazines 1741-1850* (N. Y., 1930), p. 178.
[60] *Ibid.,* p. 399.
[61] *Historical Magazine* (February, 1862), p. 41.

of Ezra Stiles, the distinguished President of Yale, but
was his literary executor. He wrote a biography of Stiles
in 1798, and study of the many papers left by Stiles
stimulated the younger man to write his own history.

In his preface the historian says: "A new world has
been discovered which has been receiving inhabitants
from the old, more than three hundred years. A new empire has arisen which has been a theatre of great actions
and stupendous events. That remarkable discovery, those
events and actions can now be accurately ascertained,
without recourse to such legends, as have darkened and
disfigured the early annals of most nations." But, while
local histories of particular portions of America have
been written, Holmes went on to say, "no attempt has
been made to give even the outline of its entire history.
. . . It has been uniformly my aim to trace facts, as much
as possible to their source. Original authorities, therefore, when they could be obtained, have always had preference."

The work in its later edition is in two volumes divided into three parts, which are again subdivided. The
first part treats of the European discoveries and settlements. Part II, which runs over into the second volume,
is concerned with the Anglo-American colonies, and is arranged in six periods. The first four cover the periods
from the founding of Virginia to the Plymouth settlement, then from 1620 to the New England confederation
of 1643, thence to the revolution of 1689, and to the settlement of Georgia in 1732. The critical attitude of a later
New England to the witchcraft episode is fully indicated
by Holmes's statement: "This part of the history of our
country furnished an affecting proof of the imbecility of
the human mind, and of the potent influence of the passions." He took a rather comprehensive view of the subject, however, and his remarks on witchcraft in America
and England are an interesting precedent for the posi-

tion taken by Professor George L. Kittredge a hundred years later in his apologia for the Puritans. The fifth period of Holmes's work carries the chronology forward some thirty years to the Peace of Paris, and the last runs from 1763 to the Declaration of Independence. Part III continues the annals to the organization of the Federal government in 1789, and the final section is to the "completion of the fiftieth year of the Independence of the United States in 1826." His materials on the war are largely concerned with its military aspects, and in these pages his work partakes more of the character of a narrative history. The author closes with the assurance of divine interference to secure the glory of America. Quoting Washington, he says: "Every step by which they [the United States] have advanced to the character of an independent nation, seems to have been distinguished by some token of providential agency."

Although Holmes had wished that his book might be more than a chronology, it proved to be little more than that. Events are treated year by year, and it belongs to the school of Thomas Prince's *Chronology*. It has the latter's merit, too, in its concern for accuracy, and it contains a good bibliography. This work, the first published by an American to cover the whole field of our history, was, despite its many deficiencies, a significant advance in American historiography. In a summary of American historical writing that appeared in the *North American Review*, April, 1838, it was said of Holmes that all students of our history owed him gratitude. He is the link, said the writer, "that connects the men of an earlier generation Belknap, Hutchinson, Stiles, Trumbull, and the rest with the scholars of our own." A reviewer of the first edition of the *Annals* thought Holmes had done as well as might be expected to dress up the barren bones of our early history; the material in the post-Revolution-

ary period was found meager and unsatisfactory.⁶² It was
pointed out by Jared Sparks, in a review of the later edition, that the annalist had kept close to his intention to
tell what happened without informing the reader "what
should have been or . . . with dissertations on causes
and consequences, or professing to have any deep wisdom
in detecting the hidden policy of rulers, or the mysteries
of local and general politics." Holmes, it was said, had
touched on every important point in American history,
and his citations would enable any student to pursue his
own investigations further. "It is the best repository of
history, chronology, and biographical knowledge respecting America," said Sparks, "that can be found embodied
in one work." ⁶³ Bancroft had high praise for the work
of Holmes, a judgment echoed by Winsor more than
eighty years after the *Annals* had appeared. "It is a book
still to inspire confidence," wrote Winsor. Holmes made
good use of the increased collections that came to Boston
and Harvard between the dates of the first and second
editions of his *Annals*.

The writer's style, sometimes unhappy, invited the
editorial blue pencil in his younger as well as in his later
years. When Holmes was a student at Yale he contributed to a literary publication, *Clio,* edited by Juliana
Smith, sister of a classmate, who once remarked of his
writing: "The Pegasus he rides is a sorry steed that has
lost its wings and is badly shod." ⁶⁴ His descendants,
Oliver Wendell and Justice Holmes, have more fortunately sat astride winged thoroughbreds.⁶⁵

⁶² *The Monthly Anthology,* III, 372; IV, 101.
⁶³ *N. A. Rev.* (October, 1829), pp. 429-441.
⁶⁴ Helen E. Smith, *Colonial Days and Ways* (N. Y., 1900), pp. 282-283.
⁶⁵ See, however, M. A. DeWolfe Howe's ascription of the epic poem
"Yaratildia," 1796, to Holmes, Mass. Hist. Soc. *Proc.,* LXII, 155. See
memoir of Holmes in Mass. Hist. Soc. *Colls.,* 3d ser., VII, 274 ff.

Timothy Pitkin

In 1828 Timothy Pitkin brought out a two-volume work called *A Political and Civil History of the United States of America, from the Year 1763 to . . . 1797.* There were five chapters that gave "a summary view of the political and civil state" of the colonies up to 1763. Over a hundred pages of documentary source material were appended to the volumes, and in the body of the text much of the same matter was imbedded.

In his preface Pitkin wrote that since Americans were sufficiently acquainted with the military events of the Revolutionary period, "a connected view of the political and civil transactions of our country, unmixed with military events, except so far as the latter had an influence on the former, was a desirable object." Pitkin said his sources were the colonial histories and original records: "In our researches respecting colonial history we have felt the want of many papers which could only be found in the office of the board of trade and plantations in England"; but he did make use of the works of George Chalmers. The libraries of Yale and Harvard rendered Pitkin aid, and the private papers of leading figures of the Revolution furnished him with much information. He did not aim "to present a philosophical history" but rather "a plain and connected . . . impartial account of the principal political and civil transactions of the United States during a most interesting period of their history."

At the end of his introductory chapters Pitkin has a few lines, still worth reading, on the differences between European and American character. "Though the motives and views of those who settled in the different colonies, were different, yet their situation in their new places of abode, being, in many respects, similar, naturally produced in all an energy of character, and a spirit of independence, unknown, in the great mass of the people they had left in Europe. . . . Every man was a freeholder, and his freehold was at his own disposal. Attached to the farm on which he lived, and from which he supported himself and his family, he had every inducement to secure and defend it. . . . This independent condition of the colonists, with respect to the tenure of their lands, combined with that equality which existed among them, arising from an equal distribution of property, a general diffusion of knowledge, and a share which all had in the government, naturally produced a love of liberty, an independence of character, and a jealousy of power, which ultimately led, under divine Providence, to that revolution, which placed them among the nations of the earth.'' [66]

Pitkin adheres to his promise to confine the annals of military events to the barest minimum, and he gives a lengthy treatment of the negotiations between the colonies and England, between the new states and France, the formation of the Confederation and the internal difficulties of the newly organized American governments. Pitkin's personal interest in finance led him to stress the problems of public credit, and the measures taken to restore it. He writes from the standpoint of a Hamiltonian Federalist: ''While Congress were . . . forming a government for the territory, and laying the foundation of future new states at the west [northwest ordinance] they had lost all authority over the old states at the east. . . . The general government . . . was totally inefficient, and the authority of the state governments greatly weakened, and in some instances almost destroyed.'' ''The only remedy that promised relief, was an essential alteration in the national compact. No amendments, however, could be made to the confederation, without the assent of every state in the union. Experience had proved that no relief

[66] I, 154.

could be expected from this quarter.'' [67] Then followed
the Constitutional Convention, which was called, asserts
Pitkin, largely because of the ''insurrection in Massachusetts,'' Shays' Rebellion, in 1786. ''This open and formidable opposition to the laws,'' he writes, ''threatened not
only the destruction of the government of that state, but
of the union.'' ''Fortunately the state of Massachusetts
by the firmness of its governor and legislature, and the
patriotism of individuals . . . was able to suppress the
insurrection, without the aid of the Federal arm,'' which
had already been promised.

The chapter on the convention at Philadelphia, which
discussed, among other things, the differences between
the Constitution and the Articles of Confederation and
the public reaction to the proposed new form of government, can still be read with profit. The policies of the
Federalists, designed to strengthen the national government, are treated at length. Although Pitkin manages
usually to mask his own opinions, in the case of Shays'
Rebellion, as in the treatment of the Whisky Rebellion,
he shows his obvious Federalist sympathy. His history
ends with Washington's Farewell Address, an ''inestimable legacy which the father of his country'' left to
Americans.

Pitkin's work ranks far beyond most of the histories
published up to that time, showing a power of organization and discrimination in choice of material that few
could match. He did place, perhaps, a disproportionate
emphasis on New England. Although it contains no writing of an inspired character, it is not heavy reading and
often exhibits the marks of a shrewd intelligence. There
were many books, written long years after on the same
period that Pitkin covered, which added little to what he
wrote.

[67] II, 213-214.

Another of his publications is *A Statistical View of the Commerce of the United States of America; its connection with Agriculture and Manufactures* . . . (Hartford, 1816). This work, still esteemed, is an example of the growing spirit of commercial enterprise after the War of 1812.

The first chapter gives a résumé of the period up to the Revolution; the rest of the book is concerned with the following years down to his own day. Pitkin reveals the characteristic American pride in bigness of every kind. "Since the establishment of the present government," he says, "the progress of national as well as individual wealth has kept pace with the increase of population; and until the commencement of commercial restrictions in December, 1807, and the declaration of war against Great Britain, in 1812, no nation it is believed, had ever increased so rapidly in wealth as the United States." [68] His specialty was commercial activities, and the many valuable tables of statistics he left us are important information for our early national history. Pitkin's fame as a statistician has eclipsed his reputation as a historian, but his achievement in the *Political and Civil History of the United States of America* deserved a better fate.

THREE EUROPEAN HISTORIANS OF AMERICA

That American history interested Englishmen in the eighteenth century was, of course, not surprising—the colonies were part of the empire. A common background and the similarity of institutions help to explain the continued interest of England in American history. Students of other lands, Germany and France particularly, were also drawn to this theme, which gained in attractiveness as a result of the Revolution. Probably the most impor-

[68] Pp. 32-33.

tant of the works published by Europeans were those by
Ebeling, Grahame, and Botta, although it was the latter's
volumes that were the best known. During the colonial
period histories of America written by Englishmen were
as well known to Americans as those written by natives.
The Revolution in some respects made Americans more
provincial (the rise of nationalism brought results in the
United States similar to those elsewhere) so that scholarly writings by Englishmen and others on America often
secured very little of an audience here. This, however,
was not always so, as the wide acquaintance with Botta's
work attests. It was true, unfortunately, for the volumes
of James Grahame and Christophe D. Ebeling; these
works might have greatly benefited American students
had they known them better.

Ebeling was born in 1741, educated at Göttingen, and
became a professor of Greek and history in the Gymnasium at Hamburg. Early in life he became interested in
America, and for forty years he labored on various works
relating to the new world. He wrote to a friend in after
years that he had spent a good part of his life, all his
money, and even much of his health collecting materials
on the United States.[69] He was remarkably thorough in
the search for Americana, and it is supposed that he had
the best collection of late eighteenth-century American
newspapers in existence. Ebeling, who referred to himself as a "Cosmopolite,"[70] had a wide circle of correspondents in the United States, including Ramsay, Belknap, Morse, Ezra Stiles, Abiel Holmes, and William
Bentley. Over a long period Ebeling worked on his history, which was planned as a study of American civilization. Delay in getting books from the United States so
hindered him at times that he wrote to Bentley, "My

[69] "Letters of C. D. Ebeling," Amer. Antiq. Soc. *Proc.* (October, 1925),
p. 413, April 17, 1812.
[70] *Loc. cit.*, p. 310.

America goes on slowly.'' [71] Ebeling's interest in America was not only to write a better history than was then in existence, but also to furnish for the benefit of a reactionary Europe a ''faithful picture of a truly free republic.'' Between 1793 and 1816 Ebeling's *Erdbeschreibung und Geschichte von Amerika* appeared in seven bulky volumes. It was in reality an unintegrated social history. It was the most inclusive work done on America by a European up to that time, and surpassed works written by Americans themselves. Ebeling was also associated with other literary ventures relating to America— the *Amerikanische Bibliothek* which stressed geography, and the *Amerikanisches Magazin* which acquainted Germans with American constitutional documents, books, and miscellaneous news of life overseas. Harvard's purchase of Ebeling's great library and collection of maps in 1818 made it the foremost repository of American history. Abiel Holmes and other students used it, so that this German scholar, working under a severe handicap thousands of miles from the scene of his intellectual interests, ultimately did contribute to the development of American historical writing.[72]

Charles W. Botta, born in 1766, was a Piedmontese whose medical practice was sidetracked by his interest in politics and history. He wrote various historical works, but to Americans he was best known as the author of a *History of the War of Independence of the United States of America,* which was originally published in Italian (1809) in four volumes. An Italian edition was reviewed in a Philadelphia magazine,[73] which spoke of it as the best history of the Revolution ever written. Translated by

---

[71] *Loc. cit.,* p. 371, June 29, 1805.

[72] In addition to the letters referred to in Amer. Antiq. Soc. *Proc.,* see also letters in Mass. Hist. Soc. *Proc.,* 2d ser., VIII; 6th ser., IV.

[73] *Analectic* (May, 1815); see John Adams's discussion, *Works,* X, pp. 171-172.

George A. Otis in 1820, it immediately became the subject of extensive correspondence among Americans, who
anxiously awaited each new publication on the Revolution. Botta followed classical models by putting speeches
into the mouths of characters who may or may not have
uttered them. As was seemly for a European writing such
a history, Botta gave much space to the world-wide character of the American Revolution, an approach which
pleased John Adams. Irish discontent was related to
the struggle, and other episodes attracted Botta to such
lengths that at one point he interrupted himself by saying that "it is time to return upon the American continent." [74] It was his great dependence upon English and
French sources that undoubtedly influenced Botta to
adopt such an approach. Americans, of course, were de-
lighted with Botta's enthusiastic republicanism, and Jefferson thought it would be "the common manual of our
Revolutionary History." [75] When Jared Sparks met
Botta in Paris in 1828, he testified to the latter's careful
workmanship, which was evidently well rewarded, for
fourteen editions of the *American Revolution* had been
sold in one year.[76] Madison, like Adams, felt that a complete view of the Revolution involved exploration of the
archives of the nations that participated in it, directly or
indirectly, and, in a note to the American translator, he
spoke of the impetus that Botta's work would give to a
more critical study of the Revolution.[77] Madison noted
flaws in Botta's work and mentioned in particular his
failure to credit John Adams with a proper share in the
debates on the proposal for independence. Despite its obvious shortcomings, not until Bancroft's volumes appeared was there an American narrative that could com-

[74] Otis trans., 7th edn., 1837, II, 173.
[75] See page 167.
[76] Adams, *Jared Sparks*, II, 93.
[77] *Letters and Other Writings of James Madison,* 1865 edn., III, 177,
July 3, 1820; also 203-204, January, 1821.

pete with the fame of Botta's history of the Revolution.

At the time when Americans were complaining to one another about the lack of interest in their history, a Scotsman was writing a history of the colonies which, when published, was to be accepted by critical authority as the best in the field until Bancroft's volumes began to appear. It has been pointed out by more than one critic that Bancroft never adequately recognized the work of Grahame as his predecessor.[78] James Grahame was born in Glasgow in 1790, and an inherited love of the spirit of liberty turned him to a study of American history. In his diary, June, 1824, Grahame wrote: "I have had some thoughts of writing the history of North America; from . . . colonization till the Revolution. . . . The subject seems to me grand and noble. It was not a thirst of gold or of conquest, but piety and virtue, that laid the foundation of those settlements. The soil was not made by its planters a scene of vice and crime, but of manly enterprise . . . [and] good morals. . . ." The Revolution in America, Grahame went on to write, was not promoted by infidelity as that in France; on the contrary, he said, the American Revolution in large part was caused by religious men.

It was in 1824 that Grahame began the composition of his history. "History is everything," he wrote to a correspondent. "Religion, science, literature, whatever men do or think, falls within the scope of history. I ardently desire to make it a religious work, and in writing, to keep the chief end of man mainly in view." The library of George Chalmers, a fellow historian of America, was opened to Grahame. Taking his work very seriously, he went to Göttingen, where, he tells us, books were available that he could not get in England. The first two volumes of *The History of the United States of North Amer-*

---

[78] *Historical Magazine* (February, 1867), pp. 102-105.

ica from the plantation of the British Colonies till their assumption of National Independence were published in 1827; they carried the narrative to the period of the Revolution of 1689. Although his work was neglected in England, Grahame went on with his history.

Perhaps the first significant welcome accorded Grahame's history was that extended by Charles Francis Adams in 1831 in the *North American Review*. Adams remarked that the lack of interest in Grahame arose in part from the fact that England had not noticed the work, and, as Americans often took their cue from English critical comment they, too, passed the work by in silence. Adams said that Grahame's book was the best "that has anywhere appeared upon the early history of the United States." Adams was critical of the conventional philosophical history, and in a comparison he made with the works of Robertson and Chalmers, Grahame stood out to advantage. John Quincy Adams spoke with similar enthusiasm of Grahame's work, which he told Jared Sparks was "the only true history of the early settlements of the colonies." [79] Sparks, however, was contemptuous of Grahame as an historian.[80] In 1836 the remaining two volumes of Grahame's history appeared, and again they met with ill-merited neglect.

The historian writes with intense devotion to American principles and institutions, and adopts throughout a high moral tone. Curiously, Grahame never visited the United States, and his friendships included but few Americans. Honors came to him, however, from Harvard and from the Royal Academy of Nantes. Grahame once said that "the depths of my heart are with the primitive Puritans and the Scottish Covenanters," but he was opposed to their idea of the close relation between church

[79] Adams, *Jared Sparks*, I, 554.
[80] *Ibid.*, II, 217.

and state. Despite his admiration for America, Grahame did write in his preface, "I am far from thinking, . . . that every part of the conduct of the American states . . . was pure and blameless."

Volume I deals with Virginia and New England. It has a fair description of the policy of the Navigation Acts, not very much unlike that given by American historians fifty years later. English colonial policy, says Grahame, "on the whole, was much less illiberal and oppressive than that which any other nation of Europe had ever been known to pursue.[81] Trained as a lawyer, Grahame paid especial attention to the laws when he wrote colonial social history, to which he devotes a few pages. His work compares very favorably with the early volumes of Bancroft, whom he regarded as a friendly rival. The second volume covers the middle colonies—Maryland, and the two Carolinas. A very interesting appendix is found at the end of this volume. It deals with the state and prospects of the North American provinces at the close of the seventeenth century, and includes also opinions of colonists respecting the sovereignty and policy of Great Britain. (Bancroft and Osgood included, in their volumes on the seventeenth century, similar surveys.)

Volume III continues the narrative to 1763, and the fourth completes it with the Declaration of Independence. Like nearly all histories of this period, Grahame's is mainly a political narrative, but, again like some of these histories, sections are added on what we, today, call social history. Appendix II to the eighth book of Volume III is on the state of the population, the laws, trade, and manners in the colonies about 1733. "British oppression and intolerance, which had founded most of the North American colonies," said Grahame, "still continued to augment the numbers and influence the sentiments of their inhabitants." The fourth volume goes back into

[81] I, 112.

the years already treated in the preceding volume, in order to pick up the story of the Seven Years' War, and then continues to 1776. Long before later historians, who seemed to rediscover the fact, Grahame showed how the British intention to introduce the episcopal establishment in the colonies aroused intense opposition in New England. An appendix (III) is included in the fourth volume on the condition of the colonies about 1764. These appendices, not integrally related to the rest of the narrative, are like the chapters on culture or social and economic progress that have concluded more recent historical works.

Grahame makes some penetrating observations on the relative positions of the colonies and Great Britain. "Even although no other subject of quarrel had presented itself," he writes,[82] "the commercial restrictions alone must in process of time have occasioned the disruption of the American provinces from the British empire." There is a good examination of the constitutional aspects of the Stamp Act controversy, and the author included a reference to a phase of history in this period which attracted Carl Becker and Arthur M. Schlesinger many years later. "The supporters of colonial rights in the higher classes of society at New York," said Grahame, "were struck with alarm at the riotous outrage committed by their townsmen, [in the Stamp Act riots] and perceived the expediency of constituting prudent leaders for the management and control of the multitude." [83] Grahame mentioned again the danger of the proposal to establish the episcopal hierarchy about 1768.[84] With the fervor that native Americans summoned in their annual Fourth of July oratory, he heralded the Declaration of Independence. "While European sovereigns were insulting and violating every sanction and safeguard of na-

[82] IV, 172.
[83] P. 230.
[84] P. 317.

tional right and human liberty by the infamous partition of Poland, a revolutionary principle of nobler nature and vindictive destiny was developed to the earnest and wondering eyes of the world, in America.''

Grahame's work was praised by competent American critics, but some held that, because it was the work of a foreigner, it could not have penetrated to the heart of American history. Grahame vigorously replied to this contention, maintaining that a foreigner might well be fitted to portray more impartially than a native, the history of a particular country. He died in 1842, and three years later a second edition of his history appeared with an appreciative memoir by Josiah Quincy. There were some Americans, at least, who held it no bar to excellence in writing their history that a historian should have been born in Scotland.

VI

SPARKS, BANCROFT, PALFREY, HILDRETH

With Sparks and Bancroft the student meets the individuals whose contributions did more than those of any others to establish American historical writing on a firmer footing. They told the American people what they wished to hear about their past. In their histories and biographies, Sparks, Bancroft, and Palfrey glowingly narrated in detail the conquest of a vast territory and the victories in behalf of political and religious freedom. The certainty of older historians that God was on the side of Protestant battalions was not much weakened in the nineteenth century, despite the growth of religious tolerance and the widening of historical perspective. Narratives dramatized the clash of personalities in debate or war, and the conflicts of ideas were usually presented in a manner that reflected the ideological controversies of the historians' own generation. The economic foundations on which many of the conflicts were based were inadequately handled by filiopietistic historians. In their writings the ideals of freedom which they praised flowered unrelated

to the soil from which they sprang. Hildreth, more than
Sparks, Bancroft, or Palfrey, came down to earth.

JARED SPARKS

Jared Sparks and the American Republic began
their careers together in 1789. Heir to the traditions that
had already been woven around the struggle out of which
the Republic was born, Sparks labored to conserve the
documents and to tell the story of the War for Independence. It was his reading of Franklin's autobiography, we
are told, that first inspired him.[1] Sparks was born in the
poverty of the small-farmer class of Connecticut, but his
early brilliance at school opened the path to a richer life.
When he was eighteen he was teaching in a country
school for eight dollars a month. Friendly intercession
gained for him an education at Phillips Academy, in
Exeter, New Hampshire, and then at Harvard, from
which he was graduated in 1815. During his undergraduate days he read very widely and was far ahead of his
younger classmates.

Soon after his graduation he was teaching mathematics and natural history at Harvard. In 1817 he became managing editor of the two-year-old *North American Review,* but before this time he had been steadily
reading in theology. These were the exciting days of Unitarianism, whose supporters fervently looked to the day
when a reasonable religion would be the chosen faith of
those yet bound by Calvinism. Sparks, who had entered
the ministry, accepted the call that Baltimore issued for a
Unitarian pastor because he thought he saw in the South
fertile soil for his religious fervor. After four years of
hard work, and little progress, Sparks was forced to give
up his charge.

[1] Adams, *Life and Writings of Jared Sparks,* I, 6.

Although he had performed his ministerial duties diligently, Sparks clung to his literary interests and his association with the *North American Review*. During his stay in Baltimore he had also served as chaplain of the House of Representatives for two years, and his acquaintance with the leading public figures of his day was to be of great value in his later career as a historian.

In the year of his return to Boston, 1823, Sparks became the owner of the *North American Review,* and with his first number in January, 1824, set a high standard of editing. Although his aim was to publish a national periodical with contributors from all over the country, he had little success in this direction, for most of his contributions came from Boston or near by. The members of an exclusive "Literary and Social Club," founded by Prescott in 1818, supplied material for the *Review,* and a "North American Review Club" dictated for a time the magazine's policy. Among Sparks's innovations was the practice of paying for articles, at the rate of one dollar a page. The *Review,* for a long time the leading magazine in the country, exercised great power over the destiny of new books, and writers often awaited with nervous anxiety the judgment of editor Sparks. After seven years with the *Review,* he sold his remaining share of the property (he had disposed of a fourth in 1826) for a good price at a time when the *Review* had three thousand subscribers. In his editing of the magazine, as in his later editing of the letters of famous men, Sparks revealed a fatal weakness. As Bassett put it, "he was not willing to offend the mighty."

His historical interests developed during the years of his pastorate in Baltimore, when he wrote articles of a historical nature for the *North American Review*. At that time Sparks also became interested in the career of the famous Connecticut traveler, John Ledyard, and although his intended biography of Ledyard was delayed for some

years, it probably served to keep Sparks's historical associations active. In a letter, written in 1819, Sparks said
that he had sent to London for additional material about
Ledyard. He had been attracted to Ledyard because of
his own intense interest in travel.[2] Three years later
Sparks was still waiting for some European materials,
and he wrote to a friend that Ledyard "moves slowly." [3]

In any event, although it is not certain what directed
Sparks to the study and writing of history, it is known
that he was thinking rather seriously about it in 1823. In
the summer of that year he wrote in his diary: "Meditating on the importance of having a new history of America. Thought I might undertake it some time or other. No
ordinary task to do it properly. I would go to the foundation, and read everything on the subject. The Ebeling
Library at Harvard University, the collection of books in
the Boston Athenaeum and Historical Society, afford
facilities which cannot be enjoyed elsewhere." His duties
as editor of the *Review* prevented him from devoting
much energy to history, but the subject was never far
from his mind. A former schoolmate, Charles Folsom,
who was running a press in Cambridge, wrote to Sparks
(1824) that he intended to publish a complete edition of
Washington's writings. Folsom wished to know who, in
the South, could best aid him in the publication.

Sparks communicated with Supreme Court Justice
Bushrod Washington, nephew of the First President, in
whose care at Mount Vernon were many Washington letters. Although this letter, written in Folsom's behalf, received a refusal, Sparks decided to publish the letters
under his own name, if he were given access to the great
collection. The *if* was of serious magnitude, for despite
the intercession of distinguished friends, particularly of
Justice Story, Sparks found it difficult to get Justice

[2] Adams, *Sparks,* I, 165.
[3] *Ibid.,* 202.

Washington's permission to see the letters. Meanwhile Sparks became interested in the whole field of the Revolution, and in the spring and fall of 1826 he traveled through the Atlantic States, inspecting the archives for material bearing on this great theme. He became more than ever convinced of the necessity for a study of the Revolution. "I have got a passion for Revolutionary history," he wrote, "and the more I look into it the more I am convinced that no complete history of the American Revolution has been written. The materials have never been collected; they are still in the archives of the states, and in the hands of individuals." [4]

Permission having finally been obtained, Sparks arrived at Mount Vernon in January, 1827, to study the 40,000 Washington letters. When he was permitted to take them to Boston for a more thorough study, the New England literary capital acclaimed with delight this coup that had brought him and the city so much distinction. It is interesting to note that as a result of the attention Sparks won for the Washington collection, the government bought it and eventually deposited the manuscripts in the Library of Congress.

The First President's letters launched Sparks into a number of enterprises of a historical nature, on all of which he worked while preparing the edition of Washington. During these years he even thought of editing the papers of Alexander Hamilton, Lafayette, and John Jay. The range of his activities between 1827 and 1840 exacted a great toll on his energy. In view of his academic obligations after 1840 it is not surprising that from that date to his death, in 1866, Sparks's work was small in volume and in no way comparable to that done in his earlier days.

As time passes Sparks will probably be remembered

[4] *Ibid.*, 509.

less as a historian than as a discoverer and collector of
the documents from which history is written. He attracted attention to the sources of our history and, together with George Bancroft and Peter Force, he stimulated interest in private as well as public collections. His
tour of the State archives in 1826 gave him a better
knowledge of the materials for American history than
any other individual then possessed. Over a period of
three and a half months Sparks traveled some 3500 miles
on his tour of archival exploration, and wherever he went
he stimulated interest in American history.[5]

In European archives he continued his quest for documents bearing on the Revolution. Thus was inaugurated
for American scholars the practice, now traditional, of
going to Europe for sources of American history. Sparks,
landing in England in the spring of 1828, was certainly
one of the earliest Americans to examine the British side
of the Revolutionary struggle. Despite the letters of distinguished men, intended to aid Sparks in gaining access
to the government archives, many precious weeks slid by
before he finally won the coveted permission. In London
several private collections, including the papers of the
Earl of Shelburne, were opened to Sparks's examination.
He also went to Paris for a few months, where he worked
under difficult conditions to unearth from the archives
the story of French participation in the War for American Independence. Lafayette was Sparks's host for a few
weeks, and every morning, as the distinguished general
told the historian of his memories of Washington and the
Revolution, Sparks wrote down the gist of these conversations.[6] To the aged James Madison, who was very
much interested in historical activities, he confided the
project of "A History of the Alliance between France
and the United States during the American Revolution,"

[5] *Ibid.*, 508-509.
[6] *Ibid.*, II, 117.

to be based on the material in American and French archives.[7]

His most productive years saw the publication of the
long-deferred *Life and Travels of John Ledyard* (1828),
and, in 1829-1830, *The Diplomatic Correspondence of the
American Revolution* in twelve volumes. This work, done
under a Federal contract by which the government took a
large number of copies, proved profitable to Sparks. In
1832 he brought out three volumes on *The Life of Gouverneur Morris* of which the first was the biography, and the
remaining two contained selections from Morris's papers
and correspondence. This work, which was rapidly completed, has not been favorably noticed by succeeding generations. This and other historical labors were looked
upon by Sparks as contributions to his major interest—
the history of the American Revolution. Between 1834
and 1837 appeared the twelve volumes of *The Life and
Writings of George Washington*. There was a note of
relief in the entry in Sparks's journal, July 22, 1837:
"Finished the 'Life of Washington' and sent the last
sheet of the manuscript to the printer. The whole work
. . . is now completed."[8] Although the first volume is
the biography, Sparks published it last in order to get
the benefit of the closest association with all the manuscripts in his possession. The letters of Washington
written before the Revolution are in Volume II, and in
the next volumes, through the eighth, are the letters, official and private, written during the war period. The private letters, written from the close of the war to the beginning of his first presidential term, are in Volume IX;
the next two volumes contain the public and private letters written during his term of office. In the last volume
are Washington's speeches, proclamations, and messages
to Congress. In an outline of his plan of publication,

[7] *Ibid.*, p. 232; January 17, 1832.
[8] *Ibid.*, p. 278.

Sparks had written to Bushrod Washington that he did not intend to publish any of the private letters, "except such as you, and other judicious persons, may deem in accordance with the dignity of the work, as containing interesting facts or developing traits of the author's mind and character." [9]

In his preface to the life of Washington, Sparks disclaims any intention of writing an "historical biography"—"after the able, accurate, and comprehensive work of Chief Justice Marshall, it would be presumptuous," thought Sparks. "Anecdotes are interwoven, and such incidents of a private and personal nature as are known; but it must be confessed, that these are more rare than could be desired." He takes a dig at some of his many competing Washington biographers: "I have seen many particulars of this description which I knew not to be true, and others which I did not believe. These have been avoided; nor have I stated any fact for which I was not convinced there was credible authority. If this forbearance has been practised at the expense of the reader's entertainment, he must submit to the sacrifice as due to truth and the dignity of the subject." Years afterward, answering a query of Edward Everett as to the credibility of Parson Weems's *Washington,* Sparks replied that he had never referred to Weems's biography because he had "little confidence in the genuineness or accuracy of his statements." [10]

The largest part of Sparks's biography deals with Washington's services in the Revolutionary War. Some sentences are exceedingly moderate for the patriotic temper of his day—"the constitution, as it came from the hands of its framers, was regarded by no one as theoretically perfect." Some of his remarks on the character of Washington are very appropriate: "Wisdom, judgment,

[9] *Ibid.,* I, 398; January 16, 1826.
[10] *Ibid.,* II, 517; January 11, 1864.

prudence, and firmness were his predominant traits.''
''He deliberated slowly, but decided surely; and when
his decision was once formed, he seldom reversed it, and
never relaxed from the execution of a measure till it was
completed.'' ''It is the happy combination of rare talents
and qualities, the harmonious union of the intellectual
and moral powers, rather than the dazzling splendor of
any one trait, which constitute the grandeur of his character.''

Before the last of the Washington volumes was off
the press, the first of the volumes of *The Works of Benjamin Franklin; with Notes and a Life of the Author* was
in process of publication. During the four years, 1836-
1840, ten volumes appeared, of which nine are devoted to
letters and papers, and one is reserved for a life of
Franklin. In this biography, which is adjudged to be
Sparks's best work, after his *Washington,* a new characterization of the Philadelphia patriarch emerges. Formerly Franklin was presented as a cunning, insincere individual, whereas in Sparks's hands he becomes a wise,
honorable, and patient soul. As early as 1832, Bancroft,
with his usual enthusiasm, had urged Sparks to write the
life of Franklin to ''gain the glory of being the vindi-
cator of his fame to all posterity.'' ''Defend in a permanent form the honor that has been wantonly assailed by
the invidious.'' [11]

Sparks carried on the biography where Franklin's
autobiography ended. Franklin, writes Sparks, ''possessed a perfect mastery over the faculties of his understanding and over his passions.'' ''It was as fortunate
for the world, as it was for his own fame, that the benev-
olence of such a man was limited only by his means and
opportunities of doing good, and that, in every sphere of
action through a long course of years his single aim was
to promote the happiness of his fellow men by enlarging

[11] *Ibid.,* p. 191.

their knowledge, improving their condition, teaching them practical lessons of wisdom and prudence and inculcating the principles of rectitude and the habits of a virtuous life.''

Edward Channing, a later successor of Sparks at Harvard, wrote that the *Washington* and *Franklin* were ''a monument to his industry and his historical insight.'' But the edition of Franklin was by no means complete, for Sparks was unable to gain access to a large collection in London possessed by Franklin's descendants. In justice to Sparks, however, it should be mentioned that he foresaw that it was possible that more of Franklin's papers might be unearthed. Many years elapsed before a more inclusive edition of Franklin's writings was published, but even this modern work of Albert H. Smyth is far from complete.

While Sparks was busy publishing the biographies and correspondence of these leading Americans, he was also engaged in editing, between 1834 and 1838, a series of ten volumes in *The Library of American Biography*. Sparks had written in his journal, July 28, 1832: ''I have been thinking of a project for a new publication to be entitled 'A Library of American Biography.' '' This was to be a series of prominent lives from different periods, serving in a measure as a connected history of the country.[12] With his usual tartness, John Quincy Adams pointed out that Sanderson's *Lives of the Signers of the Declaration of Independence* were all eulogies. ''Is it intended that your 'Library of Biography' should be so?'' he asked Sparks.[13] Sparks was too good a historian to echo the blatancy of Sanderson, but he catered sufficiently to the current patriotic taste to insure success for his venture. He followed it up with a second series of fifteen volumes (1844-1847), likewise written for the popular

12 *Ibid.*, p. 189.
13 *Ibid.*, p. 193.

taste, which at that time demanded biographies of those Americans who had played important parts in the making of the Republic.

Sparks's great interest in biography came from his belief, shared by some writers of our own day, that a nation's history can be told through biographies of its leading men. He had a high standard—for his time—of the art of biography. The subject, he said, was to be kept before the reader always, and the incidents of his life "made to follow each other in consecutive order." This type of biographical writing, as distinguished from others, like memoirs, was rather difficult, wrote Sparks, because it required "a clear and spirited style, discrimination in selecting facts, and judgment in arranging them so as to preserve just proportions." Sixty biographies were included in these twenty-five volumes. It is interesting to observe that the eight biographies written by Sparks were evenly divided between explorers and American Revolutionary figures, thus reflecting the two major interests of his literary life.

A later publication, which appeared in 1853, although it had been planned years earlier, was the four-volume *Correspondence of the American Revolution; being Letters of Eminent Men to George Washington.* This work had been projected when Sparks was looking over Washington's papers, and required little preparation when the time for publication arrived.

The library of nearly seventy volumes associated with the name of Sparks accounts for the high station that he occupies in American historiography. The few volumes of Abiel Holmes, Timothy Pitkin, David Ramsay and William Gordon, available before Sparks began publication indicate the vast gaps that he filled. It is true that the comparatively temporary nature of Sparks's work has necessitated more research in the fields in which he labored. The vast range of his activity, however, altered completely the character of our historical literature and indicated the direction that much contemporary and subsequent research was to take. Thirty years after Sparks died, a careful student, Moses Coit Tyler, wrote that a tendency prevailed "to forget or undervalue his important and indeed almost herculean labors, as a pioneer in American historical scholarship." [14] The publication of the biography of Sparks by Herbert B. Adams, in 1893, regained for him something of his rightful due.

Fortunately for Sparks, he brought out his volumes at a time when there was intense public interest in documents. Through all his historical enterprises he kept in mind the plan of writing a documentary history of the Revolution. Early in his career, when he was reveling in the riches of Washington's papers, Sparks told Madison that he would write a history of the American Revolution "comprehending its causes and origin, its military, civil, and diplomatic features." [15] Later, when he was finishing the edition of Franklin, he hoped that his editing career had ended: "I have planned a history of the American Revolution, on an extended scale," he writes, "having studied that subject at the fountain-head for ten years. I know not when it will be executed." [16] Not long afterward he said, again: "I am preparing to write a formidable history of the American Revolution." Sparks had not the requisite good health and energy to realize his dream, and the "Documentary History of the Revolution" was never written.

It has previously been intimated that much of the work done by Sparks was impermanent, particularly that done in his editorial capacity. Progressive as he was in many ways, he clung to a custom that more farsighted

[14] M. C. Tyler, *Literary History of the American Revolution* (2 vols., N. Y., 1897), II, 362, note 2.

[15] Adams, *Sparks*, II, 209; May 12, 1827.

[16] *Ibid.*, p. 346; August 23, 1898.

editors were already abandoning. It is unfair to compare Sparks with Parson Weems, who presented much fiction in the guise of history, and yet fundamentally their purposes were somewhat similar. For both authors, the lives of great men, particularly Washington, were sermons continually exhorting lesser mortals to nobler personal achievements. Not all aspects of Washington's life, nor all his words were fit to be sacred sermons, and rather than exhibit Washington in all his humanity, Sparks excised or altered his language to fit the character created by a worshipful America. A number of critics, who were also acquainted with Washington's letters in their originals, engaged Sparks in controversy, over what Lord Mahon, historian of England, called his "embellishments" of the language of the First President. In justice to Sparks, who was defended by so distinguished a historian as John Gorham Palfrey, it should be said that only rarely did editors then insist on literal reproduction; the common practice was to dress up the words of eminent men, lest the curious public see their idol in dishabille. Another accusation leveled against Sparks in his edition of Washington was that he left out of the letters expressions unfavorable to New Englanders.

Sparks's frailties as an editor were clearly seen in the *Diplomatic Correspondence of the Revolution.* Since it was obviously a book of reference, there was no need for altering the text of these documents in order to exhibit the nobility of any individual character. When a new edition of this correspondence was proposed some twenty years after the death of Sparks, it was found that he had not included letters that referred to a projected substitution of Marshal Broglie for Washington as commander in chief in 1776-1777.[17] The mistakes of Sparks as an editor are the errors committed by most pioneers

[17] Francis Wharton, *The Revolutionary Diplomatic Correspondence of the United States,* 6 vols., Washington, 1889, preface to Vol. I.

in any field of activity. A grateful posterity recognizes the worth of the chart he made of a field that had lain largely in obscurity.

Although Sparks's name is associated with a large body of historical work, most of it was of an editorial nature. What creative writing he did had many shortcomings. It lacked the sparkle of Bancroft, and it is clear that he did not belong by temperament to the New England school of literary historians which included Prescott and Motley. The heavy emphasis that Sparks placed on original sources, particularly manuscript materials, drew praise from Prescott, who noted Bancroft's lesser dependence on such matter in his early volumes. Bancroft, said Prescott privately, ''is sketchy, episodical, given to building castles in the air,'' while Sparks, he said was ''on *terra firma.''* [18]

The readers of his day rewarded him well with their patronage, which assured Sparks a comfortable livelihood. We are told on good authority that more than 600,000 copies of works bearing his name as editor or author were sold in his lifetime. [19] History vied with fiction in public appeal, and the foresight of Sparks was well rewarded when he picked the subject that would yield the most fertile returns—Revolutionary history. Here was the same rich drama—struggles for liberty and conquest of new lands—that provided materials for the works of Bancroft, Prescott, Motley, and Parkman. They wrote when sagas of liberty and conquest were not dim-remembered tales of half-forgotten ancestors, but when these epics were part of the very fabric of their lives. At that time America was in the process of winning vast new regions beyond the Mississippi, and Americans prided themselves on the welcome they gave liberty-loving revolutionaries who fled European reaction.

[18] Adams, *Sparks,* II, 292-293, note 1; February 1, 1841.
[19] W. R. Dean, *Historical Magazine* (May, 1866).

The later years of Sparks's life, which were unproductive of literature, were partly spent in association with Harvard. In keeping with the progressive spirit of his day, Sparks, like others who had been to Europe, was interested in new educational ideas. Many Harvard graduates wanted to reform their alma mater, and they were particularly anxious to establish a university. Soon after his return from Europe, Sparks wrote to George Bancroft in 1829: "The lower, or the school-part of this seminary is an inherent ingredient and must from the necessity of the case keep down the upper, or university-part. Neither money, nor talents, nor both combined, can remedy this defect. Now let us have a university without the school part; let us have an establishment where we can teach young men something about the operations of their own minds, the doings of the world, and the business of life. Europe is full of such institutions; it is time for one at least in America." Many years were to elapse, however, before institutions of university standing were created in the United States.

In 1839 Sparks was appointed the McLean Professor of History at Harvard, and thus became the holder of the first chair distinctly devoted to that subject in the United States. His duties were not exacting; his lectures were delivered only four months a year. In his first term he gave a course of lectures on the American Revolution, covering the period from 1763 to 1783, and in following years he gave an additional course. He also gave courses of public lectures on the American Revolution, in Boston, New York, and elsewhere. So popular was the subject that it was not unusual for the speaker to have an audience of 2000.[20] College instruction in history, however, is but little indebted to Sparks, who though interested in better teaching, anxiously awaited the end of the school

[20] Adams, *Sparks,* II, 419.

year to be off on projects of research. It is more the pity, therefore, that he allowed himself to become further involved by accepting the presidency of Harvard in 1849. He was not adapted to handling the many details of this position. Ill health added to his difficulties, and, after a scant four years, he resigned. For thirteen years thereafter he lived in retirement at Cambridge till his death in 1866. In that time only the four-volume *Correspondence of the American Revolution* appeared, but Sparks, the dean of American historians, was kept busy answering many inquiries that frittered away his energies.

Not all his correspondence, however, was inconsequential. Historians and public figures wrote to him for advice and information, and younger authors sought the guidance that so willingly came from the older man. John Gilmary Shea dedicated to Sparks *The Discovery and Exploration of the Mississippi Valley,* and the New England historian then successfully urged Shea to write the history of the early Catholic missions in Canada and the West.[21] "It is a noble subject," said Sparks some years before Parkman illumined its nobility. Sparks was generous in his praise of William Henry Trescot of South Carolina, who published an essay on the *Diplomacy of the American Revolution: An Historical Study* (1852). He urged Trescot to write a diplomatic history of the administrations of Washington and Adams; Trescot did so, and sent Sparks the completed work in 1858. He was then encouraged to continue the diplomatic history of the United States to the Treaty of Ghent and beyond, but he did no more, and the task was left for Henry Adams.[22]

In the enthusiasm of his younger years Sparks wrote to Bancroft in 1825: "My absorbing passion is for books, knowledge, and thought; I would not exchange it for all

---

[21] *Ibid.,* p. 557, and note 2.
[22] *Ibid.,* pp. 558-559; see also Trescot mss. in Library of Congress, letters from Richard Rush.

the wealth of the Indies." The anticlimactic character of the last twenty-five years of Sparks's life of diverted energy is a sad commentary on the impermanence of youthful fire.[23]

GEORGE BANCROFT[*]

George Bancroft was eleven years younger than Jared Sparks, having been born in 1800, but he outlived Sparks by twenty-five years. Thus his life encompassed the largest part of the whole first century of the American Republic, the spirit of which he faithfully mirrored. He was born in Worcester, Massachusetts, where his father, Rev. Aaron Bancroft, was a noted liberal clergyman leaning to Unitarianism. Aaron Bancroft wrote one of the many biographies of Washington which appeared during the years immediately following the President's death. This *Life of Washington,* published in 1807, was widely read and went through several editions in America and Europe. The author indicated in his preface that his book was not written "for men of erudition, but for the unlettered portion of the community," and though he entertained "no expectation of acquiring literary fame," he hoped "to escape the disgrace of having written an useless book." Perhaps the most useful achievement of the elder Bancroft was the impulse to historical study that he communicated to his more illustrious son, who, on his mother's side, was descended from that Captain Benjamin Church who won his fame in the Indian war against King Philip and later wrote a chronicle of this struggle.

[23] See Adams, *Jared Sparks;* Bassett, "Jared Sparks" in *Middle Group of American Historians;* Howe, *Letters of George Bancroft;* and Roger Wolcott, *Correspondence of William Hickling Prescott 1834-1847* (Boston, 1925).

[*] This section on Bancroft is substantially the same as the material published in the *New England Quarterly,* December, 1934.

George Bancroft was a promising youngster. When he completed his studies at Harvard, after preparatory work at Phillips Academy, Exeter, he was not yet seventeen years old. Edward Everett, one of Bancroft's instructors, had gone to Europe to travel and study at Göttingen. While abroad, he urged President Kirkland of Harvard to send Bancroft to the German university. Through the generosity of a few Harvard men a sufficient sum of money was raised to enable Bancroft to spend four years in Europe. He gained his doctor's degree in 1820 and the following year he attended lectures in Berlin.

Soon after his return in 1822 he accepted the position of tutor in Greek at Harvard, but his unconventional character, strengthened by the acquisition of foreign manners, antagonized a number of influential people. Ralph Waldo Emerson was more discriminating in his judgment of Bancroft. The young doctor, as was then customary, delivered some sermons, after which Emerson wrote, ''He needs a great deal of cutting and pruning, but we think him an infant Hercules. All who know him agree in this, that he has improved his time thoroughly at Göttingen. He has become a perfect Greek scholar, and knows well all that he pretends to know; as to divinity, he has never studied, but was approbated abroad.''

With George Ticknor, who had also studied at Göttingen, and was a fellow member of the Harvard faculty, Bancroft immediately began a campaign to reform the teaching methods of the college. Germany had inspired these younger men with newer pedagogic ideas with which they rashly hoped to supplant the uninspiring student recitations. But conservatism had its way for the time being, and Bancroft was sick at heart. In May, 1823, he wrote to a friend: ''Our hopes of a reform at college have pretty much blown over. . . . I have found College a sickening and wearisome place. Not one spring of comfort have I to draw from. My state has been nothing but trouble, trouble, trouble, and I am heartily glad that the end of the year is coming so soon.'' In his own classes, however, Bancroft did institute changes to the advantage of learning, but it was evident that he and Harvard were at the parting of the ways.

With Joseph Green Cogswell, who had studied at Göttingen and was then, in 1823, working in the Harvard Library, Bancroft formed a partnership to organize a school based on the model of the German Gymnasium. This idea was not new; four years earlier, Bancroft had written to President Kirkland from Göttingen that he might open a high school on his return. ''I would gladly be instrumental in the good cause of improving our institutions of education,'' he wrote, ''and it is our schools, which cry out most loudly for reformation.'' To that friend of historians, Samuel A. Eliot, Bancroft confided his plans. The aim of the new Round Hill School at Northampton, Massachusetts, he said, was to contribute to ''the moral and intellectual maturity of the mind of each boy we take charge of; and the means are to be first and foremost instruction in the classics. . . . We call our establishment a school, and we mean to consider ourselves as schoolmasters. We might indeed assume a pompous name, speak of instituting a gymnasium; but let the name be modest. I like the sound of the word Schoolmaster.''

For eleven years (1823-1834), Bancroft's school attracted attention and support as a worthy educational experiment—even from Harvard, with which his relations had been rather unpleasant. The modernity of some of the pedagogical practices at Round Hill are noticed in the remarks of Cogswell: ''I do not form any classes but allow every one to get as much of any book which he is studying, as he can do, in the time assigned for the exercise, telling him that he may recite as soon as he is ready, but cautioning him at the same time, that the least failure sends him back, and obliges him to wait till the rest have been brought to trial." Bancroft himself left the school in 1831, convinced of his own limitations as a teacher, but in many ways he was a different personality from the highly imaginative, excitable young Harvard tutor of nine years before. For one thing, he was already interested in the very practical and great game of politics.

The earliest publication of the future historian was a slender volume of *Poems* in 1823, and he lived long enough to rue this youthful indiscretion. For his Round Hill School he prepared adaptations of the better German textbooks which later gained popularity elsewhere in the United States. One of the books which Bancroft translated was by his old Göttingen master, Arnold H. L. Heeren, *Reflections on the Politics of Ancient Greece* (1824). "The business of translating," thought Bancroft, was "but an humble one; and yet it may be the surest method of increasing the number of good books which are in the hands of our countrymen. None can be offered more directly interesting to them, than those which relate to political institutions." Bancroft hoped that scholars would accept his translation of Heeren's work as "an earnest of his desire to do something . . . for the advancement of learning in our common country." During these years, and in later life as well, Bancroft was an important agent in spreading a knowledge of German culture in the United States.

In 1828 Bancroft wrote to President Kirkland of a projected course in history to be based largely on the volumes of Heeren. "For my own country," he added, "I should venture to write outlines." Not all the pertinent volumes of Heeren were translated, but in the latter part of the same year appeared the *Geschichte des Euro-*

paischen Staatensystem in two volumes under the title
*History of the Political System of Europe and its Colo-
nies, from the Discovery of America to the Independence
of the American Continent.* To suit American tastes
Bancroft had obviously adopted a title not in the original.
The last part of the comprehensive course in history was
to be the volume on America, and although it was not
written as part of this plan, it is not unlikely that there
lay the genesis of the future *History of the United States.*

Other literary activities that occupied the attention
of Bancroft before the first volume of his history appeared in 1834 were the many articles and reviews that
appeared in the *North American Review.* In his relations
with its editor, Jared Sparks, Bancroft was sometimes
deeply hurt because his contributions were adjudged too
harshly critical or because the editor took unusual liberties with the blue pencil. When Sparks made many
changes in his article on Goethe, Bancroft wrote him: "If
I mistake not the character of the American public, there
is no need of keeping back any truth from it. The public
is willing to be shocked. Ask yourself if a thing appears
good to your mind; and doubt not, the objections which
may arise from the fear that this or the other will be
offended, will prove groundless."

Despite much bickering, Sparks remained a good
friend to the younger Bancroft, to whom he wrote in
1826: "You must not work yourself to death, nor be too
greedy after the treasures of this world. But you are
doing great things, and the fruits of your labors are to
appear not in the present time only, but in the future
ages."

The older man's remarks were to the point, for Bancroft was already determined that wealth as well as fame
should be the rewards of a literary career. He was turning more and more to local history and subjects of con-

temporary interest, probably in part as a result of Sparks's influence.

Another phase of his literary activities during these years brought him before the public eye in the role of politician. His earliest political opinions give no indication of his later affiliations; quite the contrary, indeed, for they linked him with the older traditions of New England Federalism. But on July 4, 1826, Bancroft delivered at Northampton, Massachusetts, one of the numerous orations made on that day to celebrate the fiftieth year of the nation's birth. Therein he told of the advance of republicanism throughout the world, and, on behalf of the United States, laid claim to the largest contributions to its progress. The speaker extolled the Jeffersonian doctrine in phrases that shortly were to alienate him from his conservative surroundings. "We hold it best," he declared, "that the laws should favor the diffusion of property and its acquisition, not the concentration of it in the hands of a few to the impoverishment of the many. We give the power to the many in the hope and to the end, that they may use it for their own benefit; that they may always so legislate, as to open the fairest career to industry, and promote an equality founded on the safe and equitable influence of the laws."

Bancroft's article in the *North American Review*, in 1831, a study of the report of the Committee on Ways and Means on the Bank of the United States, largely determined the course of his political life. His support of Jackson's position that the Bank's charter should not be extended did not represent the policy of the *Review* and antagonized New England opinion. The editor of the magazine, Alexander H. Everett, in obvious contradiction to the tenor of Bancroft's contribution appended the following: "The expediency of renewing the charter of the present National Bank has not been brought into [this] discussion. On this question our opinion is decidedly in the affirmative; and we propose in a future paper to assign the reasons which lead us to that conclusion." The article which followed, strongly supporting the Bank, was not by Bancroft. He prepared a clearer statement of his position, in another paper, but it was unacceptable to the editor. Bancroft was thenceforth marked for high preferment among the politicians in the Jacksonian democracy, who well knew how to use his literary talents.

For a time, in 1834, Bancroft was a prospective Whig candidate for Congress, but withdrew to run under the workingman's emblem for the lower house of the Massachusetts General Court. Although he was defeated and bitterly attacked by the Whigs, he succeeded in drawing attention to his standard. That same year the first volume of his history brought him national distinction, and he was soon exchanging letters with such prominent political figures as William L. Marcy and Van Buren, whom he supported in the election of 1836. In 1837, he was named collector of the port of Boston, in which office he remained until the Whig administration four years later. He was now an acknowledged member in the national councils of his party.

Bancroft's decision to desert the schoolroom was a fortunate one, for otherwise his history would probably never have been written. The constant strain on his nerves and the lack of time would have been too much of a handicap. In April, 1833, he wrote to Sparks in his lively way: "History thrives . . . you will be pleased with the researches I have fearlessly undertaken. I am by degrees getting clear insight into the old times, and sometimes discover errors even in Chalmers." [24]

In the preface to his first volume Bancroft writes: "I have formed the design of writing a History of the United States from the Discovery of the American Con-

[24] Adams, *Sparks,* II, 190, note 1.

tinent to the present time. As the moment arrives for publishing a portion of the work, I am impressed more strongly than ever with a sense of the grandeur and vastness of the subject; and am ready to charge myself with presumption for venturing on so bold an enterprise. I can find for myself no excuse but in the sincerity with which I have sought to collect truth from trustworthy documents and testimony. I have desired to give to the work the interest of authenticity. I have applied, as I have proceeded, the principles of historical skepticism, and, not allowing myself to grow weary in comparing witnesses, or consulting codes of laws, I have endeavored to impart originality to my narrative, by deriving it from writings and sources which were the contemporaries of the events that are described. Where different nations or different parties have been engaged in the same scenes I have not failed to examine their respective reports. Such an investigation on any country would be laborious; I need not say how much the labor is increased by the extent of our republic, the differences in the origin and early government of its component parts, and the multiplicity of topics, which require to be discussed and arranged.''

In this preface Bancroft also states the theme on which the later pages played their variations: ''The spirit of the colonies demanded freedom from the beginning.'' He is critical of those American historians who, so he says, have taken on faith statements of earlier writers, and have not consulted the sources themselves. He had not forgotten the training he had received in Germany. In discussing the credibility of various contradictory sources, in one instance, Bancroft refers to memory as ''an easy dupe,'' and tradition as ''a careless story teller.'' ''An account,'' he continues, ''to be of highest value, must be written immediately at the time of the event. The eyewitness, the earwitness often persuade memory into a belief of inventions." The long note on the speech of James Otis in connection with the writs of assistance is an excellent example of Bancroft's critical evaluation of sources.

In his introduction he glorifies the North American republic. "The United States," he declares, "constitute an essential portion of a great political system, embracing all the civilized nations of the earth. At a period when the force of moral opinion is rapidly increasing, they have the precedence in the practice and the defence of the equal rights of man." Although the United States was part of a system extending over the earth, to Bancroft it was the leader among all nations. The confidence of the young Republic never spoke with greater assurance.

This first volume treats of the expansion of Europe into America and the history of the colonies to the restoration of the Stuarts. In writing of the establishment of St. Augustine, Bancroft states that "it sprung from the unrelenting bigotry of the Spanish king." "In its transition from the bigoted policy of Philip II to the American principles of religious liberty" it was of striking interest to Americans. "Its origin should be carefully remembered," continues Bancroft, "for it is a fixed point, from which to measure the liberal influence of time; the progress of modern civilization; the victories of the American mind, in its contest for the interests of humanity." [25] Abounding in rhetorical excursions, Bancroft could sometimes write simply and impressively, as in his reference to the failure of Raleigh to plant a colony: "If America had no English town, it soon had English graves." As might be expected, Roger Williams is assigned an especially distinguished place in Bancroft's list of worthies. In one of his many asides, Bancroft

[25] Long afterwards, Henry Adams also spoke of fixed points in measuring the movement of time.

pauses to exclaim: "History has ever celebrated the heroes who have won laurels in scenes of carnage. Has it no place for the founders of states; the wise legislators, who struck the rock in the wilderness, so that the waters of liberty gushed forth in copious and perennial fountains?" In a eulogy on the Quakers, Bancroft takes to task their persecutors, writing with the proud tolerance of a descendant of Puritans: "The fears of one class of men are not the measure of the rights of another." In this, and in later volumes, Bancroft's sense of proportion is at variance with the modern temper, for he gives far too much space to religion and to the sharp disputes among its various votaries.

Devoting nearly all his time to history for the next six years, Bancroft worked rapidly and brought out a second volume in 1837 and a third in 1840. Politics and the need for more extended research postponed the appearance of the fourth and fifth volumes until 1852. Two years later the sixth was published; in 1858 came the seventh and in 1860, the eighth. Bancroft's reserves of energy were copious: the ninth and tenth volumes, which conclude the story of the Revolution, appeared in 1874. The title of the first volume had promised a history to the "present time," but for such a task life was too short —even for the long-lived Bancroft—and the later volumes bear the title *History of the United States from the Discovery of the American Continent.*

The second volume carries the narrative chronologically to 1689. In this and in other volumes, Bancroft, like Palfrey, gives more attention to contemporary conditions in England than do most later historians. Running through the text are statements which show Bancroft's preoccupation with the American Revolution. Writing of the hanging of the regicide, Hugh Peter, "for opposition to monarchy," Bancroft observes: "The blood of Massachusetts was destined to flow freely on the field of battle for the same cause; the streams were first opened beneath the gallows.'' At another point he pauses to write history backward: ''The Navigation Act contained a pledge of the ultimate independence of America''; at still another: ''Bacon's rebellion . . . was the early harbinger of American independence and American nationality.'' Bancroft liked sweeping phrases and used them more skillfully than has often been acknowledged: ''Tyranny and injustice peopled America with men nurtured in suffering and adversity. The history of our colonization is the history of the crimes of Europe.'' [26] He salutes the rise of the Quakers in comparable language as ''one of the memorable events in the history of man. It marks the moment when intellectual freedom was claimed unconditionally by the people as an inalienable birthright.''

Bancroft concludes his second volume with a chapter entitled ''The Result thus Far,'' which brings to mind the later practice of Osgood, who ends his volumes on the seventeenth century in similar fashion. There is a note of pride in the sentence: ''Thus have we traced, almost exclusively from contemporary documents and records, the colonization of the twelve oldest states of our Union.'' In this summary Bancroft presents points of view strikingly similar to those of later scholars. He dimly anticipates Freeman and the latter's disciples, Herbert Baxter Adams, John Fiske, and others—men who believed that they could find the roots of American institutions in Germany's primitive communities. (''Of the nations of the European world, the chief emigration was from that Germanic race most famed for the love of personal independence.'') Like a younger contemporary, Francis Parkman, Bancroft celebrates the glories of the Anglo-Saxon mind. Another sentence anticipates Thomas

[26] Cf. Voltaire's phrase, ''The history of great events in the world is scarcely more than a history of crimes.''

C. Hall, who stresses America's indebtedness to the Lollards. "When America traces the lineage of her intellectual freedom," writes Bancroft, "she acknowledges the benefactions of Wickliffe." "We have written the origin of our country; we are now to pursue the history of its wardship," he concludes. "The period through which we have passed shows why we are a free people; the coming period will show why we are a united people."

According to a notice which precedes the text, this third volume was supposed to complete the history of the colonization of the United States. In arranging his subject, Bancroft had kept in mind his belief that "the great drama of their Independence opens with the attempts of France and England to carry the peace of Aix-la-Chapelle into effect." He asks that judgment be suspended for the moment if there is any question as to the propriety of his choice of chronological divisions. Although this book was planned to cover the period from 1689 to 1748, there is really very little on the colonies in the eighteenth century. The volume is concerned mainly with the Indians and the colonial wars. The disproportionate amount of space reserved for the civilization of the Indians probably reflects the extent of contemporary American interest in the life of the red man, who, in 1840, was still a vital factor in our history. This work was much inferior to the first and second volumes. It had no central theme, and the author wandered from one subject to another. For many years to come this was the neglected period of our colonial history.

The fourth volume introduces the first epoch of the American Revolution and has for subtitle *The Overthrow of the European Colonial System, 1748-1763*. There is a distinct speeding up of the tempo in this volume, and here, as before, Bancroft's tendency to look toward the future is marked. "The hour of revolution was at hand, promising freedom to conscience and dominion to intelligence. History, escaping from the dictates of authority and the jars of insulated interests, enters upon new and unthought-of domains of culture and equality, the happier society where power springs freshly from ever-renewed consent.'' The author quotes John Adams to the effect that ''the history of the American Revolution is indeed the history of mankind during that epoch.'' Scattered through his pages are many observations that indicate how superior his concepts of historical writing were to those of Prince and Abiel Holmes. He insists, for example, that it is the idea of continuity ''which gives vitality to history. No period of time has a separate being; no public opinion can escape the influence of previous intelligence.''

In writing the history of the American Revolution, Bancroft felt that he was ''bound to keep faith with the ashes of its heroes.'' This war was ''a civil war'' in which men of the same ancestry were pitted against one another, ''yet for the advancement of the principles of everlasting peace and universal brotherhood. A new plebeian democracy took its place by the side of the proudest empires. Religion was disenthralled from civil institutions. . . . Industry was commissioned to follow the bent of its own genius.''

The fifth volume, which begins the second epoch of the American Revolution, is captioned *How Great Britain Estranged America,* and covers the years 1763-1766. The first seventy-five pages or so Bancroft devoted to a picture of eighteenth-century life in Europe, stressing the English aristocracy in particular. The approach, which emphasizes the difficulty of mutual understanding between England and the colonies, is not unlike that of Charles M. Andrews in his *Colonial Background of the American Revolution.* The volume covers the storm over the Stamp Act and the debates in Parliament over the question of the taxation of America.

Bancroft's sixth volume, completing the history of the causes of the American Revolution, carries the sequence of events down to May, 1774. This volume, and the fourth and fifth, tells of the rise of the union of the United States, the change in the colonial policy of France, and the results of the British plan to strengthen English power in America. "The penal Acts of 1774," says Bancroft, "dissolved the moral connection between the two countries, and began the civil war." Prefacing this volume is a list of the materials owned by or made available to Bancroft in the course of his researches, and of this list he describes the papers of Samuel Adams as "the most valuable acquisition of all . . . they unfold the manner in which resistance to Great Britain grew into a system, and they perfectly represent the sentiments and the reasonings of the time." As the chief engineer of revolutionary activity, Adams is accorded a high place by Bancroft, and Hutchinson is treated with scorn.

The seventh and eighth volumes, covering the third epoch of the American Revolution (*America Declares Itself Independent*), contain detailed narratives of two years: May, 1774, to July 4, 1776. The rising tide of sentiment and the spirit of the Revolution are described with skill and proportion in these pages; probably no general historical work has ever done it better. The papers of the committees of correspondence, which Bancroft had in his possession, enabled him to give a graphic account of their activities. Contrary to the conventional opinion of Bancroft's work (based often on hearsay only), the historian was by no means eager to give offense to England. Discussing this very subject of animus, Bancroft writes: "The tone of our writers has often been deferentially forbearing; those of our countrymen who have written most fully of the war of our revolution, brought to their task no prejudices against England, and while they gladly recall the relations of kindred, no one of them has written a line with gall." [27]

The ninth and tenth volumes carry the story from 1776 to 1778 and then on to the treaty of peace. In the preface to the ninth volume, the author writes of getting "masses of papers from Germany," and he also indicates his indebtedness to Jared Sparks, who often read proof for him. In the midst of his narrative of military affairs, Bancroft includes a chapter on the constitutions of the American States, but all the volumes on the Revolution are concerned, in the main, with the war. In writing of the many causes which made the French alliance possible, Bancroft thinks that "the force which brought all influences harmoniously together was the movement of intellectual freedom. We are arrived at the largest generalization thus far in the history of America." The sense of proportion which the author shows in this ninth volume— the inclusion of a large-scale study of European intervention—suggests the possibility of the influence of John Adams, who long before had proposed a similar approach to the period. The tenth volume contains several chapters on the internal history of the states, which comprise one of the few digressions from the story of the war. The title of one of the chapters—"The King of Spain Baffled by the Backwoodsmen of Virginia 1778-1779"—reveals an interesting aspect of the working of Bancroft's mind: he always tried to lift events out of their provincial settings to give them international significance.

The early volumes are a paean to liberty and democracy. The first, according to Professor Jameson, was "redolent of the ideas of the new Jacksonian democracy —its exuberant confidence, its uncritical self-laudation, its optimistic hopes." [28] As a clear expression of con-

[27] Bancroft, *History,* VIII, 121-122.
[28] J. Franklin Jameson, *The History of Historical Writing in America* (Boston, 1891), p. 104.

temporary spirit, the book created an immediate sensation. Edward Everett enthusiastically wrote to Bancroft: "You have written a work which will last while the memory of America lasts; and which will instantly take its place among the classics of our language. It is full of learning, information, common sense, and philosophy; full of taste and eloquence, full of life and power. You give us not wretched pasteboard men, not a sort of chronological table, with the dates written out at length, after the manner of most historians:—but you give us real, individual, living men and women with their passions, interests and peculiarities." [29] Emerson declared, "It is noble matter, and I am heartily glad to have it nobly treated," and Prescott placed Bancroft with the "great historical writers of the age." [30]

The chorus of American praise was not echoed with equal intensity in Europe. Heeren wrote from Germany praising Bancroft's regard for sources, and expressing amazement at the mass of materials he had used. "You have chosen a great subject, it is a life work." Carlyle liked the color of the work, but added "all things have light *and* shadow," and remarked, "I should say that your didactic theoretic manner gratified me generally much less." Hallam thought "a more moderate tone would carry more weight"; while Guizot qualified his praise of Bancroft's work with the reference that it was "très démocratique." Even some Americans, at least privately, were keenly critical of Bancroft's achievement. John Quincy Adams noted in his *Diary* for September 27, 1840, that the historian's treatment of the Navigation Act of 1651 was a "very lame account," and he disapproved also of his "florid panegyric" upon the first settlers of Virginia. Bancroft's morality was "ostenta-

[29] Howe, *Life and Letters*, pp. 205-206.
[30] W. H. Prescott, *Biographical and Critical Miscellanies* (N. Y., 1845), p. 337.

tious," "but very defective"; yet his "transcendent talents" and "brilliant imagination" deserved acknowledgment.

Bancroft's work at once became the standard history of the United States. Within ten years the first volume had reached its tenth edition, and in 1878 the twenty-sixth edition was published. The following volumes ran through twenty editions, or more, before 1875; the later volumes also sold well. A modern generation knows scarcely more of his history than the author's name. Careful scholarship is dissatisfied with "his loud and uncritical Americanism" and with his omission of certain factors, particularly the economic conflicts.

It should be remembered, however, that Bancroft began writing at a time when history was something more than an investigation into the past. It was supposed to give instruction. The philosophic historians of the eighteenth century, in whose tradition Bancroft was largely reared, were not interested in history for history's sake.[31] These historians, as Professor J. B. Black remarks, desired that history should "prove something," should "take us somewhere," should "provide us with a view of the world and human life." The idea of "progress" animated the thought of this school, and Bancroft was an apt pupil. He saw in the United States the goal to which civilization everywhere should aspire. "The inference that there is progress in human affairs is . . . warranted." "The trust of our race has ever been in the coming of better times."[32] In other respects, too, Bancroft was akin to these eighteenth-century spirits who fancied that the moral world was "swayed by general laws. . . . Event succeeds event according to their influence . . . they form the guiding principle of civilization," arranging "checkered groups in clear and har-

[31] J. B. Black, *The Art of History* (London, 1926).
[32] Bancroft, *History* (1852), III, 398.

monious order." One could not, however, know "the tendency of the ages" intuitively, but must engage in disinterested research. Bancroft's kinship to earlier and to later writers—to Lord Acton, for example—is found in his notion that "as a consequence of the tendency of the race towards unity and universality, the organization of society must more and more conform to the principle of freedom." [33] Years later, when Bancroft was minister to Germany, Von Ranke told him that in his classes he referred to his history as "the best book ever written from the democratic point of view." In response Bancroft observed, "If there is democracy in the history it is not subjective, but objective as they say here, and so has necessarily its place in history and gives its colour as it should." [34]

In later life Bancroft took Carlyle's criticism to heart and rewrote his early volumes. Although he dimmed, somewhat, the brilliance of their "light," even in old age he could see little "shadow" in America. Although the tone of the work became more moderate as it advanced, showing a notable improvement in craftsmanship, Bancroft's volumes continued "to vote for Jackson," according to Dr. Jameson. That "cutting and pruning" which Emerson had thought necessary to Bancroft's development when he was still a young man teaching at Harvard, should have been urged openly upon him all his life.

The last volumes contain mainly the history of military and diplomatic movements during the Revolution, and here Bancroft is at his best. Some sections on this period are so good, in fact, that even the present-day student should be aware of their value. His weaknesses are more obvious when he writes on the internal de-

[33] *The Necessity, the Reality, and the Promise of the Progress of the Human Race:* Address at the New York Historical Society, 1854.
[34] Howe, *Life and Letters,* II, 183.

velopment of the colonies or on their relationship to the mother country. His treatment of the colonies in the eighteenth century is very sketchy, some three chapters sufficing for the story of British administration, apart from its concern with military affairs. In their struggle with king and parliament the colonists were right, and their opponents wrong. Bancroft belonged to that school of historians which the late Professor Osgood called "prosecuting attorneys."

What invalidates most of Bancroft's material on the colonial period is the point of view which he adopts as a clue to America's early history. A philosophic historian must have "some great principle of action . . . that may give unity, and at the same time, importance to the theme." "Such a principle," wrote Prescott in his favorable review of Bancroft's third volume, "did exist in that tendency to independence, which however feeble, till fanned by the breath of persecution into a blaze, was nevertheless the vivifying principle . . . of our ante-revolutionary annals." [35] Like most other students of his day, Bancroft was interested in colonial history not so much for its own sake, as for a background of the Revolution. Critical opinion encouraged that viewpoint. "What Mr. Bancroft has done for the Colonial history," said Prescott, "is, after all, but preparation for a richer theme, the history of the War of Independence, a subject which finds its origin in the remote past, its results in the infinite future." The most erudite student of American history, Jared Sparks, made a similar approach, but with deeper understanding. Once, when he was exploring State archives, he wrote: "The more we look into the history of the colonies, the more clearly we shall see that the Revolution was not the work of a few years only, but began with the first settlement of the country; the seeds

[35] Prescott, *Biographical and Critical Miscellanies,* p. 307.

of liberty, when first planted here, were the seeds of the Revolution; they sprang forth by degrees; they came to maturity gradually; and when the great crisis took place, the whole nation were prepared to govern themselves, because they always had in reality governed themselves."[36] Earlier than Prescott and Sparks, a writer in *The Monthly Anthology* asserted that after the first colonists made their settlements, no other great events remained for an historian to describe until the Revolution.[37]

Bancroft became involved in many arguments with his critics, especially over statements in his ninth volume dealing with the military history of the Revolution. Descendants of the generals, Greene, Schuyler, Sullivan, and others, believed that the historian had been unfair in his criticisms of the military conduct of their ancestors, and a long battle of words developed into the "War of the Grandfathers." Some of the criticisms of the grandsons were ultimately accepted by Bancroft and incorporated in his revision.

In the years following 1840, Bancroft devoted so much of his time to public life that history frequently must have been only an incident in a busy career. Bancroft was always careful to see that the virtue of having voted right was rewarded. Polk named him Secretary of the Navy after the election of 1844, although Bancroft's preference was for a diplomatic post. His chief claim to remembrance as Secretary of the Navy was the fact that he established the Naval Academy at Annapolis. In 1846 he was sent as minister to England. Although he did little historical writing during the next three years, he was very busy collecting materials. He wrote Prescott that people had "heaped" him "full of documents"; the daughter of Lord North let him see her father's papers; the papers of the Duke of Grafton and Lord Dartmouth

[36] Adams, *Sparks*, I, 494.
[37] *The Monthly Anthology*, III (1806), 372.

were likewise opened for his inspection. Bancroft also made a number of trips to Paris to gather material. He had desired a diplomatic post because he hoped thus to gain access to material in Europe, and when the Whigs won the election of 1848, Bancroft knew it would not be long before he would be returning to the United States.

During the next eighteen years (1849 to 1867), Bancroft divided his time between his homes in New York and Newport. Social life made many demands upon him, but during this period he brought out five volumes of his history. An interval of fourteen years separated the eighth volume from the ninth and tenth, which were published in 1874. Politics did not absorb him as it had formerly done because, as a Northern Democrat opposed to the dominant proslavery influence, he was not in sympathy with the guiding spirits of his party. His re-entrance to active political life was in part the reward for an unusual service which he performed for Andrew Johnson. It was not until forty years later that Professor Dunning discovered that Bancroft had written the message which the new President sent to Congress in December, 1865. The author of this state paper was given the congenial ministerial post in Berlin, where he remained from 1867 to 1874. The friendship of Bismarck made him a man of distinction in the German capital. The Jacksonian of the eighteen thirties became the Junker of the eighteen seventies. Yet there had always been a contradiction between his private life and his political philosophy. He liked the distinctions of the aristocracy, while he heatedly defended the idea of American democracy. As early as 1823 he had written President Kirkland: "I love to observe the bustle of the world, but I detest mixing in it. I like to watch the shouts of the multitude but had rather not scream with them."

After his diplomatic career was over, Bancroft decided to continue his history down to the adoption of the

Federal Constitution. He was far advanced in years, now, but his small stature bore their weight well. In 1882 he published two volumes entitled the *History of the Formation of the Constitution of the United States of America.* Bancroft used manuscripts in widely scattered archives for these volumes, and he also had access to the private papers of some of the participants in the Constitutional Convention. Moreover, Madison, before his death in 1836, had given Bancroft his personal observations on the Constitution.

The subject of his narrative, says Bancroft, "has perfect unity, and falls of itself into five epochs or acts" —The Confederation; On the way to a Federal Convention 1783-1787; The Federal Convention; The People of the States in Judgment on the Constitution, 1787-1788; The Federal Government, June, 1789. This old man, now past eighty, continued to write in very much the spirit of the young author of thirty. "In America," he concludes, "a new people had risen up without king, or princes, or nobles, knowing nothing of titles and little of landlords, the plough being for the most part in the hands of free holders of the soil. They were more sincerely religious, better educated, of serener minds, and of purer morals than the men of any former republic. [Their constitution] excelled every one known before; and . . . secured itself against violence and revolution by providing a peaceful method for every needed reform."

Bancroft lived through the Civil War and evidently had no desire to remember its violence when he was writing history. The uncritical nature of many of its pages and the complete neglect of economic factors have been noted by many students. Andrew C. McLaughlin, after paying tribute to Bancroft's "painstaking research," declares that because of the older historian's "tone of exaltation with which it is almost impossible to write truthful history . . . the reader fails to get the right idea of the years of the Confederation.'' Probably more valuable than the text itself are the appendices of hitherto unprinted materials which comprise half of the two volumes.

Bancroft worked also on a final edition of his history, which was to undergo a more thorough revision than had been given to the *Centenary Edition* of 1876. The volumes on the Constitution were joined with those that had been written earlier, and, after many changes in style and much compression of text, the whole history was reissued in six volumes—*The Author's Last Revision* (1883-1885). In spite of the discipline of literary restraint, in principle his work remained unchanged. According to John Spencer Bassett, ''His book remains our great defense of the rise of American nationality, our most fervent great apology for the war of independence in all its untutored Americanism.''

Although Bancroft made a great many transcripts of papers in European collections, rigorous critics have pointed out that he did not always use this material wisely. His biographer states that, following a practice of his day, he ''did not scruple to compile from separate reports and offer as continuous deliverances the speeches ascribed to Pitt, Conway, Grenville, and Mansfield of 1766.'' Sydney G. Fisher, in a paper on the ''Legendary and Myth-making Process in Histories of the American Revolution,'' says of Bancroft, in a hypercritical vein, ''His researches for material both in this country and in Europe are described by his friends as the most remarkable ever made. Documents and sources of information closed to all others were, we are assured, open to him. But strange to say, we see no result of this in his published work. Nor can any subsequent investigator profit by his labors; the wondrous and mysterious sources of information remain mysterious, and many of his opinions are difficult to support with the evidence which the investigators are able to find.'' [38] Certainly some of the British papers he used should have given Bancroft another side of the controversy that preceded the outbreak of the Revolution.

Some years before he died in 1891, a newer standard of historical scholarship had dated Bancroft's volumes in the opinion of professional students of history, but he was still acknowledged everywhere as the greatest American historian. Under the influence of the rigorous ''scientific'' school of history, pre-eminently exemplified by Von Ranke, American scholars of the 1880's, and thereafter, went to extremes in ridiculing Bancroft and in making apologies for him. It is time, however, not merely to count his faults but to measure them. Bancroft belonged to that period which witnessed, both in America and in Europe, the publication of important nationalist histories resulting largely from the revolutions of 1830. It is slightly disconcerting to hear Bancroft criticized for the very fault which was often overlooked in German historians—the idols of his American detractors. Bismarck is said to have thought that ''next to the Prussian army, it was the German professors of history who had done the most to create the new Germany under the hegemony of Prussia.''

Bancroft, with all his faults, brought order out of the records of America's past and placed the history of his own country in some sort of definite relation to that of Europe. That nearly everything he wrote has been rewritten is no very serious indictment—now that it begins to look as if all history would have to be done over time and again for the delight of each new generation and to the dismay of the old. A biographer of Bancroft suggests that the permanent value of his history ''may well be found to be as much in its presentation of the American point of view in the period in which it took

[38] American Philosophical Society *Proceedings,* LI (1912), 69.

form as in its record of an earlier time.'' A reviewer of
Mr. Howe's *Life and Letters of George Bancroft* stated:
''His position as Father of American History is as un-
shaken as is that of Herodotus among the Greeks.'' [39] It
is to the credit of modern historians of America that even
before the third generation they had learned to avoid the
sins of the father. But it is ungracious of them to ignore
his virtues.[40]

JOHN GORHAM PALFREY

In that last decade of the eighteenth century, which
saw the birth of Jared Sparks and George Bancroft, was
born another son of New England who was to become
pre-eminently *its* historian. John Gorham Palfrey was
born in Boston, in 1796, and pursued his collegiate studies
at Harvard, from which he was graduated in 1815 with
his fellow classmate Sparks. He tells us that from his
youth he was interested in the past of New England; his
commencement oration was ''Republican Institutions as
affecting Private Character.'' That valuable outlet for
New England writers, the *North American Review,* was
edited for a time by Palfrey.

The first three volumes of Palfrey's *History of New
England,* with the subtitle ''during the Stuart Dynasty,''
appeared between 1858 and 1864; they were dedicated to
his lifelong friend, Jared Sparks. In the preface to his
first volume Palfrey said that his intention was ''to relate in several volumes the history of the people of New
England.'' The emigration to New England and the establishment of a social system in the new surroundings
are the themes of the first volume. The historian had two

---

[39] *Harvard Graduates' Magazine,* XVI (June, 1908), 652.
[40] M. A. De Wolfe Howe, *Life and Letters of George Bancroft* (2 vols.,
N. Y., 1908); J. S. Bassett, *The Middle Group of American Historians*
(N. Y., 1917); N. H. Dawes and F. T. Nichols, ''Revaluing Bancroft,'' *New
England Quarterly* (June, 1933).

main objectives: to trace in detail the interrelations, both hostile and friendly, among the New England colonies, and to write a narrative of those concurrent events in the homeland which affected the lives of the colonists. "I have thought," he writes in his preface, "that the course of early events in New England required often to be interpreted by bringing to view their relations to earlier and contemporaneous transactions in the parent country."

The historian who wrote two hundred years after the first decades of Puritan settlement fought again the political and theological battles that had disturbed his ancestors. "The name of Mrs. Ann Hutchinson," to him, "is dismally conspicuous in the early history of New England." Toward the events of 1689 Palfrey exhibited the traditional provincial attitude which constantly interpreted the relations between the colonists and the crown as a conflict between "patriots" and "tyrants." He writes apologetically of the witchcraft episode, and seeks to palliate it by referring to contemporary conditions in Europe.

In the preface to his third volume, Palfrey said he was finishing the history of New England "down to the time of her First Revolution." Now almost seventy, he was thinking of laying down his pen, since he had realized his ambition to contribute to the welfare of his country "by reviving the image of the ancient virtue of New England." But eleven years after the publication of Volume III in 1864, Palfrey, despite his advanced age, brought out the fourth volume, called the *History of New England from the Revolution of the Seventeenth Century*. It was dedicated to Charles Francis Adams, whose son, Charles Francis, Jr., was later to be one of Palfrey's severest critics. In his history, says Palfrey, he "follows the strenuous action of intelligent and honest men in building up a free, strong, enlightened and happy state.

. . . Each generation trains the next in the lessons of liberty, and advances it to farther attainments; and when the time comes for the result of the modest process to be disclosed, behold the establishment of the political independence of America, and the boundless spread of principles which are working for good in the politics of the world.'' Thus in his eightieth year, in 1875, the historian was expanding his commencement oration delivered sixty years earlier on ''Republican Institutions as affecting Private Character.''

The anxiety of nearly all nineteenth-century American historians to see in the events of this period, 1689-1740, indications of the later Revolution, vitiates their work as well as Palfrey's. The disproportion of space given to the forty years after 1700—some three hundred pages, compared with the three volumes on the seventeenth century—indicates the author's hurry to reach the Revolutionary period. For the student at the end of the nineteenth century, Palfrey's work was most useful because of its many details, but, apart from a treatment of the Great Awakening in religion, his volumes are rather weak on social and economic history.

Palfrey had a premonition that he would never be able to finish his history. ''The plan of my work,'' he says in Volume IV, in a pathetically hopeful mood, ''would be accomplished by the completion of one more volume, bringing down the narrative to the opening of the War of Independence.'' Despite his fears, Palfrey was able substantially to finish the manuscript of his last volume, the fifth, before he died in 1881; it was not published, however, until 1890. This volume covers the thirty-five years after 1740, concentrating heavily on the period after 1760. It is apparent that the declining vigor of the historian, already evident in the fourth volume, barely enabled him to carry on the research necessary for his last effort. This fifth volume is more like an anecdotal history, e.g., Chapter XIII, "Events in New Hampshire, Connecticut and Rhode Island." The comparatively good organization and consecutive narrative of the earlier volumes are largely missing in the last; the latter is the work of an old man who finds it hard to fix his attention for long.

In a tribute to Palfrey, Judge E. R. Hoar of the Massachusetts Historical Society said of him: "His excellence as the historian of New England and her people is largely due to the strong flavor that was in him of the soil and the race."[41] From his researches in England, Palfrey was able to get much valuable information in state papers, reports, correspondence, and the like, and yet, what Palfrey had once said of Hutchinson and his history might with greater appropriateness be said of his own work: "All the details of his subject were vividly before him; [but] he did not understand his subject." In the discourse that he delivered before the Massachusetts Historical Society in 1844, in which he discussed Hutchinson, Palfrey said: "The founders of New England left a rich inheritance to their children, but in nothing so precious as in the memory of their wise and steady virtue. May there never be baseness to affront that memory!"[42] It was Palfrey's self-appointed task to exalt that memory by patient, scholarly investigation. But, as a fellow New Englander, Charles Francis Adams, wrote, Palfrey was devoid of skepticism, was "a victim almost of that terrible New England conscience" that guided his pen.[43] This leading representative of the filiopietistic school of historians set up an impermanent monument as a token of his ancestor worship.

[41] Mass. Hist. Soc. *Proc.,* XVIII (May, 1881).
[42] Mass. Hist. Soc. *Colls.,* 3d ser., Vol. IX.
[43] "The Sifted Grain and the Grain Sifters," *Amer. Hist. Rev.,* VI.

Richard Hildreth

Bancroft's fame so overshadowed other historians of America that their writings were almost completely eclipsed in their own day. This was even more true in after years. However, he did not have the field entirely to himself, and the works of some of his contemporaries have fared better than his own at the hands of a more critical posterity. One of these historians was Richard Hildreth, another of Harvard's sons. This graduate of 1826, it is said, had thought of writing a history of the United States in his student days. The work he eventually wrote was not published, however, until 1849. Before then he had been editor of an influential Boston paper, the *Atlas,* and had written an antislavery novel and a campaign biography of General Harrison.

The History of the United States of America, from the Discovery of the Continent to the organization of government under the Federal Constitution 1497-1789 was published in three volumes. Hildreth's opening words in the "Advertisement" to his volumes state in unambiguous language just where he stood: "Of centennial sermons and Fourth-of-July orations, whether professedly such or in the guise of history, there are more than enough. It is due to our fathers and ourselves, it is due to truth and philosophy, to present for once, on the historic stage, the founders of our American nation unbedaubed with patriotic rouge, wrapped up in no fine-spun cloaks of excuses and apology, without stilts, buskins, tinsel, or bedizzenment, in their own proper persons, often rude, hard, narrow, superstitious, and mistaken, but always earnest, downright, manly and sincere. The result of their labors is eulogy enough; their best apology is to tell their story exactly as it was." Hildreth says he does not think it "necessary to distract the reader's attention, and to increase the size and cost of the book, by a parade of references,'' but he does list the printed sources he used. The proud author calls the reader's attention to the fact that, in 1849, ''no other work on American history, except mere compends and abridgments, embraces the same extent of time.'' It will be remembered that Bancroft had as yet published but three volumes, which brought him only to the middle of the eighteenth century. ''Nowhere else,'' says Hildreth, ''can be found in the same distinct completeness the curious and instructive story of New England theocracy, the financial, economical, and political history of the colonies and the Revolution, the origin and shaping of our existing laws and institutions, state and national, the progressive, social, and intellectual development of our people.''

The latter statement, however, was not completely justified in the text of Hildreth's work. The narrative is, in the main, political history, but interspersed through his pages, Hildreth touches upon manners, schools, immigration, etc. His writing is often hardheaded and matter of fact. Volume I, called ''Colonial 1497-1688,'' details the voyages of discovery and the settlements of the various colonies. Unlike many other writers, he refused to be enthusiastic about the Quakers. Their ''divine illumination superior to reason,'' was ''in fact, but a whimsical, superstitious, ill-informed, passionate, narrow, ill-regulated reason, right no doubt, upon many important points, but often exaggerated; unwilling or unable to justify itself by argument or fact. . . .''

Volume II carries the narrative forward to 1773. Hildreth's remarks on the effect of the revolution of 1689 on America are very interesting in the light of subsequent research. ''By strengthening the Parliament, and increasing the influence of the manufacturing class, it exposed the American plantations to increased danger of mercantile and parliamentary tyranny, of which, in the acts of trade, they already had a foretaste—a tyranny far more energetic, persevering, grasping, and more to be dreaded than any probable exercise of merely regal authority." Hildreth did not like Cotton Mather, whose "application," he says, "was equal to that of a German professor." During the witchcraft episode, "his eagerness to believe invited imposture. His excessive vanity and strong prejudices made him easy game." Hildreth's caution, however, prompted him to remind his readers of contemporary belief in animal magnetism, and such like, lest they "hurry too much to triumph over the past." A large part of this second volume is given up to the story of the struggles between the French and the English for the control of the Mississippi Valley. The events of the 1760's are told in an unsensational manner, and, in some instances, from a point of view that finds approbation today. Writing of the Boston Stamp Act riots, this contemporary of Bancroft says: "As commonly happens on such occasions, the immediate actors in these scenes were persons of no note, the dregs of the population." Their "revolutionary acts, designed to intimidate," were "melancholy forerunners of civil war." Hildreth refers thus to the Boston massacre, "for so it was called, exaggerated into a ferocious and unprovoked assault by brutal soldiers on a defenseless people." The last words of the volume indicate that Hildreth had no love for the tales of war, then so frequently the staple of historical writing. He thought that the "strong passions which revolutions and war of necessity arouse, operated as a sudden severe check to the intellectual development of the people, or rather, turned that development almost exclusively into military and political channels. Of statesmen and soldiers, men great in action, we shall presently find enough. Thinkers are the product of quieter times."

The revolutionary years 1773-1789 are the subject of Volume III. The conservative temperament of Hildreth

was not betrayed into emotional excesses when he reached
the stirring events of these years. "There were in all
the colonies many wealthy and influential men, who had
joined indeed, in protesting against the usurpations of the
mother country, but who were greatly disinclined to anything like a decided rupture." The historian takes note,
however, of "the domineering spirit of the British ministry and nation," and pays quiet tribute to the New
England yeomanry, "full of the spirit and energy of
freemen," "who fought for their farms and firesides."
Hildreth considers at some length the projects for reconciliation with the mother country, before and during the
war. The narration of events during the period of hostilities takes up a great part of the volume. There is frequent reference to the financial difficulties of the colonists, and the internal dissensions of the American
armies. The last third of Volume III covers the problems
of constitution-making for the states and for a united
people, and boundary controversies between the states.
Hildreth handles impartially the question of the loyalists but his interpretation of Shays' Rebellion and similar outbursts is Federalist in tone. These were the events,
he says, that led to the formation of the Federal Constitution. The Constitutional Convention, as a whole, writes
Hildreth, "represented in a marked manner, the talent,
intelligence, and especially the conservative sentiment
of the country. . . . The public creditors, especially,
demanded some authority able to make the people
pay. . . ." Although some eminent men opposed the Constitution, more numerous among its opponents were "the
advocates of paper money, and of stop and tender laws"
who "took the same side, as did all those whose ruined
and desperate circumstances led them to prefer disturbance and revolution to the preservation of social
order." [44]

[44] P. 535.

Shortly after publishing his three volumes on American history to 1789, Hildreth brought out, in 1851, a second series of three more volumes which continued the narrative "to the end of the sixteenth Congress" (1821). "In dealing with our colonial and revolutionary annals," he says, "a great difficulty had to be encountered in the mythic and heroic character . . . with which in the popular idea, the fathers and founders of our American Republic have been invested." "To pass from these mythical and heroic times to those which form the subject of the present volumes is like suddenly dropping from the golden to the brazen and iron ages of the poets." In this period, however, the "damnatory element" usually plays the larger part in "rhetorical effusions." Hildreth notes that some conspicuous personages during the Revolution were described as possessed of "superhuman magnanimity and disinterestedness," who became later "mere ordinary mortals, objects of sharp, bitter, and often unmerited obloquy." Although the historian states that his narrative is not "tricked out in the gaudy tinsel of a meretricious rhetoric, nor stretched nor shortened to suit the purposes of any partial political theory," his friendliness for the Federalists is clearly evidenced.

This fourth volume of Hildreth's history covers Washington's administrations. Jefferson is painted shrewdly, but unsympathetically: "To sail before the wind as a popular favorite [was] the great object of his ambition." John Adams, on the other hand, wished "rather to guide public opinion than merely to sail before it." Hamilton, "the real leader of the Federal party," is described as "a very sagacious observer of mankind, and possessed of practical talents of the highest order." He was wise in recognizing that the greater danger to the Union lay in the "resistance of the states to federal power than executive usurpation," but Hildreth thought Hamilton mistaken in believing that a president and senate chosen for life or good behavior would strengthen the government. The Hamilton-Jefferson feud is given considerable space in these pages.

In a very interesting examination of party divisions, Hildreth writes that "the only real controversy was as to the amount of democracy, which safely could be and ought to be infused into the republican system adopted as well by the Union as by the separate states." The "natural aristocracy" of America comprised the judiciary, lawyers, great landowners in the Middle States, the "clergy and the leading members of the great religious sects," merchants and capitalists, "mostly men who had raised themselves by their own superior energy and sagacity to a position above the vulgar level." These generally supported Hamilton's measures. The "natural democracy" in America consisted largely of small landowners, "men who cultivated their own farms with their own hands." Political divisions in the United States, as elsewhere, remarks Hildreth, "have arisen not so much from any direct contest between the principles of aristocracy and democracy, as from the factions into which the natural aristocracy has split; the democracy chiefly making itself felt by the occasional unanimity with which it has thrown itself into the scale of one or other such contending factions." Usually, however, there is no such unanimity, but a majority of the "natural democracy" under the influence of the "natural aristocracy" has been won to the side of the latter. The international relations of America's early national years receive extended treatment.

The fifth volume of Hildreth's history opens with the inauguration of Adams and closes with the troubling international events of 1807. His sympathies are with the Federalists and England: "Insults and injuries which, coming from Great Britain, would have set the whole country on fire, were submitted to with all the patience

and even pleasure with which an overfond lover sometimes allows himself to be trampled upon and plundered
by an imperious and profligate mistress." [45] Again, referring to events a few years later, he writes: "The manly
resistance made by the Federalists to the insults and aggressions of France seemed to give them a hold upon the
public mind such as they had never possessed before." [46]

Nearly all that Hildreth has to say about Jefferson
is definitely colored by hostility. Jefferson was "willing
to risk . . . the destruction even of the Union itself" in
1798 because of his hatred of the administration, says Hildreth.[47] On the other hand, he ridicules the allegations of
danger arising from the meeting of the Hartford Convention in 1814. He attributes the downfall of the Federalists
to exhaustion, resulting from unusual efforts to awaken
and "prepare the country to resist the aggressions of
France"—surely an insufficient explanation. Great praise
is awarded to the Federalists: "The whole machinery of
the Federal government, as it now operates, must be considered as their work." When the Republicans or Democrats came into power, despite their earlier criticisms,
they immediately adopted most of this machinery, "testimony as irrefragable as it was reluctant, that however
the so-called Republican leaders might excel the Federalists in the arts of popularity, the best thing they could
do, in the constructive part of politics, was humbly to
copy the models they had once calumniated." In Washington, Hamilton, and Jay, America had "a trio not to
be matched, in fact, not to be approached, in our history,
if indeed, in any other." [48] The New England historian

[45] P. 104.

[46] P. 325.

[47] In another volume, *Despotism in America: An Inquiry into the
Nature, Results and Legal Basis of the slaveholding System in the United
States* (1854), Hildreth was very friendly to Jefferson as a democrat, but
hostile to him as a plantation owner.

[48] P. 527.

refers to the "four years of vexatious and ruinous commercial restrictions" in Jefferson's administrations, followed by "two years and a half of most disastrous and aimless war, ending in a near approach to national bankruptcy, and seriously threatening, had it not been unexpectedly brought to a close, the dismemberment of the Union."

Hildreth's last volume closes with the Missouri Compromise. The historian's dislike for the Jeffersonians never wanes: "In forcing upon the country the total abandonment of the export trade, if not by a political trick, at least by sudden surprise, without opportunity for deliberation . . . Jefferson and Madison, with all their professed abhorrence of executive dictation, had ventured on an exercise of executive influence and authority such as neither Washington nor Adams had ever dreamed of." The shrewdness of some of Hildreth's judgments, verified by later students, is demonstrated in his remarks on the War of 1812, which he thought "an offensive war, voluntarily undertaken on the part of the United States to compel Great Britain, by the invasion and conquest of her Canadian territories, to respect our maritime rights." Hildreth charges that threats against Madison's re-election drove him to take the lead, and thus permitted a declaration of war to be carried in Congress. A little less than half of the volume is concerned with the events connected with the war.

Hildreth's interpretation of the controversy over the admission of Missouri is decidedly Northern. The leaders of the Hartford Convention had a just provocation, "the provocation on the part of the South was their not being allowed to spread what they admitted to be a terrible evil over the whole territory west of the Mississippi." In Northern men this action was termed "moral treason," he says bitingly, but "in Southern representatives was but a manly refusal to submit to a domineering interfer-

ence with constitutional rights." It is from the Missouri
question, writes Hildreth in conclusion, in 1851, that "recent American politics take their departure." During the
last few years of his life Hildreth watched the American
political scene from Trieste, whither he had been sent as
consul by President Lincoln. He died in Italy in 1865.

Hildreth's forthright statements are refreshing, if
not always agreeable, to the historical sense. Self-
consciously he wrote of the offense he gave to New England, "region of set formality and hereditary grimace"
by his "undress portraits of our colonial progenitors";
he was a little proud of "bursting the thin, shining bubble
so assiduously blown up by so many windy mouths, of a
colonial golden age of fabulous purity and virtue." In
another volume, not part of his history, he refers to the
"moral oligarchy" in early New England, and he anticipates later students with the observation that "the history of the contest in New England between Democracy
on the one hand and the priestly and legal alliance on the
other, has never yet been written." He notes that because
of its apparent lack of dramatic episodes it had not
strongly attracted the attention of political writers, who
supposed that the progress of American democracy, had
been "quiet, silent and almost unresisted," whereas, according to Hildreth, it was a "most violent and bitter
struggle." [49] Hildreth's writing is more nearly in accord
with present-day interpretations than is that of Bancroft.
Theodore Parker, one of America's ablest critics, was on
the whole favorably impressed by Hildreth's work, but
believed that the historian was better on the colonial
period than on the Revolutionary years. He objected to
the insufficiency of philosophical history in the narrative.[50]

[49] *Despotism in America,* pp. 13-14.
[50] See essay on Hildreth in Theodore Parker, *The American Scholar*
(Boston, 1907).

Partly in answer to those who complained of a lack of "philosophy" in his history, Hildreth published a very interesting volume on the *Theory of Politics: an Inquiry into the Foundations of Governments, and the Causes and Progress of Political Revolutions* (1853). The economic interpretation of history, which he had already followed to some extent in his six volumes, is here more thoroughly elaborated. His familiarity with leading European revolutionary thinkers is clearly apparent, and his analysis of the causes of revolts and political alignments is sharp indeed.[51] Although he does not regard wealth as the sole element of political power, he does consider it to be the most important, able to buy up all the needed props for its own perpetuation. The few rich could easily combine "to act together with energy and effect," paralyzing the opposition by bribing the leaders of the mass of the people.[52] The only hope for the latter, he says, is for a split among the aristocracy, and then alliance with one of the factions.[53]

In referring to the French Revolution of 1848, Hildreth speaks of the Socialist demands for the full return to labor of the value of the product created. If labor were the sole source of wealth, he asks, "why should not the wealth thus produced go exclusively to those whose labor has called it into existence, instead of sticking to the fingers of capitalists and speculators?"[54] He goes on to point out that rather than fight the socialists, property holders preferred the establishment of the French Empire.

His concluding chapter, "Hopes and Hints as to the Future," is largely Marxian in its argument. "The clergy, the nobles, the kings, the burghers have all had their turn. Is there never to be an Age of the People—of the working classes?" asks Hildreth. "Is the sugges-

[51] See pp. 203-204, 206.   [53] P. 155.
[52] Pp. 151-152.   [54] P. 225.

tion too extravagant that the new period commencing with the middle of this current century is destined to be that age?'' Social changes already taking place, he says, showed signs of the approaching Age of the People. To be above the ''servile position'' in which they have long been held, the people must have ''a vastly greater portion than they have ever yet possessed of those primary elements of power, sagacity, force of will, and knowledge, to be backed by the secondary elements of wealth and combination.'' Hildreth emphasizes the distribution of the annual returns of labor as of much more importance than the distribution of the actually accumulated wealth. ''But no redistribution even of that—though it might sweep away the existing comfortable class,'' he continues, ''would suffice, very materially to elevate the condition of the great body of the people.'' What is really needed is a ''great increase in the amount both of accumulated wealth and of annual products.''

Hildreth was more of an Owenite than a Marxian socialist; he believed in a process of social change which was evolutionary and not revolutionary. He warns the rulers of society that ''this socialist question of the distribution of wealth once raised is not to be blinked out of sight'' nor ''settled by declamations and denunciations, and mutual recriminations any more than by bayonets and artillery.'' He thinks it is a question for ''philosophers,'' but meanwhile Hildreth urges the party of progress not to act, ''for which it is at present disqualified by internal dissensions,'' but to deliberate and discuss various measures. The student of radical thinking in America might well turn to this and other little-known writings of Hildreth; to most scholars his half-dozen volumes of history are apparently his chief claim to remembrance.

So critical a student as Channing, writing as late as 1917, said that the historical work of Hildreth ''remains to this day the most satisfactory account of the administrations of Washington and John Adams''; ''it gives the facts accurately and in usable form.'' But it is well to remember that in his last three volumes he saw most of America's history as it emanated from the nation's capital; he rarely left the Atlantic coast, and then not to go west but east to Paris and London. Many writers in after years owed a large debt to Hildreth for the organization of his material (poor as it was) and the philosophic grasp that he sometimes displayed.

Hildreth's work was well known to the college students in the last decades of the nineteenth century, but early in the twentieth century his volumes, along with those of Bancroft, were allowed to gather dust upon the shelves. New viewpoints on American history and changed ideas as to the proper content of historical narratives outmoded these distinguished historians.

VII

TUCKER, GAYARRÉ—IRVING, BENTON

GEORGE TUCKER

Historical writing in the South never showed the continuity of vigor apparent in New England. Southerners who might have been expected to write history sometimes excused their inactivity with the remark that they were so occupied with the tasks of governing that they had no time to pore over the records of the past—"that they who are acting history themselves, care not to read the histories of other men."[1] However, the number of publications in the South was not small. Histories of value had been written in the colonial period, but not until near the close of the first quarter of the nineteenth century was there something of a reawakening of interest in historical writing. This was part of a general movement observable throughout the country at the time, but it was also an expression of the South's desire for independent intellectual expression.[2] This desire grew stronger as the sectional division grew sharper in the

---

[1] E. M. Coulter, "What the South has done about its History," *The Journal of Southern History* (February, 1936), p. 5.

[2] See *Southern Literary Messenger* (August, 1834), Vol. I, No. 1.

next three decades and as the South sought economic and cultural independence.

All the Southern States had their historians, and they were particularly anxious to celebrate the achievements of their communities in the Revolutionary struggle. Burk's history of Virginia and Ramsay's history of South Carolina have been mentioned. Major General William Moultrie wrote his *Memoirs of the American Revolution . . . ,*[3] as it was fought in the Carolinas and Georgia. A fellow Revolutionist, the famous ''Light-Horse Harry'' Lee, also gave to posterity his interesting *Memoirs of the War in the Southern Department of the United States.*[4] These works contain more than the record of the authors' personal experiences, for they are fairly extensive historical narratives. Other historians were also busy: the versatile doctor, Hugh Williamson, published a *History of North Carolina*[5] which was not highly regarded, and Hugh McCall wrote *The History of Georgia.*[6] Maryland had a historian in 1837 in John L. Bozman, who recorded in two volumes the colony's first thirty years. Historians had already appeared in the newer States to the west—John Haywood in Tennessee, 1823, and Humphrey Marshall, in Kentucky, 1824. Alabama's history was written by Albert J. Pickett (1851).[7] Another history of South Carolina was written in 1840 by one of the South's most distinguished literary figures, William Gilmore Simms. Historical societies were founded in the South, some few individuals also preserved papers, and some of the periodicals, the *Southern Literary Messenger, DeBow's Review,* and the *Southern Quarterly Review,* published much historical material. But the South did not have the zest for history that was

---

[3] 2 vols., N. Y., 1802.   [5] 2 vols., 1812.
[4] Phila., 1812.   [6] 2 vols., 1811, 1816.
[7] See Ralph L. Rusk, *The Literature of the Middle Western Frontier* (2 vols., N. Y., 1925), I, 242-249, for historical writing in this period.

everywhere apparent in New England. No one had yet surveyed the South as a whole nor had anyone written the history of the nation.

It was a source of some dismay that no Southern Bancroft had appeared, but finally George Tucker attempted to satisfy the need with *The History of the United States from their Colonization to the end of the twenty-sixth Congress in 1841*,[8] a title similar to Hildreth's. Tucker, who had been born in Bermuda and educated at the College of William and Mary, was a person of talented versatility. He had been a member of Congress, a professor of ethics in the University of Virginia, a writer on economics, and a biographer of Jefferson before he turned to the history of the United States when he was seventy-five years old. Tucker had known many of the leaders in American life—Jay, Marshall, John Randolph, and others—and this gave him something of a personal contact with the course of American history. Before publishing his life of Jefferson, Tucker had many conversations with Madison. Although a Jeffersonian disciple, his biography was fairly impartial and is still held in high esteem. Tucker was living in Philadelphia when, in his old age, he began to write a history of the United States, and his contemporaries tell us that his mental vigor was matched by his physical vitality.

In "A Discourse" before the Virginia Historical and Philosophical Society, Tucker had said that the modern historian, unlike the earlier writer who treated only of politics and war, "aims to make us acquainted with the progress of society and the arts of civilization . . . — everything indeed, which is connected with the happiness or dignity of man." With others of his day Tucker believed that lessons of wisdom were to be drawn from history. He was active in promoting the care of documentary materials for history and urged that original papers

[8] 4 vols., 1856.

bearing on the settlement of the West be collected and preserved before it might be too late. He pointed out, as others were doing at this time, that materials on Virginia's colonial history were to be sought in English archives.[9] When he finally came to write his history of the United States, however, Tucker wrote pretty much in the manner of the historians whom he had once thought outdated. In the preface to his work he said he had been preparing his materials for more than six years, and, while he tried to be impartial in his viewpoint, he laid no claim to being free from party prejudices.

In his first volume Tucker rapidly disposes of the colonial period in some hundred pages (out of more than six hundred) in order to reach the Revolution. He takes the occasion to defend slavery [10] and furnishes a useful corrective to contemporary writing by pointing to the similarities, rather than the differences, among the colonies on the eve of the Revolution. Tucker writes in praise of parties to whose clashing tendencies, he says, the United States "owe the highest civil freedom which is compatible with the salutary restraints of law and order." In a fair analysis of Jefferson and Hamilton, this belated Southern Jeffersonian says that the influence of Hamilton's political principles had almost disappeared, whereas those of Jefferson had gained greatly in prestige. Tucker's narrative does not begin to be detailed until he reaches the establishment of the new government under the Constitution. For the colonial period his main authorities were Grahame, Hildreth, and Bancroft, and for the Revolution he relied on Gordon, Marshall's *Washington,* the *Annual Register,* and Jared Sparks.

The second volume begins with John Adams's administration and ends with Madison's first term, while the third volume continues the history through the ad-

9 *Southern Literary Messenger* (April, 1835), pp. 408-420.
10 P. 98.

ministration of John Quincy Adams. Tucker, it is interesting to note, is rather critical of the Hartford Convention,[11] but he writes a friendly estimate of the second Adams. In his later pages he makes use of more firsthand materials, such as the *Annals of Congress*. In fact, it is a kind of Congressional history of the United States and, as such, is a forerunner of the better-known work by James Schouler. It is also akin to the earlier *Annals* of Abiel Holmes.

In the fourth volume Tucker gives extended treatment to Jackson's administrations, on which he sometimes writes shrewdly and well. The most striking feature of his administrations, says the historian, was "that its presiding officer was unceasingly engaged in a series of angry controversies, which, whatever was their origin, always assumed more or less of a personal character." It could hardly be doubted, says Tucker, that Jackson's popularity "was rather increased than diminished by his belligerent propensities."[12]

In an interesting concluding chapter, "Present and Future Condition of the United States," Tucker defends the right of the South to deal with the slave question without interference from the North. "But suppose that the present unfortunate discrepancy on Negro slavery should continue unchanged [and] that the manufacturing States will forget that they now have the advantages of the free trade and restrictive systems united, which they must lose in case of a separation—which consideration also applies to the agricultural States . . ." —will the States, queries Tucker, who have so much to gain from Union, separate?[13] He utters a pathetically vain hope that the Union may continue, but at the same time he speaks of the South's intention to guard its institutions.

Tucker's history, written from the Southern point of

[11] III, 131.   [13] IV, 432.
[12] IV, 139.

view, naturally emphasizes problems that had a sectional bearing, but it is probably as dependable as contemporary works written by Northerners. It is one of history's minor ironies that Tucker's volumes were largely ignored by the audience he addressed, who continued to read their own history as written by Northerners.

CHARLES E. A. GAYARRÉ

The finest historian the South produced before the Civil War was probably Gayarré. At the time Charles Etienne Arthur Gayarré was growing to manhood, historical interests were gaining in importance in various parts of the country. In his own community, Louisiana, he had before him the example of Judge François Xavier Martin, who had compiled a *History of Louisiana*. Gayarré, of Spanish and French descent, was born in 1805 in New Orleans, where his family had played an important part in the affairs of the old colony. As a young man, he was sent to Philadelphia to study law and was admitted to the bar. He was active in public life in the judiciary and in the United States Senate, but ill-health caused his retirement.

Gayarré translated and adapted Martin's history, bringing it out in 1830 with the title *Essai Historique sur la Louisiane*. This historical romance, for it was not conventional history, covered the period to 1815 and displayed a literary skill that was to be an outstanding characteristic of all Gayarré's important work. While regaining his health in France he prepared his *Histoire de la Louisiane*, which was published in 1846-1847 in two volumes. It was written in French to preserve the flavor of the original documents from which extracts were taken; these he joined together with a slender thread of narrative covering events to 1769. Partly under the inspiration of Walter Scott, who was a great favorite in the South, Gayarré turned to the popularization of history. His next publication, wider in its popular appeal, written in English, was *The Poetry, or the Romance of the History of Louisiana* (1848) in which fiction and history are closely interwoven. To the detriment of his fame, at least among serious historians, Gayarré used this as the first volume of his larger history. The second and third more firmly fixed his place as an accurate historian and gifted writer. These volumes, written in the form of lectures, delivered as a series, "Louisiana: its Colonial History and Romance," were later brought together under the title *History of Louisiana: The French Domination*.[14]

In the preface to his third series of lectures, Gayarré made light of his earlier publication on the "Romance of the History of Louisiana," and said that he had checked his imagination, "that boon companion with whom I had been gamboling," and "took to the plough," turning himself "to a more serious and useful occupation." Gayarré had also been preparing materials on the later periods of Louisiana's history and in 1854 brought out the *History of Louisiana: The Spanish Domination.* The next volume, the *History of Louisiana: The American Domination,* was ready a few years later, but, because of the Civil War, publication was delayed until 1866. Other productions came from his pen, including a suggestive study of Philip II of Spain (1866), and, in later life, an autobiographical novel.

Gayarré used the manuscripts in the archives of the French Ministry of Marine and the Colonies, hitherto scarcely used by American historians. As Secretary of State for Louisiana, 1846-1853, he built up the State Library with purchases of historical materials, some from the Spanish archives being incorporated in his history. Written to a large extent from original documents,

[14] 2 vols., 1854.

Gayarré's volumes were far in advance of most of the work then being done in the United States. The volume on the Spanish domination is perhaps his best: the period was congenial to him; he said that people enjoyed living in Louisiana during the Spanish domination; and the exciting years from 1769 to 1805 contained material well suited to his literary powers. The *American Domination* describes the introduction of American institutions to a Europeanized Louisiana. This volume, on which Gayarré expended much care, covers the period 1803-1816, and a supplementary chapter briefly sketches the years to 1861. Gayarré tied his personal fortunes to those of his beloved Louisiana during the Civil War, and it was with a great sense of tragedy that he issued this volume on the American domination: "My task as historian is done," he wrote, "but my love, as thy son, shall cling to thee in poverty and sorrow, and nestle in thy scarred bosom with more rapturous constancy then when thy face was beaming with joy and hope. . . ."

George Bancroft, in a note to Gayarré, said he had given his State "an authentic history such as scarce any other in the Union possesses. I have for years been making ms. and other collections," said Bancroft, "and the best that I have found appears in your volumes." [15] In the long-drawn-out years from the Civil War to his death in 1895, Gayarré eked out a difficult living—sad epilogue to a valuable, productive life. The work of his earlier days places him with American writers of the first rank; not until the present generation has the South been favored with historians of similar distinction. [16]

[15] La. Hist. Soc. *Publications,* "Gayarré Memorial Number," Vol. II, Part IV (March, 1906).

[16] See *Louisiana Historical Quarterly* (January, 1929), containing Gayarré autobiography and bibliography.

BIOGRAPHY

In the second quarter of the nineteenth century American interest in biography as well as history was very great, and, in addition to the many individual volumes issuing from the press, practically all periodicals included extensive sections of biographical material. Such was the eagerness with which readers awaited this literature that the New York *Mirror* referred to a contemporary phrase coined to describe it—"biography mania."[17] Unquestionably the memoirs of old Revolutionaries stimulated this interest, but biographical writing had, of course, a long tradition in colonial America, reaching at least as far back as Cotton Mather. Members of the Massachusetts historical circle at the end of the eighteenth century planned biographical dictionaries; the advice of Belknap, who later brought one out, was solicited by John Eliot, who projected such a dictionary in eight parts, dealing with statesmen, scholars, military men, physicians, and other prominent men.[18] In 1810 *The Monthly Anthology* of Boston[19] ran a discussion of biographical dictionaries, which included John Eliot's and William Allen's, both issued the year before. Some years later, in the first number of Philadelphia's *American Quarterly Review*[20] an article on American biography listed four more biographical dictionaries in addition to Eliot's and Allen's.[21] John Sanderson's *Biography of the Signers to the Declaration of Independence*[22] was an especially noteworthy publication, but John Quincy Adams had little use for it because of its excessively eulogistic tone.[23]

A writer in the *American Quarterly Review* criti-

---

[17] 1830, quoted in F. L. Mott, *History of American Magazines,* p. 421.
[18] Mass. Hist. Soc. *Colls.,* 6th ser., IV, 210-215; July 3, 1781.
[19] Vol. VIII.
[20] March, 1827.
[21] See also June, 1827.
[22] 9 vols., 1820-1827.
[23] Adams, *Sparks,* II, 193.

cized the modern biographer who included everything in his work: "He prefixes an historical introduction, and happy it is, if his retrospect do not extend to the Deluge, or sweep over the civilized world." The biographer, it was complained, "rarely leads you into the private lodgings of the hero—never places before you the poor reasonable animal, as naked as nature made him; but represents him uniformly as a demigod." English biographies, as well as Marshall's *Washington,* Tudor's *Otis,* and Wirt's *Patrick Henry,* were criticized for their misplaced, voluminous materials which only served to "overlay or obscure the individuals designated in the title pages." Jared Sparks was also critical of these fulsome biographies. "Should the future historian rely on these alone for his authority," he wrote, "our descendants of the tenth generation will have the pride of looking back upon the most immaculate chapter of statesmen and heroes that have adorned the annals of any nation." [24] Sparks took advantage of the public interest in biography to issue *The Library of American Biography,* and in announcing it he expressed the commonly accepted belief that "biography is only another form of history." "It admits of no embellishments that would give it the air of fiction," he said, with an implied rebuke to Parson Weems and others, "and yet its office is but half done, unless it mingles entertainment with instruction"—and thus he was less removed from Weems than he supposed. [25] Washington Irving likewise thought that "one of the most salutary purposes of history" was "that of furnishing examples of what human genius and laudable enterprise may accomplish." [26]

[24] *N. A. Rev.* (January, 1830), p. 4.
[25] Vol. I, 1834.
[26] *Christopher Columbus,* 1850 edn., I, 56.

Washington Irving

The career of the First President invited many biographers in the early part of the nineteenth century, including the most famous literary personage of his day— Washington Irving. Irving's amusing caricature of the Dutch in *A History of New York* (1809), besides revealing his historical interests, was an impetus to research among his contemporaries. Irving was casting about for a theme fit for his pen which might also prove financially profitable, and he turned to a life of Washington. Before he had started on this project, however, he was drawn off in 1826 on an exciting biographical quest of another figure who was of perennial interest to Americans—Christopher Columbus.

Alexander H. Everett, minister to Spain and also a student of history, suggested to Irving that an English version of Navarrete's collection of materials on Columbus "by one of our own country would be peculiarly desirable." Fernández de Navarrete, perhaps the most learned student of the era of exploration, was then publishing a series of volumes on the Spanish voyages and discoveries. Irving seized the opportunity and prepared himself for his task by making his home with the great bibliographer, Obadiah Rich, then acting as American consul. In Madrid he made a closer study of the Spanish language and feasted on the treasures of the greatest Hispano-American library in existence. Irving soon saw that the English reading public would not be so much interested in a translation of Navarrete's documents as it would in a popular biography of Columbus. He worked with unflagging industry on the biography and seemed to enjoy it. "And so ends the year 1826," he wrote in his diary, "which has been a year of the hardest application and toil of the pen I have ever passed. I feel more satisfied, however, with the manner in which I have passed it than I have been with that of many gayer years, and close this year of my life in better humor with myself than I have often done.'' [27]

The acquisition of additional information forced him to rewrite many parts of his *Columbus*. ''It is a kind of work that will not bear hurrying,'' he said.[28] He wrote that he had collated all the works he could find on his subject, printed and in manuscript, and had compared them ''with original documents, those sure lights of historical research.'' [29] His pretensions to scholarship were greater than his achievement, for in the main his work was based on Navarrete. After two years he completed it and in 1828 *The History of the Life and Voyages of Christopher Columbus* was published. In addition to the biography of the great discoverer, Irving later brought out another work on the companions of Columbus.

The vigor and charm of the biography substantiate Irving's statement that he enjoyed writing it. His admiration for Columbus is obvious; the description of the voyage of discovery is well done; and the narrative of the homeward voyage and the reception at Palos is particularly moving. Irving's success was immediate and he appeared especially pleased at the reception accorded the biography in America.[30]

He now returned to the biography of Washington after abandoning a plan for a history of the United States. He thought a life of Washington, ''if tolerably executed, must be a valuable and lasting property. I shall take my own time to execute it,'' he said, ''and will spare no

[27] Pierre M. Irving, *The Life and Letters of Washington Irving*, II, 254.

[28] *Ibid.*, II, 257; February 22, 1827.

[29] *Christopher Columbus*, p. xv.

[30] *Letters of Washington Irving to Henry Brevoort*, p. 419; December 20, 1828.

pains. It must be my great and crowning labor.'' [31] For
many years thereafter the *Washington* kept Irving busy
intermittently, but he did not work on it as conscientiously
as he had on the *Columbus*. At length, in 1855, the first
volume appeared, with excuses by the author for its delayed publication. It deals with Washington's life before
the Revolution, and, like the succeeding volumes, is in
reality a history of the times in which the subject of the
biography lived. Although the work failed to come up to
Irving's expectations—it is not his ''crowning labor''—it
does on occasion reveal a keen insight into Washington.
In one instance, for example, Irving remarks that it is
worthy of note ''that the early popularity of Washington
was not the result of brilliant achievements, nor signal
success; on the contrary it rose among trials and re-
verses, and may almost be said to have been the fruit of
defeats.'' [32]

After the favorable reception that greeted this first
volume, Irving was impatient to get on with the second.
''I live only in the Revolution,'' he said to his nephew.
''My desire is to give everything vividly, but to avoid all
melodramatic effect.[33] The second, third, and fourth volumes carry the story down to 1783; the last few pages
in Volume IV rush through the years 1783-1789.[34] The
fifth volume (1859) is on Washington's presidential administrations and his last years. Despite the length of his
work, Irving added very little to the earlier biographies
by Marshall and Sparks. In fact, he did not pretend to
tap unused sources. Sparks found the volumes entertaining and instructive but did not think they should be

[31] *Life and Letters of Washington Irving,* II, 424-425; December 18,
1829.
[32] *Ibid.,* I, 212.
[33] *Ibid.,* IV, 196.
[34] A note to the third volume says that the original plan to complete
the biography in three volumes had been abandoned in favor of a larger
work.

passed off as a life of Washington. "Indeed," he said, the work "can scarcely be called history; it is rather a delineation of striking events, adorned with amusing incidents and anecdotes." [35] Although Irving's *Washington* as a whole was not greeted with unusual enthusiasm, his *Columbus* long remained a favorite with the general public and scholars. Even when, in after years, much new material had been unearthed, Henry Harrisse and Edward G. Bourne, two of the leading students of the literature of discovery, had kind words for Irving's *Columbus*.[36]

THOMAS HART BENTON

In the period before the Civil War few of the men making history also wrote it. On occasion they recorded, in letters or diaries, the passing scene, but they rarely produced a consecutive narrative. One of the most important publications of a combined autobiographical and historical character which appeared in this period is Thomas Hart Benton's *Thirty Years' View; or, A History of the Working of the American Government for Thirty Years, from 1820 to 1850.*[37] Benton, who had been in the Senate, worked on these volumes in his retirement, and historians have recognized them as of the first importance. He also completed another important work, the *Abridgement of the Debates of Congress from 1789 to 1856* (1857-1861).

Benton was in the Senate during the period he surveyed in the *Thirty Years' View,* and in addition to his own speeches and recollections he used as source materials the debates of Congress, Jackson's papers, and other documents. As an active member of the Senate, he tells us, he "had an inside view of transactions of which

[35] Adams, *Sparks,* II, 508-509.
[36] S. T. Williams, *The Life of Washington Irving* (2 vols., N. Y., 1935), I, Chap. XIII; II, 227-231, 296-308.
[37] 2 vols., 1854, 1856.

the public only saw the outside.'' He saw how measures
were promoted or thwarted and knew the secrets of political ''wirepulling.'' His is not a ''regular history,'' Benton informs the reader, ''but a political work, to show the
practical working of the government.''

The modern historian who wishes to penetrate beneath the surface of events and get clues worth pursuing
can find no better guide than Benton. Charles A. and
Mary R. Beard, in their *The Rise of American Civilization,* for example, were well aware of his value. In analyzing legislation relating to the disposition of public lands,
a problem in which he was vitally interested, Benton said
that many members of Congress then (1820) debating
relief from debts contracted in the purchase of lands,
were themselves ''among the public land debtors, and
entitled to the relief to be granted.'' [38] In discussing the
tariff bill of 1828, Benton quotes the remarkable speech
of Representative McDuffie in opposition: ''Do we not
perceive at this very moment,'' said McDuffie, ''the extraordinary and melancholy spectacle of less than one
hundred thousand capitalists . . . exercising an absolute
and despotic control over the opinions of eight millions
of free citizens, and the fortunes and destinies of ten millions?'' [39] Benton goes on to refer to the many allusions
''coupling manufacturing capitalists and politicians in
pressing this bill.'' He points out that the South, which
had once been very prosperous, later grew slowly, whereas
the North grew rapidly until it became ''a money lender
to the South.''

Most of the first volume of the *Thirty Years' View* is
on the presidency of Jackson. Benton had promised Jackson, his hero, that he would write a review of his administrations.[40] Here, as one would expect, are long sections
on the Bank of the United States and a history of Ben-

[38] I, 12.   [40] I, 734.
[39] I, 101.

ton's opposition to it. He points to the interesting fact that in the sphere of foreign diplomacy, where Jackson's impetuosity was most to be feared, the President was successful.[41] In his sketches of fellow members of Congress he sometimes presents excellent characterizations; that of John Randolph of Roanoake, for example, is notable. Throughout his work Benton digresses to point out alleged flaws in de Tocqueville's estimate of American democracy.

The second volume begins with Van Buren's inauguration. In the course of the author's observations on politics he again returns to a discussion of the comparative prosperity of North and South, and notes the latter's discontent. The figures on the commerce of the two sections from 1760 to 1832 show the great inferiority of a South dissatisfied with the Union, whose laws benefited the North at her expense. It is this belief of "an incompatibility of interest," says Benton, "which constitutes the danger to the Union, and which statesmen should confront and grapple with"; and there is no "danger to slave property, which has continued to aggrandize in value. . . ."[42] Dissatisfaction with the distribution of wealth as effected by the laws "was the point on which Southern discontent broke out—on which it openly rested until 1835, when it was shifted to the danger to slave property.[43] Benton's appeal to the North to preserve the Union was largely based on the pecuniary advantage to be derived from it.

There is a cry of exultation in the chapter headed "Last Notice of the Bank of the United States." [44] For ten long years, writes Benton, "the name of this bank had resounded in the two Halls of Congress . . . ," and for the first time (1841) a session passed in which its name was not once mentioned. "Alas," says this bitter

[41] I, 601-608.   [43] II, 133.
[42] II, 132.   [44] II, 365.

foe, "the great bank had run its career of audacity, crime, oppression and corruption." [45] On another subject, the Oregon Territory, Benton quotes the prophetic remarks of Calhoun, who spoke, in 1843, of the advantages of the region in trading with China and Japan. Markets will be opened for European and American trade, and, concluded Calhoun, "what has taken place in China, will, in a few years, be followed in Japan and all the eastern portions of that continent." [46]

The *Thirty Years' View* is to a large degree autobiographical. It is not a wholly accurate presentation of the anti-Jackson standpoint, but it is what Benton intended it to be, a guide to the practical working of the government. The student today might well make better use of that guide than did many of the historians of yesterday.

[45] *Ibid.*
[46] II, 471.

VIII

FRANCIS PARKMAN

While Bancroft and Gayarré were enriching American literature with their volumes, a younger contemporary was preparing himself for the task of narrating the Anglo-French conflict for control of North America. In spirit Francis Parkman belongs to the romantic school of historians with their dramatic presentation of adventurous deeds, and yet his volumes have been so acceptable to the generations who have followed that his place is more that of a transition figure. His scrupulous care in the use of sources has not been surpassed by later writers, and his literary gifts have been the envy of a host of historians.

Parkman was born in Boston in 1823, the son of a prominent Unitarian clergyman. He was graduated from Harvard in 1844, but his education seems to have been largely the result of his own direction. He loved fine writing and read widely in the established English classics; his favorite books, however, were those on American Indians. Thus early did he indulge his love of the forest, which he knew intimately at firsthand, and which was to be a main theme in his life work. In an autobio-

graphical note, written late in life, he said: "Before the
end of the sophomore year my various schemes had
crystallized into a plan of writing a story of what was
then known as the 'Old French War'—that is, the war
that ended in the conquest of Canada—for here, as it
seemed to me, the forest drama was more stirring and
the forest stage more thronged with appropriate actors
than in any other passage of our history. It was not till
some years later that I enlarged the plan to include the
whole course of the American conflict between France
and England, or, in other words, the history of the American forest; for this was the light in which I regarded it.
My theme fascinated me, and I was haunted with wilderness images day and night." Two ideas possessed him:
"One was to paint the forest and its tenants in true and
vivid colors; the other was to realize a certain ideal of
manhood, a little medieval, but nevertheless good." Parkman once explained to a fellow historian, M. Pierre
Margry, who had asked him how he had come to write
the history of the French in America, that it had come
from two tastes—books and the forest. These, he had
found, "could be reconciled, could be made even mutually helpful, in the field of Franco-American history."

In his vacations from classroom studies Parkman
took long walks through his beloved woods, tracing the
battle lines that still scarred the now peaceful forest.
Here was the stage on which had been enacted the drama
of Indian warfare, which he was to re-create with such
superb artistry. The notes that he made in his student
diaries were the historical materials of his riper years.
On July 17, 1842, he wrote: "I went this morning to see
William Henry. The old fort is much larger than I had
thought; the earthen mounds cover many acres." "In
the rear, a hundred or two yards distant, is a gloomy
wood of pines, where the lines of Montcalm can easily
be traced." The summer of his junior year he spent in

collecting historical information, mainly from local in-habitants, on a tour that took him through Lake George, Montreal, Quebec, and the White Mountains.

In the fall of 1843 his health, which had not been too robust and had been injured "by numerous drenchings in the forest of Maine," was such that it was considered more advisable to send him to Europe than back to Har-vard. Although of New England Puritan ancestry, and often critical of Catholicism, he gained a deep respect for the latter faith by his personal contacts in Italy. This knowledge served him usefully when he came to write of the Catholic Church. In Sicily he was greatly im-pressed by "the Church of the Benedictines." "This and others not unlike it have impressed me with new ideas of the Catholic religion. Not exactly, for I reverenced it before as the religion of generations of brave and great men, but now I honor it for itself. They are mistaken who sneer at its ceremonies as a mere mechanical force; they have a powerful and salutary effect on the mind."

Parkman returned to take his bachelor's degree with his class, and then went on to study law at the request of his father. But nonlegal literature was more attractive, particularly American history, travels, Colden's work on the five Indian nations, and the like. He stole time from law studies to write Indian tales that were printed by the *Knickerbocker* magazine in New York. "In the way of preparation and preliminary to my principal under-taking," Parkman tells us, "I now resolved to write the history of the Indian war under Pontiac, as offering peculiar opportunities for exhibiting forest life and In-dian character. . . ." In the summer of 1845 on a trip to the West he gathered much material that went into *The Conspiracy of Pontiac*. He wormed information out of old settlers, talked with Indians, and studied the to-pography of the region near Detroit. His correspondence on historical subjects was already very extensive, and he had decided to devote himself almost entirely to history. His desire to see the Indian in his native state unchanged by contact with white civilization, "as a necessary part of training for my work," he said, brought him farther west in 1846. Although the trip was in preparation for historical writing, it incidentally resulted in a notable book of travel and adventure—*The Oregon Trail*.

Parkman's health was worse after his Western trip and from that time on it was always in an uncertain state. Few people, however, were aware of his suffering. Only after his death was it generally known that he began the volume on Pontiac's conspiracy at a time when his health was particularly poor and when his eyesight was so affected that he used a frame constructed like a gridiron to guide his black crayon. "For the first half year the rate of composition averaged about six lines a day. The portion of the book thus composed was afterwards partially rewritten." He also dictated much of his work, and as time passed his health improved so that he worked faster, "and the history was complete in about two years and a half." With the aid of his amanuensis, Mrs. Parkman, the historian wrote to his friend Charles Eliot Norton in June, 1850: "Pontiac is about three quarters through, and I hope will see the light within a year. I calculated at starting it would take four years to finish it, which, at the pace I was then writing, was about a straight calculation, for I was then handsomely used up, soul and body on the rack, and with no external means or appliances to help me on."

The Conspiracy of Pontiac appeared in 1851, although it had been finished almost a year before. The manuscript had been read in part by Jared Sparks, whose comments furnish something of a measure of the difference between the ideals of the older and the newer historians. The *Pontiac*, wrote Sparks, "affords a striking picture of the influence of war and religious bigotry upon savage and semibarbarous minds.'' But Parkman's failure to draw moral lessons prompted this statement from Sparks: ''Although you relate events in the true spirit of calmness and justice, yet I am not sure but a word or two of indignation now and then, at such unnatural and inhuman developments of the inner man [as the massacre of the Indians by the Paxton Boys] would be expected of a historian, who enters deeply into the merits of his subjects.''

Theodore Parker wrote a criticism of the *Pontiac* at the request of his friend Parkman. Parker's observations were keen and are worth noting because of many misconceptions which persist about Parkman's understanding of the Indian. ''You evidently have a fondness for the Indian,'' said Parker, ''—not a romantic fondness, but one that has been tempered by sight of the fact. Yet I do not think you do the Indian quite justice; you side rather too strongly with the white man and against the red. I think you bring out the vices of the Indians with more prominence than those of the European— which were yet less excusable.'' ''It seems to me that the whites are not censured so much as they deserve for their conduct toward the Indians in these particulars''—rum, women, treachery, and cruelty.

In the preface to *The Conspiracy of Pontiac* Parkman writes, ''The conquest of Canada was an event of momentous consequence in American history. It changed the political aspect of the continent, prepared a way for the independence of the British colonies, rescued the vast tracts of the interior from the rule of military despotism, and gave them, eventually, to the keeping of an ordered democracy. Yet to the red natives of the soil its results were wholly disastrous.'' To rescue from oblivion their struggle against the menace of the advancing colonists was the object of his work. ''It aims to portray the American forest and the American Indian at the period when both received their final doom.''

The difficulties that Parkman faced in writing this, as well as the other volumes of his series, are made clear in language fitting his subject. ''The field of history was uncultured and unreclaimed, and the labor that awaited me was like that of the border settler, who, before he builds his rugged dwelling, must fell the forest-trees, burn the undergrowth, clear the ground, and hew the fallen trunks to due proportion.''

The character of the Indian, as Parker had noted, receives less than a just appraisal at the hands of the historian—''Ambition, revenge, envy, jealousy, are his ruling passions.'' It is a proud white man who writes these words on the Indian: ''He will not learn the arts of civilization, and he and his forest must perish together.'' After an examination of Indian civilization, Parkman studies the English and French rivals, and then moves on to the climax of his story, the onslaught of Pontiac. ''Canada, the offspring of Church and State . . . languished, in spite of all [support] from the lack of vital sap and energy. The colonies of England, outcast and neglected, but strong in native vigor and self-confiding courage, grew yet more strong with conflict and with striving, and developed the rugged proportions and unwieldy strength of a youthful giant.'' ''In every quality of efficiency and strength, the Canadian fell miserably below his rival; but in all that pleases the eye and interests the imagination, he far surpassed him.'' Lesser characters and minor themes are introduced in support of the main plotter, Pontiac, who holds the center of the stage.

Pontiac, the leading chief of the Ottawas, determined to make war upon the victorious English who were now spilling over into the diminishing lands of the Indians. ''Already their best hunting grounds were invaded, and from the eastern ridges of the Alleghanies they might see, from far and near, the smoke of the settlers' clearings, rising in tall columns from the dark-green bosom of the forest." Pontiac, "though capable of acts of magnanimity . . . was a thorough savage, with a wider range of intellect than those around him, but sharing all their passions and prejudices, their fierceness and treachery. His faults were the faults of his race; and they cannot eclipse his nobler qualities." The modern reader, further removed from the Indian than Parkman was, will oppose the injustice of the remarks that Pontiac was "the Satan of this forest Paradise." The implication of innocent white Eves and Adams is scarcely warranted.

The cries of warriors, the attacks on frontier posts, and the sickening details of border warfare fill most of the pages of Pontiac, particularly the chieftain's long but futile siege of Detroit. Failure to capture the fort meant disaster to the plans of Pontiac. Gradually his allies fell away and the great leader was forced to make his peace with the English.

Although Parkman planned immediately to get to work on the beginnings of his story of the Anglo-French struggle, ill-health again intervened to force him to turn to less exacting pursuits. It was in this period that he wrote a novel, *Vassall Morton,* which was largely autobiographical, and a book on roses. Like Bancroft, Parkman had a deep devotion to flowers, and the specimens he raised in his garden brought him wide renown.

The *Pioneers of France in the New World* was published in 1865, but by this time Parkman had also written large parts of some of the later volumes. In the introduction to this volume the author wrote that the earlier narratives of his proposed series would be devoted to " 'France in the New World'—the attempt of Feudalism, monarchy and Rome to master a continent. . . . These banded powers, pushing into the wilderness their indom-

itable soldiers and devoted priests, unveiled the secrets
of the barbarous continent, pierced the forests, traced
and mapped out the streams, planted their emblems, built
their forts, and claimed all as their own. New France
was all head. Under King, Noble, and Jesuit, the lank,
lean body would not thrive. Even Commerce wore the
sword, decked itself with badges of nobility, aspired to
forest seignories and hordes of savage retainers.''

Against this combination ''an adverse power was
strengthening and widening with slow, but steadfast
growth, full of blood and muscle,—a body without a
head.'' It was a case of ''Liberty and Absolutism, New
England and New France.'' When writing of the failure
to plant a Huguenot colony in Florida, Parkman adds:
''To plant religious freedom on this Western soil was
not the mission of France. It was for her to rear in
Northern forests the banner of Absolutism and of Rome;
while among the rocks of Massachusetts, England and
Calvin fronted her in dogged opposition.'' Parkman,
however, could see the faults in his ancestral home. ''Politically, she was free; socially, she suffered from that
subtile and searching oppression which the dominant
opinion of a free community may exercise over the members who compose it''; ''in defiance of the four Gospels,
assiduity in pursuit of gain was promoted to the rank
of a duty, and thrift and godliness were linked in equiv-
ocal wedlock.'' ''The French dominion,'' he writes mistakenly, ''is a memory of the past.'' Parkman neglected
to note the tenacity of French culture in perpetuating
itself in Canada.

His statement of his main sources in the *Pioneers*
applies to all his volumes; among them were the archives
of France and other countries, the recently printed colonial records and other publications often exceedingly
rare. The footnotes are not a fair index to his preparation, for much of his reading was of an illustrative char-

444

acter—to "clothe the skeleton with flesh," as Parkman himself expressed it. "If at times it may seem that range has been allowed to fancy, it is so in appearance only; since the minutest details of narrative or description rest on authentic documents or on personal observation." Despite his great physical handicaps, the historian meant "if possible to carry the present design to its completion." Each volume, he said, "will form a separate and independent work." Parkman's friend and biographer, C. H. Farnham, suggests that "possibly it was the uncertainty of his life and working power that led him to cast his subject in monographs, enabling him to finish the work in pieces as he went along." It was Parkman's ultimate intention to remold his monographs into a continuous narrative.

The *Pioneers of France in the New World* is divided into two parts—the Huguenots in Florida, and Champlain and his companions. The bitter struggles between the Spaniards and the French for Florida are detailed in all their horror of massacre and countermassacre. "This pious butcher [Menendez] wept with emotion as he recounted the favors which Heaven had showered upon [his] enterprise." "It was he who crushed French Protestantism in America." The vengeance that Dominique de Gourgues visited upon the Spaniards is described in milder words; in fact his exploit is termed "romantic," but his courage was sullied by "implacable cruelty."

In the foreword to the second part of the volume ("Champlain and His Associates") Parkman writes, in the third person: "For the basis of descriptive passages he is indebted to early tastes and habits which long since made him familiar with most of the localities of the narrative." And he also felt a kinship with all the chivalrous characters whose burning enthusiasm glowed in his pages. Parkman speaks feelingly of Champlain, who "belonged rather to the Middle Age than to the seventeenth century.'' ''The *preux chevalier,* the crusader, the romance-loving explorer, the curious knowledge-seeking traveller, the practical navigator, all claimed their share in him.'' ''With the life of the faithful soldier closes the opening period of New France. Heroes of another stamp succeed; and it remains to tell hereafter the story of their devoted lives, their faults, their follies, and their virtues.''

The high praise with which the *Pioneers* was received was repeated with even more emphasis when the subsequent volumes appeared. Shorter intervals separated their publication—*The Jesuits in North America in the Seventeenth Century,* 1867; *La Salle and the Discovery of the Great West,* 1869; *The Old Regime in Canada,* 1874; *Count Frontenac and New France under Louis XIV,* 1877; *Montcalm and Wolfe,* 1884. The last work indicates that Parkman had leaped over a half century to write the final act of his great drama, which he considered more important than the events of the intervening years.

In the preface to his volume on the Jesuits, the historian sought to ''reproduce an image of the past with photographic clearness and truth.'' The introductory chapter is on the civilization of the Indians among whom the Jesuits labored. Much of Parkman's information came from the Jesuits' written records of their experiences. A large part of the book is made up of sketches of individual Jesuits, and the trials and tortures they endured for their faith. In particular he singles out Isaac Jogues, ''one of the purest examples of Roman Catholic virtue which this Western continent has seen.'' In the chapter ''Priest and Puritan,'' Parkman returns to his frequent comparison of the two competing civilizations, with the usual advantage on the side of New England. In conclusion, he writes: ''The cause of the failure of the Jesuits is obvious. The guns and tomahawks of the Iro-

quois . . . were the ruin of their hopes.'' The defeat of
the Jesuits meant that the West would not be settled
under the auspices of the French, and hence ''Liberty,''
typified by New England, would eventually triumph.

La Salle and the Discovery of the Great West was
completely revised and partly rewritten when much new
material on the explorer was published under the editorship of M. Pierre Margry, Director of the Archives of
the Marine and Colonies at Paris. The character of La
Salle had a powerful attraction for Parkman, who admired ''the strong personality'' of the Frenchman that
''would not yield to the shaping hand [of the Jesuits]
and who by a necessity of his nature, could obey no in-
itiative but his own,'' a man with an ''intense longing
for action and achievement.''

In contrast to the ascetic Marquette, La Salle ''with
feet firm planted on the hard earth, breathes the self-
relying energies of modern practical enterprise''—''he
would leave barren and frozen Canada behind, and lead
France and civilization into the valley of the Mississippi.'' ''Neither the English nor the Jesuits should conquer that rich domain; the one must rest content with
the country east of the Alleghanies and the other with
the forests, savages, and beaver-skins of the northern.
It was for him to call into light the latent riches of the
great West.'' La Salle's aims of settlement were in conflict with the plans of the Jesuits, and from first to last
they set themselves against him because they regarded
him as their most dangerous rival for the control of the
West.

The story of the services of La Salle's friends and
the machinations of his enemies is an exciting one as
Parkman tells it, and it provides the background for the
climactic ''Success of La Salle,'' Chapter XX. ''Again
they embarked; and with every stage of their adventurous progress the mystery of this vast New World was

more and more unveiled. More and more they entered the
realms of spring. The hazy sunlight, the warm and
drowsy air, the tender foliage, the opening flowers, be-
tokened the reviving life of Nature.'' The journey was
at an end in the beginning of April's second week, 1682.
As La Salle ''drifted down the turbid current, between
the low and marshy shores, the brackish water changed
to brine, and the breeze grew fresh with the salt breath
of the sea. Then the broad bosom of the great Gulf
opened on his sight, tossing its restless billows, limitless,
voiceless, lonely as when born of chaos, without a soul,
without a sign of life.'' Parkman takes leave of the leader
slain by conspiring subordinates, with the epitaph: ''He
belonged not to the age of the knight-errant and the
saint, but to the modern world of practical study and
practical action. He was the hero not of a principle, nor
of a faith, but simply of a fixed idea and a determined
purpose.'' ''His whole life was a fight with adversity.''
''America owes him an enduring memory; for in this
masculine figure she sees the pioneer who guided her to
the possession of her richest heritage.''

Parkman's purpose in *The Old Regime in Canada*
was to show how the French monarchy attempted to
fasten its hold on its American colony, its partial success, and its eventual failure. ''In the present book we
examine the political and social machine; in the next
volume of the series we shall see this machine in action.''
Three sections make up the volume: La Tour and
D'Aunay, the feudal chiefs of Acadia; ''Canada a Mission''; ''The Colony and the King.'' Ordinarily Parkman
is less interested in the slow process of establishing a
civilization than he is in its unusual, colorful incidents.
In this last section, however, he comes closest to modern
interests in social history, with chapters on ''Paternal
Government,'' ''Marriage and Population,'' ''The New
Home,'' ''Canadian Feudalism,'' ''Trade and Industry,''

"Priests and People," "Morals and Manners." The
writing in these chapters necessarily has less of the glow
that lights the pages of frontier battles, but the material
is well organized. "One great fact stands out conspicuous in Canadian history," writes Parkman, "—the
Church of Rome. More even than the royal power, she
shaped the character and the destinies of the colony."
"The royal government was transient; the Church was
permanent." The historian's pride of Anglo-Saxon ancestry dictated the concluding words: "A happier calamity never befell a people than the conquest of Canada
by the British arms."

In the preface to the next volume in his series Parkman says: "The events recounted in this book group
themselves in the main about a single figure, that of
Count Frontenac, the most remarkable man who ever represented the crown of France in the New World." The
first important struggle between the rival powers came
under his rule. He organized a "grand scheme of military
occupation by which France strove to envelop and hold
in check the industrial populations of the English colonies."

In his *Old Regime in Canada* Parkman explains that
he had attempted to "show from what inherent causes
this wilderness empire of the Great Monarch fell at last
before a foe, superior indeed in numbers, but lacking all
the forces that belong to a system of civil and military
centralization." In his *Count Frontenac* the author
claims to "show how valiantly, and for a time how successfully, New France battled against a fate which her
own organic fault made inevitable. Her history is a great
and significant drama, enacted among untamed forests,
with a distant gleam of courtly splendors and the regal
pomp of Versailles." Because his collection of materials
(on what was chronologically the last section of his
work), was "now rather formidable," Parkman decided

to pass over a period "of less decisive importance" to write on the collapse of French power in America. Thinking of his health, the historian said that if the material "is to be used at all, it had better be used at once."

Montcalm and Wolfe, which came next as the result of this decision, was acclaimed by the public as the finest book in the series, a judgment in which Parkman concurred. "The names on the title page," writes the author of the two volumes, "stand as representative of the two nations whose final contest for the control of North America is the subject of the book." The historian notes here what was equally applicable to his other works— "the subject has been studied as much from life and in the open air as the library table."

In this, as in other volumes, Parkman compares the combatants, and finds "that in making Canada a citadel of the state religion . . . the clerical monitors of the Crown robbed their country of a trans-Atlantic empire. New France could not grow with a priest on guard at the gate to let in none but such as pleased him." "France built its best colony on a principle of exclusion, and failed; England reversed the system, and succeeded." While noting the "hardy virtues of a masculine race" that populated New England, Parkman also observes that "Puritanism was not an unmixed blessing. . . . It strove to crush out not only what is evil, but much that is innocent and salutary." The historian's great ability to make generalizations containing a large factor of truth is thus revealed: "Pennsylvania was feudal in form, and not in spirit; Virginia in spirit, and not in form; New England in neither; and New York largely in both." The English colonies represented the future, fighting against the past, typified by French Canada, "moral and intellectual life" against "moral and intellectual torpor"; it was a fatal struggle of "barren absolutism against a liberty, crude, incoherent, and chaotic, yet full of prolific vitality.''

Some of the topics he was to treat again in the *A Half Century of Conflict* found a place in *Montcalm and Wolfe*. These subjects are introduced as background for the climactic struggle at Quebec. In this volume the partiality that sometimes motivated Parkman may be noticed in the more sympathetic treatment of the New Englander, William Shirley, than of the New Yorker, William Johnson. Not until near the end of Volume I does Montcalm appear on the American scene. The chivalrous Frenchman, shocked at the barbarous behavior of his Indian allies at Fort William Henry in 1757, cried, ''Kill me, but spare the English who are under my protection.''

Throughout this book, as frequently in his other volumes, Parkman keeps an eye on the European aspects of the colonial wars. The glitter of Versailles casts a remote light in the darkness of the American woods, and the imperial-minded Pitt, ''this British Roman,'' finds an important place in the description of the Anglo-French struggle. In his usual manner with the men he liked, Parkman describes the character of Wolfe at some length. ''The ardent and indomitable Wolfe,'' who ''had been the life of the siege'' of Louisburg, enters the story in the early part of Parkman's second volume. The historian's own fondness for things military attracted him to the young commander, who seemed ''always to have been at his best in the thick of battle; most complete in his mastery over himself and over others.'' ''Wherever there was need of a quick eye, a prompt decision, and a bold dash, there his lank figure was always in the front.'' The volume is half finished before Wolfe is at Quebec. The long siege wasted his frame, but ''through torment and languor and the heats of fever, the mind of Wolfe dwelt on the capture of Quebec.'' No writing could be more dra-

matic and more filled with suspense than the description
of the successful attempt to scale the heights of Abraham. On the Plains of Abraham, two gallant soldiers,
Montcalm and Wolfe, gave their lives for their rival
sovereigns.

Toward the very close of his narrative, with a reference to the broad scale of operations, Parkman mentions what modern students wish he had elaborated
further: "Now [1762] more than ever before, the war
appeared in its true character. It was a contest for maritime and colonial ascendency; and England saw herself
confronted by both her great rivals at once." "With the
Peace of Paris ended the checkered story of New France;
a story which would have been a history if faults of constitution and the bigotry and folly of rulers had not
dwarfed it to an episode."

Praise from those who were fitted to speak on history came in abundance when *Montcalm and Wolfe* was
published. Parkman's writing gained from the restraint
that an advancing maturity brought. "The book puts you
in the front rank of living English historians," wrote
Henry Adams. "Of its style and narrative the highest
praise is that they are on a level with its thoroughness
of study. Taken as a whole, your works are now dignified
by proportions and completeness which can be hardly
paralleled by the 'literary baggage' of any other historical writer in the language known to me to-day." E. L.
Godkin, editor of *The Nation,* wrote to Parkman that
he had never "been so much enchained by a historical
book." "No one else does nearly as much for American
literature." Henry James, Lowell, and the aged George
Bancroft paid their tributes, and Theodore Roosevelt
asked permission to dedicate his own work, *The Winning
of the West,* to Parkman.

In 1889 Parkman wrote to his friend the Abbé Cas-
grain, the Canadian historian, that although his health

was better, "it is still an open question whether I shall ever manage to supply the missing link between the *Montcalm and Wolfe* and its predecessor *Count Frontenac*." Fortunately he was able to return to his task, and in 1892 *A Half Century of Conflict* was published in two volumes. "The long day's work was done," concludes Sedgwick, Parkman's biographer.

Of his last volumes Parkman wrote: "The nature of the subject does not permit an unbroken thread of narrative, and the unity of the book lies in its being throughout, in one form or another, an illustration of the singularly contrasted characters and methods of the rival claimants to North America." "Queen Anne's War" and "The Tormented Frontier" are two of the chapters; in fact, most of Volume I is a tale of warfare wherever the French and English met. This book has less of the vibrant writing of the other volumes, and one senses the author's hurry to finish his task. He was now a tired man. Parkman always liked to spin his story around some central character, and because he had none in *A Half Century of Conflict,* it is supposed that he was not much interested in the book.

Although he means to be fair to the French, whose political and religious system he believed to be mistaken, Parkman's Anglo-Saxon view here, as elsewhere, pervades his writing. The American denied the validity of a French criticism, that he saw "Canadian defects through a microscope, and merits through a diminishing glass." He did not mind sectarian criticisms of his work. "Some of the Catholics and some of the Puritans sputter at the book [*The Jesuits in North America*]—others take it very kindly only regretting that the heretical author will probably be damned." [1]

His sympathy for his aristocratic heroes, cast in a

---

[1] Don C. Seitz, *Letters from Parkman to E. G. Squier* (1911), p. 45; October 24, 1867.

medieval mold, stemmed from his own political convictions. "I do not object to a good constitutional monarchy," he once wrote to a correspondent, "but prefer a
conservative republic, where intelligence and character,
and not numbers hold the reins of power." To his friend
Pierre Margry he spoke with glee of the conservative
victory in a municipal election. "Fortunately the low
and socialistic elements—for we have them thanks to the
emigration of 200,000 Irish to Boston—have suffered a
defeat." [2] The historian's attitude toward martial affairs
explains something of his love for the pageantry of war.
In the midst of the Civil War period Parkman wrote to
a Boston newspaper that the military instincts are "always strongest in the strongest and richest nature."
Even as a youth on his first trip to Europe, in 1843, he
wrote in his diary: "Here in this old world I seem, thank
Heaven, to be carried about half a century backwards
in time." "Above all, there is no canting of peace. A
wholesome system of coercion is manifest in all directions." On another occasion the historian wrote in his
Pioneers that "the story of New France is, from the first,
a story of war."

Thousands of manuscript pages of copies of records
in foreign archives constituted only one type of source
used by the indefatigable historian. "While engaged on
these books," wrote Parkman, "I made many journeys
in the United States and Canada in search of material,
and went four times to Europe with a similar object."
Some seventy volumes of manuscripts were among his
gifts to the Massachusetts Historical Society. In addition
to his own work Parkman stimulated historical scholarship by active membership in various organizations and
by causing valuable documents to be published. He also

2 "Letters of Francis Parkman to Pierre Margry," Smith College "Studies in History" (1923), VIII, Nos. 3 and 4; December 15, 1875.

served for a number of years on the Corporation of Harvard College.

Godkin correctly placed a high estimate on the value of Parkman's contribution to American literature, and for historians the New Englander's inspiration has an undying quality. "Faithfulness to the truth of history," Parkman once wrote, "involves far more than a research, however patient and scrupulous, into special facts. Such facts may be detailed with the most minute exactness, and yet the narrative, taken as a whole, may be unmeaning or untrue. The narrator must seek to imbue himself with the life and spirit of the time. He must study events in their bearings near and remote; in the character, habits, and manners of those who took part in them. He must himself be, as it were, a sharer or a spectator of the action he describes." John Fiske was probably right when he said of Parkman: "Of all American historians he is the most deeply and peculiarly American, yet he is at the same time the broadest and most cosmopolitan." Modern students find that Parkman's volumes, written in a romantic realm, do not quite fulfill the highest ideal of historical writing. But even though details of his narrative may be altered by supplemental studies, the main structure of his work seems built for permanence. It was a half-blind historian who made us see the heroism and villainy that stained with blood the green carpeted wilderness he loved as much as life itself.[3]

---

[3] Henry D. Sedgwick, *Francis Parkman* (Boston, 1904).

Charles H. Farnham, *Life of Parkman* (Boston, 1900).

Of the many commemorative papers on Parkman's centennial, see Joseph Schafer, *Miss. Valley Hist. Rev.* (March, 1924).

See introduction and full bibliography in Wilbur L. Schramm, *Francis Parkman* (N. Y., 1937), American Writers Series, Harry Hayden Clark, ed.

IX

THE RISE OF THE "SCIENTIFIC SCHOOL"

When Bancroft died in 1891, he had outlived his own school of historical writing by more than a decade. In a survey of American historical teaching in the 1880's, Francis N. Thorpe wrote: "Bancroft and Hildreth are our historians, but our history is yet to be written. The revival of historical studies in our generation is a step toward that consummation—the production of a complete history of America." Changes in historical writing are in abundant evidence in the 1880's—restrained expression, caution in statement and a broader consideration of the social and economic background of American history. With the passing of our more youthful writing went, perhaps, a certain exuberance and spontaneity whose charm made literature of history. More than one observer has regretted the passing of our younger days, and many are concerned lest our matured history writing die of old age.

Signs of the newer trend appeared near the middle of the last century. Although several states had earlier provided for the teaching of history in the public schools, a more important place for it in the curriculum was not

assured until after the Civil War. In the heat of the nationalism that came as the war's aftermath, North,
South, and West joined in prescribing American history.[1]
Following the example of Noah Webster, compilers of
children's books substituted materials on American history for the conventional biblical stories that had been
the staple reading matter.[2] About this time, Benson J.
Lossing and Thomas Wentworth Higginson were satisfying popular historical tastes by many articles in *Harper's Magazine*. Lossing, in his *Pictorial Field Book of
the Revolution,* sketched in prose as well as in pictures
those incidents and scenes which were dear to American
memory. The editor of *Harper's,* musing over the uncertainty of our historical knowledge, remarked, ''How hard
it is to know the truth when we have all the documents
and live among the men and events. But when a hundred
years hence any man's interpretation of them must be
trusted, is it not clear that we should not be too swift to
believe, until we know exactly the sympathies and character of the historian?''[3]

The expansive growth of historical societies and the
vitalizing of those that had existed almost in name alone
were other marked features of this past generation of
historiography. The creation and publication of collections of documents by these societies were of great aid
to scholars. Contemporary with the vast collections of
source materials that were being made in England, Germany, France, and Spain, individuals and states were
similarly engaged in gathering the materials that would
illumine the early history of the American nation. The
unfinished enterprise of Peter Force, whose *American
Archives* was not even the torso of the huge body of ma-

[1] B. L. Pierce, *Public Opinion and the Teaching of History* (N. Y.,
1926), Chap. II.
[2] Rolla M. Tryon, *The Social Sciences as School Subjects* (N. Y., 1935),
p. 117.
[3] 1861-1862, XXIV, 413.

terials he had envisaged, revealed the wealth that lay at hand for the historical craftsman. The publications of colonial records by New York, Pennsylvania, North Carolina, and other states, better organized than Force's work, were blessings to historians. A *Bibliography of the various Historical Societies throughout the United States,* published in 1868, showed how much work had been done in publishing documents and in writing local history.[4]

Collections on the era of discovery and exploration—"the great subject," as one of the munificent collectors, John Carter Brown, called it—were of special importance. For the first time American scholars, as a group, dug to the foundations of a subject, uncovering original sources upon which they based their narratives. Abandoning the preconceptions of earlier writers and speaking with caution, these scholars mark a transition from the older to the newer historical school. The interest of Americans in the period of discovery and exploration was but the local manifestation of a scholarly activity then in progress in Europe and Latin America.[5]

Noted collectors, like John C. Brown, James Lenox, Samuel L. M. Barlow, and others, were enthusiastic bibliophiles and made available to students extremely rare materials. A number of writers turned their attention to various episodes in the early history of the new world. John Gilmary Shea made studies in early French exploration and edited the *Jesuit Relations* (1857-1866). James C. Brevoort brought out his *Verrazano, the Navigator* in 1874, and the following year another phase of this theme was presented by Henry C. Murphy, a noted

---

[4] W. H. Whitmore, *Historical Magazine* (September, 1868).

[5] Friedrich Weber, *Beiträge zur Charakteristik der älteren geschichschreiber über Spanish-Amerika* . . . (Leipzig, 1911), pp. 22-27. See also article by J. C. Brevoort, "Spanish-American Documents Printed or Inedited," *Magazine of American History* (1879). It shows the vigorous effect on scholarship caused by the publication of these documents.

book collector, in *The Voyage of Verrazano*. The learned Harvard librarian and cartographer, Justin Winsor, wrote a biography of Columbus (1891), and then brought out in rapid succession three volumes on the exploration and settlement of the Ohio and Mississippi valleys. The first of these volumes was *Cartier to Frontenac;*[6] the second was *The Mississippi Basin*,[7] which continued the narrative of the Anglo-French struggle to 1763; and the last was *The Westward Movement: the Colonies and the Republic West of the Alleghanies*.[8] Winsor's interests were not those of Parkman; he was concerned rather with maps and documents for their own sake. A work of great value, whose publication was largely the result of Parkman's vigorous aid, were the six volumes of sources on French colonial history edited by Pierre Margry.[9] More important than these writings were the contributions of Henry Harrisse, which extended over more than forty years.

Harrisse was born in Paris in 1830, came to the United States as a child, and studied at the University of South Carolina. He qualified for the bar and spent some time in Chicago, where he vainly tried to earn a living. Eventually he left for New York and in the latter city he became a close friend of Barlow, who inspired in Harrisse a love for the study of the period of discovery. "Next to Christianity," thought Barlow, "the discovery of the New World was the greatest event of our era."[10] He was constantly emphasizing to students the necessity of consulting the original sources. "Even if there is . . . only one of our fellow-beings who longs to know the truth regarding the discovery and historical commencements

[6] Boston, 1894.
[7] Boston, 1895.
[8] Boston, 1897.
[9] *Découvertes et établissements des Français dans l'ouest et dans le sud de l'Amérique Septentrionale 1614-1754* (1876-1886).
[10] H. Harrisse, *The Late S. L. M. Barlow* (1889), p. 11.

of the New World, the book should be written," said Barlow. And then Harrisse wrote, in reference to himself : "Mr. Barlow made one proselyte, and . . . the task will be continued to the last." [11]

Harrisse, who saw a magnificent theme for the pen of a historian in the rise, decline, and fall of the Spanish empire in America, recognized that bibliographical studies had first to be made. His *Notes on Columbus* (1866), based on the collections in the libraries of Barlow and others, was a good beginning, and encouragement from collectors led him to undertake a more ambitious project, the *Bibliotheca Americana Vetustissima —A Description of Works relating to America published between the years 1492 and 1551* (1866). Dedicated to Barlow, who had inspired it, the volume, printed in the luxurious manner so dear to the collector, made known to the student over three hundred important items on the period. Harrisse tells us that he unearthed these rarities in various parts of the country, sometimes finding them "in the dusty garret of a dilapidated church," where he pored "over them when the thermometer stood below zero." [12] Although the great importance of his work was recognized by a small circle, the general reader was uninterested, and in disgust Harrisse moved soon after to Paris. Now, at last, financial success as a lawyer made it possible for Harrisse to devote most of his time to his studies. Moreover, in Paris he was warmly welcomed by French scholars, among them Ernest Renan.

The fruits of his labor are amassed in thirty volumes and many pamphlets touching various phases of his chosen subject. Six years after his bibliography of Americana was published he issued a volume of *Additions* (1872), and his introduction reveals how eagerly he had combed the libraries of Europe for material. He

[11] *Ibid.,* p. 15.
[12] P. liv.

found to his surprise that no library in Europe could compare with some private American libraries in the collection of books on the early history of the new world.[13] In referring to Humboldt's *Examen Critique,* Harrisse had said that it was "the greatest monument ever erected to the early history of this continent." [14] A tribute of similar distinction was later paid to his own publication, *The Discovery of North America* (1892).[15] Edward G. Bourne, who was well qualified to pass judgment, said that Harrisse's work was "the greatest contribution to the history of American geography since Humboldt's *Examen.*" Harrisse's lavish volume is a critical, documentary, and historical investigation, and its careful analyses of conflicting evidence show the marks of the legal mind. In addition to its cartographical studies it contains biographies of many of the pilots who made their voyages westward.

The discoverers who claim most of Harrisse's attention are Columbus, Cabot, and Vespucius. His *Christophe Colomb* [16] is an advance over earlier studies because of the publication of new documents and because of his customary sharp criticism of the sources. This, like his other works, is less a narrative than a study in historical criticism. *Jean et Sebastien Cabot* had appeared in 1882, but some years later Harrisse revised it and brought out another publication, *John Cabot: The Discoverer of North America and Sebastian His Son* (1896), in which the son is held up to scorn. "Sebastian Cabot," writes Harrisse, "was a man capable of disguising the truth,

---

[13] P. v.

[14] *Bibliotheca Americana Vetustissima,* p. xlii.

[15] Professor Clarence H. Haring doubts Harrisse's familiarity with the Spanish language, *Trade and Navigation Between Spain and the Indies* (Cambridge, 1918), p. xxii, but José T. Medina, the great bibliographer and historian, said Harrisse was the real founder of the modern school of historians of the era of discovery and exploration, *Bibliotheca Hispano-Americana, 1493-1810* (Santiago de Chile), VI, cxvii.

[16] 2 vols., 1884.

whenever it was to his interest to do so." [17] Harrisse gathered much material on Vespucius and worked up some of it, but he did not live to present it in a form comparable with his other publications. In the course of his researches Harrisse entered into a number of controversies.[18] While subsequent scholars have not accepted all his conclusions, it is probably correct to say that no one in his day was more familiar with the literature of discovery and exploration than the transplanted peppery American. Years before he died in 1910, he had written that "his task will be continued to the last," and with monkish zeal he held to his vow. Few Americans have made contributions to the literature of history and geography as important as those of the lawyer-scholar Harrisse.[19]

Study of the materials of the age of exploration aroused interest in historical writing among a limited few. A more general incentive was the Civil War, which stimulated interest in the whole field of American history, particularly in the national period. Some sought escape from the passions aroused by the war by returning to study the foundations of the Union which had just been preserved. Even during the war the *Historical Magazine* was writing that it closed publication of its sixth volume in 1862, "in the midst of a struggle which will for the next century be a matter of historic research and examination, and which in its overwhelming importance seems to banish for a season the study of the past." Yet, said the editor, "our past history, now more than ever claims, and is receiving the attention of think-

[17] P. 115.

[18] See his *Americus Vespucius,* 1895, critical of Clements Markham and C. H. Coote.

[19] See, for biographical details, A. Growoll, *Henry Harrisse.* See also notice and bibliography by H. Cordier in *Bulletin du Bibliophile et du Bibliothécaire* (1910), as well as letters to Ildebrando Rossi in *La Bibliofilia,* XXVIII, 1927, pp. 258-267, and autobiographical letter to S. L. M. Barlow from Paris, 1884, in ms. in the N.Y.P.L.

ing men.'' In the same magazine, soon after the war, a contribution appeared that revealed unusual foresight. ''It is really only now,'' said the writer, ''that we are beginning to know for certain what were the undoubted facts in our revolutionary history of 1776. It will require fifty years of painstaking and painful waiting—fifty years of a new conscience and the . . . disrobing of passion . . .'' before the true history of the war of secession will appear.[20] While the war was still in progress William H. Trescot, the historian of American diplomacy, was thinking of preserving materials for the future student. ''It is only by a rigid and impartial scrutiny of all the testimony,'' said Trescot, ''that the future historian can reach the positive truth.'' The manuscript that he wrote in 1861 he referred to as ''only a contribution to the materials of that future history.''[21]

The approach of the centennial in 1876 was another impetus to historical writing. In his diary Moses Coit Tyler betrays his annoyance because his volumes on American literature would not be ready in time. Carl Schurz told Samuel Bowles, the famous newspaper editor, that a Philadelphia publisher had asked him to prepare a political history of the United States in time for the centennial year. Although he would not do it on such a schedule, Schurz said he was intending to undertake it. He preferred, however, a Boston publisher, because he liked ''the literary atmosphere . . . and the great libraries of Boston,'' and would do his work there. Bowles said that a political history was greatly needed, and told Schurz that he was the best man to write it.[22]

Publication of periodicals like the *Magazine of American History* (1877) and the *Pennsylvania Maga-*

[20] *Historical Magazine* (May, 1866), pp. 166-167.
[21] ''Trescot Papers,'' Library of Congress; August, 1870.
[22] November 27, 1874, December 3, 1874; F. Bancroft, ed., *Speeches, Correspondence and Political Papers of Carl Schurz*, Vol. III.

zine of History and Biography (1877) attested to the awakened interest of Americans in their past. Martha J. Lamb, historian of New York City, and editor of the *Magazine of American History* from 1883 to her death in 1893, was a particularly active figure in stimulating historical writing. Earlier than these publications was *The Historical Magazine* (1857-1875), in whose editing Henry B. Dawson and John G. Shea had a large share. The preface of the first volume stated that it was an "organ for historical societies and a medium of inter-communication for literary men." This magazine was perhaps the periodical that came nearest to satisfying the need later filled by the *American Historical Review*. Samuel G. Drake, the Boston bookseller, antiquary, and editor, was influential in awakening historical interest; not least among his labors was his editorial supervision of the early volumes of the *New England Historical and Genealogical Register*. Memoirs of leading participants in the Civil War published in periodicals and books also intensified public interest in history. Colonel Alexander K. McClure published in the *Philadelphia Weekly Times* a series of articles by Civil War personalities. Other editors likewise ran articles in their journals, but the most famous series of all was the one published by the *Century Magazine* (1885-1888), under the editorship of Clarence C. Buel. These articles, later brought together in book form with the title *Battles and Leaders of the Civil War,* were immensely popular and aroused widespread discussion.[23]

Publication of archival material, so important a feature of the earlier decades in historiography, was continued in the later period. The bibliographical activity of these decades was of transcendent importance, the names of Henry Harrisse, Joseph Sabin, Paul L. Ford,

[23] See Century Collection, ms. letters, N.Y.P.L.

and Justin Winsor standing to the fore. The prospectus of Sabin's *A Dictionary of Books relating to America* was announced in 1866, and in 1868 the first volume of this classic bibliography began to come out. "Should I wait to make this bibliography as full and exact on all points as I trust it will generally be found, I should never complete it," he said. Sabin never did live to complete it, but Robert Vail and the dean of American bibliographers, Wilberforce Eames, recently finished it. Another great work is the *American Bibliography, 1639-1820* compiled by Charles Evans. Only twelve volumes, including items down through 1799, were published. The editorial activities of John Gilmary Shea made available many rare imprints, and Charles Deane of the Massachusetts Historical Society was setting a high standard for editors in these years with his literal printing of Bradford's history of the Plymouth settlement, perhaps the most important original source of American history to have appeared since Winthrop's *Journal*. An example of the acuteness of historical criticism then a characteristic of many students was Horace Binney's *An Inquiry into the Formation of Washington's Farewell Address* (1859). The widening scope of historical interests, long before McMaster wrote, is noticed in the observation of a Virginia student who complained that histories of kings, rulers, and statesmen abounded but "the People rarely appear upon the stage." He thought that the time had arrived for a history of the people.[24]

On a smaller scale than Bancroft's, historians wrote narratives of their states or described some particular aspect of history. Edmund B. O'Callaghan and John R. Brodhead wrote on New York, Samuel G. Arnold on the *History of Rhode Island and Providence Plantations*,[25] John S. Barry covered the *History of Massachusetts*

[24] *Va. Hist. Reg.*, 1848, I, 69.
[25] 2 vols., N. Y., 1859.

(1492-1820) in three volumes.[26] Francis L. Hawks published the *History of North Carolina* in two volumes [27]
and Charles Campbell brought out a good history of Virginia just before the Civil War.[28] Narratives and collections of documents in religious history shed much light
on the subject as a whole. Very important work in this
field was done by Hawks and William S. Perry, in collaboration and also separately. Perry's *Historical Collections relating to the American Colonial Church* [29]
brought to the attention of students many papers hitherto
inaccessible. Charles W. Baird wrote on *The History of
the Huguenot Emigration to America.*[30] John G. Shea
dealt with the Catholic Church in America; Abel Stevens
published three volumes on Methodism (1858-1861); and
Henry M. Dexter compiled a valuable bibliography and
lectured on the literature of Congregationalism, which
was the subject of a volume he published in 1880. A work
of great value on all Protestant sects, *Annals of the
American Pulpit,*[31] was edited by William B. Sprague.
At this time, too, Moses Coit Tyler wrote his history of
colonial literature. On another subject, *The American
Loyalists* (1847), Lorenzo Sabine gave to Americans a
new viewpoint on the Revolution and its combatants.[32]
An interesting preliminary essay examined the classes
in colonial society and their political allegiance. Sabine's
Loyalists, which appeared in a revised and enlarged edition in 1864, had a great influence on later writers and
was of extreme importance in rescuing the Tories from
traditional obloquy. A century of America's history was
better understood because of the publication of the

---

[26] Boston, 1855-1857.
[27] Fayetteville, 1857-1858.
[28] Phila., 1860.
[29] 5 vols., 1870-1878.
[30] 2 vols., 1885.
[31] 10 vols., 1856-1868.
[32] *The Life of Peter Van Schaack* by his son, H. C. Van Schaack, in
1842 was called "the first attempt to present to the public of the United
States a justificatory memoir of one of the Tories in the Revolution." See
C. F. Adams, *N. A. Rev.* (July, 1842).

Works of John Adams [33] and the *Memoirs* of John Quincy Adams.[34] In 1865 *The Historical Magazine,* which was so valuable to historical scholars for nearly two decades, said that ten years previously historical students and collectors were comparatively few, but that now, "a change great beyond all precedent, and too rapid perhaps to be enduring, has come." "The class of buyers has extended in numbers, and risen in point of taste." [35]

HISTORY TEACHING IN THE COLLEGES

More important than these factors in promoting a newer historical writing was the change that occurred in history teaching in American colleges and universities. Up to this time, and indeed for the rest of the nineteenth century, many of the narratives read by the public were written by nonacademic historians. Bancroft, Hildreth, Prescott, Motley, Parkman, Rhodes, and others were not schoolmen. Not until the last few years of the century do we observe a preponderant influence exerted by the academicians in American historiography, but the colleges and universities before this had begun to affect historical interests. Young students came back from Europe in increasing numbers determined to apply to the schools at home what they had learned in the old world. Even in earlier years men like Sparks at Harvard, William Dew at William and Mary, and Francis Lieber at South Carolina (later at Columbia) had given historical lectures of high quality, but these were isolated instances. Because of their intellectual pre-eminence in history and constitutional law, such men as Sparks and Lieber also acted as clearing houses for the ideas of contemporaries.[36] They realized the need, too, for better his-

[33] 10 vols., Boston, 1850-1856.   [35] P. 167; May, 1865.
[34] 12 vols., Phila., 1874-1877.
[36] C. B. Robson, "Papers of Francis Lieber," *Huntington Library Bulletin* (February, 1933), p. 147.

torical texts, and Lieber sought to fill that need.[37] When Sparks's advice was requested by the newly created New York University, he drew attention to the necessity of studying American history. At the same time he was in correspondence with his friend George Ticknor on a problem of common interest—improvement in college teaching.[38] Sparks had accepted the Harvard professorship in 1838 on condition that he teach nothing but history. The promising beginning in the improvement of history teaching which he made was, however, cut short by his acceptance of the presidency of Harvard in 1849. Throughout America pedagogy was in a sorry plight. Even gifted professors, according to Andrew D. White, taught history by having their pupils repeat from memory the dates in a manual or by having them recite its words.

The complaint which William Ellery Channing uttered in 1830 in his *Remarks on National Literature* had not lost its point. He granted that Americans were generous in spreading elementary education, but, he added, "we fall behind many in provision for the liberal training of the intellect, for forming great scholars, for communicating that profound knowledge, and that thirst for higher truths, which can alone originate a commanding literature. The truth ought to be known. There is among us much superficial knowledge, but little severe, persevering research; . . . little resolute devotion to a high intellectual culture. . . . Few among us can be said to have followed out any great subject of thought patiently, laboriously, so as to know thoroughly what others have discovered and taught, concerning it, and thus to occupy a ground from which new views may be gained." Conditions were later improved, thanks largely to the important contributions of American colleges.

It was from Europe that Americans drew their in-

[37] Adams, *Sparks,* II, 427, 1835.
[38] *Ibid.,* II, 361-363, 1835.

spiration for a fuller intellectual life. American and European intellectual relations were always very close, but never more so than in this period. What we need, said Henry Adams, writing home from London to his brother Charles Francis, "is a *school*. We want a national set of young men like ourselves or better, to start new influences not only in politics, but in literature, in law, in society, and throughout the whole social organism of the country—a national school of our own generation. And that is what America has no power to create. In England the universities centralize ability and London gives a field. So in France, Paris encourages and combines these influences. But with us, we should need at least six perfect geniuses placed, or rather, spotted over the country and all working together; whereas our generation as yet has not produced one nor the promise of one. It's all random, insulated work, for special and temporary and personal purposes, and we have no means, power or hope of combined action for any unselfish end. One man who has real ability may do a great deal," said Adams, "but we ought to have a more concentrated power of influence than any that now exists.[39] The "geniuses" that Henry Adams so ardently desired for America very soon appeared.

Andrew D. White and Daniel C. Gilman had gone abroad in 1853 and had studied European educational methods. White, after three years' absence, during which time he heard lectures under French and German masters, went to the University of Michigan to institute the first historical courses, in an American school, that represented the modern trend. He introduced his students to valuable reading outside of their textbooks, and from the rich library he had already begun to collect he read the language of the original sources. It interested his stu-

[39] W. C. Ford, ed., *A Cycle of Adams Letters* (2 vols., Boston, 1920), I, 196; November 21, 1862.

dents, he tells us, "far more than any quotation at second hand could do." Contemporaneously, H. W. Torrey and E. W. Gurney were reinvigorating the study of history at Harvard. History was placed at the forefront of studies in Michigan, and, when White accepted the presidency of the newly established Cornell University, he carried there his enthusiasm for his favorite subject. "The historical works of Buckle, Lecky and Draper, which were then appearing," said White, "gave me a new and fruitful impulse; but most stimulating of all was the atmosphere coming from the great thought of Darwin and Spencer— an atmosphere in which history became less and less a matter of annals, and more and more a record of the unfolding of humanity." Lecky's history of rationalism stirred progressive minds in America. Henry C. Lea, the historian of the Inquisition, and one of the greatest scholars the United States has ever produced, thought that Lecky's book would aid in developing a school "in which history may be taught as it should be. We have had enough annalists to chronicle political intrigues and military achievements," said Lea, "but that which constitutes the inner life of a people and from which there are to be drawn the lessons of the past that will guide us in the future, has hitherto been too much neglected." [40]

Auguste Comte, the founder of sociology, had thought it possible, by applying the methods of natural science to history, to discover the laws of historical development and thus foretell the future. He criticized the earlier historians with their too-colorful political episodes and romantic attachment to great personalities. He advocated instead a study of society as a whole and believed that all peoples had a mass psyche which underlay the group mores. [41] Buckle believed that Comte had done more than any

[40] *A Memoir of William E. H. Lecky* by His Wife (London, 1909), pp. 51-52.

[41] For the early influence of Comte in America, see R. L. Hawkins, *Auguste Comte and the United States 1816-1853* (Cambridge, 1936).

other writer to raise the standard of history, and his general support of the French scholar's point of view helped to strengthen the latter's hold in English-speaking countries.[42] John Stuart Mill, whom the young Henry Adams considered "the ablest man in England," deeply affected American thought. Mill and de Tocqueville were "the two high priests of our faith," confessed Adams.[43] The influence of Buckle was particularly great, and many fell under his spell. Theodore Parker was one of his earliest American correspondents, and Moses Coit Tyler once wrote of having been "obsessed . . . for weeks together" by the English historian.[44] Americans were decidedly attracted to Buckle's thesis on the relationship between environment and the development of humanity, but a number of years passed before they applied his ideas to their own history. In his chapter in Winsor's "Narrative and Critical History of America" and in more complete form in his volume *Nature and Man in America* (1891) Nathaniel S. Shaler was one of the first to note geographical influences in American history. A few years later, in 1903, Ellen C. Semple published one of the best of these interpretive volumes in her *American History and Its Geographic Conditions*. At the same time the famous historian of the trails, Archer B. Hulbert, was editing the *Historic Highways of America*,[45] which emphasized geographical determinism in American history.

Buckle, Lecky, and John W. Draper [46] were not alone in opening new perspectives to the young student. Semi-

[42] Henry T. Buckle, *History of Civilization in England* (1882 edn., 3 vols.), I, 5, note.

[43] *A Cycle of Adams Letters,* I, 253, 281.

[44] John Weiss, *Life and Correspondence of Theodore Parker* (Boston, 1864), I, 467 ff.; Howard M. Jones, *The Life of Moses Coit Tyler* (Ann Arbor, 1933), p. 141.

[45] 16 vols., Cleveland, 1902-1905.

[46] A professor of chemistry in New York University, Draper was the author of a *History of the Intellectual Development of Europe* (1863), which had a wide influence because of its evolutionary approach to historical writing.

nar study provided a thrilling experience to Americans abroad and this new delight in scholarship infused their teaching with unwonted zest. Herbert Baxter Adams, recalling student days in Berlin, spoke of the seminar with particular warmth. "There the student appears, fortified by books and documents borrowed from the University library, and prepared with his brief of points and citations, like a lawyer about to plead a case in the court room. . . . Authorities are discussed; parallel sources of information are cited; old opinions are exploded; standard histories are riddled by criticism, and new values are established. This process of destruction and reconstruction requires considerable literary apparatus, and the professor's study-table is usually covered with many evidences of the battle of books."[47]

Charles K. Adams, a former student of White, introduced a seminar at Michigan in 1869, and two years later Henry Adams inaugurated the seminar method at Harvard. The work of Henry Adams was of great value despite his own disparagement of his seven years' stay at Harvard. Several of his students were awarded Harvard's first Ph.D.'s, and among them were some whose names are well known in the literature of history and economics—J. Laurence Laughlin, Henry Osborn Taylor and Edward Channing. Most of Adams's students became historians, and, aside from Torrey and Gurney, Harvard's history department was for many years after his departure conducted by his former pupils. Adams was proud of "baking" his first "batch of doctors of philosophy" in 1876. To one of them, Henry Cabot Lodge, he wrote: "I believe that my scholars will compare favorably with any others, English, German, French or Italian. I look with more hope on the future of the world as I see how good our material is." The volume of *Essays in*

[47] "Seminary Libraries and University Extension," Johns Hopkins University. "Studies in History and Political Science" (1887), V, 445.

Anglo-Saxon Law (1876) by Adams and his students
"was the first original historical work ever accomplished
by American university students working in a systematic
and thoroughly scientific way under proper direction"—
this, at least, was the observation of a co-worker, Herbert
Baxter Adams, who was more familiar with academic
activities in history than any other teacher of his day.[48]
Daniel C. Gilman thought that this Harvard volume may
have given Herbert Baxter Adams at Johns Hopkins the
idea for his own later *Studies.*[49]

Most of the younger men in the decades of the 1870's
and 1880's were under the strong influence of John Richard Green and Edward Freeman. Green's *Short History
of England,* in particular, was a great success in America.[50] James Ford Rhodes believed that Green had more
readers in America than any other historian except Macaulay, and added that his power to shape the opinions
of the reading public ranked him with Gibbon, Carlyle,
and Macaulay.[51] The whole range of knowledge in these
years felt the impact of Darwinism, and principles of relationship and continuity were sought in every subject.
Edward L. Youmans, a champion of the new thought in
America, wrote to Spencer in 1871, the same year in
which the *Descent of Man* was published: "Things are
going here furiously. I have never known anything like it.
Ten thousand *Descent of Man* have been printed, and I
guess they are nearly all gone. Five or six thousand of
(Huxley's) *Lay Sermons* have been printed . . . the
progress of liberal thought is remarkable. Everybody is
asking for explanation." [52] "A new epoch in the study of

[48] *Ibid.,* p. 451.
[49] *Herbert B. Adams: Tributes of Friends,* 1902, p. 55.
[50] *Letters of John Richard Green,* ed. by Leslie Stephen, pp. 387, 395.
[51] James F. Rhodes, *Historical Essays* (N. Y., 1909), "John Richard Green."
[52] Quoted in Sidney Ratner, "Evolution and the Rise of Scientific Spirit in America," *Philosophy of Science* (January, 1936), p. 113.

history dates" from the publication of *The Origin of Species,* said Charles Francis Adams, who added, "Human history has become part of a comprehensible cosmogony, and its area vastly extended.[53] It was felt that the idea of unity and continuity was as applicable to the history of the new world as it was to that of the old.

As a result of attending the lectures of the leading scholars of France and Germany, American students at this time laid great stress on the history of institutions, constitutions, social organization, legal theory, public law, administration, and government. Henry Adams, who introduced to Harvard the habit of emphasizing institutional history, was thus akin in historical spirit to his contemporaries, Maine and Stubbs, Waitz and Fustel de Coulanges. Institutional history continued to be heavily emphasized at Harvard during the last thirty years of the nineteenth century; Ephraim Emerton was the only one at that university who stressed *Kulturgeschichte.* In the seminar of Herbert Baxter Adams at Johns Hopkins, students read on the wall before them the statement of Freeman: "History is past politics and politics present history." They were surrounded by portraits of men whose ideas fecundated their own—Pertz, Freeman, Bluntschli, and others. Bluntschli, who had been the master of Adams at Heidelberg, was interested mainly in political science. Broader fields of investigation were indicated by McMaster, who gave history a prominent position at the University of Pennsylvania. He sent his students to the original documents that were the sources of his own great work: annals, debates, journals, publications of Congress, pamphlets, newspapers, and the like.

The discontent that Ticknor fifty years earlier had felt when he compared his attainments with European contemporaries was still being experienced by Ameri-

[53] Mass. Hist. Soc. *Proc.,* "Historians and Historical Societies," 2d ser., XIII, 89-90.

cans. "Every day I feel anew," wrote Ticknor in 1815, "what a mortifying distance there is between a European and an American scholar. We do not yet know what a Greek scholar is; we do not even know the process by which a man is to be made one." Then he added, with prophetic insight, "I am sure, if there is any faith to be given to the signs of the times, two or three generations at least must pass away before we make the discovery and succeed in the experiment.[54] The generations had now passed, the discovery had been widely made and the experiment had already met with some success. The wish that the German historian of America, Christophe D. Ebeling, had expressed in 1817, was now beginning to be realized. He was writing at the time about the work of four Americans, Everett, Ticknor, Cogswell, and Augustus Thorndike, then studying at Göttingen, and added: "I hope they will be the means of a learned intercourse between the worthies of the United States and Germany."[55]

In his later years Ticknor revealed to his friend, the eminent geologist Sir Charles Lyell, something of the intellectual excitement then stirring in the scholastic world. He referred to the establishment of the Museum of Comparative Zoology at Cambridge and his own interest in it, because, he said, "I think such an institution will tend . . . to lay the foundation for a real university among us, where all the great divisions of human knowledge shall be duly represented and taught. I had a vision of such an establishment forty years ago, when I came fresh from . . . Göttingen; but that was too soon. Nobody listened to me. Now, however, when we have the best law school in the country, one of the best observatories in the world, a good medical school, and a good botanical

[54] *Life, Letters and Journals of George Ticknor,* I, 73, note.
[55] Am. Antiq. Soc. *Proc.,* "Letters of C. D. Ebeling" (October, 1925); to Joseph McKean, June 11, 1817.

garden, I think the Lawrence Scientific School, with the Zoological and Paleontological Museum, may push through a true university and bring up the Greek, Latin, mathematics, history, philosophy, etc., to their proper level. At least I hope so, and mean to work for it." [56]

Flushed with confidence, young American scholars came back from Europe to their colleges and universities, and, in the reorganizations of curricula that were then being effected, they made an important place for history. In a report to the trustees of Cornell in 1872, President White had bemoaned the fact that an American had to attend the lectures of Édouard de Laboulaye at the Collège de France or of Karl Neumann in Berlin to learn American history. [57] But it was not long before American history came into its own. Chairs for history alone were created, and new courses were instituted. Moses Coit Tyler held the first professorship of American history established in 1881 at Cornell, and in these years, writes Charles K. Adams, American universities were more advanced than Scottish universities, and hardly behind Oxford and Cambridge in the teaching of history. In the last two years of his teaching career, Henry Adams gave in succession the two courses on American history, separated by the year 1789, "which" as Emerton says, "have been Harvard classics ever since." With the sophistication that belonged as well to other teachers of his generation, Henry Adams wrote amusingly to his English friend, Charles Milnes Gaskell: [58] "I am reading hard for a new course in American colonial history . . . in which I am to expose British tyranny and cruelty with a degree of patriotic fervor which, I flatter myself, has rarely been equalled." In a report on the study of history in American

[56] *Life, Letters and Journals,* II, 422; May 17, 1859.

[57] The former published in three volumes a history of the United States in 1862-1866; Neumann also brought out a three-volume history in 1866.

[58] June 22, 1874.

colleges in 1887, Herbert Baxter Adams said that a student need no longer go abroad for instruction; it was available at Harvard, whose historical work, he thought, rivaled that of a German university.

When native faculties were more firmly established, students began to be trained in America in larger numbers, especially at Johns Hopkins under Herbert Baxter Adams and at Columbia under John W. Burgess after 1880. Both Adams and Burgess had studied in the vigorous atmosphere of Amherst, where they came under the influence of President Julius H. Seelye. Adams, in characteristic fashion, once described the process of adapting the rooms occupied by the biology department for his history seminar: "The old tables which had once been used for the dissection of cats and turtles were planed down, covered with green baize, and converted into desks for the dissection of government documents and other materials for American institutional history." [59] In a retrospective view, J. Franklin Jameson spoke of the "revelation" that Johns Hopkins was in 1876. Entrance into its atmosphere "was to those who went there in its earliest days," he said, "like the opening of the Pacific before the eyes of Balboa and his men. Here were no dated classes, no campus, no sports, no dormitories, no gulf between teacher and student where all were students, no compulsion toward work where all were eager." [60] The lengthy bibliography printed in the memorial volume to Herbert Baxter Adams revealed the scope of the Johns Hopkins influence in the last quarter of the nineteenth century. In a tribute to his teacher, Frederick J. Turner said of Adams that his importance lay not in the keenness of his scholarship nor in the critical character of his investigations, but in the power to

[59] Johns Hopkins University "Studies," V, 455.
[60] The Dial (1902), p. 144.

inspire "men with enthusiasm for serious historical work and in bringing out the best that was in them." [61]

The works of many scholars in these years were published in the Johns Hopkins University "Studies in Historical and Political Science," and in the Columbia University "Studies in History, Economics and Public Law." Adams, who was the editor of the Hopkins volumes, included in the "Studies" several papers on academic work in history in various European countries, which indicated the extent of American interest in contemporary teaching elsewhere. Adams and others also stressed the need of training students in political science in preparation for leadership in public life. Articles on American historical literature during the 1870's and 1880's were to be found in the *Revue Historique* and in the *Historische Zeitschrift* to which J. Franklin Jameson contributed. "Seminary Notes on Recent Historical Literature" in the Johns Hopkins "Studies" [62] was a general review of the work in American history, thus performing a service for the student that the *American Historical Review* was to do continuously after its first publication in 1895. Charles K. Adams brought to the student a guide to historical literature with the publication in 1882 of his *Manual.* The work of a librarian like Justin Winsor was of great value in supplementing the efforts of Channing and Hart to establish the high place of American history at Harvard. When the latter began teaching in 1883, the books of Hildreth and von Holst were the only available histories of the United States covering the period since the Revolution. Channing and Hart, through their *Guide to the Study of American History* [63] and their many publications of rare documents mapped out huge fields of our history. In 1887 *The Nation* directed attention to a neg-

[61] *Herbert B. Adams: Tributes of Friends,* 1902, p. 45.
[62] VIII, 1890.
[63] Boston, 1896, and later revised with F. J. Turner (1912).

lected subject—immigration—and urged the composition of full histories of the various immigrant groups in the United States. "Their social, religious, literary and other characteristics," it said, "will be of great value to future historians in analyzing the national peculiarities of the American people . . ." [64]

The editorial labors of Benjamin F. Stevens, Reuben G. Thwaites, Worthington C. and Paul Leicester Ford, and Victor H. Paltsits were of great assistance to historical writing, and their volumes fixed more firmly a high standard of editing. Among the many services of J. Franklin Jameson to historical scholarship has been his work in connection with the historical division of the Carnegie Institution of Washington. One of the recommendations made by a committee which included Dr. Jameson, Charles Francis Adams, and Andrew C. McLaughlin, was the creation of an Institute of Historical Research to supervise certain projects, particularly the editing of valuable manuscripts and the publication of guides to materials on American history in European depositories. Other projects included an atlas of American geography, and a dictionary of national biography comparable with England's.[65] Years passed before very much materialized, but eventually these and other publications came from the press, and some are still in progress.

The invigoration of the intellectual life that America experienced in the period after the Civil War resulted in the formation of a number of societies among scholars in the social sciences.[66] The founding of the American Historical Association in 1884, the establishment of the *Political Science Quarterly* in 1886, and the publication of the

[64] February 22, 1877.
[65] Carnegie Institution of Washington, *Year Book,* No. 1, 1902, pp. 227-230.
[66] G. B. Goode, "The Origin of the National Scientific and Educational Institutions of the U. S.," Amer. Hist. Assn. *Papers* (1890), Vol. IV, Part II.

American Historical Review a few years later were signs of the change that had come over our native historical writing. High standards of craftsmanship were promoted, and the vigorous criticisms of recognized scholars were often a healthy stimulus to their younger colleagues.

Books have changed in content since McMaster brought the "people" into his narrative. The aspirations and defeats of the multitude have become as much the legitimate theme of the latter-day historian as were the intricate developments of constitutional theory to the historian of an earlier day. "Our history is not in Congress alone," wrote a colleague of McMaster in 1887; "that is, indeed, a very small part of it. Our discoveries, our inventions, our agrarian interests, our settlements westward, our educational affairs, the work of the church, the organization of charities, the growth of corporations, the conflict of races and for races, at times in our history, are all sources for research." [67] At about this same time Henry Adams was writing to an English friend, "Society is getting new tastes, and history of the old school has not many years to live. I am willing enough to write history for a new school; but new men will doubtless do it better, or at least make it more to the public taste." Charles Francis Adams, in 1899, also thought "that the day of the general historian of the old school" was over, and prophesied the increasing importance of the monograph." [68]

New points of view were suggested by Frederick Jackson Turner, stressing the influence of the frontier in American history. The economic interpretation of some phases of American history was reinforced by a reading of Karl Marx, although Marx had little direct influence on American historical writing. Economists, particularly Thorstein Veblen, were among the first of the American

[67] F. N. Thorpe, "The Study of History in American Colleges and Universities," Bur. of Educ., *Circular of Information* (1887), No. 2, p. 252.
[68] Mass. Hist. Soc. *Proc.,* 2d ser., XIII, 89-115.

scholars to appreciate the significance of Marx. Professor Edwin R. A. Seligman's *The Economic Interpretation of History* (a small volume published in 1902) was an analysis of the theory, and noted the applications that had already been made of it in English, French, and American historical writing. Although critical of a rigid economic determinism, Professor Seligman spoke of the great importance of the economic interpretation of history, noting that the "entire history of the United States to the Civil War was at the bottom a struggle between two economic principles." Wherever one turns in the writings of recent historical investigation, he observes, "we are confronted by the overwhelming importance attached by the younger and abler scholars to the economic factor in political and social progress." [69] Few writers have gone so far in their strict Marxian interpretation as A. M. Simons, in his *Social Forces in American History;* [70] Gustavus Myers, in *The History of the Great American Fortunes;* [71] Herman Schlüter, in *Lincoln, Labor and Slavery;* [72] or Lewis Corey, in his suggestive studies of American capitalism. Before the rise of this group, American historians had a long tradition which embraced the economic among other factors determining the course of history. It goes back at least to Belknap, Marshall, Pitkin, Benton, and, more decidedly, Hildreth. In a sense, Marx merely reminded Americans of their own tradition.

No one has done more to impress his fellow scholars with the value of this approach than Charles A. Beard, who was, however, anticipated by J. Allen Smith, who wrote *The Spirit of American Government* in 1907. Herbert L. Osgood of Columbia, one of Beard's teachers, was aware of the difference between his generation and the newer one. "Men of my generation," said Osgood, "grew

[69] P. 86.
[70] N. Y., 1911.
[71] 3 vols., Chicago, 1911.
[72] N. Y., 1913.

up in the midst of great constitutional and institutional debates and our interest turned to institutional history. Profound economic questions have now arisen and students of the younger generation, true to their age, will occupy themselves with economic aspects of history." [73] Osgood's forecast was correct, and a large number of publications have appeared interpreting various episodes from an economic standpoint. A scholar who has spanned Osgood's generation and the present, J. Franklin Jameson, has written a splendid short survey of *The American Revolution Considered as a Social Movement*.[74] Arthur M. Schlesinger and Charles M. Andrews made important studies of the relationship of the merchants to the American Revolution, while Beard's volumes, the *Economic Interpretation of the Constitution* and *Economic Origins of Jeffersonian Democracy,* disturbed the comforting quiet of academic halls. Dr. Beard made good use of a work published twenty years earlier by Orin G. Libby on *The Geographical Distribution of the Vote of the Thirteen States on the Federal Constitution 1787-1788*.[75] New light was thrown on the background of the Civil War by students who saw more in it than a constitutional struggle. Episodes in the history of labor have recently found historians more accurate than were Rhodes, Oberholtzer, and others. Henry David in *The History of the Haymarket Affair* [76] and J. Walter Coleman in *The Molly Maguire Riots* [77] have shown how distorted by antilabor sentiments were the interpretations of earlier writers.

The scientific developments of the nineteenth century, with their facile general principles that explained so much, stirred the students of history to seek a like universal generalization in their own field. No one tackled the

---

[73] *Amer. Hist. Rev.* (October, 1935), p. 81.
[74] Princeton, 1926.
[75] University of Wisconsin *Bulletin,* "Economics, Political Science, and History Series" (1894), Vol. I, No. 1.
[76] N. Y., 1936. [77] Richmond, 1936.

problem with greater virtuosity than Henry Adams, who found in the second law of thermodynamics a destructive blow to current social thinking. As he expressed it: "It was absurd for social science to teach progress while physical science was committed to destruction." [78] But such efforts to relate history and science, valuable as they are, run afoul of the fact that scientific truths change, and that historical theories resting on them thus have transitory bases. A recognition of the special character of the organism of human society has made some scholars wary of drawing analogies between it and other organisms in nature.[79]

Historians are still making important contributions to their subject by correlating human progress with advances in science, but the most significant of the newer approaches to history is the "collective psychological," advanced by Karl Lamprecht. According to this school the historian can understand the historical development of any age only in the light of its collective psychology, and the burden rests upon him to uncover the factors "which create and shape the collective view of life and determine the nature of the group struggle for existence and improvement." [80] Lamprecht's influence turned scholars back to intellectual history (which had attracted Condorcet in the eighteenth century) and, under the leadership of James Harvey Robinson, American students published a number of valuable studies. Outstanding in this field are Preserved Smith and Carl Becker. The latter has greatly enriched our perception of the spirit of the eighteenth century by his study of the philosophes and his analysis of *The Declaration of Independence*.[81]

[78] *A Letter to American Teachers of History* (1910).
[79] Charles A. Beard and Alfred Vagts, "Currents of Thought in Historiography," *Amer. Hist. Rev.* (April, 1937).
[80] Harry E. Barnes, *The New History and the Social Studies* (New York, 1925), pp. 36, 198-203.
[81] N. Y., 1922.

Historians have increased enormously the scope of their narratives and have measurably deepened their understanding of the past by levying upon the contributions of colleagues in archaeology, geography, anthropology, ethnography, economics, psychology, and, particularly, sociology. The line has been drawn rather thin between the historian and the sociologist; in fact, the dominant group writing history today may be spoken of as the "sociological school of historians." [82]

The accumulation of vast quantities of source and monographic materials has made it more and more difficult for any one person to master the whole field of our history. It is the opinion of many that Edward Channing's survey of American history in its entirety will be the last attempted by an individual. Unfortunately death stopped him before his narrative caught up with contemporary America. The trend has been steadily in the direction of co-operative endeavor, and we may look forward to a continuing series of comprehensive histories written by groups of individuals treating separate periods. The result, however, is often little more than a group of monographs thrown together and serves to emphasize the need for an integrated synthesis of the whole of American history. It must be a courageous spirit who will dare, alone, to scan the whole of our history and set himself the task of writing its record.

BIBLIOGRAPHY

C. K. Adams, "Recent Historical Work in the Colleges and Universities of Europe and America," *Papers,* Amer. Hist. Assn. (January, 1890), pp. 39-65. This is the best survey of what happened after 1860. See also Prof. J. A. Woodburn, *Journal,* Illinois State Historical Society, XV (1922), pp. 439 ff.; An-

[82] See Carl Becker, "Some Aspects of the Influence of Social Problems and Ideas upon the Study and Writing of History," *The American Journal of Sociology,* XVIII, 641 ff.

drew D. White, *Autobiography* (2 vols., N. Y., 1905); *Letters
of Henry Adams, 1858-1891* (Boston, 1930), edited by W. C.
Ford; Arthur M. Schlesinger, *New Viewpoints in American His-
tory* (N. Y., 1922); see John S. Bassett, "The Present State of
History-writing" in *The Writing of History* (N. Y., 1926);
William A. Dunning, "A Generation of American Historiog-
raphy," *Ann. Rep.* of the Amer. Hist. Assn. for the year 1917;
Charles M. Andrews, "These Forty Years," *Amer. Hist. Rev.*
(January, 1925).

X

HENRY ADAMS

The historians of the "scientific school" were trained for the most part in the university seminars of Europe and America, and their writings began to assume real significance in the 1880's and 1890's. Henry Adams may well be said to have inaugurated this period in American historiography. The fluency of his style places him with the literary historians, while his vigorous critical standards, comparative objectivity, and influence over academicians prompt his classification with the later group. Although contemporaries like John Fiske and the bibliographers Harrisse and Winsor produced works that were valuable to the historians of the newer day, they, far more than Adams, were holdovers from a former era.

The Adams family has been lavish in its contributions to American political and literary life. Its most important gift to historical literature was the *History of the United States* by Henry Adams. This representative of the fourth generation, one of the most interesting of them all, was born in 1838. He followed the family educational tradition in going to Harvard, and, after travel abroad, returned to America, where, among other activities, he wrote some historical articles for the *North American Review.*

In 1871 President Eliot invited Adams to become assistant professor of history at Harvard and to give a course on the Middle Ages. As Adams expressed it in the *Education,* "between Gurney's classical courses and Torrey's modern ones, lay a gap of a thousand years which Adams was expected to fill." "I have nine hours a week in the lecture room," he wrote to his friend C. M. Gaskell, "and am absolutely free to teach what I please within the dates 800-1649." [1] Despite his own gloomy judgments of his work, he filled the gap well, according to the testimony of some of his illustrious students. "He was the greatest teacher that I ever encountered," was Edward Channing's tribute. His use of the seminar method in teaching, following the German model, was of great value in stimulating productive research, but he was not satisfied with his work and left after seven years at Harvard. Long after, he wrote to Dr. Jameson about his teaching: "I became over-poweringly conscious that any further pretence on my part of acting as instructor would be something worse than humbug, unless I could clear my mind in regard to what I wanted to teach. As History stands, it is a sort of Chinese Play without end and without lesson." [2] In retrospect these pedagogical years "seemed to him lost," but at the time of "baking" his batch of doctors of philosophy in 1876, Adams saw the world and himself in a rosier light.[3] In his last year at Harvard, Adams gave a course in the history of the United States 1789-1840, from which it is believed came his later writings on this period. Many years after, Lindsay Swift, an Adams student, recalled that his teacher

[1] *Letters of Henry Adams, 1858-1891,* September 29, 1870.
[2] November 17, 1896; quoted in R. F. Nichols, "The Dynamic Interpretation of History," *New England Quarterly* (June, 1935).
[3] *Letters,* June 30, 1876.

would assign students to debate on various selected subjects, asking the sons of Federalist ancestors to exchange
sides with sons of Republican ancestors. "To this day,"
said Swift, "I do not know which side Henry Adams favored—Federalist or Republican." [4]

As an Adams he came by his interest in the early national history of the United States quite naturally, and in
1877 he brought out the *Documents Relating to New England Federalism 1800-1815*. In 1879 he published a biography of Albert Gallatin and in three additional volumes
edited his papers. This *Life,* not yet superseded, was a
happy augury for more important work to come. Less beneficial to Adams's reputation was the biography of John
Randolph, a bitter enemy of his grandfather, John Quincy,
whose prejudice was inherited by the grandson. "I am
bored to death," wrote Adams to John Hay, "by correcting the proofs of a very dull book about John Randolph, the fault of which is in the enforced obligation to
take that lunatic monkey *au sérieux.*" [5]

After "ten or a dozen years to Jefferson and Madison," says Adams in the *Education,* he brought out between 1889 and 1891 his nine volumes covering their administrations. He had been gathering materials for the
work in America and in Europe during the 1870's and in
May, 1880, he wrote to Henry Cabot Lodge, a former
student: "I foresee a good history if I have health and
leisure the next five years, and if nothing happens to my
collections of material. My belief is that I can make something permanent out of it, but, as time passes, I get into a
habit of working only for the work's sake and disliking
the idea of completing and publishing." He planned at
first six volumes for the sixteen years. "If it proves a
dull story, I will condense, but it's wildly interesting, at
least to me—which is not quite the same thing as interest-

[4] Mass. Hist. Soc. *Proc.,* V, 69.
[5] *Letters,* September 3, 1882.

ing the public." [6] Adams lost interest in the history after his wife died in 1885, but by 1888 he was able to write with some relief to a friend, "Midsummer has come, the straw-berries and roses have dropped and faded, my last half-dozen chapters are begun. . . ." [7]

Historical scholars immediately recognized this work as one of the most significant that America had produced. Volumes I and II cover approximately Jefferson's first administration, and the opening chapters on American society in 1800 are of unusual interest. After two chapters on "Physical and Economical Conditions" and "Popular Characteristics" Adams describes the intellectual life of various sections of the country, and concludes with a chapter on "American Ideals"; he then begins his political narrative with Jefferson's inauguration.

The presentation of the materials of social history has never been done more interestingly than in these first six chapters. "Among the numerous difficulties with which the Union was to struggle," writes Adams, "and which were to form the interest of American history, the disproportion between the physical obstacles and the material means for overcoming them was one of the most striking." Native writers who were acutely observant, Adams notes, stated that "the American mind, except in politics, seemed . . . in a condition of unnatural sluggishness." The Congregational clergy, though yet respected, "had ceased to be leaders of thought," he writes. In a novel, *Democracy*, which he had written a few years earlier, Adams indicated a rather tenuous belief in that form of government. In his *History* his conviction on this subject has grown weaker rather than stronger. He suggests, however, that "the future direction of the New England intellect seemed already suggested by the im-

[6] *Letters*, May 13, July 9, 1880.
[7] July 15.

possibility of going further in the line of President
Dwight and Fisher Ames," who were extremely conservative. Adams thinks that "innovation was the most useful purpose which New York could serve in human interests, and never was a city better fitted for its work."
Society in New York, "in spite of its aristocratic mixture, was democratic by instinct." Pennsylvania appears
to be "the model democratic society of the world."

The words with which Adams portrays Jefferson
describe the historian as well: the Virginian's "true delight was in an intellectual life of science and art," and
"he shrank from whatever was rough and coarse."
Adams preferred Jefferson to Hamilton: "I dislike Hamilton because I always feel the adventurer in him," he
once wrote to Lodge.[8] Looking at the country as a whole,
Adams thought that "American society might be both
sober and sad, but except for negro slavery it was sound
and healthy in every part"; "the American stood in the
world a new order of man." No one has written better
than Adams on "American Ideals," and in that chapter
he posed questions which democracy has not yet answered. In winged prose Adams re-created the dream of
every American to fashion humanity anew. When he was
composing his manuscript, Adams said he did not intend
to give "interest to the society of America in itself, but
to try for it by way of contrast with the artificial society
of Europe, as one might contrast a stripped prize fighter
with a life-guardsman in helmet and breast-plate, jack-
boots and a big black horse."[9]

Very skillfully Adams assembles the important personages at Jefferson's inauguration, and then he goes on
to discuss the organization of the new government. In a
short time, says the historian, "the energy of reform was
exhausted . . . and . . . complications of a new and un-

[8] *Letters,* May 15, 1876.
[9] *Letters,* May 21, 1881.

expected kind began, which henceforward caused the chief interest of politics to centre in foreign affairs." Thereafter to the end of his first volume and on into the second, Adams winds his way over the tortuous path of American, Spanish, and French diplomacy. "Between the Americans and the Spaniards no permanent friendship could exist," Adams writes. "Their systems were at war, even when the nations were at peace"; the Americans "were persistent aggressors." Many of these pages seem to belong more to the history of Europe than they do to that of the United States, but Adams undoubtedly felt they were necessary for the background of his narrative. "The essence and genius of Jefferson's statesmanship lay in peace," and the tenacity of his hold on this idea is the clue "to whatever seemed inconsistent, feeble, or deceptive in his administration." The failure of Napoleon to crush the Negro revolt in Haiti forced him to give up plans of a colonial empire in America and led him to sell Louisiana to the United States. Adams lingers delightedly over the theatricals with which Napoleon invested the sale of the territory. The constitutional difficulties into which the purchase of Louisiana plunged the Jeffersonian Republicans seem to amuse Adams, but he feels sorry for Jefferson. Privately, he thought Jefferson "a character of comedy." [10] With incisive strokes Adams reaches the heart of the debate over Louisiana, whose acquisition "profoundly altered the relations of the States and the character of their nationality."

The historian remarks that Jefferson's "extraordinary success" in foreign affairs in 1803 was paralleled in domestic affairs. The web of the conspiracy of Massachusetts Federalists to detach New England from the Union is disentangled by his critical analysis. Quickly disposing of problems of internal politics, Adams again

[10] *Letters,* to John Hay, September 3, 1882.

turns to diplomatic questions, which take up nearly the entire second half of volume two. "Jefferson's overmastering passion," we are told, "was to obtain West Florida." In fact Adams goes further and places Monroe and Madison among those who could not "resist the impulse to seize it." Difficulties with England soon overshadowed the negotiations for Florida. "To the world at large nothing in the relations of the United States with England, France, or Spain seemed alarming," thinks Adams. "The world knew little of what was taking place." With the will to know that always characterized him, Adams found out what was going on behind the scenes, but the drama played out before the reader has much of the rarefied air of the drawing room. The millions of lives affected by this diplomacy do not appear on the stage, even in the role of extras.

In the opening chapter of his third volume Adams briefly considers some of the achievements in internal improvement. Here, too, the historian follows his bent in the dissection of ideas. This son of the Adams family generously writes that Jefferson, beginning his second term, "might reasonably ask what name recorded in history would stand higher than his own for qualities of the noblest order in statesmanship." Returning to the field of diplomacy, Adams remarks that the national government during Jefferson's and Madison's administrations "was in the main controlled by ideas and interests peculiar to the region south of the Potomac, and only to be understood from a Southern stand-point. Especially its foreign relations were guided by motives in which the Northern people felt little sympathy."

It is characteristic that in writing on domestic affairs in 1806 Adams should give most of his space to the internal reaction to questions of foreign relationships. It is especially interesting to observe the historian's emphasis on American concern with international affairs in spite of his own remark that the ''United States moved steadily toward their separate objects, caring little for any politics except their own.'' Nowhere does Adams more clearly reveal the gulf that separates him from many contemporary historians than when he writes: ''Every day a million men went to their work, every evening they came home with some work accomplished; but the result was matter for a census rather than for history.'' Historians of today are inclined to think that the life and work of a people are as much the proper subjects of historical discourse as are minute details of diplomacy. A third of Volume III follows the tangled skein of Burr's conspiracy to set up an independent state in the West.

With Volume IV Adams is fully launched on the troubled sea of Anglo-American relations. Beginning with the incidents of the ''Chesapeake'' and the ''Leopard,'' the historian measures the rising tide of resentment in each country toward the other, discusses the imposition and eventual failure of the embargo, and closes with the retirement of Jefferson. A clue to the policy of the administration toward the navy may be found in the fact that the President ''did not love the deck of a man-of-war or enjoy the sound of a boatswain's whistle; the ocean was not his element.'' As a result of the attack on the ''Chesapeake,'' says Adams, ''for the first time in their history the people of the United States learned, in June, 1807, the feeling of a true national emotion.''

Adams, who clung to the original meaning of the word history, ''inquiry,'' restlessly sought to know the psychology of nations. England expected her opponents to fight, and if they would not ''she took them to be cowardly or mean.'' The American administration, he says, ''had shown over and over again that no provocation would make [it] fight; and from the moment that this attitude was understood, America became fair prey.''

Mingled with English contempt, however, was a "vague alarm" aroused by American threats to British commercial and naval supremacy. One effect of the events of these months, says Adams, was to make the Federalists a "British faction in secret league with George Canning." Jefferson preferred the embargo to war, with its dangerous influence on government, but, notes Adams, "personal liberties and rights of property were more directly curtailed in the United States by embargo than in Great Britain by centuries of almost continuous foreign war." The chapter on "The Cost of Embargo" is a splendid example of Adams's philosophic approach to history.

In Volumes V and VI Adams carries the reader at a rapid pace through the further ramifications of American diplomacy with England and France, finally leading up to the War of 1812. John Hay, who was his closest friend (but not his severest critic), wrote that these volumes "take the cake. There is a gathering strength and interest in these later volumes that is nothing short of exciting. The style is perfect, if perfect is a proper word applied to anything so vivid, so flexible and so powerful." The opening pages of the fifth volume touch briefly on the economic significance of the embargo and nonimportation acts: "American manufactures owed more to Jefferson and Virginians, who disliked them, than to Northern statesmen, who merely encouraged them after they were established." The shifting status of Anglo-American relations was thus summed up: "As Canning frowned or smiled, faction rose to frenzy or lay down to slumber throughout the United States." Canning, the English minister, is the evil genius throughout these protracted maneuvers; the harm he did was "more than three generations could wholly repair."

Turning back to the domestic scene, Adams takes note of Henry Clay's maiden speech as a Senatorial "war hawk." He observes that it "marked the appearance of a school which was for fifty years to express the national ideals of statesmanship"; thereafter "the Union and the Fathers were rarely omitted from any popular harangue." The historian, descendant of diplomats, moved with easy grace in Congressional halls, Napoleon's court, and the council rooms of the English Parliament. He well understood how impulses originating in one place were communicated to the others, and he carefully measured these forces.

Returning for a brief moment to the American Atlantic seaboard to assess the results of the census of 1810, the author remarks that "the tendency toward city life, if not yet unduly great, was worth noticing, especially because it was confined to the seaboard States of the North." Politically the government of the United States had reached by March 4, 1811, "the lowest point of its long decline" that began with Jefferson's second administration. In foreign affairs, however, Madison acted with more vigor than he did in handling domestic problems. The successful diplomacy of John Quincy Adams at the court of the Russian Tsar, in securing American trading rights over the objections of Napoleon, reflected favorably on Madison's administration.

There is an Olympian viewpoint in Adams's writing which puts to shame the scribbling of lesser historical gods. Here is his overture to 1812: "As in the year 1754 a petty fight between two French and English scouting parties on the banks of the Youghiogheny River, far in the American wilderness, began a war that changed the balance of the world, so in 1811 an encounter in the Indian country, on the banks of the Wabash, began a fresh convulsion which ended only with the fall of Napoleon. The battle of Tippecanoe was a premature outbreak of the great wars of 1812." The young Republicans, says Adams, "were bent on war with England, they were will-

ing to face debt and probably bankruptcy on the chance
of creating a nation, of conquering Canada, and carrying the American flag to Mobile and Key West." This
New England historian, reflecting his region's hostility
toward the war, writes critically of it, saying that probably four-fifths of the American people thought it could
have been avoided. Madison's first term ended with "the
country more than ever distracted, and as little able to
negotiate as to conquer."

In the latter half of Volume VI and on through the
following volumes, including the first chapters of the
ninth, Adams follows the trail of war on land and sea;
the parliamentary and diplomatic battles that accompanied the martial events hover in the background of his
pages. Napoleon, whose enigmatic character strongly attracted the author, plays almost as important a part in
Adams's interpretation of American history as does the
President. The historian, at home on the sea, describes
with keen delight American naval successes, which he
attributes to the superiority of American naval architecture. Adams suggests also that the privateers which
inflicted great damage on English commerce "contributed more than the regular navy to bring about a disposition for peace in the British classes most responsible
for the war." "The quasi-blockade of the British coasts"
that they maintained in 1813 "became a real and serious
blockade in 1814" and even the "Thames itself seemed
hardly safe." The incompetence of the American military
strategy, except in a few instances, filled Adams with
disgust.

In New England opposition to the war was increasing. At the beginning of 1814, Adams estimated that
"nearly one half of the five New England states supported the war, but were paralyzed by the other half,
which opposed it." The national government itself was
approaching exhaustion because of the lack of money and

men to carry on the war. The Massachusetts Federalists now felt that they could stop the war. In his treatment of the Hartford Convention, Adams was moderately critical, but he took pains to show the contributions of Massachusetts to the war in a light more favorable than most writers were accustomed to do. In England also it appears that "the war had lost public favor." The treaty finally reached actually left all the points in dispute "to be settled by time, the final negotiator, whose decision they [the Americans] could safely trust."

More than a half of the last volume is a characterization of American society at about 1815, a treatment similar to the first chapters in Volume I. "The long, exciting and splendid panorama of revolution and war, which for twenty-five years absorbed the world's attention and dwarfed all other interests, vanished more quickly in America than in Europe, and left fewer elements of disturbance." Prosperity in America "put an end to faction," but New England did not share very much in this wealth. In fact the end of the war brought distress to Massachusetts, whose influence in politics suffered a sharp decline, whereas the South and West gained rapidly in economic and political importance. The Americans of 1815 were far less interested in the Rights of Man, which had troubled them in 1801, than they were in the price of cotton. "Every one felt that real distinctions of party no longer existed," writes Adams. In 1800 there was indifference to internal improvements; sixteen years later people everywhere were actively interested in these projects. Although population was doubling within twenty-three years, wealth was doubling within twenty. Americans "with almost the certainty of a mathematical formula, knowing the rate of increase of population and of wealth . . . could read in advance their economical history for at least a hundred years."

"The movement of thought, more interesting than

the movement of population or of wealth," writes Adams characteristically, "was equally well defined." In religion, excitement tending to emotionalism was clearly in evidence, except in New England, where "the old intellectual pre-eminence . . . developed a quality both new and distinctive" in Unitarianism. Although in religion society tended to develop more divisions, in politics public opinion slowly moved in a fixed direction of emphasis on national sovereignty. Harvard College was at this time stimulating intellectual activity in many directions; "the American mind, as far as it went, showed both freshness and originality." The Americans, thinks Adams, "had as a people little instinct of beauty; but their intelligence in its higher as in its lower forms was both quick and refined." The historian finds that by 1817 "the difference between Europe and America was decided," and in his political character, the American "was a new variety of man." Adams, along with McMaster and Turner, noted that "the South and West gave to society a character more aggressively American than had been known before." Although "the traits of American character were fixed" as was the rate of population growth, Adams observed that the concern of history thereafter was "to know what kind of people these millions were to be." For an answer he thought that "history required another century of experience."

One of the reasons that prompted Adams to write American history was his desire to establish history as an exact science, and he thought that the development of America furnished the best data for such a theory. Like others of his generation he felt the pervasive influence of Darwin and the noted geologist Sir Charles Lyell. "By rights, he [Adams] should have been a Marxist," he tells us in the *Education,* "but some narrow trait of the New England nature seemed to blight socialism, and he tried in vain to make himself a convert. He did the next best thing, he became a Comteist within the limits of evolution.'' Throughout his volumes Adams uses the terminology of the physicist, and often with marked effect. Edward Channing, a vigorous critic, termed the work of Adams a ''masterpiece,'' and paid it the tribute of abandoning his own plans to write on Jefferson's first administration when he saw some advance sheets of the *History*.

All students praise the handling of diplomatic questions by Adams, who had a good knowledge of domestic and foreign manuscript materials. It is almost equally true, however, that many students have found fault with his treatment of internal affairs, which generally ignored the West and showed only a slight perception of the economic motivation in politics. In fact, large stretches of the *History* are but a series of political episodes placed in executive chambers or in legislative halls in Europe and America. In his almost exclusive devotion to Congressional proceedings as an expression of American politics, Adams is a contemporary of Schouler, but he is infinitely superior to the latter in his skill of composition and analysis. Like a dart of lightning Adams's keen analysis illumines dark corners and often leaves in its wake blasted reputations.

The historian was at his best in treating individuals, but, like most of the Adams family, he was uneasy and unsympathetic in handling masses. ''Democracies in history,'' he once wrote, ''always suffered from the necessity of uniting with much of the purest and best in human nature a mass of ignorance and brutality lying at the bottom of all societies.'' The peace of his aristocratic soul was troubled by the disquieting symptoms he observed in American life. Adams at one time wrote to his brother, Charles Francis, Jr., that he was preparing an article on political ''rings'': ''I am going to make it monumental, a piece of history and a blow at democracy." [11] Adams was no Whitman to draw a turbulent democracy to his breast. The later volumes, it may be noted, are more critical than the earlier ones. "They were written . . . in a very different frame of mind from that in which the work was begun," Adams admitted. The history, as a whole, he said, "belongs to the *me* of 1870; a strangely different being from the *me* of 1890." [12]

Twenty years before the publication of his history Adams had adopted the seminar method in his teaching. The generalizations that he freely scattered about in his volumes have also been the seeds from which more books have grown. In his *Education* he wrote that he had "published a dozen volumes of American history . . . to satisfy himself whether, by the severest process of stating, with the least possible comment, such facts as seemed sure, in such order as seemed rigorously consequent, he could fix for a familiar moment a necessary sequence of human movement"; but he complains he "had toiled in vain." The historian of today, who also knows how difficult it is to follow clues through chaos, can sympathize with Adams, but he is nevertheless thankful that the dozen volumes were written, for they mark one of the highest achievements in American historiography.

[11] *Letters,* January 27, 1869.
[12] *Ibid.,* January 2, February 6, 1891.

XI

THE NATIONALIST SCHOOL

The generation that grew up in the period after the Civil War read the stories of its conflicts in voluminous tomes and in lengthy serials published in magazines and newspapers. The historian looking for a fit theme for his pen turned away from the fields of colonial history, already fully harvested he thought, and eagerly seized upon the middle period. Some went back to the Revolution for a running start, but James Ford Rhodes began with the year 1850. A Southerner had prophesied that to the South's overflowing cup would be added the bitter taste of having the history of the war written by Northerners; the publications, for many years after, verified his prediction. Not until very recently has that irrepressible conflict been viewed with other eyes, and only in our day has the prophecy—that fifty years would elapse before the true history of the war would be written— been fulfilled.

Although many of the historians who wrote on this period were trained in the use of documents and the weighing of evidence, they did not feel their task completed with the mere statement of facts. They donned the judicial robe also, and despite prior professions of impartiality, they passed sentence, with varying degrees of moderation, upon the offending South. These prosecuting historians, worshiping that new deity, the national state, and believing in the essential immorality of slaveholding, indicted the South on two counts—as the assailant of nationality and as the defender of a decadent civilization. The marriage of the States had apparently been made in heaven and that dark Satan, the slavocracy, was the evil spirit that spread discord. For the most part the narratives they wrote are of conflicting constitutional interpretations—the mingled shouts of the slavery and antislavery forces and the murmurs of the compromisers seeking to stave off the armed struggle. Infrequently did these historians turn to the population outside the legislative halls or behind the battle lines—that population which was to receive its due meed of attention when McMaster, a younger contemporary of Von Holst, Schouler, and Rhodes, began to publish his history.

The deification of the national state was closely related to the glorification of the role of Anglo-Saxon peoples in furthering political progress. Darwinism apparently sanctioned the spread of Anglo-Saxon civilization because it had seemed the fittest to survive, and it was to the advantage of other peoples to pattern themselves after this dominant group—or else succumb in the inevitable struggle between them.

Before Darwin and Spencer supplied scientific terminology to the literary world, American historians had already preached the superiority of certain groups. In the eyes of Bancroft, Parkman, and Motley, liberty, political and religious, and the orderly progress of modern civilization were largely due to the efforts of Anglo-Saxon Protestants. Other peoples, it was argued, were obviously of inferior stock. The English historian Freeman, whose ideas had so strong a hold on many Americans, expressed himself on this point with characteristic positiveness. America would be a grand land, he said, "if only every Irishman would kill a negro, and be hanged for it."[1] John Fiske, an ardent disciple of Darwin, Spencer and Freeman, was convinced that American Anglo-Saxons had evolved the most suitable practice of political organization—Federalism. Burgess, too, was a strong believer in the racial superiority of Anglo-Saxons and in their surpassing political wisdom. In his work, *Political Science and Comparative Constitutional Law*[2] Burgess asserts that the Teutonic peoples, because of their pre-eminence in building national states, must "assume the leadership in the establishment and administration of states"—not only over backward, i.e., barbaric peoples, but also over any people politically incompetent. With less emphasis Von Holst and McMaster held the same ideas. Their histories gave coherence to the sentiment of nationalism, and in the books of Burgess and Alfred T. Mahan writers found an arsenal whose weapons, though literary, prepared the way in the 1890's for the real instruments of war.[3]

HERMANN VON HOLST

Hermann Von Holst, whose history of the United States belongs to the intensely patriotic period that marked the coming of age of American nationalism, was born in 1841, in Livonia, a Baltic province of Russia inhabited by many Germans. As a young man he went to the university at Heidelberg, where he took his Ph.D. in 1865. Hostile to the Russian regime, he sought the freedom of America in 1867. Although his first months

---

[1] *The Life and Letters of Edward A. Freeman* (N. Y., 1895), II, 242.
[2] 2 vols., 1890.
[3] Cf. J. W. Pratt, "The Ideology of American Expansion," in *Essays in Honor of William E. Dodd* (Chicago, 1935).

brought the bitter experiences common to all penniless immigrants, he soon gained a measure of financial security by tutoring and by writing for various periodicals. He projected a work on the evils of absolutism and participated actively in Republican politics in New York. He had not been in America very long when his friends, the noted Professor Heinrich Von Sybel and the well-known student of American life, Friedrich Kapp, commended Von Holst to some Bremen merchants who commissioned him to write informative essays on the United States. From the small beginning of some newspaper and magazine articles that Von Holst wrote later grew the *Constitutional and Political History of the United States.*[4]

In Germany his writings drew attention to him as an authority on America, and in 1872 he became a professor at the new University of Strassburg, lecturing on American history and constitutional law. The first volume of his history was published in Germany in 1873 and brought him the professorship of modern history at Freiburg the next year. Four years later, and subsequently again, Von Holst made short trips to America to gather additional historical material and to lecture at several universities. For a few years he was also a member of the Baden legislature. He finally took up permanent residence in America, and from 1892 until his death in 1904, Von Holst served as head of the department of history at the University of Chicago. He gave up his teaching, however, five years before his death. The history he wrote was used for some time as a textbook, but the English translation did not always accurately reflect the original German. In addition to his history, Von Holst wrote biographies of Calhoun, for whom he had great respect, and of John Brown. In 1885 he published his *Constitutional Law of the United States.* One

[4] 7 vols. and index vol. (Chicago, 1876-1892).

who knew him well said that he "valued history chiefly
for its practical bearing on current problems," and that
a "stern morality" guided his judgments on the past and
the present. Von Holst was no believer in the virtues of
that "objective history" so much talked of and written
about in his day. He held it a distinct right of the historian to measure events and men according to his own
political and moral beliefs.

With the confidence that most authors have in
their own impartiality, Von Holst wrote in his preface:
"I venture to assert that among all the works covering
about as large a ground as mine, there is not one to be
found which has been written with as much soberness of
mind." On the other hand Von Holst stated that all his
sources were printed works, and hence "no new facts
are to be found in the work, and I even cannot claim that
new views of importance have presented themselves to
my mind." He was perhaps unduly modest in this statement, and possibly deserved the encomium of his American translator, who said that his was "the most important work on the internal history of the United States
that has emanated from the European press." Von Holst
felt that he had an advantage over American historians
because of his foreign birth, but for the Frenchman, de
Tocqueville, he had small respect, considering him a
"doctrinarian."

A brief section of Von Holst's *Constitutional and
Political History of the United States* covers the years
under the Confederation, written from his nationalist
standpoint. The objections of the "particularists" to
Federalism are thus dismissed: "Their arguments bor-
dered on the extremest absurdity and their assumptions
might have excited the loudest merriment, were it not
that the question was one of life or death to the nation."
In his earliest pages the historian, who proclaimed his
sobriety of mind, indicates the strength of his feeling on

the "slavocracy," which warped most of his work, when he refers to the "evil consciences" of proslavery advocates. The thesis upon which most of his book rests is here stated: slavery was "the rock on which the Union was broken to pieces." On the themes of slavery, and national sovereignty versus state rights, Von Holst constructed his work: "The slave holding interest knit mesh after mesh in the net in which it sought to entangle the Union, but men did not or would not see this." [5] Von Holst, who was a contemporary of Bismarck and thoroughly imbued with the nationalistic spirit, was, of course, a partisan of Hamilton. Jefferson, on the other hand, "was always ready to sacrifice much of his favorite theories to his feverish thirst for power and distinction." The usually staunch upholder of nationality is very lenient in his judgment of the Hartford Convention of 1814.

A discussion of "The Economic Contrast between the Free and Slave States" (later drawn upon by McMaster) gives a doleful picture of Southern life. "Everything was considered in reference to the 'peculiar institution,' " says Von Holst, "and therefore hostile distrust of everything was felt, because this institution was in ever sharper contradiction with the spirit of the age." The different industrial systems in North and South drove them farther and farther apart. In a long discussion of the nullification movement of 1832 which closes the volume, Von Holst, quoting Bismarck, writes: "Conquered and conquerors brought down punishment upon themselves because they did not understand one thing, or, if they understood it, would not live up to it; 'Sovereignty can only be a unit and it must remain a unit,— the sovereignty of law.' "

The second volume of the translation, *Jackson's Administration—Annexation of Texas*, continues the nar-

[5] P. 324.

rative to 1846 and in greater detail than that in Volume I. Von Holst's characterization of Jackson has found wide acceptance: "Since Louis XIV, the maxim, *l'état, c'est moi*, has scarcely found a second time, so ingenuous and complete an expression as in Andrew Jackson. The only difference is that it was translated from the language of monarchy into the language of republicanism." Although the historian gives considerable space to the panic of 1837, he soon returns to the main interest of his study—slavery and the constitution. His comment on the election of Harrison is typical: "The person who wished to read the future of the country from the numbers of the presidential election of 1840, should not have stopped at the electoral vote and at the numbers which went beyond a million. Weightier than these were the not quite seven thousand votes cast for Birney and Earle, the candidates of the liberty party." In his treatment of the annexation of Texas, Von Holst adopts the view, conventional with antislavery writers, that the expansionist movement was solely the result of Southern desires for more slave territory. With forced imagery, Von Holst writes of the Congressional process of annexation: "The bridal dress in which Calhoun had led the beloved of the slavocracy to the Union was the torn and tattered constitution of the United States."

Around the struggle with Mexico and the Compromise of 1850, Von Holst wove the narrative of the preceding four years. This volume was delayed for a year (July, 1878 to July, 1879), during which the author, aided by a grant from the Prussian Academy of Sciences, gathered additional material in America and traveled through the South and Far West to acquaint himself further with the country.

The caption, "Polk Weaves the Warp of the Mexican War," indicates Von Holst's approach. He suggests the effect of annexation on the growth of abolition sentiment: "The long struggle over annexation had opened many eyes which had hitherto been struck with blindness. The thorn of the political rule of the slave holding interest had been pressed deeper into the flesh of many, and a still greater number, by a louder and clearer condemnation of slavery 'on principle' sought refuge from their own consciences for having allowed or helped the slavocracy again to win a victory." Von Holst thus refers to the Southern domination of American politics: "Questions which had hitherto been hotly debated, were now settled, in accordance with the views of the South, almost without a struggle." In the discussion with England over Oregon, Polk is pictured in an unfavorable light.

Over the writing of Von Holst hangs an air of conspiracy, the tenseness of the modern "thriller." In his reference to the events preceding the war with Mexico, Von Holst says that Congress and the President were "participants in the guilt of the dark work which had been so busily and cunningly carried on in the White House." Ethics and the writing of history are closely allied in the words of Von Holst, who refers to the "bold immorality, with which the leading Democratic politicians . . . devised and carried to its conclusion the whole affair of the war." The narrative inevitably leads up to the remark that Polk "purposely brought on the war," but the author adds, too, that Congress was in accord "with his crooked policy."

In view of his whole approach, it is amusing to find Von Holst defending "manifest destiny" and writing that "history cannot decide . . . questions by the code of private morals." This son of a Bismarckian generation could write bluntly of an established law of historic growth—that "decayed or decaying peoples must give way when they clash in a conflict of interests with peoples who are still on the ascending path of their historic mission, and that violence must often be the judge to decide such litigation between nations." [6]

The last pages of Volume III compare the North and South economically, and Von Holst finds the latter at a great disadvantage. He says that intellectual life in the North was also superior to that in the South. He regards as most significant, not the fact that in every respect the South was behind the North, "but that the forces which had caused it to remain so far in the rear still continue to operate, and that it would therefore necessarily fall still further behind." Von Holst is always the strong protagonist of urban capitalism and to the end of his life believed in a thoroughgoing laissez-faire doctrine. He looked upon the proletariat of great cities as a necessary evil. Here and there in his work there are glimpses of an economic interpretation of history, but, in general, morality rather than economics is his key to an understanding of the past.

The six years that followed the Compromise of 1850 (treated in one volume in the German edition, and in two in the American translation), the historian declares "are the most important in the development of the irrepressible conflict between the North and the South." Politicians, he finds, were powerless in these years, "in the presence of the progressive and sternly logical development of actual circumstances." Thus does American history move on toward the inevitable tragedy with the precision of Greek drama.

In a long-drawn-out discussion Von Holst notes how deeply the disputes over the Compromise of 1850 had affected public sentiment nearly everywhere. As for the election of 1852, he concludes that Pierce won because "the great majority of the people had become possessed

[6] Later in the 1890's Von Holst opposed American expansionist tendencies; Eric F. Goldman, "Hermann E. Von Holst," *Miss. Valley Hist. Rev.* (March, 1937), p. 515.

by the quietistic conservative spirit, and did not wish their repose to be disturbed by any further contention as to the price paid for it." Modern students have seriously modified the statement that "the disruption of the Whig party on account of the slavery question was the beginning of a new formation of parties on the basis of the slavery question and this formation was the beginning of the end of *this* Union." Douglas with his "moral hollowness" is the villain in the drama of the Kansas-Nebraska bill, whose fourteenth section, Von Holst decides, was "from the first word to the last, constitutionally and politically, a fraud" whose "ultimate consequences . . . brought the Union and slavery simultaneously face to face with the question of existence, in such a way that the conflict of interests and principles could no longer find its final settlement in words, but was forced to seek it in deeds."

The fifth volume of the American edition covers the two years to Buchanan's election. The expansionist sentiment of this period was due, writes Von Holst, to the slavocracy. Although unable to secure Cuba, "the progressive fraction of the slavocracy which grew from year to year in weight and numbers, awaited only a new opportunity to take up the frustrated annexation project again, and they were resolved to create the opportunity if it did not offer of itself." In a long section on the growing opposition to immigration and Catholicism by the Know-Nothing party, Von Holst, although unsympathetic to the Catholics, points out the danger of Know-Nothingism to American institutions. He drew a distinction between Anglo-Saxon immigrants—in particular, the Germans, who surpassed all others—and the Irish, who belonged "to the lowest stage of culture." He notes, too, that nativism, as typified by the Know-Nothing movement, was an attempt to divert attention from the slavery question.

Von Holst describes the history of these years in phrases suggestive of military tactics. The South under all circumstances during this period was "certain that none of the positions it had won could be wrested from it, for no hostile resolution of the house of representatives would receive the assent of the senate or the sanction of the president." But the South, in order to be victorious, needed to be on the offensive and show a confidence in victory, "and assurance of victory was best manifested by its coming forward with new and bold demands." The Kansas troubles were all due to the slavocracy, which "in the name of law and order, and behind the protecting shield of the president . . . carried on with blood and iron, in the territorial domain of the Union" the propagation of slavery. The lurid glow of Von Holst's partisan prose is a vivid reflection of "Bleeding Kansas."

Buchanan's election, it was written, had been bought by a more binding pledge to the slavocracy, and, adds Von Holst, the "declaration of the Republicans that the era of compromises was forever closed, was answered from the South by the declaration that the time when the continuance of the slave states in the Union could be purchased by concessions, was forever past."

The three years to 1859 bring Von Holst up to his concluding volume. After a comparatively brief treatment of the Dred Scott Decision, which, in the historian's view, was "the greatest political atrocity of which a court had ever been guilty," and following the author's debate with Taney, the narrative moves on to a chapter on the Lecompton Convention. The scorching words with which Von Holst indignantly castigates the slavocracy in Kansas have lost none of their burning quality since they were written. Through these pages Kansas stalks like Banquo's ghost. The historian hears the voices of the unlaid ghosts of free-soilers threatening the slavocracy with an early grave. When Von Holst came to write of the "irrepressible conflict," "Lincoln loomed up higher and firmer, while . . . fragments of Douglas's armor strewed the ground."

In one of his infrequent departures from Congressional history, Von Holst takes stock of the country's economic position in 1857, and he uses a good part of his space to reflect on the low standard of morality in railroad finance in that decade. The Mormons are considered almost exclusively in their relation to the national government. The volume concludes on the mournful note that the "funeral bells of the democratic party were tolling" when the Thirty-fifth Congress ended, "and hence the history of the Thirty-sixth Congress could not but become the knell of the Union."

Before his history goes on to toll the knell of the parting Union, Von Holst prefaces his seventh and final volume with a tribute to the famous historian Von Sybel, who had provided the original impulse to the *Constitutional and Political History of the United States*. Writing in 1892, Von Holst considered as the valuable fruits of his labors of twenty-three years, not only the "rich recognition" that his work had met, but also the "abundant and violent opposition it encountered."

From the two crowded years beginning with the events at Harpers Ferry and running to Lincoln's inauguration, the historian picked his materials for this last volume. The prose swings into poetic rhythm as it touches on the man John Brown, with his "homely realism" and "great, ideal loftiness of soul." The reader is taken through the many details of the political conventions of the presidential year, which put "four parties in the field; one with a national, single-faced head; two double-faced ones with the same name, and one with no face at all." Buchanan, who did not have "the moral courage to do his duty" in suppressing the insurrection, is the object of Von Holst's severe criticism; and his policy of noncoercion is thoroughly ridiculed. "His dread of assuming any responsibility," says the historian, "was as great as his delusion with regard to his own infallibility." With the failure to preserve the already broken Union by compromise measures, its restoration, concludes Von Holst in his characteristic language, "could be effected only by blood and iron." With Lincoln's inauguration "the restoration of a Union incomparably stronger, more majestic and richer in promise for the future, was beyond a question, for the cornerstones of the new foundation were to be the burial mounds of the three dark powers which unbound the furies of civil war: the doctrine of non-coercion, the slavocratic interpretation of state sovereignty, and slavery."

This professor, German even during his American university years, glowering at his class, "always striking hard, always striving to emphasize the great things," performed a pioneer task and stimulated much research. If it might be said of McMaster that he discovered the value of the newspaper as a historical source, with equal truth it might be said of Von Holst that he was among the first to appreciate the significance of the records of Congressional debates, although he, too, made good use of newspapers. The reader soon discovers, however, that Von Holst's work is really only a history of the slavery contest, with but few references to other phases of American life. The mass of materials that he collected was designed to show that slavery was the principal question before the American people after 1830. Even before he reached his last volume, Von Holst's work had begun to lose its hold on the more critical generation of American historians. His obvious antislavery bias can do no harm to the present-day reader, who has learned his history from other and more temperate sources. It

is possible that the pain which racked the body of Von
Holst for so many years made it difficult for the professor to write dispassionately.[7] The decades since Von
Holst wrote have added dust to his unused volumes so
that today they seem to have become objects of archaeo-
logical excavation rather than tools of historical research.[8]

JAMES SCHOULER

In the years that marked the growing maturity of
American historiography James Schouler's *History of
the United States under the Constitution* began to appear. "To write without fear or favor," he said in 1880,
"has long been my cherished wish." "For more than
fifteen years past I have, as a diversion from graver
professional tasks, pursued special studies for that period which ends with the War of 1812." Schouler's reason for writing his history was that no comprehensive
narrative existed "from which one may safely gather
the later record of our country's career," with the partial exception of Hildreth's work, for which he has high
praise. Although testifying to Hildreth's general accuracy, Schouler differed from him "in many particulars,
and most widely as to estimates of our political leaders
and their motives." Schouler, a Harvard graduate and
the author of legal texts, became interested in constitutional history about 1864. He says that he wanted to
begin where Bancroft "had seemingly laid down his pen"
and to "supply the connecting link between the American
Revolution and the Civil War." It was his distinction
to be the first historian to bridge the gap from the beginnings of the nation to the end of Reconstruction by
a continuous narrative. Schouler was also the author of

---

[7] See A. B. Hart in *Pol. Sci. Quart.* (1890) on Von Holst.

[8] A good essay on Von Holst is to be found in the *Miss. Valley Hist.
Rev.* (March, 1937), by Eric F. Goldman; there is also one in *The Nation*
(January 28, 1904).

biographies of Jefferson and Hamilton and of a useful study on *Americans of 1776*.[9]

In a strictly chronological arrangement, largely devoted to political events, Schouler begins his work with some introductory remarks on the States under the Articles of Confederation, and concludes his first volume with the passing of John Adams's administration. The Constitutional Convention was, says Schouler, "the protest of liberty protected by law against liberty independent of it." The historian halts his narrative at various points to portray the several leaders: Washington's character is described in seven pages of writing that are imitative of a decadent classicism. Schouler is less sympathetic to Hamilton than is Hildreth, and therefore, by the usual rules of American historical writing, he is more friendly to Jefferson.

In many respects Schouler's arrangement seems to be nothing more than an enlargement of the older method of writing historical chronicles as practiced by Prince and Abiel Holmes. History, he once said, "is the record of consecutive events . . . of consecutive public events," and to his mind "the only clear law of history is that of motion incessantly onward."[10] His divisions are based upon the succession of presidential administrations. He introduces, rather clumsily, some pages on Congressional discussions of slavery in 1790 by saying, "The slavery question deserves attention in connection with the angry debates of this session." Schouler's attitude on slavery, which colored his later narrative strongly, is early revealed: "That an institution, both wasteful and unrighteous, should have been suffered by wise statesmen to fasten its poisonous fangs so deeply into the vitals of a republic whose essential foundation was freedom, is one

[9] N. Y., 1906.

[10] Amer. Hist. Assn. *Papers,* "The Spirit of Historical Research" (July, 1890), pp. 98-99.

of those political facts which only the theory of human imperfection can well explain, so inevitable must have been the final catastrophe.'' The treaty negotiated by Jay with England is criticized on the ground that it surrendered too much. ''A Party Tyranny'' is the caption for the years when the Federalists sponsored the Alien and Sedition Acts, but Schouler pays a generous tribute to the character of John Adams, who ''was in closer sympathy with the people than most leaders of the party to which he belonged, and a more genuine American.''

In the note to his second volume, which concludes with Monroe's election and which appeared in 1882, the author wrote that he would continue his history down to the Civil War, and ''deal impartially with men and events.'' Schouler's statement that ''Jefferson proceeded moderately, and by no means maliciously, in the matter of removals from office'' seems just. In discussing the latter part of Jefferson's second administration, Schouler writes: ''Six years of Jefferson had fixed immutably the republican character of these institutions, and vindicated this American experiment as never before.'' A long chapter, ''The United States of America in 1809,'' describes this ''miniature golden age of American history.'' ''The phenomenon of Jefferson's administration,'' writes Schouler, ''was undoubtedly the development of a West,'' whose population in the Mississippi Valley in after years was ''to assert a great, if not the greatest, influence in national affairs.'' These pages broke fresh ground, but plowed neither deeply nor very widely.

With much zest Schouler swings back to his political narrative leading up to the War of 1812. '' 'On to Canada' had been the cry of the war party for years,'' but this is his only reference to what is today considered one of the chief objects of the war. The author finds that ''the disaffection of the New England States is a sad episode of the war for history to contemplate, nor can the impartial historian on that topic hope to escape controversy.'' The military and naval episodes are quickly disposed of. The last five of the seventeen years covered by the volume are assigned less than a quarter of its pages. Schouler was reluctant to use space on proceedings outside of Congress. In Volume III, published in 1885, the author declared that he was constantly aiming ''to furnish in the true sense a history of the people of the United States, their virtues, their errors, and their wonderful development.'' The next fourteen years to 1831 are the subject of the volume. In his discussion of changes in political parties, Schouler reveals no deep understanding of political motivation; for him it is the old drama, perhaps melodrama, of bitter personal rivalries, ''jostling ambitions, intrigues to overthrow one administration and bring in another.'' Bancroft's literary mantle was seized by Schouler, who wore it ungracefully: ''Proud in our annals was the year 1818, when the whole nation felt itself soaring upward in a new atmosphere, exhilarated and bold, like an eagle loosened from confinement.'' The historian asserts that ''the Missouri Compromise must be pronounced a surrender to the slave power'' if ''viewed from the stand-point of a stern morality.'' But he decides that ''this point of view is not just to the honor and statesmanship of the times,'' because the Constitution itself was to blame. Through rose-colored glasses Schouler viewed the end of Monroe's administration, when ''the whole mechanism of society moved in perfect order. The democracy ruled, but it was a democracy in which jealousies found no root, and the abler and more virtuous of the community took the lead.'' Soon, however, ''fiercer passions rule once more the hearts of men.''

Jackson's victory four years later was a triumph ''of popular principles, and in a sense of the military, or at least the mobilizing spirit in politics''; but ''out of all the infamous abuse, scandal, and vilification heaped upon him, Adams emerged pure as refined gold.'' In his last few pages, for which he is in considerable debt to de Tocqueville, Schouler considers some aspects of American social history. Although he writes that ''we are now at the portal of an epoch full of eager progress and the crowding, trampling ranks of humanity,'' to him that humanity remains but an abstraction.

The fourth volume of the history, published in 1889, narrates the events of the years 1831 to 1847. Bancroft, who was in Polk's Cabinet, furnished Schouler with information on national politics. Schouler again states that he had ''endeavored to learn the whole truth as others have not learned it before,'' but adds, somewhat naïvely —as if judgment were always easy—''it is not in my nature to be impartial as between right and wrong, honorable and dishonorable public conduct.''

The discussion of the United States in 1831, with which the historian closed his previous volume, is continued in the fourth: ''The leading feature of American society as a whole,'' he writes, ''was its commonplaceness, the unpicturesque level it afforded.'' The shrewdness of his comments on industrial life is perhaps attributable to his experience in the business world. The West, scarcely mentioned up to this time by general historians, is given a little space in these pages: ''The phenomenon of American development was the growth of the great West.'' New England's influence, however, in fashioning and ruling Northern society was strongest. She ''was a sort of education, a great generator of ideas for American society.'' It should be noted, too, that Schouler was not entirely unsympathetic to Southern society.

Schouler's thoughts on nullification are clothed in language redolent of medieval chivalry: ''These were glorious days for the constitution's allied defenders; the one matchless in debate, the other terrible in action and clad in popular confidence like a coat of mail.'' Schouler's whole treatment of the nullification controversy in the tradition of Von Holst is so warped by a nationalist bias that, today, it appears almost useless to the student. Writing of politics in 1834, he used words that McMaster deemed of sufficient value to include in his own work later: ''Mobs were taking the law into their own hands, and settling local disputes after nature's fashion.'' But the indulgent Schouler added: ''Let us pardon something to the spirit of American liberty, which was now taking a new and freer flight.'' His introduction to a discussion of the annexation of Texas is characteristic. ''A dark chapter opens in our national history,'' and this whole episode is interpreted from the view of Southern desires for more slave territory. Over most of these pages, in fact, Schouler casts the heavy shadow of slavery.

In 1891 Schouler published the volume which he had originally planned as the last, concluding it with the outbreak of the Civil War. From his usual position Schouler surveys the struggle with Mexico: ''The glory of the Mexican War was the glory of the South, like the Texan conquest before it . . . to add largely to the area of slavery by annexations from Mexico was regarded by slaveholders as a necessary means of strengthening their power against Northern encroachments.'' The conventional Whig disapproval of Webster's Seventh of March speech is expressed here: ''He . . . bargained away his moral conviction for the sake of national harmony.''

The military adventures in Central America and Cuba were, to Schouler, ''that cormorant appetite for seizing weak sovereignties,'' a ''misguided policy of robbery and subjugation which seeks to conceal its cruel features under the mask of manifest destiny.'' In the six years before 1861, he says, the American people were mainly absorbed in the slavery controversy. Franklin Pierce is excoriated for being "an abject devotee of the slave holders." John Brown was utterly "irrational," but his treatment revealed the slave master's "innate tyranny and cruelty towards an adversary."

In his closing lines Schouler is more temperate in his remarks about the conflict between North and South. " 'Conspiracy,' 'treason,' were names at first applied, all too narrowly, to those who struggled to break from the Union. 'Rebellion' is a more enduring and appropriate word. . . . We must divest ourselves of the false impression [which he himself does much to convey, however] that the crime of a few Southern leaders produced the real mischief."

After an interval of a few years Schouler returned to his historical narrative and brought out a volume on the Civil War. This sixth volume had the benefit of his own youthful impressions of the events he describes. Although he tries "to do full justice" to the motives of both sections, he admits that, "I have not suppressed my personal convictions as to the real merits of this sanguinary strife, nor amiably shifted the ground of discussion." It was not necessary for Schouler to indicate what his personal convictions were; his earlier volumes had done that sufficiently. At the end of his previous volume he had discountenanced the use of the word "conspiracy" in connection with the war, but he had forgotten this injunction when he wrote, "There was something of a conspiracy, however, in the present Southern movement for breaking up the Union." The larger part of the volume chronicles the military events and political history incidental to the war.

Fourteen years after he had said that he was finished with his historical narrative, Schouler, at the age of seventy-four, picked up his pen again to add a seventh volume on the period of Reconstruction. His main purpose was to vindicate the "much maligned" President Johnson. For the material on Grant's administrations, Schouler says that he had largely depended on the work of Rhodes, although personal reminiscences of life in Washington were also a useful source. It may be pointed out in passing that in his last volumes Schouler drew very heavily upon the work of Rhodes, largely ignoring Dunning's studies in Reconstruction. It is interesting to observe that in the notice given to recent publications designed to rehabilitate Johnson, the early work of Schouler seems to have been generally forgotten. Like Rhodes, Schouler severely condemned the Military Reconstruction Act because it forcibly uprooted "State governments already advanced towards natural conditions of self-rule," and replanted them "on a new political basis utterly impracticable and ruinous."

The first third of the volume scarcely deals with the history of Reconstruction. That subject is usually lost sight of in the defense of Johnson's character and motives. Most of the remainder of the volume treats essentially of Northern politics, and has comparatively little to do with the Southern side of the Reconstruction period. As a partisan of Tilden, Schouler gives considerable space to the election of 1876. "Iniquitous as we must deem that electoral figuring which placed Hayes instead of Tilden in the White House," he concludes, "it was probably better, under all the circumstances, for the peace of the country and the safe re-establishment of all the ex-Confederate States as loyal once more."

Throughout his history Schouler has conventional heroes and villains. Lincoln is one of his greatest heroes; opposed to him is Davis, a "gloomy despot." In an age apparently less susceptible to Carlyle, professional historians, at least, have no regard for such literary fare. Aside from a few references to passing events in other parts of the country, Schouler's history might almost have been written from a spectator's seat in Congress. A stern Scotch morality pervades his writing, and he once pleaded: "Whatever may have been my imperfections as a narrator of events . . . I trust it may be said of me that I have written with a constant purpose to be just and truthful." Unfortunately historical truths are not constant, and Schouler, one of "the terrible just," was in reality less just than some of his contemporaries who had learned to look more dispassionately at American history.[11]

JOHN W. BURGESS

John W. Burgess is more likely to be remembered for his work in founding and building up the School of Political Science at Columbia University and his many years of teaching service, than for his contributions to American history. Burgess came from a family of Tennessee slaveowners who were, however, Whig Unionists. One of his students, William R. Shepherd, wrote that "American nationhood . . . was an inspiration of the boy's childhood, an ideal of his later years." America, Burgess felt, "was a great creative and regenerative force for the welfare of mankind."[12]

After a lengthy service in the Union Army, young Burgess went to Amherst, where he came under the observant eye of Julius H. Seelye. For a short time after his graduation, in 1867, he studied and practiced law in Massachusetts, and, following a brief teaching career at Knox College in Illinois, he left for Germany. Under the patronage of George Bancroft, Burgess studied with Germany's greatest masters of history and public law,

[11] For autobiography, see *Historical Briefs,* "James Schouler" (N. Y., 1896); also see L. E. Ellis, "James Schouler," *Miss. Valley Hist. Rev.,* Vol. XVI.

[12] See Shepherd in *American Masters of Social Science* (N. Y., 1927), ed. H. W. Odum.

Mommsen, Curtius, Von Ranke, Droysen, and Rudolph Von Gneist, the leading student of English law and government. Of these it was Von Gneist who had the most profound influence in directing Burgess's career.[13]

Amherst called Burgess from Germany in 1873 to a newly established professorship of history and political science. In this small but influential New England college he instituted the German seminar, which studied various problems and phases of the constitutional history of Europe and the United States. (These studies were the beginings of the volumes that Burgess wrote on American history.) Less than three years later he was invited to give a course of lectures in the Law School at Columbia College in New York. At this time there was no institution of "university" rank in the United States. In 1876 Burgess went to Columbia to teach constitutional history and international law, beginning an academic association that lasted to his death in 1931. After many tribulations the "Faculty and School of Political Science" was organized in 1880. "Thank God the University is born," cabled a friendly trustee to Burgess, who was then in Paris. From that time, this graduate school has had a great influence on the growth of scholarship.

Although Burgess was the author of a number of studies in political science, his several volumes on nineteenth-century America are more important for the student of historical writing. The publishing house of Charles Scribner's Sons, believing that the time was ripe for a fairer treatment of the struggle between the North and South, turned to Burgess as the man best suited by birth and training for the task,[14] and in a spirit of "sacred duty" to his country he fulfilled the obligation.

In the preface to his volume on *The Middle Period*

[13] J. W. Burgess, *Reminiscences of an American Scholar* (N. Y., 1934), p. 131.
[14] *Reminiscences*, p. 289.

1817-1858 [15] Burgess writes that it is high time that the history of those years "should be undertaken in a thoroughly impartial spirit. The continued misunderstanding between the North and the South is an ever present menace to the welfare of both sections and of the entire nation." The author admits his prejudices against secession and slavery, but attempts to present opposing opinion. He carefully avoided all the histories written immediately after the end of the Civil War, and, like a true son of German scholarship, claims to have used no secondary material. To the present-day student, his remarks on impartial writing sound amusingly irreconcilable with his statement that this history must be written by an American and a Northerner "and from the Northern point of view," because it is, in the main, "the correct view." The stern moralist thus speaks: "The time has come when the men of the South should acknowledge that they were in error in their attempt to destroy the Union and it is unmanly in them not to do so." Although his early environment made him sympathetic to Southern people and their leaders, Burgess writes that "not one scintilla of justification for secession and rebellion must be expected." "I am writing a political history," he says. The main theme in *The Middle Period,* as Burgess sees it, is the struggle between the Northerners, who wished to adapt the government to changing conditions, and the Southerners, who clung to the beliefs of the framers of the Constitution.

The Civil War and the Constitution 1859-1865, [16] appearing in two volumes, is largely a history of military events and of some of the political questions raised by the struggle. He also traces the development of constitutional law towards nationalism during these years. Although Burgess dislikes extremists on both sides, espe-

[15] N. Y., 1897.
[16] N. Y., 1901.

cially John Brown, he continues to maintain that the cause of secession was "constitutionally and morally indefensible." In his chapter on "Secession" he criticizes the constitutional arguments of the secessionists, which were "from every point of view, a mere jugglery with words." From his friend Mrs. Jefferson Davis, and from her husband's papers, Burgess gleaned some valuable information.

In the volume *Reconstruction and the Constitution, 1866-1876* [17] Burgess is largely interested in an examination of the means used to reconstruct the defeated States. "In my preface to 'The Middle Period,'" he says, "I wrote that the re-establishment of a real national brotherhood between the North and South, could be attained only on the basis of a sincere and genuine acknowledgment by the South that secession was an error as well as a failure. I come now to supplement this contention with the proposition that a corresponding acknowledgment on the part of the North in regard to Reconstruction . . . is equally necessary." The author maintains that the purpose of Reconstruction, "to secure the civil rights of the newly emancipated race," was praiseworthy, but that "erroneous means were chosen." The South should have been placed under a territorial civil government "until the white race in those districts should have sufficiently recovered from its temporary disloyalty to the Union to be intrusted again with the powers of . . . government." Insisting that there is a "vast difference in political capacity between races," Burgess believes that it was "the white man's mission, his duty and his right, to hold the reins of political power in his own hands for the civilization of the world and the welfare of mankind." An epilogue to this historical trilogy is a small book, *The Administration of President Hayes*,[18] in which

[17] N. Y., 1902.
[18] N. Y., 1916.

Burgess highly praises the executive for re-establishing "constitutional normality."

Although he was intensely nationalist in his writing, Burgess saw the danger of nationalism in practice. In his volume on *The Reconciliation of Government with Liberty* [19] he concluded: "It is high time for us to call a halt on our present course of increasing the sphere of government and decreasing that of liberty." Recent historical investigation has played havoc with Burgess's theses on the great sectional struggle in America, and students with an economic interpretation have filled many gaps in his story. His colleague and former student, William A. Dunning, also wrote more penetratingly on some of the constitutional questions involved. Posterity's verdict will probably be that Burgess gave us not so much history as historians.

JAMES FORD RHODES

The era of the Civil War was obviously of intense interest to the historically minded person who had grown to manhood during the years of strife. Schouler and Burgess wrote its story as they saw it from a Northern judgment seat. James Ford Rhodes's stand was nearer Mason and Dixon's line, but his view, too, was somewhat obscured by the traditional viewpoint.

Rhodes had very unusual opportunities to write the history of the period he chose for his theme. He was born in Cleveland, 1848, where his father was a person of importance in the coal and iron industry. Stephen A. Douglas was a frequent visitor at the Rhodes home and, through many other similar contacts, Rhodes was able to write much of his history at firsthand. A conversation with Judge E. R. Hoar, for example, enabled Rhodes to account for President Grant's personal honesty, "while

[19] N. Y., 1915.

keeping such bad company.''[20] During his school days
the Civil War was a daily topic of conversation, and his
father's influence made the young Rhodes a ''sturdy
Democrat.'' The elder Rhodes was a delegate to the Democratic convention of 1860 in Charleston. A business associate and brother-in-law of the younger Rhodes was Mark
Hanna. Rhodes's interest in history was aroused, he tells
us, when he entered New York University in 1865, and attended the classes of Benjamin N. Martin. The latter suggested stimulating reading to Rhodes, who reveled in
Buckle's *History of Civilization* and Draper's *Intellectual Development of Europe.* As he read the last words
of Buckle's famous volumes, the young student ''resolved
some day to write a history.''

Rhodes entered on a business career in 1870, but he
retained a lively interest in literature which the compan-
ionship of John Hay strongly fostered. ''One evening in
1877, while reading Hildreth's *History of the United
States,''* Rhodes remarks in an autobiographical sketch,
''I laid down my book and said to myself why should I
not write a 'History of the United States'?'' From then
on, despite the cares of business, he kept elaborate notes
of his reading. ''I resolved that as soon as I should have
gained a competence, I would retire from business and
devote myself to history and literature.'' In 1885 Rhodes
kept his resolution, retired from business, and then
plunged into a heavy schedule of reading. His interest in
history was stimulated by the publication of several articles he wrote for the *Magazine of Western History,* then
published in Cleveland. One of the articles was a lengthy
review of the second volume of McMaster's *History of
the United States,* and another was a study of Woodrow
Wilson's *Congressional Government.*

Two years later Rhodes started in earnest the prep-

[20] Century Collection, N.Y.P.L., letter to R. U. Johnson; October 22,
1908.

aration for his history. He began the work of composition in 1888, and in three years was ready with the manuscript of the first two volumes. The same year, 1891, Rhodes moved to Cambridge and later to Boston, whose atmosphere and library facilities he found more suitable than those of Cleveland.

The two volumes, which appeared in 1892, and the following three, carried on their title pages the description, *History of the United States from the Compromise of 1850*.[21] In his first volume Rhodes says his plan is to write the history of the United States from the Compromise to the inauguration of Grover Cleveland in 1885, which marked the return to power of the Democrats. This period, he says, "ranks next in importance to the formative period—to the declaration and conquest of independence and the adoption of the Constitution." For eleven years before the Civil War, Negro slavery "engrossed the whole attention of the country." "It will be my aim," says Rhodes, "to recount the causes of the triumph of the Republican party in the presidential election of 1860, and to make clear how the revolution in public opinion was brought about that led to this result. Under a constitutional government the history of political parties is the civil history of the country." Rhodes thinks that the year when the Democrats were victors with Cleveland was a "fitting close of this historical inquiry, for by that time the great questions which had their origin in the war had been settled as far as they could be by legislation or executive direction."

Volume I treats the years from 1850 to 1854 and is largely concerned with describing the influence of slavery upon politics. The historian underestimates the danger of secession in this period; studies that have appeared since 1892 have noted the serious nature of such a move at this

[21] Quotations are by permission of The Macmillan Company, publishers.

time. In Volume II, which carries the story to 1860, much space is given to the elections that were held in the second half of the decade of the fifties. Like Von Holst, Rhodes adopts an antislavery view and confesses that he has been "profoundly influenced" by the former's work. As a supporter of unionism against secessionist theory, Rhodes writes from the standpoint of a nationalist, but *The Nation* reviewer, who referred to Rhodes's treatment of slavery, said, "We doubt whether a fairer view of the subject can be met with in so moderate a space." Rhodes used newspapers freely for some of his sources. Another reviewer of authority thought that "possibly the next century will see a fairer treatment, but we have no right to expect that in this generation a book will be written more free from passion and prejudice." Burgess of Columbia University thought Rhodes was too strongly prejudiced against slavery, and severely criticized him for the perpetuation of the John Brown cult. Because Burgess called Brown one of a "class of common criminals," "a murderer," Rhodes and Von Holst were drawn to each other in a common sympathy.

The publication of these two volumes of his *History* won for Rhodes a well-merited distinction throughout the country. His position as a man of letters was assured to the end of his life, in 1927, and he was also well known as a genial companion who joined enthusiastically in all kinds of social functions. Despite the solicitation of editors and publishers, Rhodes could not be turned aside from his main task. In 1896 he declined Lord Acton's invitation to write the American volume of the *Cambridge Modern History,* with the statement that he needed twenty years more to complete his history and therefore must devote all his energies to it alone.

He was always conscious of his style, studying to improve it, feeling he had need to make up for his earlier business years that had been lost to literature. He con-

fided to a friend: "After my four or five hours of composition daily I try to read two or three for style—Shakespeare, the Bible, Burke, Webster, Lowell and Hawthorne
are just now my guides; and I am reading Frederick the
Great for method." Rhodes was proud of his acceptance
in the best Boston literary circle, but sometimes the
reader senses the historian's lack of assurance: "Please
the élite, the rest will follow," he wrote in 1898. "I am
aspiring for culture and wish to be a scholar." Even in
his later years Rhodes rather self-consciously wrote of
acquiring culture.

In 1895 the third volume of the history, dedicated to
Justin Winsor, was published. It treats of the years 1860
to 1862 and includes a long chapter, well written, on social and economic conditions. Rhodes was sensitive about
his treatment of the Southern leaders. "My estimate of
Lee is wholly sincere," he wrote to Dr. Frederick Bancroft, "and I shall be sorry if it shocks many of my old
friends who bore the brunt and burden of the war and
to whom Lee's 'traitorous conduct' obliterated in their
minds all his virtues." "But an historian cannot be partisan." Yet in the same letter Rhodes evidently felt no in-
consistency when he added: "You and I are far enough
away from the Civil War to look upon the actors without bitterness, convinced though we may be that in the
grand balance of right and wrong, the right was on the
side of the North. Agreement on such a main point will
make up for any differences we may have as to Webster,
Seward and J. Brown."

The year before this volume appeared, Rhodes said
to Edward L. Pierce, Sumner's biographer: "My history
has grown on me, and I shall close the third volume in the
blaze of glory of our victories of the early part of
'62. . . ." He thought he might have reached the Emancipation Proclamation if it had not been for the material
Pierce had given him, "but that and my other studies

have enabled me to give somewhat of freshness to my treatment of English sentiment, of which I am glad, as considerable of my work is commonplace enough from following the beaten track. But if the beaten track is true it is better to follow it than to get out of it for the purpose of making a sensation.''[22]

Volume IV, which carries the story another two years to 1864, appeared in 1899. This is mainly a narrative of the military and naval history of the Civil War, but the diplomatic incidents with England and the re-election of Lincoln are also included. Rhodes gained much knowledge of this period from conversations with participants in its leading events. In the *American Historical Review,* Dunning of Columbia said of Rhodes: ''In guiding us through the central heat of the Civil War, he never loses the clearness of head and the calmness of spirit with which he brought us up to the conflagration.''

Five years intervened before the fifth volume was published, and another two years elapsed before the sixth and seventh appeared in 1906. Volume V, which covers the period 1864 to 1866, contains chapters on society in the North and in the South, although, as Rhodes indicates at the start, most of his work is a political history, substantially chronological in treatment. To the criticisms of Charles Francis Adams on this volume, Rhodes admitted that he had not sufficient knowledge to grapple with the question of sea power. The title of his work was changed in the last two volumes (partly because of a suggestion of Charles Francis Adams) by the addition of the words *To the Final Restoration of Home Rule at the South in 1877;* this altered his original intention to carry the story to Cleveland's first inauguration. In the preface to the sixth volume, which covers the years 1866 to 1872, the author writes: ''Reflection has . . . convinced me

[22] *Amer. Hist. Rev.* (July, 1931).

that a more natural close for this history is the account of the final restoration of home rule in the South"—soon after the inauguration of Hayes. Rhodes believed that questions other than the Southern issue must be treated after 1877, but he stated that he "had a lack of basic knowledge" to attack the social questions involved. He suggested that he might continue his writing after "a systematic study of the history of Europe during the eighteenth and nineteenth centuries" to gain the broader background that he felt later American history required.

Rhodes closes his seventh volume on an optimistic note that lacks, somewhat, the impartial spirit he had earlier prescribed for historians. His history, he writes, "has covered twenty-seven years of pregnant events; the compromise on slavery devised by great statesmen; its upsetting by an ambitious Northern Senator; the formation of the Republican party; the agitation of slavery; Southern arrogance and aggression; the election of Lincoln; the refusal of the South to abide by the decision of the ballot-box; the Civil War; the great work of Lincoln; the abolition of slavery; the defeat of the South; Reconstruction based upon universal negro suffrage; the oppression of the South by the North; the final triumph of Southern intelligence and character over the ignorance and corruption that so long had thriven under Northern misconceptions." "The United States of 1877 was a better country than the United States of 1850. For slavery was abolished, the doctrine of secession was dead, and Lincoln's character and fame had become a possession of the nation."

William G. Brown, well qualified to speak on the subject, said that Rhodes's seventh volume was "the best history yet written of Reconstruction," but criticized it for its digressions. Brown's remarks on this volume might also be applied to the previous ones. He said that Rhodes's writing possessed a "heavy, awkward strength" and that the historian was "at his best when investigating and judging causes and men; not when he confronts the stirring scenes and occasions which a historian of a more artistic bent would welcome as opportunities."

Some of the historian's omissions are very serious. He pays little attention to the westward movement after the war and, curiously enough, despite his early business career, displays no interest in economic history. He was apparently uninfluenced by the work of Turner; there is nothing in Volume I on the interplay of politics and federal grants for railroads. Andrew Johnson today seems a more important personality than Rhodes was willing to concede. He should have devoted less space to the failures of the Reconstruction period and paid more attention to such successes as the institution of a public school system. Negro students of the Reconstruction period have claimed that Rhodes magnified the virtues and minimized the faults of Democrats, whereas for Republicans, especially when colored, he did the reverse.[23] Dunning thought that in the later volumes Rhodes had lost something of the Western vantage point of observation on American history, possibly because of his removal to Boston.

Rhodes disclaimed any intention of writing a "philosophical narrative." When his friend Charles Francis Adams wrote to him gently that "no well and philosophically considered narrative of the struggle has yet appeared," Rhodes replied that "a purely narrative historian should, so far as he can, put all philosophical conditions aside. His aim is to tell a story and leave philosophy to others." He admitted to Adams, who detected a "weariness and haste" to finish the last two volumes, that his observation was probably correct, although Rhodes said he had not been conscious of those feelings at the time.

Aside from its position as a standard treatment of a

[23] J. R. Lynch, "Some Historical Errors of James Ford Rhodes," *The Journal of Negro History,* Vol. II (October, 1917).

momentous period in the history of the United States, the work of Rhodes had an immense value as balm to bitter wounds. "It is a sign that our country . . . is really getting past the time when the differences of 1861-1865 serve as red rags," wrote Professor Dodd to Rhodes. "May I say I believe your masterly *History* has done more than any other historical agency—perhaps any other agency of any sort—to bring about this state of feeling?" It is interesting to observe, too, that, in keeping with the less emotional approach to these problems which Dunning's seminar at Columbia University then inculcated, the attitude of Rhodes himself had changed, especially toward such leading figures as Jefferson Davis.

It is difficult to avoid the conclusion that a Southerner would have treated the years 1850-1877 differently. "It is a history written from the Northern point of view," remarks Lester B. Shippee,[24] "by one who was willing to acknowledge just as far as in him lay the rights on the other side, but who saw in *slavery* a great moral evil which had corrupted the greater portion of a whole society." Slavery, for Rhodes, explained "practically all the main currents of American national history down to the close of Reconstruction." It should be stated, however, that in the pages on Reconstruction, Rhodes approximates more nearly a truly nationalist viewpoint.[25]

In 1911 Rhodes was at work on the continuation of his history. "I am now living in the period 1877-1897," he wrote to a friend, "and have more original material at hand than I have eyes to read or brains to assimilate." He interrupted his study of more recent American history, at the request of his publisher, to write a one-volume *History of the Civil War, 1851-1865* (1917), which, he said, was not an abridgment of his three volumes on

[24] *Miss. Valley Hist. Rev.,* VIII, 133 ff.
[25] Cf. N. W. Stephenson, "Mr. Rhodes as Historian," *Yale Review* (July, 1921).

the period, "but a fresh study of the subject on which
I have used my work as one of many authorities." Much
material, which had been difficult or even impossible of
access when he was writing his larger work, was now
available. But his interest in historical writing was ebbing
fast. To Charles H. Firth, of Oxford, Rhodes said, "I
published in 1917 a History of the Civil War which you
will not care for, but I will send you next autumn the continuation of my History telling the tale from 1877 to
1899. I shall go on with it if life and health be spared,
but I am indifferent whether I publish any more or not."
*The History of the United States from Hayes to McKin-
ley, 1877-1896* was not published until 1919, and was followed three years later by *The McKinley and Roosevelt
Administrations, 1897-1909.*

It was a misfortune to publish these two volumes,
for they are far below the standard set by Rhodes's
earlier work. He shows no understanding of the great
economic changes that had come over the United States
since 1877, and his strong property sense colors his view
of the labor struggles in these decades. Even in his own
chosen field of political history he exhibits no critical
approach to the events and personalities that fall within
the scope of the later volumes. Rhodes knew many of the
leading characters in American life who are portrayed
in these volumes, and his appraisal of their actions is
warped by friendly indulgence. It is a pity that he did
not remember what he had written to Edward L. Pierce
thirty years earlier: "Undue leniency in judging men's
actions is [in the historian] as distinct a vice as undue
severity." It would have been better for his fame if that
indifference to further publication, of which Rhodes had
spoken, had resulted in the suppression of the manuscript
of the last two volumes.

Although he did not number his readers in the large
figures accredited to Fiske and George Bancroft, those

that he had were people who contributed most to molding public opinion—teachers, editors, political leaders.
Rhodes had a high conception of a historian's calling:
"Natural ability being presupposed, the qualities necessary for an historian are diligence, accuracy, love of
truth, impartiality, the thorough digestion of his materials by careful selection and long meditating, and the
compression of his narrative into the smallest compass
consistent with the life of his story." [26] In his earlier
years, at least, Rhodes tried to live up to his own expressed standards, and his position among the leading
American historians is still secure.[27]

John Fiske

John Fiske, whose career as academician and as public lecturer had in it elements of both the older and the
newer schools of historians, ranged over the whole field
of American history. He was essentially a literary, philosophical historian, but his work has some kinship with
the "scientific" group. Fiske, although dead but little
more than thirty years, seems curiously outdated. The
intellectual battles he helped fight and win—he was a
student who frequently appeared on the platform before
large public audiences—have been largely forgotten by a
generation that has taken its victorious heritage for
granted.

Fiske was born in Hartford, Connecticut, in 1842.
He was a very precocious youngster, studying languages
and reading history at an early age, and while still a
child he wrote a lengthy history. In 1860 he went to Harvard, where he quickly earned a reputation as an intellectual radical. Accidentally he discovered the work of

[26] Essay on "History."
[27] See M. A. DeWolfe Howe, *James Ford Rhodes* (N. Y., 1929); also
Rhodes, *Historical Essays* (N. Y., 1909).

Herbert Spencer in a Boston bookshop that year and immediately subscribed for his volumes. For the rest of his life Fiske remained an ardent follower of Spencer and Darwin and became an active champion of the theory of evolution in the United States. Even before his graduation from college, Fiske announced his advanced position on the doctrine of evolution when he published two important articles in the *North American Review* in which he pointed out some fallacies in Buckle's *History of Civilization.*

When Eliot became President of Harvard, Fiske was invited to give a course of lectures on "The Positive Philosophy." He visited England in 1873-74, where he wrote *The Outlines of Cosmic Philosophy,* a revision of his Harvard lectures. Fiske himself contributed an idea of importance when he pointed out how the long infancy of humans influenced the social organization of the family. The English leaders in the fight for evolution were heartened by the support of Fiske, the leading exponent of these new ideas in America. To the end of his days, however, Fiske was still trying to harmonize his religious beliefs and ideals with the latest doctrines of science.

After a service of almost seven years as Harvard librarian, Fiske left in 1879 to enter upon a career as lecturer in history that has perhaps no parallel in America. It had been rumored two years earlier that Fiske was to be appointed to the history department at Harvard, but opposition to his unconventional ideas prevented the appointment. His successful series of lectures on "America's Place in History" in 1879 given in the Old South Church in Boston determined the future course of his life.

In one of his works, *The American Revolution,* Fiske wrote in his preface: "In the course of my work as Assistant Librarian of Harvard University in 1872 and the next few years, I had occasion to overhaul what was called the American Room, and to superintend, or revise, the cataloguing of some twenty thousand volumes and pamphlets relating to America. In the course of this work my attention was called more and more to sundry problems and speculations connected with the transplantation of European communities to American soil, their development under new conditions and the effect of all this upon the general progress of civilization. The study of aboriginal America itself had already presented to me many other interesting problems in connection with primitive culture.'' Fiske saw in America's development an excellent illustration of the theory of evolution applied to the history of civilization, and he popularized his thesis in his historical lectures and writings. He had a clear perception of the contemporary appropriateness of such lectures. ''The centennial has started it,'' he wrote, ''and I have started in at the right time.'' He thoroughly enjoyed his experiences as a lecturer, and wrote, after one appearance, ''The applause was great. I had a sort of sense that I was fascinating the people and it was delicious beyond expression.'' In the year that Fiske made his American debut as a lecturer in history, he gave the same series in London with astonishing success. The report of his popularity in London preceded Fiske's arrival home in the summer of 1879, and many applications for lectures awaited him from all over the country. Two years later he was lecturing on ''American Political Ideas'' under the auspices of Washington University in St. Louis. These lectures appeared in book form in 1885.

Meanwhile Fiske was thinking of writing a history of the American people from Columbus's discovery to the end of the Civil War. The work was to be in three volumes and modeled after John Richard Green's *Short History of the English People*. He even made arrangements for publication of his history, but within a short time he realized that it had to be written on a much larger scale.

When his publisher refused to arrange for a history of greater scope, Fiske canceled his agreement. The materials he had already gathered were used later to comprise two volumes in the co-operative *A History of All Nations*.[28]

In the winter of 1883-1884 he gave a course of lectures on "The American Revolution," followed shortly by a new series on the six years succeeding the Revolutionary War, which Fiske called "The Critical Period of American History." In 1886 he became one of the editors of Appleton's *Cyclopedia of American Biography*, for which he wrote twenty-four articles, and in the same year made several contributions to the *Atlantic Monthly*.

The next year he turned back to earlier American history to prepare a lecture series on "The Beginnings of New England," which he opened with a lengthy survey of political ideas among the civilizations of the Orient, Rome, and England. In 1888 *The Critical Period of American History* was published. Fiske took account of the difficulties facing the new nation and made a number of sketches of the leaders in the Constitutional Convention. The historian went on to discuss the motives that prompted the States to accept the Constitution, and included a vivid description of Washington's inauguration. This volume is probably the best of Fiske's works from the standpoint of interpretation, even though it lacks documentation. Contemporary readers received *The Critical Period* with much favor, and John Morley's review (which sounds amusing in view of his own ponderous biography of Gladstone) said of Fiske: "He knows how to tell a story in a free, clear and lively style, and he has not the terrible defect of insisting on telling us everything, or telling us more than we want to know."

Fiske now planned to write a history in five divisions: "The Epoch of American Discovery"; "The Pe-

[28] J. H. Wright, ed., 24 vols., Phila., 1905.

riod of Colonization''; ''The Revolutionary War''; ''The Critical Period''; ''The Establishment of the Federal Government and Its Development.'' Of these, the third and fourth and part of the second were already completed. Houghton Mifflin Company, his publishers, made it possible for him to shorten his schedule of five or more months of lectures each year in order to devote most of his time to research and the writing of his history. Before long *The Beginnings of New England* and *The American Revolution* were ready for the press. One sixth of the former book, which has as a subtitle the ''Puritan Theocracy in Its Relation to Civil and Religious History,'' explains why the world's political center of gravity shifted from the Mediterranean and the Rhine to the Atlantic and the Mississippi, from the Latins to English-speaking peoples. Unlike some modern students of the subject, Fiske saw little of the economic motive in the settlement of New England. In his preface he writes: ''It has been my aim to give the outline of such a narrative as to indicate the principles at work in the history of New England down to the Revolution of 1689.'' Love of the dramatic made Fiske give disproportionate space to some subjects. For example, nearly fifty pages are devoted to King Philip's War out of a total of less than three hundred. The outworn character of his point of view may be measured by a chapter with the heading ''The Tyranny of Andros.'' Today the episode is described as an incident in imperial reorganization.

The American Revolution is largely a military history and reveals nothing of the internal developments in the colonies. In the traditional manner, George III is burdened with the chief responsibility for bringing on the war. The much-reviled king is to Fiske a typical villain: ''Scantly endowed with human sympathy, and almost boorishly stiff in his ordinary unstudied manner, he could be smooth as oil whenever he liked.'' ''He had little faith in human honour or rectitude, and in pursuing an end he was seldom deterred by scruples." Fiske believes that "it is historically correct to regard him as the person chiefly responsible for the quarrel."

In 1890, at the Lowell Institute of Boston, Fiske gave a course of twelve lectures on "The Discovery, Conquest and Colonization of America." These lectures outlined the two volumes which appeared in 1892, dedicated to the English historian Edward A. Freeman. These were, perhaps, Fiske's most careful work, and some critics have regarded them as the best of his writings, particularly because of his use of source material. The researches of Henry Harrisse were extremely useful to him. From the viewpoint of documentation, this book, alone among his many works, approximates modern historical standards, but in his usual digressive manner, Fiske referred to many details of small significance. Phillips Brooks thought the chapter on Las Casas "the finest piece of historical narrative in the English language," and James Ford Rhodes exclaimed with too much enthusiasm that "the *Discovery of America* is a great book; it is the greatest historical work I have ever read by an American except the *Rise of the Dutch Republic*." A reviewer in the New York *Sun* thought this book of Fiske's "the most valuable contribution to history that has been made by an American," even when measured alongside the work of Bancroft and Prescott.

In his two volumes Fiske allotted a very large proportion of space to pre-Columbian civilization, which was a reflection of contemporary interest in primitive peoples. He tells us that it was his study of prehistoric Europe and of early Aryan institutions that led him to study American aborigines. He thought that he might thus shed further light on the conclusions of the Aryan school of anthropologists.

The uncritical character of much of Fiske's research

may be seen in his *Old Virginia and her Neighbors*
(1897), where his unquestioned faith in the truthfulness
of John Smith betrays a too-credulous mind. Competent
critics were unfavorably disposed toward *The Dutch and
Quaker Colonies in America* (1899). Osgood said that
when Fiske "crosses the threshold of the eighteenth century, his narrative becomes so sketchy as to lose nearly
all its value." "He can only express the pious belief that
such and such things are so; the proving of them requires
activity of an order different from that of telling a pretty
story or sketching the results of earlier investigations."

Fiske's *New France and New England* (1901) has
very little documentation and, like the work on the American Revolution, is largely a military history. *The Mississippi Valley in the Civil War* (1900), the result of another lecture series, is also a military history. Fiske obviously devoted much of his lecturing and writing to military history because that phase of the subject can be
made most interesting to the widest number of people.
Another work on *Civil Government in the United States*
is dominated by the outmoded evolutionary theory that
traced the origins of the New England township to Greek
and Roman institutions.

His fondness for playing with ideas sometimes led
him to an unwarranted speculation upon the motives of
men. Fiske had a wide acquaintance with monographic
literature and other secondary materials bearing on his
various subjects, but his use of primary sources was limited. It is well known that he frequently borrowed from
some and summarized the research of others without acknowledgment. His *Critical Period,* in particular, suffers
from these frailties.

It is scarcely surprising that Fiske often showed
little direct knowledge of the sources. His tempo of life
prohibited leisurely examination of large masses of materials and, besides, his grandiose view of history pre-

cluded close observation of any particular period. Fiske had, however, something of value to say on this subject. His remarks referred to Freeman, but they were probably intended also as a justification of his own wide range of historical writing. Freeman, he said, ''was remarkably free from the common habit—common even among eminent historians—of concentrating his attention upon some exceptionally brilliant period or so-called 'classical age,' to the exclusion of other ages that went before and came after. Such a habit is fatal to all correct understanding of history, even that of the ages upon which attention is thus unwisely concentrated.''

In 1901, because of his great reputation, Fiske was invited to be the American representative at the millenial celebration in King Alfred's honor. He chose to speak on ''The Beginnings of Federalism in New England, as related to the Expansion of Alfred's World,'' but he did not live to deliver the address in September when it was scheduled.

Fiske has been acclaimed by a competent student as ''one of the most important intellectual influences in America in the last quarter of the nineteenth century'' [29] because of his activities in bringing to Americans the products of advanced European thought. But in his historical as in his scientific writing he gives no indications of original genius. His influence, however, exerted through lectures and writings, stimulated youthful Americans to a study of their own history. Charles M. Andrews, as a young scholar,[30] felt the popular reaction to Fiske, who brought into a dull period of historical writing, provincial in tone, the volumes that captivated the American public. ''He vitalized it [American history], bringing it out of its isolation into touch with the forces of world history. He was almost the first to give . . .

[29] J. T. Adams in *Dictionary of American Biography*.
[30] C. M. Andrews, *Amer. Hist. Rev.* (1925).

reality to the men and events of our past and accomplished a remarkable feat when he turned the American people from Prescott, Irving, *et al.*, whose subjects lay chiefly outside the limits of the present United States, and caused them to read with enjoyment books that dealt with their own origin and growth. Nothing that Fiske wrote is great history, but much of it is good history," concludes Professor Andrews, "and his place in American historiography is one of great merit and dignity." Robert L. Schuyler sums up his contribution with precision: "Both in his philosophical and in his historical work he was rather the live wire that diffuses knowledge than the dynamo that generates it." [31]

[31] *Pol. Sci. Quart.* (1918). See John Spencer Clark, *Life and Letters of John Fiske* (2 vols., Boston, 1917); T. B. Sanders, "John Fiske," *Miss. Valley Hist. Rev.* (September, 1930).

XII

TWO HISTORIANS OF THE PEOPLE

JOHN BACH MCMASTER

While a number of writers in the last decades of the nineteenth century were conventionally narrating the political and constitutional history of the period following the Revolution, another historian emerged whose volumes were to have a remarkable influence on his own and the next generation. His work was called *A History of the People of the United States, from the Revolution to the Civil War*. It won for its author, John Bach McMaster, immediate recognition in and beyond the academic world.

McMaster had given no indication of a special bent for history except for his hobby of collecting historical materials in his undergraduate days at the College of the City of New York. He was awarded his A.B. degree in 1872, and soon after he contributed two volumes to the literature of his profession, civil engineering. From 1877 to 1883 he was an instructor in civil engineering in Princeton University. It was while on a surveying trip to the West, McMaster once related, that he was impressed "with the drama of the settlement of a new land, the creation of a new empire, and determined to write its history before the spirit of the period was gone."[1] When his first volume was published, in 1883, the University of Pennsylvania invited him to occupy the specially created chair of American history—a position he held until 1922, when he became professor emeritus.

McMaster's volume, with its catholicity of subject matter, was a unique contribution to historical writing and was instantly recognized as such. Social history thus made a conspicuous and very successful debut. During the thirty years that followed the publication of Volume I the work was completed in eight volumes, and after a long interval another was added on Lincoln's administration.

The author fixes the attention of the reader instantly with his declaration that "the subject of my narrative is the history of the people." They "shall be the chief theme," although much will need to be written of political and military history. "It shall be my purpose," writes the historian, "to describe the dress, the occupations, the amusements, the literary canons of the times; to note the changes of manners and morals; to trace the growth of that humane spirit which abolished punishment for debt, which reformed the discipline of prisons and of jails, and which has, in our own time, destroyed slavery and lessened the miseries of dumb brutes." His history is to describe also the discoveries and inventions of a mechanical nature; "to tell how, under the benign influence of liberty and peace, there sprang up, in the course of a single century, a prosperity unparalleled in the annals of human affairs"; "how by a wise system of free education and a free press, knowledge was disseminated, and the arts and sciences advanced."[2]

[1] See E. P. Cheyney in *Amer. Hist. Rev.* (July, 1932).
[2] Cf. Macaulay's *History of England:* "It will be my endeavor to relate the history of the people as well as the history of the government;

In his early volumes McMaster largely fulfills his promise. Although he sets chronological limits for each of his volumes (the first runs from 1784 to 1790), the historian does not always adhere rigidly to his design; materials belonging to earlier and later years are sometimes included. McMaster's writing, rarely dull, is often fired with enthusiasm. A cross section of American civilization in 1784 takes up a large part of the first volume. "The Constitution before the People" is an excellent description of public opinion expressing itself on a matter of great importance. McMaster's discussion of Hamiltonian policies is friendly to the Federalists, and his pages on the episode known as Shays' Rebellion are unsympathetic to the debtors. The difficulties of organizing the materials of social history are made vividly clear when we observe that descriptions of Noah Webster's spelling reforms and of John Fitch's steamboat are inserted in a chapter on "The Breaking up of the Confederation." The headings of chapters are, in fact, very slight indications of their contents. Wander as he may, however, McMaster usually finds his way back to the main thought of his chapter.

Volume II, which appeared in 1885, continues the narrative to about 1803. A section, "The Beginning of Prosperity," crediting American economic well-being to the Federalists, might seem to indicate a bias. On a later page, however, the Federalists, who objected to the Louisiana Purchase, are referred to as "mere obstructionists, a sect of the political world which of all other sects is most to be despised." McMaster's attitude toward Jefferson may have been dictated by his reading of Hildreth, for he writes that Jefferson, on his return from France, "was saturated with democracy in its rankest form, and

to trace the progress of useful and ornamental arts . . . the rise of religious sects . . . the changes of literary taste . . . to portray the manners of successive generations, and not to pass by . . . even the revolutions which have taken place in dress, furniture, repasts and public amusements."

he remained to the last day of his life a servile worshipper of the people." The section headed "The Struggle for Neutrality" contains descriptions of the activities of pro-French sympathizers and their opponents—but it also has some pages on the yellow-fever outbreak in 1793, the patent office, the cotton gin, and so on. The yellow-fever epidemic five years later is again referred to in the chapter on "The Quarrel with France." In dealing with another important event of this period, the Whisky Rebellion, McMaster is friendlier to the insurgents than he is in the first volume to the rebels who followed Daniel Shays. It is surprising to find a reference to Washington's "cold heart." [3] "Time has . . . dealt gently with his memory," writes McMaster, "yet his true biography is still to be prepared." [4]

The larger part of this volume is concerned with the international problems that troubled the administrations of Washington and Adams, and the public reactions to Jay's treaty and the Genet affair. McMaster, in attempting to be impartial in his judgment, writes it "is perfectly true that the Federal party did show a singular affection for England, did submit with meekness while she held their posts, impressed their seamen, condemned their cargoes and their ships"; "but it is likewise true that the Republican party exhibited a most infatuated love for France," where, they believed, a revolution similar to their own had been effected. McMaster makes a distinction between Celtic revolutions, of which the French was one, marked by violence, and Saxon revolutions (like the American) "conducted with the sobriety, with the dignity, with the love of law and order that has ever marked the national uprisings of the Saxon race." How the Americans of 1775 would have smiled at that!

A chapter on "Town and Country Life in 1800" in-

[3] P. 212.
[4] P. 452.

cludes a mass of miscellaneous details on fire insurance, fashions, the theater, travel, and the like. McMaster here makes an interesting suggestion: "There is not, and there never was, a text-book so richly deserving a history as the [New England] Primer." Shortly thereafter Paul Leicester Ford wrote a history of that famous book. Mc-Master was one of our earliest historians to take note of the West, and his lines on the pioneers have done service for many authors.

The third volume was published in 1891. Some pages on the newly acquired Louisiana territory begin the volume, and it closes with the invasion of Canada in the War of 1812. McMaster's judgment on Burr is bitterly severe. He believes that the latter's life was marked by "a career of treason which links his name with the name of Arnold, and consigns it to everlasting infamy." A lengthy chapter is concerned with the uses to which the public lands were put. Up to this time subjects of this nature had secured very little attention in general historical works.

A chapter on the extension of democracy serves as a prelude to a similar discussion in a later volume. The adoption of Ohio's constitution, writes McMaster, "was another triumph for the rights of man. . . . No person could, in 1803, look over our country without beholding on every hand the lingering remains of monarchy, of aristocracy, of class rule. But he must indeed have been a careless observer if he failed to notice the boldness with which those remains were attacked, and the rapidity with which they were being swept away." There was little of democracy in the seaboard States, "but the leaven of Revolution was quietly at work," and restrictions were gradually removed. The opening of a new century brought with it "a great reform in manners, in customs, in institutions, in laws." "East of the Alleghanies long-established precedents, time-honored usages, the presence of a ruling class . . . checked the spread of the new faith. West of the Alleghanies no such difficulties were met." Half the volume tells of the events leading up to the war, impressment and the embargo. McMaster, like Hildreth before him, also noted, as a cause of the conflict, the movement for expansion to Canada.

Before narrating the episodes of the war, the historian asks leave of the reader "to describe the marvellous prosperity which, in spite of embargoes, in spite of acts of non-intercourse and acts of non-importation, of confiscations, of burnings, of plunderings, of the unwise conduct of congresses, presidents, and legislatures, had during these nine-and-twenty years been built up by the thrift, the energy, the self-reliance of the people." A long section on internal improvements details the activity in canal and road building and the construction of steamboats. The rise of manufactures and the demand for a protective tariff are recounted along with the beginnings of an organized labor movement.

In 1895 the fourth volume of McMaster's history was published; it carries the narrative through the Missouri Compromise, but a third of its six hundred pages describes the military and naval events of 1812 to 1814. For these two of the eight years covered by the volume, the historian set aside half its pages. Not often is McMaster guilty of the literary pompousness with which he opens his chapter on "Disorders of the Currency": "From the long story of battles and sieges and civil strife it is delightful to be able to turn once more to the narration of the triumphs of peace." He goes on to say, despite his own pages on internal improvements, westward migration, and the like, that "from 1793 to 1815 the questions which occupied the public mind were our neutral rights, orders in council, French decrees, impressment, embargoes, treaties, non-intercourse acts, admiralty decisions, blockades, the conduct of England, the conduct of France, the insolence of the French directory, the triumphs, the ambition, and the treachery of Napoleon. Henceforth, for many years to come, the questions of the day were to be the state of the currency, the national bank, manufactures, the tariff, internal improvements, interstate commerce, the public lands, the astonishing growth of the West, the rights of the States, extension of slavery, and the true place of the Supreme Court in our system of government.'' The announcement of peace opened ''a new era in our national history.''

In ''The Routes of Transportation'' McMaster, once a teacher of engineering, turns again to one of his favorite aspects of social history which, in this volume, gets far less attention than political and martial history. Monroe must have been convinced after his tour of the country, believes the historian, that the questions facing him were ''of home, not of foreign origin; and that in settling those questions the West would have a most decisive influence.'' There are illuminating pages, here, on the westward rush in these years. Instead of looking toward Europe, the seaboard inhabitants ''now on a sudden veered around and faced the Mississippi Valley,'' and ''an era of internal improvements opened which did far more to cement the Union and join the East and West inseparably than did the Constitution and the laws.'' A very important chapter on ''Pauperism and Crime'' is related to the economic distress of the postwar years. This was the period of a great humanitarian movement to mitigate the harshness of the laws against debtors, to promote temperance, and to reform prison conditions.

In his fifth volume, published in 1900, McMaster continues his history to approximately 1830. After running through the political events of Monroe's second administration and installing John Quincy Adams in the presidency, the historian picks up the story of other phases of American social life in this decade. ''The condition of the workingman,'' he writes, ''stood in need of betterment.

In the general advance made by society in fifty years he had shared but little.'' The organizations of labor and utopian communities are the themes of the next few pages. ''Ten years of rapid industrial development had brought into prominence problems of urban life and municipal government . . . new and quite beyond solution in 1825.'' From a consideration of the growing complexity of urban life, McMaster moves on to frontier life: ''Common hardships, common poverty, common ignorance, and the utter inability to get anything more out of life than coarse food, coarse clothes, and a rude shelter, reduced all to a level of absolute equality which existed nowhere else.'' McMaster inclines to the belief that because religion had a firm hold on frontier regions, ''nowhere else was the standard of morality higher or more fully attained.''

A chapter on ''The Industrial Revolution'' follows one on the Negro problem and the rise of a militant anti-slavery movement. While the North was vigorously cultivating ''every art and science which could add to the wealth, increase the prosperity and comfort of the people, and develop the material resources of the country,'' the South was indifferent to these forces that were changing civilization. McMaster's main interest in the industrial revolution was to show how it operated in effecting a strong antagonism between North and South. In a chapter on literature that runs back to colonial days, the historian gathered together pages on magazines, popular fiction, and ''moral books'' intended, says McMaster, ''to inculcate a morality of the most unhealthy sort.'' His remarks on the charges of American literary subserviency to England are sensible; the preference of American readers for English authors, he says, ''was not subserviency, but sound literary judgment.'' The criticism leveled by the British at the United States takes up a complete chapter, which precedes one on ''The Common

School in the First Half Century." In a discussion of political ideas, the author finds that the problems of wider suffrage and States' rights were of paramount importance.

McMaster is near the end of the fifth volume before he returns to his political narrative with a consideration of the foreign relations of Adams's administration. He passes rather quickly to the election of Jackson, which, he remarks, "was indeed a great uprising of the people, a triumph of democracy, another political revolution the like of which the country had not seen since 1800, and no mere driving from office of a man or class of men."

In 1906 McMaster brought out his sixth volume, which covers the twelve years to 1842. After two brief chapters on some of the issues discussed in Congress, with especial attention to the Webster-Hayne debate and the nullification movement in South Carolina, he uses the census of 1830 to begin another description of American civilization. The large emigration from Europe catches the attention of the social historian: "Had it not been for the presence of the imported laborer great works of internal improvement could not have been built, and the early thirties were remarkable for the number of turnpikes, canals, and railroads constructed." On the other hand, some types of immigrants, particularly of the pauper class, created problems that were met by restrictive measures. The rise of Mormonism and the exploration of the Far West are joined together in these pages.

The political and economic questions which troubled Jackson's second administration are treated at length, and for a large part of the volume McMaster loses sight of the "People" whose history he was supposed to be recording. When he returns to them in the elections of 1834, he is somewhat critical: "The era of mob rule had fairly opened and issues of every sort were met with force." Another kind of violence arouses him to un-

wonted indignation: "By his butcheries at the Alamo and
Goliad Santa Anna had forfeited his life a hundred times
and many cried out for his execution as a murderer."
The violence that accompanied the sharpening struggle
for the abolition of slavery is chronicled in a separate
chapter. When we remember that, with the exception of
some skirmishes with Indians, the United States was at
peace, it is surprising to note the numerous references to
incidents of a violent character that marked her internal
history in this decade. McMaster's "People" were surely
a high-spirited lot, or perhaps this part of his history was
a reversion to the older type of military and political narrative, with the substitution of mobs and riots for soldiers and battles. "The Log-Cabin, Hard-Cider Campaign" is described with gusto. The Liberty party convention at Albany, McMaster says, began a political
movement that "proved to be the most important in our
history since the adoption of the Constitution." [5]

In 1910 the seventh volume, which records American
life in the 1840's, was published. The numerous financial
difficulties that followed in the wake of 1837 are chronicled in great detail and are briefly summarized in the
opening of the chapter "A Struggle for Revenue":
"While the people, the banks, the chief cities, and the
States were thus struggling under dull times, shin-
plaster currency, enforced resumption, repudiation, loss
of credit, and a load of debt, the twenty-seventh Congress
met in regular session and learned from the annual message that the Federal Treasury was empty and the Government face to face with a deficit."

The sixth census provides McMaster with another
opportunity for a view of society in the East, South, and
West in three separate chapters. As before, much space
is given to improved means of communication, and the
importance that urban life had already reached in Ameri-

[5] Cf. Von Holst, p. 342.

can civilization receives its appropriate share of attention. Emigration from Europe again gets its merited space, but interstate migration within the Union is disposed of too briefly. In the chapter on the South, which is largely given over to a description of plantation life and slavery, McMaster again draws a comparison between the North and South, and the result strongly favors the North. "Socially and industrially," he concludes, "the North and South were now two distinct peoples." A chapter headed "Social and Political Betterment" rounds out his survey of the country. The active humanitarian movement and the further extension of political democracy in this decade enlisted McMaster's literary enthusiasm, so that even though interpretations are missing in the author's vast accumulation of facts, the reader does enjoy the narrative.

The West comes into its own with this volume. More than half of the six hundred pages are concerned with westward expansion and the political problems to which it gave rise. Presidential elections are discussed with regard to the influence exerted upon them by expansionist forces. A description of routes to the newly acquired region on the Pacific and the rush to California close the volume.

In 1913 McMaster published what was to be the last volume—the eighth—covering the decade before 1861. The people, whom he had formerly followed in their daily activities of earning a livelihood, educating, and entertaining themselves, are, for the most part, now engaged in the great political debates that preceded the resort to arms. McMaster returns infrequently to the main theme of his narrative, but more often, only a few of the people, political representatives, hold the center of the stage.

The historian was usually careful to let his characters speak for themselves, and also to let his readers think for themselves, but a phrase now and then reveals his sympathy—for example, he refers to "the hateful fugitive slave law." The core of his political narrative deals with the spirit of secession in 1850, "Bleeding Kansas" and the presidential elections. In his treatment of the Lincoln-Douglas debates, McMaster leaves no room for doubt as to his own attitude. In the third debate, at Jonesboro, Douglas, "suiting himself to the feelings of his hearers . . . opened with his usual biased and partisan review of the political situation. . . ." "The Eve of Secession" is ushered in with some twenty pages on John Brown who, in 1858, made known to his friends "as wild a scheme as ever entered the head of man." With an unwonted air of speed, McMaster now hurries through the movements for, and counter movements against, secession, and then the election of 1860. Buchanan was criticized for not meeting firmly the secessionist threat. In two chapters the writer gathers some picturesque materials on "Social Ferment" which includes some pages on westward migration, a topic to which he returns in a section "On the Plains." Once again McMaster refers to the problems created by the rapid growth of cities and his pet subject of transportation. The more radical labor movement then arising is chronicled with special emphasis on the influence exerted by recent immigrants. The distress that came with 1857 is pictured realistically; no less interesting are the startling comments of Mayor Fernando Wood of New York on the crisis. "Those who produce everything get nothing," said Wood, "and those who produce nothing get everything."[6]

In 1927, when he was seventy-five years of age, McMaster brought out *A History of the People of the United States during Lincoln's Administration,* a continuation of his former work. It is for the most part a story

[6] VIII, 298.

of people at war, with only brief sections on the non-military aspects of American life during those years. There is an abundance of detail on the relations of both the North and South with England during the struggle. McMaster devotes more space to economic conditions in the South than in the North. In his treatment of the latter he writes in a chapter on "The Prosperous North," "Two years and a half of war had brought no economic or industrial suffering to the North. . . ." After the hardships of the first year, "the people soon adjusted themselves to war conditions and went on with their daily occupations more prosperous than ever." McMaster does not entirely lose sight of the westward migration which continued even during the war. Although sympathetic to the South, stricken by distress, he is critical of the Black Codes, which, he believes, were drawn "with cruel harshness and a deliberate intention to reduce the freedman as far as possible to his old state of slavery."

The pen that spilled so many words—literally millions—was busy on other works of a historical nature. Biographies of Franklin, Webster, and Stephen Girard are among the titles in McMaster's bibliography. He wrote textbooks that included far more of social history than similar books thirty years ago. Pedagogically they did for American history what James Harvey Robinson's texts were then doing for European history. Over two and a half million copies of his texts were sold. When he was preparing his biography of Webster, McMaster revealed a marked divergence from his usual descriptive manner of historical writing with its absence of interpretation. He said it was necessary to avoid earlier biographic studies. "None of them make it at all clear why Webster was a great man, they merely state the fact." His own attempt at interpretation is, however, not very

successful.[7] The historian, who has been severely criticized for his lack of organization, published on one occasion a concise little volume on *The Acquisition of Political, Social and Industrial Rights of Man in America*
(1903).

But it is on his vast *History* that his reputation must
ultimately rest. In a sense the historian glorified the
common man, the record of whose life was to be sought
in periodical and pamphlet literature. Personalities are
rarely emphasized; they are subordinated to their environment. McMaster chose Macaulay for his model in
his early years, but the further he drifted from the influence of the English historian, the more accurate his
own work seems to have become. With the improvement
in accuracy is noted a decline in the picturesque quality
of the narrative. It is difficult to avoid the conclusion
that the unusual rather than the usual attracted Mc-
Master's attention, and it is very likely that this resulted
from excessive dependence upon newspapers as a source;
newspapers have always featured the extraordinary
rather than the humdrum affairs of daily existence. The
first volumes contain many inaccuracies, especially in
some of their sweeping generalizations. It is very probable, too, that the less enduring parts of his work are
the sections on political history.

McMaster had a Gargantuan appetite for historical
facts, which, it has been said, all looked alike to him. His
was not a critical spirit that could probe into American
life with a nice discrimination and express its findings
with an economy of phrase. He was content to pile page
upon page of description. The ebullience of most of his
own generation is reflected in his pages which are pervaded with national enthusiasm. In a speech he delivered,
in 1898, on "The Social Function of the History of the

---

[7] Century Collection, N.Y.P.L., letter to R. U. Johnson, February 20,
1900.

United States," McMaster said, in words reminiscent of Bancroft: "Our national history should be presented to the student as the growth and development of a marvelous people. . . . We are a people animated by the highest and noblest ideals of humanity, of the rights of man, and no history of our country is rightly taught which does not set this forth. . . . There is no land where the people are so prosperous, so happy, so intelligent, so bent on doing what is just and right, as the people of the United States."

From first to last McMaster has had his admirers and detractors, but he lived to see a whole school of historians follow in his footsteps. Some of his sentences and paragraphs have been elaborated into monographs, but McMaster himself made little use of monographic materials, even when he wrote his later volumes, by which time special studies had become more plentiful. He was, perhaps, the first to emphasize the place of the West in American history, and in stressing economic factors he was a predecessor of Beard as well as of Turner. Roosevelt, whose *Winning of the West* owed much to McMaster, wrote of the latter's second volume to Henry Cabot Lodge: "If all of McMaster's chapters were changed round promiscuously it would not, I am confident, injure the thread of his narrative in the least. He has put much novel matter in a brilliant, attractive way; but his work is utterly disconnected, and even his researches are the reverse of exhaustive. In fact all he has done is to provide material for history." And students of both greater and lesser maturity these past fifty years have not hesitated to make good use of McMaster's bountiful offerings; beginning with John Fiske and ending with the latest novice in an American history class, they have helped themselves generously. George Bancroft, who was omitting footnotes in a new edition of his work, once advised McMaster to do likewise, because writers were in the habit of using these notes without acknowledgment. McMaster's friend Frederick D. Stone used to say, when a new volume of the history appeared, "Now we shall soon have something from John Fiske."[8]

Albert Bushnell Hart has seen at firsthand the changes in historical fashions over a longer period than any other contemporary historian, and it is his opinion that McMaster is "the founder of the modern school of historians of the United States." The disciples have not followed McMaster uncritically, but they have accepted his lead in broadening immensely the boundaries of historical inquiry.[9]

ELLIS PAXSON OBERHOLTZER

Among the many students who passed through McMaster's classes at the University of Pennsylvania in the late 1880's was Ellis Paxson Oberholtzer. The latter, who was also one of the numerous Americans who attended European universities in these years, thus received the conventional accolade of scholarship. Under the influence of McMaster, Oberholtzer turned in time to historical writing, passing through various stages as editor, biographer, and historian. He edited the series of "American Crisis" biographies, wrote a volume on *The Literary History of Philadelphia*[10] and valuable biographies of two of the most important financiers in the history of the United States—*Robert Morris*[11] and *Jay Cooke*.[12] The impress of McMaster was so strong on his disciple that it is not surprising that Oberholtzer

[8] E. P. Oberholtzer, "J. B. McMaster," *Pa. Mag. of Hist. and Biog.* (January, 1933), p. 25.

[9] William T. Hutchinson, "John Bach McMaster, Historian of the American People," *Miss. Valley Hist. Rev.* (June, 1929); review of McMaster, Vol. I, by Carl Russell Fish, in *Miss. Valley Hist. Rev.*, Vol I; and Albert B. Hart, "John Bach McMaster," *Current History* (March, 1931).

[10] Phila., 1906.   [11] N. Y., 1903.   [12] 2 vols., Phila., 1907.

should have decided to carry on his teacher's history in
the same spirit. Oberholtzer had already published the
first volume of *A History of the United States since the
Civil War* when McMaster brought out the final volume
in his own history, which covered the years of strife.
Handing a copy of his book to Oberholtzer, McMaster
said: "There, I have come up to you. It is for you to
go on." [13]

Oberholtzer did go on and published four volumes
of a projected five-volume work. A fifth volume, ending
with the assassination of McKinley, came from the press
just after Oberholtzer died in December, 1936. He did
not make any statement as to his terminal point; his is
merely "A History of the United States since the Civil
War" and as such it was the author's privilege to end
it when his fancy might so decide. Following in the footsteps of his predecessor, Oberholtzer wrote a social and
political history of the years after the Civil War without attempting much in the way of interpretation. The
same types of sources were used to depict the life of
the people—for the most part, newspapers, Congressional documents, and manuscript collections.

The first volume of Oberholtzer's history covers the
three years to 1868, and perhaps the most interesting
chapters are those on social conditions in various parts
of the country. The chapter on "The South after the
War" is in the main a tragic picture of misery and deg-
radation with but few signs of economic reconstruction.
In something of the spirit of the more modern student,
Oberholtzer speaks of President Johnson laboring "with
industry, tact and patriotism to heal the great sectional
wound." [14] A long chapter on "The Triumphant North"
describes immigration, prices, and the material wealth

[13] Oberholtzer, "John Bach McMaster," *Pa. Mag. Hist. and Biog.*
(January, 1933), p. 19.
[14] P. 143.

of the region in striking contrast with the poverty of the
South. After chapters on the Indians and on the settlement of the West, the historian returns to discuss the
conflict between Johnson and Congress; from his study
of the Johnson Papers, Oberholtzer concludes that the
President had wide popular support.[15] The writing of
this type of history frequently entails some rather sudden jumps from one subject to another, and so the reader
who is immersed in a Panama Canal project must be
prepared in the next paragraph for an enumeration of
post offices in the United States.[16]

In his second volume Oberholtzer covers a slightly
longer period than in his first—it is the four years to
1872. As might have been inferred from his attitude to
Johnson in the earlier volume, when the author comes
to write of the impeachment proceedings he reveals hostility to the Congressional radicals. His handling of financial history is very useful to the student; his own
work, in a separate biography of Jay Cooke, proved
valuable to him in this connection. Oberholtzer's sense
of proportion is frequently faulty and especially so in
his treatment of the Alabama Claims, which receive far
too much space. There is an interesting section on trans-
continental railroads, with their effects on the West, and
the volume ends with a chapter, ''The End of the Orgy,''
which is very critical of the great despoilers—Gould,
Fisk, Drew, Tweed, *et al.*

The third volume of the history includes the six
years to 1878. In accordance with his usual practice he
piles his details mass upon mass, but despite this accumulation of facts, the reader is not very much enlightened
with respect to the passing scene. For example, in a reference to California, he says that the State ''was in the
control, economically and politically, of a small oligarchy

[15] Pp. 491-492.
[16] P. 221.

of men enriched by mines, railroads and other enterprises.''[17] Another generalization is as typical: ''The
entire nation came through the year 1876 with an enlargement of view in an economical, an industrial, an
artistic and an ethnographic sense, as well as with a finer
comprehension of American history, and the purpose and
design of the government.''[18] Oberholtzer would have
done better had he developed these statements instead
of leaving them unsupported by detail. In a useful chapter on education, letters, and art, the historian indicates
his high regard for Godkin, editor of *The Nation,* whose
''moral force'' still influenced the writing of Oberholtzer
years after; the latter is in reality a Godkinite hangover
from the nineteenth century.

Volume IV, published in 1931, is bulkier than its
predecessors, and also covers more ground, extending
over the ten years to 1888. The impartiality that generally characterized McMaster is absent in the writing of
his disciple. Oberholtzer himself once expressed preference for the method of James Schouler, which would not
be ''impartial as between right and wrong, honorable
and dishonorable conduct.''[19] In his fourth volume,
Oberholtzer for the first time devotes some of his space
to labor, conditions of living, and other social problems,
but his treatment of the labor movement reveals marked
prejudice. He confuses socialism with anarchism,[20] refers to the Molly Maguires as ''black-hearted men,''[21]
and in his story of strikes in this period he is grossly unfair to labor. Without revaluing the evidence in the Haymarket Affair he is convinced that the anarchists ''merited'' their punishment.[22] His bias is apparent, too, in
his remarks on the Mormons, who are ''polygamous

[17] P. 95.
[18] Pp. 189-190.
[19] *Pa. Mag. Hist. and Biog.* (January, 1933), p. 27.
[20] P. 10.   [21] P. 11.   [22] Pp. 408-423.

fanatics,'' [23] and there is no attempt to present fairly the point of view of the cheap-money advocates of this period. A disproportionate amount of space, some hundred pages, is given to the Chinese and their effect on American political and economic life. On the other hand, useful and pertinent material is to be found in his chapter on ''The New South''—its economic life, education, suffrage, and the like.

No logical reason can be found for Oberholtzer's divisions of his volumes. The simplest and most obvious one is that when he had enough material for a volume he stopped at that point and published it. The tradition of the old political chronology may have influenced him to make his volumes coincide with presidential administrations; thus the first runs to 1868, the next to 1872, then a skip to 1878, and the fourth ends with the presidential year 1888. Historical writing as typified by Oberholtzer, whose chapters are in the nature of separate essays, is now much less in favor than it once was, for the modern student prefers a synthesis of materials to an accumulation of historical facts.

[23] P. 662.

XIII

THE IMPERIAL SCHOOL OF COLONIAL HISTORY

At the time that some historians were continuing from where Bancroft had left off, other students were beginning to question seriously the value of his work on the colonial era. Far too much emphasis, they claimed, had been laid on exploration, martial events, and the conflict between personalities. Rather, they said, should the point of view be that of institutions and their development, the organization of government, and the relationship of the colonies to the rest of the empire. It is not surprising that at a time when Americans were finishing their studies in Europe a broader perspective should have come into the writing of their own history. The American eagle had also begun to spread imperial wings, and it is thus no coincidence, perhaps, that in looking back over their past American historians should have become conscious of broader horizons. Nor were they uninfluenced by the renewed interest of Englishmen in their empire, as evidenced, in particular, in the works of Sir Charles Dilke and Sir John Seeley.

Bancroft, we have seen, was not as provincial as his

400

later critics thought him. Writers of the modern school, however, have altered so greatly our understanding of the past that American colonial history now appears as but an episode in the expansion of Europe. Osgood, Channing, Beer, and Charles M. Andrews contributed much to this revision of our historical narrative; Professor Andrews has gone the farthest in reconstructing the view of our colonial past from the vantage point of the English homeland. "The years from 1607 to 1783 were colonial before they were American or national, and our Revolution is a colonial and not an American problem," he says. To a certain degree these American historians were preceded by several British writers. The works of Trevelyan and Doyle were very provocative to their younger transatlantic contemporaries, as were the chapters on the American Revolution in William E. H. Lecky's *History of England in the Eighteenth Century.*[1] Moses C. Tyler recommended Lecky to his classes at Cornell because he considered the English historian's treatment "the very best means of getting the coming generation of American students out of the old manner of thinking upon and treating American history, which has led to so much Chauvinism among our people."[2]

GEORGE OTTO TREVELYAN

Histories of America written by Englishmen in the eighteenth century were well known on this side of the Atlantic. In the nineteenth and twentieth centuries English historical studies of America continued to be read in the United States but with less interest. After the independence of the colonies Americans came to dislike,

[1] 8 vols., London, 1878-1890.
[2] *A Memoir of W. E. H. Lecky,* pp. 185-186; A. D. White to Lecky, July 30, 1890.

or at least be indifferent to, many things English. It is
also true that a genuine scholarly English interest in
America was uncommon, and when it did exist it was
often vitiated by a bias for or against democracy. Despite their prejudice against histories of America written by Englishmen, Americans read with an almost morbid anxiety the innumerable books by British travelers
who condemned or praised the United States. Although
most English writers were attracted by the era of the
Civil War, there were some who displayed an interest
in the period when the American colonies had been part
of the British Empire. Two of the most important among
them were Trevelyan and Doyle.

George O. Trevelyan's history of the American
Revolution remains one of the best-known works on
America written by a European. He was a nephew of
Macaulay, whose influence was important in directing
Trevelyan to the study of history. For many years Tre-
velyan was a member of Parliament, and it was after his
retirement from public life that his volumes on Ameri-
can history appeared.

His interest in the American Revolution came by
way of his study of the career of the famous Parliamen-
tarian Charles James Fox. Family tradition and a personal sympathy with the customs of the late eighteenth
century enabled Trevelyan to breathe life into his picture of that society which is the background for *The
Early History of Charles James Fox* (1880). This volume, which fascinated the literary and political world,
writes the author's son, gave ''the reader the entrée as
an intimate member of a bygone aristocratic society.''

To the regret of many of his friends, who used to
say that a Parliamentary statute should be passed to
force Trevelyan to finish his biography of Fox, the historian turned to write on the American Revolution.
Trevelyan's justification for such a step was that Fox's

life between 1774 and 1782 was "inextricably interwoven with the story of the American Revolution." The actions of British public figures in these years, said the historian, could only be understood in the light of what was then happening in the colonies. Over a period of fifteen years six volumes on *The American Revolution* were published. Part I, which covers the decade before 1776, was published in 1899, and at varying intervals the other volumes appeared. The last volume, *George III and Charles James Fox, the concluding part of the American Revolution,* was published in 1914.

In a lengthy chapter, the second in Volume I, Trevelyan makes some illuminating comparisons between society in England and America in which the latter comes off very well. Commenting upon some temperamental differences, he says: "There could be no personal sympathy, and no identity of public views, between the governors in Downing Street and the governed in Pennsylvania and New England." "All who loved England wisely," thinks Trevelyan, "dwelt with satisfaction upon the prosperity of America."

The spirit of Trevelyan's approach to the Revolution is suggested in the lines he quotes from Tennyson:

> O thou, that sendest out the man
>   To rule by land and sea,
> Strong mother of a Lion-line,
> Be proud of those strong sons of thine
>   Who wrench'd their rights from thee!

The Revolution was a civil war, and the differences were not exclusively between peoples on opposite sides of the Atlantic; there were divisions among Englishmen and hostilities among Americans themselves.

Very shortly the narrative swings along the political and military route. In the second volume the writer seems to lose himself in bypaths off the main highway of the

Revolution, and frequently he stops for pen portraits of the leading protagonists, whom he brings to life with rare artistry. Trevelyan was among the earliest to incorporate in a comprehensive account of the Revolution satisfactory reference to the religious factor in bringing on the struggle. Part III of the work is subtitled "Saratoga and Brandywine, Valley Forge, England and France at War," and in the pages on military operations Trevelyan maintains his position as a vivid and picturesque writer. In the last part of his history, Fox and Burke are the heroes, and the villains include George III, Lord North, and Lord Sandwich.

An examination of the work as a whole indicates that Trevelyan's volumes are mainly a Whig interpretation of English politics contemporary with the American Revolution. The English historian did not attempt to discuss many of the internal American problems that arose during the Revolutionary years, and it is unfortunate that he neglected to use American monographic studies that would have been more valuable than Fiske and Lossing.

Englishmen have generally thought Trevelyan's narrative too favorable to Americans; even some Americans have thought so. Theodore Roosevelt, a nationalist historian if ever there was one, wrote to Trevelyan that he "had painted us a little too favorably." Roosevelt was, perhaps, one of the Englishman's most enthusiastic readers. On the receipt of one of the volumes the American President wrote to the author: "I look forward to reading it as eagerly as any girl ever looked forward to reading the last volume of a favorite novel." Trevelyan could write of aristocratic customs with old-world charm, but he could also infuse extraordinary vigor into his narrative of warfare and politics. Roosevelt liked especially Trevelyan's description of battles and characterizations of soldiers like Washington and the riflemen of

Morgan. In a typical burst of Rooseveltian enthusiasm he once wrote to Trevelyan that he had "written the final history of our Revolution."

It is the opinion of the historian's son and biographer that Trevelyan depicted English civilization during the era of the Revolution "in a pleasanter and more intimate light than any to which American readers were accustomed." To learn that many Englishmen also had once despised George III soothed American tempers. Perhaps Trevelyan's work in the future will be discussed less as a contribution to historical literature than as a factor in improving Anglo-American relations in the early years of the twentieth century.[3]

JOHN A. DOYLE

John A. Doyle was born in 1844 and in time became Fellow of All Souls College, Oxford. Throughout his life he retained a conservative, almost a Tory, outlook which was strengthened by the country life he led after the fashion of the squire of a previous generation. His interest in America appeared to have been awakened early; he won the Arnold Prize in 1869 with an essay on *The American Colonies Previous to the Declaration of Independence,* and a few years afterward wrote a textbook on United States history. He kept in touch with American historical writing and contributed reviews of transatlantic publications to English periodicals. In his first publication, the essay, Doyle wrote with vigor and insight, and he anticipated the views of Benjamin F. Wright, who maintains, as against Frederick J. Turner, that the colonists brought democracy with them and did not get it from contact with the American frontier. Speaking of the Anglo-American empire in the middle

[3] *Sir George Otto Trevelyan: A Memoir by His Son,* George Macaulay Trevelyan (London, 1932).

of the eighteenth century, Doyle thought that in it "there was apparently little of the material for national unity. Its inhabitants were not of one race or one speech, still less were their institutions or worship the same. One thread alone bound them together—the common spirit of independence and self-government. We can easily understand the democratic character of New England," he said, "but it is harder at first to see what influence extended that spirit to the southern colonies. Something is due, no doubt, to the self-reliance and freedom from restraint engendered by colonial life. But that alone is not a sufficient explanation. In truth the colonies did not become democratic; they took out democratic principles with them." [4] After a treatment of the events leading up to the Revolution (most of the small volume is concerned with the twenty years preceding 1775), Doyle concludes that "the whole key to the American Revolution lies in two facts: it was a democratic and a conservative revolution. It was the work of the people, and its end was to preserve, not to destroy or to construct afresh." [5]

In the following years Doyle made the studies that eventually led to the publication in five volumes of his history of the colonies. The first of these volumes, published in 1882, is on Virginia, Maryland, and the Carolinas in the seventeenth century. In his first sentences he indicates his unprovincial approach to his subject: "I have preferred to regard the history of the United States," he says, "as the transplantation of English ideas and institutions to a distant soil, and the adaptation of them to new wants and altered modes of life." [6] The process by which these institutions were developed was to be his main theme. The colonies were to be treated separately down to the time "when the similarity of their

[4] Pp. 95-96.   [6] P. 1.
[5] P. 216.

relations to the mother country, and the identity of their interests allow them to be dealt with collectively.'' [7] In the spirit of the modern student, Doyle writes of the significance of the transition from the period of exploration to settlement in the seventeenth century. ''We pass, as it were, from a dreamland of romance and adventure into the sober atmosphere of commercial and political records, amid which we faintly spell out the first germs of the constitutional life of British America.'' [8]

A better and more detailed treatment is made of the Puritan colonies, the subject matter of the next two volumes, published in 1886. After mentioning the more abundant material from which to reconstruct the history of New England, Doyle goes on to write of the difficulties in using the sources. Unlike the contemporary Virginian and Marylander, who spoke of his world without any ''self-conscious feeling that he was writing about the infancy of a great nation,'' the Puritan ''had an exaggerated and even a morbid sense of his responsibilities as a citizen, and an enthusiastic conviction of the greatness which awaited his new country. . . . No event in his history seemed trivial to him, since each was a step in the chain by which God was working out the great destiny of the Puritan commonwealth.'' [9] Doyle's handling of New England history is sometimes at variance with that of Palfrey—it is more detached and freer from any necessity to defend the actions of the Puritans. Doyle's attitude toward Mrs. Hutchinson is similar to that of Charles Francis Adams in his *Three Episodes of Massachusetts History;* the report of her trial, says Doyle, revealed not only ''controversial acuteness,'' but ''a conspicuous union of self-reliance with dignified sobriety and restraint.'' [10] At least one of the Puritan leaders, Winthrop, earned Doyle's unstinted praise: ''He is, on

[7] P. 3.
[8] P. 74.

[9] I, 2-3.
[10] I, 182.

a narrower stage, the counterpart of Pym and Hampden, the forerunner of Washington and Madison.''[11]

Throughout, Doyle's work is informed by generalizations which are stimulating if not always true; in one instance, for example, he wrongly assumes the existence of a ''popular party'' and a government party opposed to each other.[12] In his second volume on the Puritan colonies, Doyle observes that ''the rigid system of public morality'' set up had now to be partly undone. ''Fresh wants, material, intellectual, and spiritual, have to be satisfied; commerce brings with it gradations of wealth, intercourse with the outer world calls out new ideas and new tastes. The difference between the town and the country becomes wider. Men are no longer confined to a little circle, where the actions of each are open to the full view of his neighbours, and where all live under the pressure of an austere and exacting public opinion. To bridge over the gulf which severed the new life from the old, to modify Puritanism and to adapt it to fresh requirements, to secure change without risking disruption or violent reaction, this was the problem which New England had now to solve.''[13] In his examination of political disputes with the governors, Doyle offers a valuable corrective to the conventional, patriotic interpretation made by American historians.[14]

In the year in which Doyle died, 1907, two volumes appeared that completed his study of the colonies. One is on *The Middle Colonies,* which does for this group what the earlier volumes do for the Southern and Northern colonies. The last volume of the series, *The Colonies under the House of Hanover,* treats the colonies as a unit down to the Revolutionary period.

In his description of politics in the middle colonies, Doyle is naturally concerned with the disputes between

[11] I, 393.
[12] II, 246, 310-311.
[13] II, 125.
[14] II, 517.

Governor Cornbury and the Assembly, and he takes the opportunity to observe the similarity between executive attitudes then and sixty years later. "There is in Cornbury," he writes, "the same dull obstinacy, the same narrowness of view that we see in Gage and Dunmore. Like George III, and too many of George's Ministers, Cornbury deals with the question as though it were a mere legal controversy. . . . He wholly fails to see that the very fact of their being dissatisfied and disaffected is in itself of importance." [15] The accession of the Hanoverians is a convenient point of vantage from which the historian could take a comprehensive view of the colonies. As Doyle expresses it, the main interest during the seventeenth century is in the internal history of the colonies, in the next century it is external. "External pressure, exercised by the mother country, becomes the main factor in colonial history. . . . The result is an entire and important change in our point of view. Henceforth we can regard the colonies as an organic whole forming part of an administrative system. It is true," he adds, "that this view needs much modification when we apply it in practice." [16] In his treatment of the commercial relations between the colonies and England, Doyle takes a position similar to that of George L. Beer,[17] although he presses his point too far, perhaps, when he says there was "no desire to sacrifice the colonies to the mother country." His handling of the general problem of imperial administration is, however, inadequate. The sources that lay close at hand in British depositaries were not used by Doyle, whose references are usually to printed materials. While the volume is unsystematic and written with little spirit, it contains a fairer interpretation of the Revolutionary period than historians

[15] IV, 467-468.
[16] V, 2-3.
[17] Pp. 188-189.

were wont to make a generation ago. Doyle said that it was "the blind reliance of English statesmen on administrative methods whose doom had been plainly foretold" which was largely responsible for the eventual conflict.[18]

Most of Doyle's work is on the political history of the colonies, but on several occasions he devotes many pages to other subjects. One of his best chapters is a general survey of institutions, manners, and the economic and social life of New England in 1650.[19] The last volume, on the colonies in the eighteenth century, contains useful chapters on economic progress, religion, and literary and intellectual development. The chapter on religion is excellent and probably gave the contemporary reader the best short treatment of the subject then available. In his section on immigration[20] Doyle reveals a very strong bias against the Irish,[21] but on the whole he is not given to emphasizing his prejudices.

Charles M. Andrews, in a paper he read before the American Historical Association, referred to the volumes that Doyle had already published on the seventeenth century as "unquestionably the best that we have." High hopes were entertained for the forthcoming volumes on the eighteenth century.[22] But the work of Americans— Osgood, Beer, and Professor Andrews himself, not long after—superseded the volumes of Doyle, particularly in the handling of internal problems in the colonies and in unraveling the complexities of imperial policies. Doyle's allotment of four volumes to the seventeenth century, and one to the eighteenth is, of course, a serious distortion of the relative significance of each period for the whole development of colonial life. Although important

[18] V, 613. For his critical approach to the Revolution, see an essay on Trevelyan in John A. Doyle, *Essays on Various Subjects* (London, 1911).
[19] III, Chap. I.
[20] Chap. VII.
[21] P. 391.
[22] *Ann. Rep.* of the Amer. Hist. Assn. for the year 1898, p. 50.

when they first appeared, Doyle's volumes are rarely consulted today.

HERBERT LEVI OSGOOD

Until Osgood turned his amazing energy to a study of the American colonies, there was no dependable, comprehensive treatment of this foundation period of American nationality. A new generation was dissatisfied with Bancroft's volumes, and Fiske had fallen short of the rigorous standards which professional historians had set up for themselves in the last decades of the nineteenth century. A new orientation was demanded, and Osgood was among the first to see that a large part of American colonial history must be told with reference to the British imperial system, of which the colonies were but a portion. American colonial history, he once wrote, needed to be taken out of its isolation, and made to "appear as a natural outgrowth of the history of Europe." This departure from the conventional point of view, so orthodox today as to be part of all textbooks on early American history, was productive of important conclusions, particularly in making more understandable Britain's policy toward her colonies.

Herbert Levi Osgood was born of a New England rural family in 1855. His early education included schooling at the village academy at Wilton, and then at Amherst. The college of Osgood's undergraduate years was fortunate in having on its faculty two such individuals as Julius H. Seelye and John W. Burgess. It was the influence of Burgess, then newly returned from study with the leading German historical scholars, that directed Osgood's attention to what was soon to be his life work. The young Osgood could have received no better training at that time anywhere in the United States, and he left college conversant with the method of scientific historical investigation, and determined upon a career of scholarship. Following the advice of Burgess, after a short period of further study at Amherst and at Yale, Osgood left, in 1882, for the mecca of most young American scholars—Germany.

At Berlin Osgood listened to lectures by Adolph Wagner, Schmoller, Von Treitschke and Von Gneist, the student of the constitutional history of Prussia and England. He had the opportunity too, of hearing Von Sybel. Osgood, however, was most deeply influenced by the aged master, Von Ranke; American scholars, he once said, owed Von Ranke a debt of gratitude which could not easily be repaid. Consciously, in his maturer years, the American wrote with the style of the great German as a model—not with the intention to excite, as did the lesser Von Treitschke, but clearly to provide information and explanation.

Within a year, Osgood was on his way home to teach at his alma mater. He stayed there for a short time and then for six years he taught history in the Brooklyn High School. His location near the city made it possible for Osgood to continue his studies with Burgess, head of the Columbia School of Political Science. His earliest writings, published in the then recently organized *Political Science Quarterly*, were on radical economic theory, and included an examination of the work of Proudhon. But economic theory, in which Osgood was awarded his Ph.D. degree, was not to be his main interest. In looking over the field as yet untilled by the methods of the modern historian, Osgood believed the development of American colonial institutions a theme worthy of a scholar's lifetime, and an article on "England and the Colonies," published in 1887, in the *Political Science Quarterly*, indicated the bent of his future study. Referring to the Revolution, he wrote that "the whole struggle was but an episode in the development of the English colonial system." To root himself further in the field of his choice he went to England to study her history, and after a year's stay came back to New York to accept an appointment at Columbia University.

In the company of newly appointed professors, John Bassett Moore and William A. Dunning, who were added to an older staff that included Burgess, Seligman, and Goodnow, Osgood entered upon a scene of wider usefulness. In his early years at the University he taught both European and American history. After James Harvey Robinson and others joined the staff, however, he confined his teaching to American history. The course for which he worked out the material that later formed the body of his massive volumes on the American colonies in the seventeenth and eighteenth centuries, was called the "Political History of the Colonies and the American Revolution." In his "investigation course," as it came to be called, were born a number of doctoral dissertations on the original thirteen colonies.[23]

In his article on "England and the Colonies," and in his lectures on the American Revolution he suggested the direction that future study of that episode was to follow. Charles M. Andrews thinks that Osgood was "perhaps the very first to realize that an understanding of English commercial policy was necessary for an adequate comprehension of our own colonial development." No longer were the ministers of the King or George III himself to be at the mercy of prosecuting attorneys in the guise of historians; instead their actions were to be judged in the light of a general imperial policy. In such a light English policy was found "blundering and vacillating" but not criminal.

---

[23] Osgood's students included Charles L. Raper, W. Roy Smith, William H. Fry, Edwin P. Tanner, Edgar J. Fisher, Percy S. Flippin, William R. Shepherd, George L. Beer, Arthur E. Peterson, George W. Edwards, Charles R. Lingley, Nelson P. Mead, Charles A. Beard, Arthur M. Schlesinger, and many others.

In his critical review of John Fiske's *American Revolution* in 1891 Osgood pointed out that many decades in a new environment had wrought a new people, so that soon after the middle of the eighteenth century, "two political societies of quite different type were thus brought into conflict," and he thought the duty of a historian was "to do justice to the character and aims of both." Fiske, in Osgood's opinion, had done no better on this score than had his predecessors. Osgood then went on to say: "The truth is until American historians cease the attempt to defend a dogma, and begin in earnest the effort to understand the aristocratic society which existed in England and the democracy which was maturing here, and the causes of conflict between the two, we shall not have a satisfactory history either of the colonial period or of the revolution. The Englishmen too," he warned, "who carries his party prejudices into the work will reach no better results." There were not many teachers in America of that day who were insisting on a fairer survey of the American Revolution. In a paper on "The Study of American Colonial History," read before the American Historical Association in 1898, Osgood emphasized the fact that the seventy years following 1690 had been largely neglected by historians. "Save after the external history of the French and Indian Wars," he said, "absolutely no satisfactory work of a general character has been done. Our historians come up to that period with a fairly full and comprehensive narrative, and then they become scrappy, inconclusive, and largely worthless." Our early history, Osgood continued, must be looked at from the British as well as from the colonial standpoint; "full justice must be done to both sides."

Three articles printed in the *Political Science Quarterly* in 1896, on "The Colonial Corporation" and three the next year on "The Proprietary Province as a

Form of Colonial Government," in the *American Historical Review,* were in the nature of a plan for Osgood's first two volumes on the seventeenth century. Therein appeared only material that showed the development of institutions. Although he included matters of a seemingly different nature, such as the controversy over Anne Hutchinson, or organized religion, these were related to the organization and functions of the state. In the introduction to his first volume on the seventeenth century, he said that materials of a social or economic nature would be used only in so far as they threw light on political growth, and added, showing the strong influence of Burgess and contemporary German historical scholarship, "An attempt will be made to interpret early American history in the terms of public law." On an earlier occasion Osgood had said that the main emphasis in his study would be the political and constitutional aspects of this subject, "because it is only through law and political institutions that social forces become in the large sense operative." [24] As Osgood's biographer, Dixon Ryan Fox phrases it: "Land interests him not as something to till with spades and hoes, or to sell for profit, but as something that engenders controversy as to distribution and taxation by the different governments."

In the main his subject was to be the colonies as they were in themselves and their relation to that power that had given them birth. He thought that the history of the colonies fell into two phases: the system of chartered colonies and the system of royal provinces; and the change from one form to the other. This change, writes Osgood in the introduction to his work, "was the most important and significant transition in American history previous to the colonial revolt." From the beginning of the eighteenth century to the War for Independence, the

[24] *Ann. Rep.* of the Amer. Hist. Assn. for the year 1898, p. 68.

royal province was the prevailing form of colonial government. He insists that to understand the Revolution,
the student must know the precedents that had been
slowly established in the royal provinces. The constitutional questions that arose during the Revolutionary
crisis originated largely in the royal provinces and concerned their structure and workings.

In Volumes I and II of *The American Colonies in
the Seventeenth Century,* published in 1904, with the subtitle "The Chartered Colonies: Beginnings of Self-Government," Osgood states in his preface that he has written "an introduction to American institutional history."
He acknowledges that the original impulse to this "pioneer work in the domain of early American institutional
history" had come from his former Amherst teacher and
later colleague, John W. Burgess. His work has a double
purpose, Osgood writes: "To exhibit in outline the early
development of English colonization on its political and
administrative side"; it is likewise "a study of the origin
of English-American political institutions." This means,
naturally, that his attention was devoted to the continental colonies, and the scope of his work could not include extensive reference to the commercial and economic
aspects of colonization. For an understanding of American history it is necessary to know the varied forms
English institutions took when reproduced in America,
and how they were modified overseas. Osgood signifi-
cantly points out that the origins of American institutions are not to be found wholly in the Revolutionary
period, but in earlier forms that "had undergone steady
development for a century and a half before the date of
independence." In a paper published a few years earlier,
the Columbia historian had written that "it will be impossible—as it has been impossible in the past—to write
a satisfactory history of the Revolution till the half cen-

tury and more which preceded it shall have been thoroughly investigated."[25]

In his first volume Osgood examines Virginia as a proprietary province, and the corporate colonies of New England. Special sections are devoted to the land system, the financial system and the arrangements for defense in the New England colonies. In the earliest as well as the last of his volumes Osgood is at special pains to note intercolonial relations which were to weave close ties among the scattered colonists and prepare them for the needed co-operative activity of the Revolutionary era. Osgood's pages on religion in New England are well done, but are not distinguished by marked friendship for the Puritans.

The historian in his second volume continues his study of the proprietary province in its later forms, with reference to the various systems .of landholding, officialdom, and the relations between the governors and legislatures. He notes that the "significance of the Quakers in American history arises from the fact that their ideas coincided well with the prevailing tendencies of colonial life." "The equality and individualism of colonial life found their counterpart in Quaker tendencies and beliefs."

At the close of this volume Osgood adds some interesting conclusions about American society toward the end of the seventeenth century. He finds that the colonists by this time "in their large relations . . . were [still] subordinate to Europe" but "their personal and local concerns were as distinct from those of contemporary Europeans as time or space could well make them. In their languages and in the type and traditions of their culture they were Europeans; but they were transplanted upon a new and distant continent, and felt chiefly the

[25] *Ibid.*, p. 64. Quotations from *The American Colonies in the Seventeenth Century* are by permission of The Macmillan Company, publishers.

pressure of its environment. They had already become colonials in the full sense of the word but had not yet reached a developed American type.'' The characteristics of equality and uniformity in American society were already clearly marked, especially in the corporate colonies. In this first century of American history ''in their main outlines American institutions, both local and colonial, were fashioned.'' ''If at any time the acquired rights of self-government of the colonies at large should be imperilled, that type of political theory which had its home in New England could easily be extended to fit conditions in the provinces.'' Conditions in America predisposed the colonists in favor of self-government, and in this temper they ''faced the home government and any plans of systematic control which it might devise and seek to enforce.''

Volume III, on the seventeenth century, appeared in 1907 and is concerned with ''Imperial Control: Beginnings of the System of Royal Provinces.'' For the first time, the author notes, an attempt was made to trace the imperial system of control ''as a distinct and separate feature of colonization.'' ''Attention has been directed to the organs through which it was exercised, to the objects and ideals which were pursued, and to the obstacles which prevented their attainment.'' Osgood graciously acknowledged a debt to George Louis Beer, a former student who had been making valuable independent researches, for important suggestions relating to England's commercial policy. Osgood's most competent reviewer, Charles M. Andrews, wrote that Volume III completed ''the most important interpretation of our colonial history that has thus far been made,'' although in an earlier review of the first two volumes, he thought the author had incorporated too many details, for example, in the chapter on the New England land system. Osgood himself, in after years, agreed with Professor Andrews's statement, but remarked that he had written so fully lest he be thought to have advanced insufficient evidence.

After taking the reader through the complicated and sometimes exciting events that made royal provinces of the colonies, Osgood pens some effective generalizations in the last pages of Volume III. The changes that came toward the end of the seventeenth century were ''accomplished by a combination of executive and judicial action. It swept away assemblies and boundary lines, and aimed to undo the results of a half century of historic growth.'' For bringing about these changes the Crown and Parliament were responsible. ''Prerogative government over the colonies reached its high-water mark'' in the reign of James II, writes the historian, who adds, ''Never again was so much attempted or accomplished by this method. When, in later times, imperial pressure was again brought to bear, parliament was resorted to at every step.''

At his death in 1918, Osgood left the manuscript, practically completed, of *The American Colonies in the Eighteenth Century*. After much delay it was published in 1924 in four volumes that carry his narrative to 1763. It is ironic that these volumes, written by one of America's greatest scholars, could not find a commercial publisher. The history was too meaty for the taste of the general public and might have been denied to professional historians had not a student in grateful memory provided funds for its publication.

Osgood had stated in 1898 that the two most important themes in our history during the eighteenth century were imperial policy and colonial resistance, and, because of their constant interaction, it was difficult for him to divide arbitrarily his material as he had done for the seventeenth century. Although several chapters deal with the working of the imperial system seen from the distant view of London, most of the book is concerned with the internal history of the various colonies, and especially with the struggles between governors and assemblies.

With the beginning of the eighteenth century, writes Osgood in the preface to his volumes on that period, "the controlling fact of the situation was the gradual coalescing of the colonies into one system, under the control of the British government." He intended to trace chronologically "the development of the colonies as a whole, in their internal growth, their interrelations and their connection with Great Britain." The historian faced the difficult task of following the individual growth of each of the colonies and making clear their position as part of the British Empire. Some subjects of a general nature, like projects for colonial union, colonial wars, piracy, immigration, Indian affairs, and ecclesiastical relations, had an intercolonial significance, and Osgood treated them as "distinct wholes." The arrangement of the work was made to turn upon the succession of colonial wars and the intervals of peace in the struggle between the French and English. The author's problem in recording the history of the separate colonies was to "bring out their peculiarities and their uniformities." With pardonable pride Osgood wrote that "in scope and plan, as in much of its material, this is a pioneer work"; no longer would the decades it covered be called the "unknown period" of American history.

The colonies during the first two intercolonial wars —1690-1714—constitute Part I. Because of the strategic position that the colony of New York had in the wars with the French, her place in the history of these years tends to be especially emphasized. Osgood's interest is not so much in the military events themselves as in their effects upon governmental institutions. For example, he is at pains to show how the need for military appropriations increased the power of the New York assembly. Conditions in New England are also given considerable space in these pages. In his references to the place of the Mathers in the witchcraft episode, Osgood declares that "the Mathers must be taken as representative of declining Puritanism," a statement that today is disputed by a number of scholars.

Part I is continued into the second volume with chapters on the Northern and Middle colonies, which record their history to approximately 1715. A comprehensive section on the early extension of the Anglican Church in the colonies is included. The second half of this volume begins Part II—the colonies at peace between the second and third intercolonial wars, 1714-1740. Among the significant pages in these latter chapters are those on the attitude of English officials toward commercial questions. Up to about 1730, says Osgood, "though the cabinet and parliament were much occupied with questions of trade no new principles were evolved, though the application of those already accepted was slightly extended. Of special importance is the fact that no wholesale changes in the administrative or fiscal policy of Great Britain toward the colonies were considered or probably even mentioned in those bodies which were really responsible for the conduct of the British government." What is probably the best short survey of immigration into the colonies may be found in Volume II.

Part II runs over into Volume III, which contains studies of the later governments of Maryland, Georgia, Massachusetts, Rhode Island, New Hampshire, and Connecticut. In some respects this may be considered one of Osgood's most notable volumes, with its excellent chapters on the English Church and the Dissenters. Part III, which closes the last third of the volume, is called "The Growth of the Spirit of Independence" in the period 1749-1763. Included under that caption are chapters on the Great Awakening and one entitled "Ecclesiastical Relations at the Middle of the Century." Osgood is unsympathetic to the Great Awakening, which, he notes, had caused "no appreciable improvement in the morals of communities" and "people generally had not been made wiser in the conduct of their lives." In the closing lines on planners of colonial union, Osgood assigns Shirley a high place—"Franklin was the only colonist," he writes, "whose services in this direction were comparable with those of Shirley."

The fourth volume, which concludes Part III, carries forward the narratives of New Jersey, Pennsylvania, Virginia, South Carolina, North Carolina, and New York. Osgood gives careful attention to the problems created by the frontier; he associates the Albany Congress with westward expansion. In the last quarter of his volume he enters upon the fourth intercolonial war that was finally to settle the struggle for supremacy in favor of the English. His sane judgment on the capture of Quebec is a welcome contrast to more emotional outbursts. He remarks that the death of both commanders "lifted the event out of the realm of mere military success and defeat or of political change into that of sentiment. Wolfe in particular has been taken out of the category of ordinary men and raised to the rank of a hero. . . . But what really happened was that, backed by superior force and aided by fortunate circumstances, to which he contributed by good management, Wolfe made connections, that is, after much delay and futile experiment, he hit upon a plan which led to success, and it was crowned with a timely death, a consummation for which Wolfe helped, perhaps consciously, to prepare the stage."

Of *The American Colonies in the Eighteenth Century* Professor Andrews wrote that it was "not British history, nor yet American history in any narrow and exclusive sense of that term, but something between, more American than British and growing more and more American with every decade that passes." Unusually fine at its best, at its worst, Osgood's work was "a great reservoir of organized knowledge, material for history rather than the finished product itself." It is a fair statement that he paid insufficient attention to economic and social forces acting on the course of legislation.

Unfortunately Osgood was unable to add to his volumes on the eighteenth century those illuminating generalizations with which he concludes his volumes on the previous century. These interpretive passages give an excellent summary of his materials and his treatment, and the writing in them is better than elsewhere. His style is never ornamental, nor is it easy reading for the student who may like his history romanticized. He wrote history for historians, and did not think it was his function to make history fine literature, yet he was never obscure. Although he kept abreast of the monographic material that was published, much of it the outgrowth of his own seminar, the larger part of the historian's sources were in manuscript, particularly for his volumes on the eighteenth century. He was constantly urging state action to care for and publish local and national archives, but this movement did not gain much headway until near the end of his life.

Interest in social and intellectual history has so broadened the scope of research today that Osgood's contribution, great as it was, left a large part of the colonial story untold. Even that aspect of the relationship between the colonies and the homeland that touched commercial policy was largely left for other students, especially George Louis Beer and Charles M. Andrews, to work out. Pioneer in the modern study of the political origins of the United States, Herbert L. Osgood lived to watch and encourage other students to walk more easily over the path he had so laboriously hewn.[26]

[26] Dixon Ryan Fox, *Herbert Levi Osgood* (N. Y., 1924); Homer F. Coppock, "Herbert Levi Osgood," *Miss. Valley Hist. Rev.*, Vol. XIX.

George Louis Beer

Herbert L. Osgood and Charles M. Andrews took colonial American history out of its provincial setting and made it a part of the history of the British Empire. They were ably seconded by a younger contemporary, George Louis Beer, whose work is of the first importance. "His contributions have the merit of permanence," wrote Professor Andrews, and Robert L. Schuyler says that the work of Beer "ranks as one of the major contributions to knowledge made by American historical scholarship in the present century."

Beer was a student of Burgess, Seligman, and Osgood at Columbia University, and under Osgood's direction the young scholar turned to the study of colonial history. In 1893, when he was but twenty years old, Beer published his master's thesis on *The Commercial Policy of England toward the American Colonies*, which foreshadowed his later historical writing. This little book, on a subject hitherto largely ignored by the historians, stands perhaps alone as a complete treatment of the topic. Written with freedom from any patriotic bias, it gives a new slant to the relations of England with her colonies whose inhabitants were no longer to be viewed as people subjected to tyranny, but as participants in the mercantilist system. "Thus we can see," Beer writes in the course of his argument, "that the laying of restrictions on colonial manufactures was a necessary consequence of the mercantilist system." [27] The score of years preceding 1776, he suggests, "must be regarded as transitional, as a period during which it was to be determined whether the colonies were sufficiently mature, not only to assert, but also to maintain their independence." [28]

[27] P. 67
[28] P. 144.

Beer looked forward at an early date to rewriting his essay on an extended scale, but teaching (which he did not like) and business postponed fulfillment of this intention for a decade. In 1903 his long-planned trip to London to study the needed documents materialized. He returned the next year to begin his immense task—"to describe and explain the origins, establishment, and development of the British colonial system up to the outbreak of the disagreements that culminated in the American Revolution; to analyze the underlying principles of British colonial policy, especially in so far as they found expression in the laws of trade and navigation." The details of his plan were concerned with the English fiscal system and the part of the colonies in it, colonial economic legislation that affected the relations to the mother country, the economic life of the colonies themselves, the British official system in America and how far the laws were enforced, and the relations of economics to the political system. In the part of the plan that he lived to complete, Beer gives us only that side of American history which was seen from the mother country. Far more definitely than Osgood, Beer "deliberately took the reader from the soil of America and set him down in the midst of those who were viewing the colonies from a position 3000 miles away."

When he was in England in 1903-1904, Beer had studied for the most part documents of the eighteenth century. On his return to America he found himself better prepared, therefore, to write on the period after 1750, and thus it happened that he wrote the last volume of his projected series first. In 1907 he published his *British Colonial Policy, 1754-1765*, which remains the most widely known of his volumes. Its wealth of sources showed the impossibility of writing on this subject from the printed materials available in America; in fact, for all his volumes Beer drew largely from manuscript sources.

The center of his interest, writes the author, is the British Empire, not the rise of the United States. Beer says that on its positive side this book is "a portrayal of British policy, a study in imperial history; on its negative side it is an account of the preliminaries of the American Revolution." The imperial administrative system was now tightened, he points out, because in these years the question of defense became one of the highest importance as a result of the struggle with France. In this volume Beer gives the first satisfactory treatment of the illegal trade carried on by the colonists. In writing of the readjustment of the laws of trade between 1763 and 1765, he also adds some useful advice to the student. History, he says, "is to a great extent based on social psychology and in studying the dynamic effects of any policy on the relations of two social groups, it is frequently far more important to know what people at the time thought were the results, rather than what these naturally were." [29] The long way that Beer had moved from the interpretation of nineteenth-century nationalist historians is revealed in his conclusion that the aim of the "purely commercial regulations of the years 1764-1765 . . . was to encourage and not to restrict colonial industry." [30] This volume, in which the author leans backward in desiring to be fair to England, has played a very large part in the revision that this present generation has made of the history of the American Revolution.

Beer then turned back to the sixteenth and seventeenth centuries to seek the beginnings of the colonial system. His investigation resulted in the publication of *The Origins of the British Colonial System, 1578-1660* (1908). In this volume he shows that mercantilist principles were firmly established in practice before 1640, long in advance of theorists who evolved the doctrines of

[29] P. 201.
[30] P. 226.

mercantilism. Two more volumes appeared later (1912), as Part I of *The Old Colonial System,* which cover the years 1660-1688. Beer had planned an additional six volumes to carry the narrative to 1754, but he never found time to write on the early eighteenth century. Instead he was brought up sharply against the twentieth century when the World War broke out in 1914, and he abandoned the past for the present. Anglo-American relations, which had once been an intellectual interest to the historian, became an absorbing passion to the publicist who labored in effecting the peace settlement.

In *The Old Colonial System* Beer indicates the unity of the British imperial possessions. He defines the term "colonial system" as "that complex system of regulations whose fundamental aim was to create a self-sufficient commercial empire of mutually complementary economic parts." He is not describing the economic origins of the United States, he writes, and though his viewpoint is primarily imperial, his work is "something more and also something less than merely an economic history of the old Empire." One of his chief aims, says Beer, was to learn "precisely what the statesmen of the day sought to accomplish, what means they employed for their purposes, to what extent these instruments were adapted to the actual situation, and how the various parts of the Empire developed under these regulations." To Americans who nursed a grievance against the English, Beer brought the salutary reminder that the colonial system was not a one-sided one and that it was recognized as mutually advantageous by the ancestors of aggrieved descendants in the twentieth century. To compensate for colonial trade restrictions, England protected the colonies "and gave such of their products as were needed and wanted a monopoly of the home market."

Although Beer was much interested in economic history, he generally ignored the machinery of commerce and industrial organization; only incidentally are freight charges, insurance, prices, and the like, included in his discussion. He underestimates the place of colonies as markets, for his emphasis is rather on these territorial possessions as sources of supply.[31] He tends to over-emphasize the role of the "sea dogs" in colonization, whereas the English merchants were far more important.[32] These are, however, minor flaws in a pioneer work.

Beer's volumes will not entertain the general reader who prefers his history with a dash of the dramatic. They have rather served to instruct both English and American students of colonial history in rereading their common past. The version of that past as expounded by Professor Andrews and by Osgood and Beer has come to be the one accepted by the careful student of today. It was an appropriate climax to the life of Beer, that he, who in his earlier years sought better to understand the difficulties between the colonies and the mother country, should close his life at a time when he was promoting friendlier relations between the United States and England.[33]

CHARLES M. ANDREWS

After forty-two years of teaching, Charles M. Andrews recently retired from the Farnam Professorship of American History at Yale to be Director of Historical Publications at the University. Before his long career at Yale began, Professor Andrews had taught at Bryn Mawr and in other academic halls. The Johns Hopkins of the 1880's, aglow with the freshness of intellectual dis-

[31] See valuable article by Curtis Nettels, "Markets in the Colonial System," *New Eng. Quart.* (September, 1933).

[32] See G. B. Parks, *Richard Hakluyt*, p. 88, note 1, and *passim;* also C. M. Andrews, *The Colonial Period of American History: The Settlements,* Chap. II.

[33] *George Louis Beer: A Tribute to his Life and Work* (N. Y., 1924), chapter by C. M. Andrews, "The Historian."

covery, had drawn him as it had so many others who were to make valuable contributions to American culture. The favoring circumstance of birth and nurture—he was born and bred in New England—gave him the ideal background for a historian of the American colonies. "I am a Puritan of the Puritans," he said once in describing his ancestry.

The earliest publications of Professor Andrews indicate the bent of his later major interests, especially his study of *The River Towns of Connecticut*.[34] The emphasis in the 1880's and 1890's, as we have seen, was on institutional history, and it is not surprising that he should have been strongly attracted to the field of colonial institutions. The young scholar was critical of the behavior of the early settlers. "In all their relations with their brethren and neighbors in the Connecticut valley, the Puritans," he said, "showed little of that austere honorableness for which they are famed." [35] Before he fixed his attention almost exclusively on American colonial history, which has engaged him for more than thirty years, Professor Andrews wrote on *The Old English Manor* [36] and published two volumes on *The Historical Development of Modern Europe* [37] and a *History of England* (1903). From the particular—the Connecticut towns—he progressed to the universal; and with his studies of the American colonies he has gone back to the particular, perhaps unconsciously in keeping with his own dictum that it is necessary to treat "the particular with a full understanding of its relation to the universal." [38]

In an essay which he published in the *Yale Review* in 1893 on "Some Recent Aspects of Institutional Study," Professor Andrews gives us an idea of some studies he

[34] Johns Hopkins University, "Studies in History and Political Science," 1889.

[35] P. 26.

[36] Baltimore, 1892.

[37] 2 vols., N. Y., 1896-1898.

[38] *Yale Review* (1893).

was to make later: for example, an investigation of various phases of local economic life which he thought necessary in order to understand the causes of the Revolution. Incidentally, in this paper, he revealed himself as an exponent of the "new history," which seemingly is in process of continuous renovation. On the same program with Osgood, in 1898, before the American Historical Association, Professor Andrews made a plea for the study of American colonial history from 1690 to 1750. Like Osgood, Professor Andrews emphasized the fact that an understanding of the later period rested not on the era of settlement, but on the "middle period of conflict and experience." [39] Referring to this period, he said that it was "marked at its beginning by a strengthening of the old British colonial administration all along the line; an administration destined from this time forward to come more and more under the control of parliament and to pass from the hands of Crown and council who had hitherto directed colonial affairs. No writer," he continued, "has, however, made any proper attempt to emphasize this fact or to tell us, by careful attention to details, how the experiment worked. Yet, so far as it concerned all the colonies together, it is the most important phase in their history after 1689." In this paper he also drew the attention of his readers to the value of including the Canadian and West Indian colonies in a study of the British North American group. He believed, too, that historians had not stressed sufficiently religious influences in this period. The need of close examination of manuscripts in English repositories was likewise mentioned by Professor Andrews, because he thought that, without consulting them, no one could write a complete history of the colonies.

Much of his scholarly labor has been devoted to exploring archives in America and England, and a number of reconnaissance reports testify to his unrivaled knowl-

[39] *Ann. Rep.* of the Amer. Hist. Assn. for the year 1898, p. 50.

edge of the sources of American colonial history. *British Committees, Commissions, and Councils of Trade and Plantations 1622-1675* is one of his publications. In 1908, in conjunction with Frances G. Davenport, he brought out (under the auspices of the Carnegie Institution, Bureau of Historical Research) a *Guide to the Manuscript Materials for the History of the United States to 1783 in the British Museum [and other Depositaries]*. In a preliminary report on "Materials in British Archives for American Colonial History," Professor Andrews said: "Notwithstanding the fact that for a hundred and fifty years our colonies were a part of the British empire, no systematic attempt has ever been made by British or American historians to discover the extent and value of the material contained in British archives relating to American history." [40] Osgood, the most important co-worker of Professor Andrews in colonial history, said that the *Guide* was "one among many signs that we have entered upon a new epoch in the study of American history. It is the outgrowth of a demand for a more thorough and exhaustive investigation of the sources. It implies and will be followed by a more comprehensive and scientific treatment of the period as a whole than has been possible or even imagined. The era of partial views, and isolated efforts, whether in the collection of materials or the writing of history, is passing away."

In 1912 and 1914 Professor Andrews published, in two volumes, a *Guide to the Materials for American History, to 1783, in the Public Record Office of Great Britain.* Of further assistance to the student are some special lists which he has published: "Lists of the Journals and Acts of the Councils and Assemblies of the Thirteen Original Colonies, and the Floridas, in America, Preserved in the Public Record Office, London"; [41] "List of the Commis-

---

[40] *Amer. Hist. Rev.*, X, 325.
[41] *Ann. Rep.* of the Amer. Hist. Assn. for the year 1908, Vol. I.

sions and Instructions Issued to the Governors and Lieutenant Governors of the American and West Indian Colonies from 1609 to 1784''; [42] "List of Reports and Repre-
sentations of the Plantation Councils, 1660-1674, the
Lords of Trade, 1675-1696, and the Board of Trade, 1696-
1782, in the Public Record Office.'' [43]

While Professor Andrews has performed an immensely valuable service in providing these tools for research, he has managed also on various occasions to give
illuminating surveys of parts, and once, the whole, of the
colonial period. He contributed a volume on *Colonial
Self-Government 1652-1689* to the "American Nation"
series, and at a later date two volumes to the "Yale
Chronicles" on the *Fathers of New England* and *Colonial
Folkways*. These latter books, written for a more general
audience, contain the distillation of his deep knowledge
of colonial life. For the Home University Library, Professor Andrews wrote an excellent volume on *The Colonial Period* (1912). He observed that earlier writers on
the colonial period of American history had emphasized
the colonies to the exclusion of the mother country and
had also neglected the relations between the two. It was
his belief "that the balance should be restored, and that
if we are to understand the colonies, not only at the time
of their revolt, but also throughout their history from the
beginning, we must study the policy and administration
at home and follow continuously the efforts which were
made, on the side of Great Britain to hold the colonies
in a state of dependence and on the side of the colonies
to obtain a more or less complete control of their own
affairs.'' Thus he gives almost as much space to England
as he does to the colonies, and in another departure from
traditional treatments he includes in his survey Canada
and the West Indies, as well as the original thirteen col-

[42] *Ann. Rep.* of the Amer. Hist. Assn. for the year 1911, Vol. I.
[43] *Ann. Rep.* of the Amer. Hist. Assn. for the year 1913, Vol. I.

onies. ''No distinction existed between them in colonial times and none should be made now by the writer on colonial history.'' It is necessary to view the colonies as a whole, he says, to avoid a treatment ''which is merely provincial on one side or topical on the other.''

In 1924 [44] Professor Andrews published a volume of four essays on *The Colonial Background of the American Revolution*. It restates his earlier thesis on the dependence and interdependence of mother country and colonies which ''determined to no small extent the attitude and policy of mother country and colonies alike.'' Again he reminds his readers that historians writing of the events from 1763 to 1775 have generally ''failed to see that primarily they were but a part of the history of British colonization and should be interpreted in the light, not of the democracy that was to come years later, but of the ideas and practices regarding colonization that were in vogue in Great Britain at the time.'' [45] In his last essay, ''General Reflections,'' Professor Andrews contrasts the settled and smug ruling classes in England with the society then in the making in the colonies, and finds that a conflict was almost inevitable. The colonies, he concludes, were far more advanced, politically, socially, and morally, than the mother country and ''could not longer be held in leading strings''; ''such constitutional concessions as would have satisfied the demands of the colonists, these British statesmen could not make, because they were barred by the mental limitations of their own time and class.''

In his presidential address, ''The American Revolution,'' before the American Historical Association in 1925, Professor Andrews returned to the theme treated in his essay ''General Reflections.'' The differences that existed between England and her colonies ''in mental atti-

[44] Revised edition, 1931.
[45] P. 121.

tudes and convictions," he said, "proved in the end more
difficult to overcome than the diverging historical tendencies or bridging the three thousand miles of the Atlantic itself.[46] Immobility was the characteristic of the
English mind, particularly the official mind, in the half
century before 1775. Americans, on the other hand, were
forming a new society. In speaking of this latter process,
Professor Andrews has given us what is undoubtedly the
outline of the study he is now making of the colonies:
"The story of how this was done—how that which was
English slowly and imperceptibly merged into that which
was American—has never been adequately told; but it is
a fascinating phase of history, more interesting and en-
lightening when studied against the English background
than when construed as an American problem only. It is
the story of the gradual elimination of those elements,
feudal and proprietary, that were foreign to the normal
life of a frontier land, and of the gradual adjustment of
the colonies to the restraints and restrictions that were
imposed upon them by the commercial policy of the
mother country. It is the story also of the growth of the
colonial assemblies. . . . It is above all . . . the story of
the gradual transformation of these assemblies from
provincial councils that the home government intended
them to be into miniature parliaments. At the end of a
long struggle . . . they emerged powerful legislative bodies, as self-conscious in their way as the House of Commons in England was becoming during the same eventful
years."

In a small volume, *Our Earliest Colonial Settlements*,[47] Professor Andrews engagingly tells again of
their beginnings, emphasizing the English background of
these enterprises. Three New England colonies are discussed—Massachusetts, Rhode Island, and Connecticut;

[46] *Amer. Hist. Rev.*, XXXI, 221.
[47] N. Y., 1933. Originally delivered at New York University as lectures.

and two colonies in the South—Virginia, "a normal English colony," and Maryland, "a feudal seignory in the New World." His concluding remarks are a criticism of those historians who would read the main currents of the progress of the colonies in the products of literary men. "The meaning and significance of colonial history are to be discovered," he suggests, "not by studying selected phases of the subject, the lives of individual colonial leaders . . . but by an understanding acquired of all phases, all men, and all constructive thought, no matter how simple and unpretentious it may be, that discloses the growth of the human colonial mind."[48] These pages once more reveal the writer's gift for gracefully condensing much detailed knowledge.

In 1934 Professor Andrews published the first volume of the work, long awaited, *The Colonial Period of American History: The Settlements.* The point of view adopted years earlier is again affirmed: "I have approached the subject from the English end," he writes, "and have broadened the scope of my inquiry to include all England's colonial possessions in the west" during the seventeenth century. It was necessary to do so, he maintains, because "final conclusions must always rest upon the experiences England had with all, not a part of her colonies." The scholar must keep in mind the fundamental difference between the seventeenth and eighteenth centuries; the former "shows us an English world in America, with but little in it that can be strictly called American: the eighteenth everywhere presents to the view an Anglo-American conflict." "The colonial period of our history is not American only but Anglo-American."

Beginning with the European background Professor Andrews gives an excellent picture of the temper of English life in the sixteenth century and the emergence of an ambitious middle class whose aspirations are so intimately

[48] P. 167.

linked with settlements in far-flung places. The second chapter is especially good in its emphasis on England's commercial activities. In the first forty years of the seventeenth century rapidly accumulating capital sought newer areas for operation other than those in the older region of European trade. "Thus the early seventeenth century presents a shifting scene and a new outlook." "Medieval methods and the medieval conception of the social order were threatened at their foundations by the forces of a new individualism; in fact, medieval habits and standards were breaking through though they were not yet broken and were not to be broken for many a long year." [49]

The remainder of the volume is concerned with the first half century of the settlements of Virginia, Plymouth, Massachusetts Bay, as well as of Newfoundland, Nova Scotia, and Bermuda. Throughout there is an interrelationship among these enterprises whose essential unity may be traced to the energetic activities of the incorporated companies of the homeland. While the historian seems to stress more the material than the religious motive for colonization, he does speak of the latter as an important factor in overseas migration. He is less sympathetic to the Puritans than is Samuel E. Morison, and the social and cultural history of Massachusetts is inadequately handled. Professor Andrews's main interest, however, is institutional history and his range of knowledge here is unsurpassed.

The second volume (1936) covers the settlement and early years of Rhode Island, Connecticut, Barbados, and Maryland. Through the complexities of conflicting materials on the early years of Rhode Island Professor Andrews picks his sure way and gives on the whole a friendly, yet a dispassionately critical, estimate of Roger

[49] P. 75.

Williams. He demolishes many time-worn traditions, for example, proving that no question of a search for religious freedom entered into the founding of Connecticut, but rather "the allurement of a fertile valley." He also provides the reader with a much-needed corrective to the persistent misunderstanding of Puritan "democracy," observing that "the ideas of the Connecticut Puritans regarding the political and religious organization of society [were] far removed from the democratic ideas of later times." [50]

Professor Andrews is continually warning the student against accepting the older interpretations of Bancroft and his school, who saw in the seventeenth century the foreshadowings of the later American Revolution. Whatever rights and privileges the colonists claimed were the same that Englishmen everywhere were then claiming. It is always necessary to keep in mind the fundamental difference between the seventeenth and eighteenth centuries, for the former reveals an English world in America, "with but little in it that can strictly be called American; the eighteenth everywhere presents to the view an Anglo-American conflict." One closes these volumes with the feeling of tremendous reserve power in their author's possession; he is a judge weighing the evidence in the light of his own researches and he renders his decisions with a magistral (but not humorless) air. Professor Andrews waited a long time before giving definitive form to his work, and it is not likely that the story he has told of the institutional developments in the colonial period will be seriously modified. If there is any history being written today possessing the quality of finality, this is it.

Many of the foremost students in England and the United States now at work on the period covering Amer-

[50] P. 112.

ica's colonial era are deeply indebted to Professor Andrews, and those who have sat in his classes have profited from his inspired instruction. An expectant audience awaits the remaining volumes of his great work.[51]

EDWARD CHANNING

With Herbert L. Osgood and Charles M. Andrews, another contemporary, Edward Channing, was studying the colonial period. His field of interest in time came to embrace the whole of American history but temperamentally he appeared to be more closely attached to the colonial years and the first three decades of the Republic. In 1905 Channing brought out the first volume of *A History of the United States,* which he intended to complete in eight volumes. While he was at work on the seventh volume, which was to treat the period after the Civil War, he died suddenly in January, 1931, in his seventy-fifth year.

Channing was a descendant of some of New England's brightest intellectuals. An appropriate environment drew him to history soon after his graduation from Harvard in 1878, and five years later he was named instructor at his alma mater. His Ph.D. was one of the earliest granted in American schools, then first turning to the scientific study of history. All his academic life thereafter was associated with Harvard, where he taught a number of students who have themselves gained distinguished reputations for historical scholarship. The training he gave to students in dealing critically with historical evidence was invaluable.

Channing was anxious to have young students and

[51] L. H. Gipson, "Charles M. Andrews and the reorientation of the study of American History," *Pa. Mag. Hist. and Biog.* (July, 1935); some interesting biographical details are in Professor Andrews's paper, "Historic Doubts Regarding Early Massachusetts History," Col. Soc. Mass. *Transactions,* XXXVIII (1935), 280 ff.

the general public made acquainted with the sources for American history, and, with Albert Bushnell Hart, his colleague, he edited the "American History Leaflets." For the help of the research student, he and Professor Hart published their *Guide to the Study of American History.*[52]

Long before this, Channing had published other studies alone. *The Narragansett Planters, a Study of Causes,* a minor publication, appeared in 1886, in the Johns Hopkins "Studies," and it illustrates Channing's early skepticism of accepted traditions and his desire to go to the sources for his narrative. His *Town and County Government in the English Colonies of North America* opposes the theory of Teutonic origins of New England towns. The first careful summary of the English Acts of Trade and Navigation affecting the colonies was made by Channing in a paper before the American Antiquarian Society in 1889. He was also a contributor to Justin Winsor's *Narrative and Critical History of America.* While he was still an undergraduate, Channing was taking notes for the history he was later to write. He once said he felt he had to write a history of the United States from the sources, after listening to the dogmatic lectures of Henry Cabot Lodge, his teacher, and reading the biased history of Hildreth.[53] The studies, mentioned above, as well as many others, were to be the materials for "the Great Work," as his students called it.

In the preface to his work, Channing writes: "I have undertaken a new study of the history of the United States from the discovery of America to the close of the nineteenth century." "The growth of the nation will . . . be treated as one continuous development from the political, military, institutional, industrial, and social points of

[52] Boston, 1896.
[53] S. E. Morison on "Edward Channing" in Mass. Hist. Soc. *Proc.,* Vol. LXIV.

view." "Writers on American history have usually regarded the colonists as living a life somewhat apart from
the rest of mankind. . . . The outlook of the present
work is different. I have considered the colonies as parts
of the English empire, as having sprung from that political fabric, and as having simply pursued a course of institutional evolution unlike that of the branch of the English race which remained behind. . . . I have also thought
that the most important single fact in our development
has been the victory of the forces of union over those of
particularism." The institutions and forces making for
union, Channing thinks worthy of especial emphasis,
"for it is the triumph of these which has determined the
fate of the nation." Footnotes, and provocative notes appended to his chapters, indicate his leading sources. In a
kind of apologia, Channing writes: "The task of handling the enormous mass of the material of American history is great; the time and place of one's birth and breeding affect the judgment, and the opportunity for error is
frequent."

The first volume in his series is *The Planting of a
Nation in the New World 1000-1660.*[54] Channing's treatment of the colonies as part of the English imperial system is, perhaps, the most novel feature of the volume.
This point of view, at the time, was not held very widely;
its most noted champions, we have seen, were Herbert L.
Osgood and Charles M. Andrews. Channing was more
sympathetic to the Puritans than were some of his contemporaries in the Adams family. After noting that the
first generation of New England Puritans were very
much like those who stayed behind in the mother country,
the author writes that as a result of new conditions "the
Puritan creed only slowly assumed the sternness of aspect
which made intellectual excitation save for religious pur-

[54] Quotations from Channing's *History of the United States,* are by
permission of The Macmillan Company, publishers.

poses an impossibility." Little faith is placed in John Smith's veracity, but Channing's tribute to the tragic story of the earliest Virginia settlers is that "they were the first heroes of American history."

In the last chapter, "The Colonies in 1660," Channing touches subjects of especial interest to the social historian. He returns again to the statement he made in his preface: "The greatest fact in American history has been the union in one federal state of peoples living in widely separated regions under very different conditions of society and industry." This was effected because "the institutions and the political ideals of these communities had in them so much that was akin." Although noting similarities to English precedents, he also stresses colonial divergences from them. His conclusion, however, is that "the colonists were still Englishmen in their feelings and prejudices, in their virtues and in their vices. Contact with the wilderness and freedom from the constitutional restraints which held down Englishmen in England . . . had not yet resulted in making the colonists Americans." Many more years were to elapse before the Anglo-Americans were to turn away from English traditions and ideals.

The second volume, *A Century of Colonial History 1660-1760,* appeared in 1908. The first half of the volume discusses the political affairs of the several colonies down to near the end of the seventeenth century. Channing's likes and dislikes are rather obvious and sometimes amusing. "Had the governors been persons of force, independent means, and character," he writes, "they would have exercised an important influence upon colonial life and constitutional development. . . . Fortunately," he adds, "they were usually persons of quite opposite qualities. . . ."[55] In the chapter entitled "Beginnings of Con-

---

[55] P. 247. Recent research has strongly qualified this estimate.

stitutional Controversy,'' he pays particular attention to
New York, whose assembly fought out some of the issues
later handled in more dramatic fashion by James Otis
and Patrick Henry in a larger sphere. The latter half of
Volume II carries on the discussion of political affairs to
1760, with two chapters on Anglo-French rivalry, and five
chapters on industry and commerce, immigration, labor
(mostly slave), education and religion. In a discussion of
the Great Awakening in 1740, Channing gives vent to a
personal prejudice against Benjamin Franklin. Franklin
wrote that George Whitefield's influence over him was so
great that at the end of a meeting he contributed all the
money he had with him, and Channing comments, ''When
a religious revivalist could produce such an effect on
Benjamin Franklin, it must be conceded that he possessed remarkable power of stirring human souls.''

In concluding his volume at 1760 the historian states
that ''changed climatic conditions and environments had
already begun to alter the racial characteristics of the
descendants of the first comers from England.'' Institutional ideas and commercial interests diverged in England and the colonies. ''In all that constitutes nationality,
two nations now owed allegiance to the British crown.
The colonists were patient and long-suffering; only pro-
longed misgovernment on the part of the rulers of Britain compelled them to declare themselves independent of
that empire from which they had sprung.''

In 1912 Channing brought out Volume III, *The
American Revolution 1761-1789,* which remains, probably, the best single volume on the period. ''Commercial-
ism, the desire for advantage and profit in trade and industry,'' he writes, ''was at the bottom of the struggle
between England and America; the immutable principles
of human association were brought forward to justify
colonial resistance to British selfishness. The governing
classes of the old country wished to exploit the American

colonists . . . the Americans desired to work their lands and carry on their trade for themselves." The historian goes on to show how the colonists had drifted away from English political and social ideas, and he makes brief mention of land speculation in the Ohio Valley as a cause for unrest. In contrast to older writers, says the author, "the modern student sees in the third George no mere tyrant, no misguided monarch, but an instrument of a benign providence bringing, through pain and misery, benefit to the human race." Although Channing presents some valuable information showing the burdensome taxes under which the colonists were laboring, his judgment on the Stamp Act is that it "was eminently fair and well constructed, the sole objection to it was in the mode of its passage." This volume contains many important tables on commerce and industry. By 1774 "America was united; not that all Americans thought alike or were opposed to England, but everywhere the radical party had come to the same conclusion." The historian classifies Samuel Adams and Joseph Warren "among the most astute politicians this country has ever seen."

After the first quarter of the book the story of the events of 1775 is introduced with a note of pride: "In Europe, war was a profession; in America it was only waged for life and family." A very large portion of the pages describes the military, naval, and political events of the next seven years. The writer pays high tribute to Jefferson's work in drafting the Declaration of Independence: "Never in the whole range of the writings of political theorists has the basis of government been stated so succinctly." Although the ideas and even the words are Locke's, "the reader will go to Locke in vain for so lucid a statement of his ideas." The last part of the volume is largely devoted to "Economic Adjustment," the occurrences during the four years following the war, and the work of the Federal Convention. In contrast to those

who have painted a gloomy picture of economic life at the
time the Constitution was adopted, Channing writes that
Americans "had already regained their footing in the
commercial world and were experimenting in many directions to effect a diversification of their means of livelihood." In his final chapter, "At the End of the Era," the
author touches rather briefly on some aspects of the social history of the postrevolutionary years.

Channing required three volumes to reach the establishment of the Union; three more carried him another
seventy-five years through the crisis which threatened
that Union. Volume IV is called *Federalists and Republicans 1789-1815* (1917) and covers part of the ground formerly treated by the author in his *Jeffersonian System,*
which had appeared in the "American Nation" series.
"The twenty-five years covered in the present volume,"
writes Channing, "were distinctly a period of transition
from the old order of things to the new, from the modes
of thought and action of the seventeenth and eighteenth
centuries to those of our own times."

The first chapter is an excellent survey of American
society in the 1790's. Channing discusses at some length
the problems that confronted Washington, particularly
those created by office seekers. The author's comment is
illuminating: "The 'spoils system,' . . . instead of being
an invention of Jacksonian Democrats or Jeffersonian
Republicans, was an inheritance from the Federalist
Presidents and by them had been built up on colonial and
English precedents." Channing's inclination is in the direction of the Federalists, especially the few leaders who,
he asserts, "acted with a sagacity that the world has seldom seen"; but the historian attempts to hold the scales
severely equal in his judgment. On a later page the Federalist party is described as "reactionary from start to
finish"; and it became, he said, "more aristocratic with
each successive year." Channing's words on Hamilton

have an unmistakable ring; although "he made some of the cruelest political blunders in our history," America's debt to him cannot be overstated. "He was the organizer of exploitation, the originator of monopoly; but he did his work at the precise moment that exploitation needed to be organized and human ingenuity required excitation by hope of monopoly." However, not until the discussions over the treaties with England and Spain in 1795 did the political differences then appearing in Congress mark "the formation of the first great party organizations in our history."

Channing is more than a third through his volume before he reaches "The Revolution of 1800." The historian here takes a fling at one of the many traditions he brushed aside in the course of his work: "A change of less than two hundred and fifty votes . . . would have given New York's vote to Adams and made him President with seventy-seven votes to sixty-one for Jefferson—of such was the Revolution of 1800." Channing is rather friendly to Jefferson, and Gallatin's financial policy wins the historian's praise. The author devotes more than a chapter to the Louisiana Purchase and its problems and shows how they played havoc with Jefferson's political theories. He lingers over the international difficulties that arose during Jefferson's second administration—this period of America's history had always attracted him. The embargo, he points out, did not effect nearly so much injury as has been conventionally supposed. In fact, writes Channing, "the extension of manufacturing in New England and in other States north of Maryland, went on throughout the period of commercial warfare; and thereafter was greatly stimulated by the conflict with England." Virginia, however, suffered severely from the embargo. Channing was indebted for much in the central part of this volume to the work of Henry Adams.

The last part of Volume IV covers the war years, and here the author indulges his penchant for naval affairs, but he also devotes some space to political developments. In his treatment of the Hartford Convention he is more lenient toward New England than other writers have been. The ending of the war was greeted with delight for, he writes, "the American Nation, with its back [to Europe] and its face to the West, addressed itself to the solution of the problems of the Nineteenth Century."

In Volume V, *The Period of Transition 1815-1848,* Channing returned to a consideration of American social history which he had lost sight of in the political complications of Jefferson's and Madison's administrations. The first half of this volume, published in 1921, has chapters on nearly every important aspect of American society; toward the end, another chapter containing similar material was inserted, "Western Lands and Settlements after 1840." "The American mind, which had concerned itself only with political organization," writes the historian mistakenly, overlooking colonial interest in other matters, "suddenly turned to other problems of human existence and became renowned for fertility of invention, for greatness in the art of literary expression, and for the keenest desire for the amelioration of the lot of humanity." The first chapter deals with the changes in communication; the second is an excellent account of "The Westward March." Channing was not much impressed by Turner's ideas on the significance of the frontier. In a footnote [56] he comments: "It is remarkable how evanescent has been the influence of these new conditions, for the American people is now and has been for some years among the most conservative of the nations of the earth." A valuable chapter treats the less well-known urban migration during these years; it is followed by one on the early labor movement.

[56] P. 66, note 1.

In the longest chapter in the volume, "The Plantation System and Abolitionism," the historian shows
much sympathy for the owner of the plantation: "It is by
no means improbable . . . ," he writes, "that the slaves
were often happier than their masters." The descendant
of New England intellectuals looked upon the extreme
abolitionists with something of disdain. In a note [57] the
author refers to his great-uncle William Ellery Channing, who, in the abolition controversy, "took the middle
path that satisfies no one, but sometimes is the path of
wisdom." A chapter on "Social Readjustments" discusses the early temperance campaign, the prison reform
movement, and philanthropic activity in behalf of debtors
and the insane.

"The Changing Religious Scene" witnessed "new
doctrines, new disciplines, new modes of procedure."
Special attention is given to the increases numbered
among the Roman Catholics, Presbyterians, Baptists, and
Methodists. Paragraphs on the Millerites and Mormons
indicate further the complexity of the American religious
scene. The Mormons are treated at greater length in the
chapter "Western Lands and Settlements after 1840."
In the chapter on "Education," Channing shows the
great improvement that came in American practice and
in the facilities for advanced learning. His conclusions,
however, are excessively pessimistic: "There were more
colleges and more secondary schools [1850] in proportion
to the total population than there were in 1800 or in
1820, but so far they do not seem to have greatly affected
the average intelligence of the American people, and it
was the education of democracy and not the breeding of
scholars that underlay the whole educational movement
of that time. Indeed, by 1860, the golden age of American
scholarship was passed." The historian thinks that it

[57] P. 170.

was in the field of literature "that the renaissance of the American mind is most noticeable." Unlike narrower New England students of literature, Channing writes that "the geographical distribution of writers, readers, and students shows that all sections of the country were interested in literature, using that word in its widest meaning." The conclusion of this chapter on "Literature" is as exuberant as the former on "Education" is depressing: "This half-century in the United States in poetry, in fiction, and in history stands apart,—it is without an equal since the days of Shakespeare, Francis Bacon, and John Milton."

In the second half of Volume V, Channing picks up the thread of politics with the administrations of Monroe. These years, usually considered barren of significance, "were a formative period in our political history and in our international history of the greatest interest and of the highest importance." Then "forces were taking shape that were to determine the history of the United States down to the year 1865." The historian performs the same service for John Quincy Adams that he performed for the older Adams when he shows that the son had not been so badly beaten in 1828 as has usually been reported. He writes an acid judgment on the election whose campaign trickery he deplores: "On the whole, possibly it was more honorable to have been defeated in 1828 than to have been elected." Jackson, however, comes off very well under Channing's scrutiny.

In the chapter on "South Carolina and Nullification," the author accepts the general judgment that "the Missouri Compromise marked the end of the first chapter in the history of nationalism. From that time for forty years, the whole spirit of our development was towards dualism,—for the Missouri Compromise practically marked the division of the country into two groups, having distinctly different economic interests." The highest praise is bestowed upon Webster's "Reply to Hayne," "probably the most famous speeches ever delivered in the national Senate." Three chapters at the end of his volume cover the period of expansion to the Pacific and to the Mexican boundary. For this section of his book the author placed great reliance upon Justin H. Smith's *The War with Mexico*. He closes with the question, "Would the Republic remain one united country, or would it be divided according to the social and economic desires of the inhabitants of the several sections into which it was geographically divided?"

The way in which the country answered that question is the theme of the next volume, *The War for Southern Independence,* published in 1925. Chapter I, "A Divided Country," sets the stage for the coming drama: "By the middle of the century, two distinct social organizations had developed within the United States, the one in the South and the other in the North." Had there been proper leadership, thinks Channing, "peaceable secession might have been achieved in 1850." Few Northerners have been fairer than he in his treatment of the old South. The historian himself said that "all treatments of Southern life by Northern writers gave an entirely false assessment of the weaknesses and the strengths of the slave system." In his second chapter Channing points to the benefits derived mainly by the North from the development of California and Oregon and from overseas commerce: "Almost alone in the advancing modern world, the South stood still."

In six more chapters the author reaches the election of 1860. Webster's "Seventh of March Speech" is defended against abolitionist censure; hostility is expressed against the Fugitive Slave Law. *Uncle Tom's Cabin* is credited with enormous influence in America and Europe; it "did more than any other one thing to arouse the fears of the Southerners and impel them to fight for in-

dependence.'' The eleven years before 1859 are termed
the ''most significant in our history, for it was then that
the Southerners determined to have their own way within
the United States, or else to leave the Union . . . ; and
the people of the Northern States determined in their
own minds that the time for concessions had passed and
that there should be no more compromise with slave
power.'' John Brown is handled gently.

Two chapters carry the reader to the earliest military events of the war. ''Secession'' is a careful analysis
of opinion, North and South, in the days preceding the
open break between the sections. The last half of the
volume treats of the course of the war on land and sea,
with extended reference to the international aspects of
the American struggle, particularly British opinion toward the North and South. These chapters contain valuable material on social conditions in various parts of the
country during the war and also a study of the setting of
the Emancipation Proclamation. Here, as in other parts
of Channing's work, instead of pages devoted to unraveling some knotty problem of especial interest to the author, we might have preferred further elucidation of
some interesting remarks, such as the following: ''Looking backward, we can see that the people of the North in
1861 undertook to . . . use the legislative power that the
absence of the Secessionists from Congress placed in
their hands to build up the manufacturing industries of
the North and to extend its agricultural operations.'' ''It
may well be that the prolongation of the war for a year
or more was distinctly a lesser evil than the retardation
of Northern prosperity.'' Channing clearly indicates in
his closing lines what his outlook on the policies of Reconstruction would have been had he lived to write the
volume. ''Well would it have been,'' he says, ''had the
reconstruction of Southern society been in the hands of
these men [leading soldiers] and of others who respected

one another and were guided by Abraham Lincoln." "An assassin's bullet closed the life of this greatest of Americans and delivered the Southern people into the hands of the Radical Republican politicians of the North."

Channing's *History of the United States* deserves extended treatment because of the great influence it has and probably will continue to have on the teachers and careful writers of our history, who in turn communicate the author's ideas to their own audiences. It is difficult to find any philosophy of history in Channing's volumes, although he was aware of the writings of Karl Lamprecht and his school. Instead of especially emphasizing economic factors, he writes in one place: "Now it is more often the case to emphasize the sociological or psychical change that is wrought by changed modes of living and by the general operation of economic factors. Possibly the best way to analyze the problems of progress or of changes in human outlook would be to combine all these various factors into one, for surely one's mode of living exercises a very important influence on one's mode of thinking." [58] In his own narrative he did not follow very thoroughly this method of presentation.

It is, perhaps, not surprising that there has been a very strong sectional criticism of what may well be the last of the important New England interpretations of our history. Critics have pointed out that in his treatment of the background of the American Revolution Channing includes nothing to suggest the antagonistic views between the Atlantic coast and the back country, nor does he take account of sectional alignments in the postrevolutionary period. Van Tyne, in a review of Volume III, said that "the historical account rarely leaves the Atlantic coast." To the New England historian the Mississippi Valley is "Transappalachia." Southerners, too, would rewrite many sections of his work. When, in some of his volumes,

[58] VI, 383.

Channing does emphasize social factors, these are not always related to political developments. Charles A. Beard's remark on Channing's volume dealing with the Civil War—that it tells what doctors of philosophy think of this period—is appropriate for the other volumes of his work as well. In the main it is a history for historians, and many specialists have found in Channing's contribution materials hitherto unknown to themselves. His keenness of observation unsettled many judgments long thought permanent, and he has stimulated much new research in many fields of American history.

Channing had no illusions about the permanence of a particular historical interpretation. He once wrote that "no historian can hope to live as can a poet or an essayist, because new facts will constantly arise to invalidate his most careful conclusions." [59] Even though his own interpretation may have a temporary character, the learning that his volumes display, and the spirit of the enthusiastic scholar that they reveal, may endow them like the writings of poets and essayists, with immortality. [60]

[59] V, 305.

[60] See, in addition to the other references, Carl Russell Fish on Edward Channing in *Current History* (March, 1931); R. R. Fahrney, "Edward Channing," *Miss. Valley Hist. Rev.* (June, 1931); Charles A. Beard's review of Channing's sixth volume, in *The New Republic*, XLIV, 310.

XIV

INTERPRETIVE WRITINGS

Despite the claims of the objective historians, their writing bears—sometimes subtly, it is true—the marks of subjective reaction. Other historians, however, recognizing the impossibility of writing really objective history, and, in fact, sometimes deriding it, have written their narratives with a specific thesis in mind. Some of these writers rebelled against the tradition that the facts would speak for themselves, believing that interpretation of the facts was the truer vocation of the historian. As a result some of their works assumed the character of histories of ideas, and in the freer interpretive range their authors have allowed themselves, the more orthodox historians have found much stimulation. It was believed also that a better understanding of America's past could be gained through a study of the relationship between her literature and contemporary events.

It is true enough that most of our historical writing has been of an interpretive character, with varying degrees of emphasis on interpretation. The early writers had a theological interpretation; later Bancroft and Parkman supported the thesis of a conflict between liberty-loving people and traditionalists. In the period of the "scientific historians," interpretation was presumably tabooed, but they often vigorously advanced the thesis that the logical end toward which political evolution led was the national state.

The interpretive historian is much closer in spirit to Bancroft, Prescott, and Parkman than he is to Osgood and Channing. There is an intuitive quality that pervades this writing, some of which has helped to re-establish history as a branch of literature. Much work of an interpretive nature has been written with so distinctive an ideological viewpoint that it seems preferable to include it in a separate treatment. On occasion the interpretive historian is an excellent scholar and research student himself, and such a combination has resulted in work of unusual excellence, as it has in the case of *The Rise of American Civilization*. Beard, Parrington, Moses Coit Tyler and Woodrow Wilson sought to find some clue to American history in the working of economic and spiritual forces, and the lift of their writing bears witness to the imagination they brought into their research.

WOODROW WILSON

Woodrow Wilson is hardly remembered today as an American historian whose works were once widely read by students and the general public. His own attitude towards his historical work sufficiently accounts for the modern student's disesteem. His main interests were primarily political, and historical writing was always subordinate. Wilson once wrote to a fellow historian, Frederick J. Turner: "I love history and think there are few things so directly rewarding and worth while for their own sakes as to scan the history of one's own country with a careful eye and write of it with the all-absorbing desire to get its cream and spirit out. But, after all,

I was born a politician, and must be at the task [writing on politics] for which, by means of my historical writing I have all these years been in training.''

It is well to observe also that nearly all of Wilson's historical works were written upon the invitation or at the request of editors. ''The editors of the popular monthlies offer me such prices nowadays that I am corrupted,'' he wrote in a light vein to J. Franklin Jameson in 1900. He assured Professor Jameson, however, that he would not alter the quality ''to suit the medium.''

Like others of his generation who were entranced by John Richard Green's *A Short History of the English People,* Wilson sought to write a similar book on American history. It was Green's glory, wrote Wilson, ''to have broadened and diversified the whole scale of English history.'' [1] The Princeton University professor said that he wrote the history of the United States ''in order to learn it,'' and his interest was less in knowing what had happened than in finding out ''which way we were going.'' The history of nations appeared to him to possess a spiritual quality; it is a thing, he wrote once, ''not of institutions, but of the heart.''

Wilson was not satisfied that the facts of themselves constituted truth. The truth, he once said, ''is evoked only by such arrangements and orderings of facts as suggest meanings.'' A colorless arrangement of facts was not true to the picture, and it was the historian's task to use the facts dug up by original research workers to convey ''an impression of the truth''; obviously everything cannot be told. He added that the historian must also be an investigator, knowing ''good ore from bad.'' It was Wilson's belief that the history of every nation had a plan which it was the task of a historian to divine, and in writing of past generations he was to inject himself

[1] *Century Magazine* (September, 1895), p. 791.

into their atmosphere, "rebuilding the very stage upon which they played their parts"; the historian should know no more of the period of which he writes than the generation which then lived. It was the task of historians to judge of the sincerity of men and the righteousness of their policies. Wilson contended that picturesque writers of history have always been right in theory; they failed only in practice. Writing at a time when a reaction was beginning to set in against the dry, doctor's dissertation, he concluded that the historian needed imagination as much as scholarship. "Histories," said this professor, who had a very large general audience, "are written in order that the bulk of men may read and realize." [2] He had studied under Herbert Baxter Adams at Johns Hopkins and he resented the overemphasis on the gathering of facts to the exclusion of an interpretation of events presented with literary artistry. He was not much of a believer in scientific objectivity. Whatever the subject of his inquiry, Wilson sought to probe its inner spirit, and he always thought of the practical bearing of his work. In his postgraduate years he had been attracted to government, and in the work of his "master," Walter Bagehot, who had written on the English Constitution, Wilson found a model to guide him in his study of American political institutions. He wanted to present them as living organisms, and to write a work that would reform them. "I want to contribute to our literature, what no American has ever contributed," he said, "studies in the philosophy of our institutions. . . ." No abstract philosophy, he insisted, but something immediate in its applicability.[3] The result was his justly famous *Congressional Government*.[4]

[2] "On the Writing of History," *Century Magazine* (September, 1895), pp. 788-793.

[3] See letter to Ellen Axson, 1883, in R. S. Baker, *Life of Woodrow Wilson* (N. Y., 1927), I, 211, 214.

[4] Boston, 1885.

A History of the American People, Wilson's most important historical contribution, was published in five volumes in 1902 after a popular reception had been accorded it as a magazine serial. The great number of illustrations, sometimes irrelevantly placed in the narrative, make this history much bulkier than it need be; it might easily have fitted into two volumes. The first, *The Swarming of the English,* narrates the settlement and development of the colonies in the seventeenth century. Something of that remoteness from reality which critics in after years found in Wilson as President of the United States is noticeable in the historian. "It was the spirit of liberty and of mastery," he writes, "that made the English swarm to America." The stern morality of which his colleagues spoke at the Peace Conference in 1919 was also a characteristic of the professor.

Volume II, *Colonies and Nation,* covers the eighteenth century through the War for Independence. Within the space of a third of the volume, pages devoted mainly to military and other spectacular episodes, the historian reaches "The Parting of the Ways"; the remaining two-thirds he reserves for the next twenty years. Wilson's handling of political events leading up to the Revolution, and especially the activities of Samuel Adams, is very good, but correspondingly poor is the treatment of the economic factors. There is no presentation of the colonies, for example, as parts of an imperial system. Wilson did not attempt to utilize the work that Osgood and Beer had already done on this phase of the subject. It is interesting to observe that in this history, written mainly for popular consumption over thirty years ago, a generous interpretation of the Loyalist point of view prevails, after the manner of Moses Coit Tyler. The last third of the volume is concerned almost exclusively with the military events of the struggle.

In the third volume Wilson's narrative comes down

to the election of Jackson. The place of the West in the
new nation is given heavy emphasis in the chapter entitled "Founding a Federal Government." "The instant
cry of hot protest that came out of the West," because
of Jay's proposed surrender of the navigation of the
lower Mississippi, "apprised eastern politicians of the
new world a-making there, the new frontiers of the nation." Present-day scholarship would hardly endorse the
accuracy of the following description of Jefferson's election: "The democratic forces which had set the Revolution ablaze . . . now once again reasserted themselves
and took possession of the seats of government"; "a
revolution it was, profound and lasting." Wilson refers
to the second struggle with England as a "clumsy, fool-
hardy haphazard war." The nine volumes of Henry
Adams on Jefferson's and Madison's administrations are
compressed into swift-moving sentences that fill only a
few pages in Wilson's history.

Volume IV opens with "The Democratic Revolution" of the late 1820's and closes with the end of the
War between the States. "The new nation, its quality
subtly altered, its point of view insensibly shifted by the
movement into the West . . . for the first time chose
after its own kind and preferred General Jackson." With
a note of exultation, Wilson writes: "The people's day
had come; the people's eyes were upon everything, and
were used in a temper of criticism and mastery."

A chapter on the extension of slavery serves as the
prelude to the military hostilities between North and
South. "Half the economic questions of that day of
change," says Wilson, "took their magnitude and significance from the westward expansion." Wilson unre-
servedly acknowledges Turner's influence; the two were
close friends, and talked a great deal about the significance of the frontier. "All I ever wrote on the subject
came from him," Wilson said on one occasion. At an-

other time he wrote that our historical writing had suffered from having been done almost exclusively by Easterners. Historians from regions most shocked by Jackson's election spoke of it "as a period of degeneration, the birth-time of a deep and permanent demoralization in our politics." "But we see it differently now," said Wilson; it was "regeneration," with a change once and for all of the old order. It was the West that "set the pace," and there was to be found the true national spirit; the East, he said, was sectional.[5] Wilson's history is full of interesting generalizations about which the reader asks for more information. Writing of the events of the early 1850's, he says: "New men, a new generation, again crowded forward; parties could not dictate what they should think; parties were indeed themselves to be transformed and mastered, rather, by the new forces now free of the field." Wilson's description of the character of Jefferson Davis is almost an exact model for the characterizations that were made of the historian in his own later political career.

There is a gentleness in Wilson's treatment of his native South, before and during the war, that contrasts strangely with the sternness of his contemporary, John W. Burgess. Wilson's treatment of slavery, in some respects, antedates the similar approach of William E. Dodd and Ulrich B. Phillips: "The South had thrown her life into the scales and lost it," concludes Wilson. "The Union had been saved; it was yet to be rehabilitated." In another volume, published several years earlier, *Division and Reunion 1829-1889*,[6] Wilson redressed the usual apportionment of space in historical writings by emphasizing the South and presenting its society in a sympathetic light. His contention that there was no

[5] "The Proper Perspective of American History," *The Forum*, XIX (1895), 544-553.
[6] N. Y., 1893.

American nation until after the Civil War has profoundly affected historical interpretation.

The fifth and last volume covers the period of Reconstruction to the close of the Spanish-American War.
Wilson's judgment on the radical leaders, Stevens, Wade,
and the rest, is bitterly severe. It is hard to acquit them,
he writes, "of the charge of knowing and intending the
ruinous consequences of what they had planned." The
voice of a Southern man, who had known as a boy the
dark days of Reconstruction, speaks in these pages which
are a vigorous indictment of the Republican party.

In his chapter on the "Return to Normal Conditions" Wilson approaches more nearly present-day interest in social history with his descriptions of the
changed character of American industrial and agricultural life. Wilson's treatment of labor, particularly in
the Pullman strike, is very conservative. In fact, his history, generally speaking, shows little of the progressiv-
ism that marked his later career. Grover Cleveland was
one of the author's heroes, and these two Democrats,
temperamentally, had many things in common. A chapter, "The End of a Century," begins with Harrison's
administration. "A new sectionalism began to show itself, not political, but economic," writes Wilson, remembering his talks with Turner. Wilson's analysis of the
events leading up to the election of 1896 is very thin. In
view of Bryan's influence on Wilson's political career,
it is interesting to note that the latter is not particularly
friendly to the Nebraskan's candidacy in 1896. Wilson's
judgment does not appear to advantage, either, when
he discusses the Spanish-American War, or estimates
its results.

Throughout his work Wilson delights to character-
ize political leaders, but he is not very effective in accounting for social changes. His smoothly flowing language makes of his materials, gathered from authori-

tative sources, an attractive piece of literary craftsmanship. No extended research, however, was needed to write his history. It is of significance to note, as did Turner in his review of the volumes, that Wilson was "the first Southern scholar of adequate training and power to deal with American history as a whole in a continental spirit." Few will deny that Wilson's view of the slave region, for example, was a needed corrective to the descriptions of less catholic-minded Northern historians. It may be observed without derogation that he gave us a Wilsonian essay upon history rather than a description of the events themselves. But his volumes are no longer read, and one may with certainty conclude that Wilson will be remembered not as one who wrote history, but rather as one who made it.[7]

CHARLES A. AND MARY R. BEARD

Of American historians writing today Charles A. Beard has the widest influence, with a large audience among scholars and a larger one among the general public. In his earlier years he was associated with James Harvey Robinson in the production of textbooks of European history, which immensely improved the standard of such publications. With the same collaborator he published sources which made it possible for young students to become acquainted with the primary materials of history, and has, alone, written texts on American history and politics. Beard made at least two significant contributions of original research with his *An Economic Interpretation of the Constitution*[8] and the *Economic Origins of Jeffersonian Democracy*.[9] The former was

[7] See M. L. Daniel, "Woodrow Wilson—Historian," *Miss. Valley Hist. Rev.* (December, 1934); also an essay by Wilson, "The Truth of the Matter"; R. S. Baker, *Woodrow Wilson, Life and Letters* (N. Y., 1927-35), Vols. I-V.

[8] N. Y., 1913.   [9] N. Y., 1915.

something of a bombshell in historical circles, although years ago Hildreth and other writers had pointed to the economic factor that led to the adoption of the Constitution. Beard, however, dug up forgotten records and showed the direct relationship between the holders of the government debt and their desire for a strong government which would pay it off. While he has since admitted that he overstated the case, his work has left a lasting impression on historiography.[10]

He has been insistent in calling attention to the manner in which the milieu affects the judgment of the historian, and as a leading figure among contemporary historians he has repudiated "the conception dominant among schoolmen during the latter part of the nineteenth century and the opening years of the twentieth century— the conception that it is possible to describe the past as it actually was, somewhat as the engineer describes a single machine." In selecting and ordering materials, the personal biases and social and economic experience of historians play a determining part. In the very act of writing history, the historian performs an "Act of Faith." "He is thus in the position of a statesman dealing with public affairs; in writing he acts and in acting he makes choices, . . . with respect to some conception of the nature of things. And the degree of his influence and immortality will depend upon the length and correctness of his forecast—upon the verdict of history yet to come. His faith is at bottom a conviction that something true can be known about the movement of history and his conviction is a subjective decision, not a purely objective discovery." The historian must continue to use the scientific method, but its limitations must be recognized, for a science of history cannot be established which will re-create the past in all its fullness. The historian's

[10] See introduction to *An Economic Interpretation of the Constitution*, 1935 edn.

task today is to define his own relationship to contemporary thought, and it is his function to read the trend of the times. Beard's conjecture is that the world is moving in the direction of collectivist democracy.[11]

In 1927 Charles and Mary Beard published *The Rise of American Civilization,* in two large volumes, which might have been issued in four books of more normal size. "The history of a civilization," say the authors, "is essentially dynamic, suggesting capacities yet unexplored and hinting of emancipation from outward necessities." Their conception of history, like Voltaire's, is that it should be a stimulant to self-criticism, and an aid in producing a richer intellectual climate. A more important place is given to women than was customary in the works of most historians. The role of artistry in composition is emphasized with the remark that "the history of a civilization cannot be written by patching together constitutions, statutes, political speeches, newspaper items, private letters, memoirs, and diplomatic notes."[12] The distance that Beard had traveled since the time when a strict economic determinism had appeared of overwhelming significance to him may be measured by the statement: "The heritage, economics, politics, culture, and international filiations of any civilization are so closely woven by fate into one fabric that no human eye can discern the beginnings of its warp or woof. And any economic interpretation, any political theory, any literary criticism, any aesthetic appreciation, which ignores this perplexing fact, is of necessity superficial."[13]

The work is in two large divisions—the era of Agriculture and the era of Industry—and the authors are concerned to show the influence of these respective ways

[11] C. A. Beard, "Written History as an Act of Faith," *Amer. Hist. Rev.* (January, 1934).

[12] P. xiv. Quotations from *The Rise of American Civilization* are by permission of The Macmillan Company, publishers.

[13] I, 124.

of life on the psychology of people living them. With a grasp of the literature, often of recent publication, that astonishes even specialists, Dr. and Mrs. Beard manage to convey most vividly the interrelationship of various phases of American civilization and its dynamic quality. In certain passages which are perhaps overwritten, that dynamism is almost too self-conscious, and yet American history does tell of a people thrusting forward.

The revolt of the colonies against England, the authors assert, was an "economic, social and intellectual transformation of prime significance—the first of those modern world-shaking reconstructions in which mankind has sought to cut and fashion the tough and stubborn web of fact to fit the pattern of its dreams." [14] The writers show, too, a better understanding of the middle period than has been expressed by most. In the long perspective, they believe, this period will "appear as the most changeful, most creative, most spirited epoch between the founding of the colonies and the end of the nineteenth century." The Civil War, they point out, "was merely the culmination of the deep-running transformation that shifted the center of gravity in American society between the inauguration of Jackson and Lincoln"; and that shift resulted in the triumph of industry over agriculture.[15] The fundamental question at issue was whether the political revolution, which was anticipated by the economic change, was to be peaceful or violent.

Reference to the programs of the industrialists and the agriculturists, particularly of the South, indicates the line of cleavage between them. The American currency system was in bad shape by 1860, dangerous for business enterprise, but relatively beneficial to agrarians; the courts, too, had let down safeguards for property rights. These were the weaknesses that business enterprise was

[14] I, 296.
[15] I, 632-633.

to remedy as a result of the war. In the view of Dr. and Mrs. Beard, abolition "was a minor element in bringing on the irrepressible conflict," and of far less importance than economics.

Thus the authors reach the period of the Civil War, which they term the Second American Revolution. The program of the planter aristocracy in 1860 demanded the surrender of the Northern and Western majority "to the minority stockholders under the Constitution. It offered nothing to capitalism but capitulation. . . . Finally —and this was its revolutionary phase—it called upon the farmers and mechanics who had formed the bulk of Jacksonian Democracy in the North to acknowledge the absolute sovereignty of the planting interest. Besides driving a wedge into the nation the conditions laid down by the planters also split the Democratic party itself into two factions." [16] The results of the war are shown to be of far-reaching significance: a new power, the industrialists, was placed in the government, great changes were made in the relationship of classes, in the acquisition and distribution of wealth, in industrial development, and in the Constitution, as well, in order to safeguard these changes. "Viewed in the large, the supreme outcome of the civil strife was the destruction of the planting aristocracy which, with the aid of northern farmers and mechanics, had practically ruled the United States for a generation. A corollary to that result was the undisputed triumph of a new combination of power; northern capitalists and free farmers who emerged from the conflict richer and more numerous than ever. It was these . . . facts . . . that made the Civil War a social revolution." [17] Four billion dollars' worth of property (slaves) was destroyed without compensation—"the most stupen-

[16] II, 29-30.
[17] II, 99.

dous act of sequestration in the history of Anglo-Saxon jurisprudence.'' [18]

The remaining treatment of American history follows lines more familiar to the general student. The section on the middle period has especial freshness, although it does not offer a great deal that is new to the student already acquainted with the older work of Thomas H. Benton and the more recent work of Channing and Professor Dodd. The presentation of the material, however, here as well as elsewhere in the Beards' history, is masterly. The authors may err in minimizing the place of abolition in bringing on the war. They may overestimate the economic factor as a cause of the war with Spain, missing the full significance of the weight of public opinion manufactured by the newspapers.[19] Even with its defects, however, *The Rise of American Civilization* is likely to stand for some time as one of the most brilliant interpretations offered by historical scholarship. That this work has been referred to as an essay on American history scarcely lessens its value; almost any kind of treatment of an interpretive character will have that quality. Perhaps the special student will ask for more history and less interpretation; the general reader (and there have been a great number for the work of the Beards) likes his history written in the grand manner.

Moses Coit Tyler

Moses Coit Tyler devoted himself mainly to one aspect of American history—her literature—but so important was his contribution that students might well give as much time to him as to other writers who are more conventionally classed as historians. Tyler had been

[18] II, 100.
[19] See Joseph E. Wisan, *The Cuban Crisis as Reflected in the New York Press 1895-1898* (N. Y., 1934).

trained for the ministry, but in his late twenties he resigned, explaining in a note to a confidant, "I was not
built for a parson." In the same letter, written in 1862,
he said that he would like to devote himself exclusively
to literary pursuits: "That is my passion and I think
my mission." In his commonplace book he jotted down
the thought of writing the history of American literature.[20] Five years later he was a professor at Michigan,
and in 1871 and 1872 he was noting in his diary a plan
to write a history of the United States since the Revolution. Although Tyler gave up the ministry as a profession, his conception of the academician was somewhat
akin to that of the ardent missionary. He once maintained "that while history should be thoroughly scientific in its method, its object should be practical. To this
extent I believe in history with a tendency. My interest
in our own past is chiefly derived from my interest in our
own present and future: and I teach American history,
not so much to make historians as to make citizens and
good leaders for the state and nation." [21] Like so many
other students of his day, Tyler felt the impact of Buckle,
and he hoped to find the law of American development
through her literature.[22] During his career as professor
of English literature at the University of Michigan, and
later as professor of American history and literature at
Cornell, Tyler found time to do a vast amount of research
for his four volumes on America's literary history, to
publish a biography of Patrick Henry, and to make contributions to professional periodicals. His essay on the
American Loyalists in an early issue of the *American
Historical Review* was one of the first to strike the modern note in our changed attitude toward the Revolution.

In 1879 Tyler published, in two volumes, *A History*

[20] H. M. Jones, *Moses Coit Tyler* (Ann Arbor, 1933), p. 111.
[21] "The Study of History in American Colleges and Universities," *Circular of Information*, Bur. of Ed. (1887), No. 2, p. 156.
[22] See Jones, *Moses Coit Tyler*, p. 141.

of American Literature; the first covers the period 1607-1676, the second carries the treatment down to 1765. In his preface he states: "It is my purpose to write the history of American literature from the earliest English settlements in this country, down to the present time. I hope to accomplish the work within the space of three or four volumes." The arrangement of the work was to show how from "several isolated colonial centers, where at first each had its peculiar literary accent," there developed a "tendency toward a common national accent; until, finally, in 1765 . . . the scattered voices of the thirteen colonies were for the first time brought together and blended in one great and resolute utterance" of defiance against England. Because 1765 marked the "real ending of our colonial epoch, the real beginning of our revolutionary epoch," Tyler closes these two volumes with that year. He includes all those writers who contributed to "the evolution of thought and of style in America" during colonial days.

In a swinging prose that shows a lusty pride in his Anglo-Saxon heritage, Tyler describes the various writers in Virginia and New England, and since the latter left more literary remains, her writings take up most of the first volume. Tyler could speak with assurance upon the characteristics of these early colonial historians, poets and theologians, because a careful study of every book or pamphlet referred to had given him an intimate acquaintance with its writer. Although he could be severely critical of Puritanism, Tyler had a genuine affection for many of the writers who were nurtured in its faith, and on one occasion he wrote of the Puritan: "Though his prayers were often a snuffle, his hymns a dolorous whine, his extemporized liturgy a bleak ritual of ungainly postures and of harsh monotonous howls, yet the idea that filled and thrilled his soul was one in every way sublime, immense, imaginative, poetic—the idea of the awful omnipotent Jehovah, his inexorable justice, his holiness, the inconceivable brightness of his majesty, the vastness of his unchanging designs along the entire range of his relations with the hierarchies of heaven, the principalities and powers of the pit, and the elect and the reprobate of the sons of Adam.''

More than half of the second volume to 1765 is concerned with the literature of New England. A number of individuals are rescued from oblivion by the tender mercies of Tyler, and in some cases are revealed to be writers of genuine worth. He refers to John Wise as ''the first great American expounder of democracy in church and state,'' and he indicates the value of Nathaniel Ames, whose almanacs were superior to those of Franklin. Two chapters on literature in the middle colonies, and in the provinces further south, precede the final chapter on ''General Literary Forces in the Colonial Time.'' This last includes some excellent observations on American journalism and the colonial colleges.

Although these two volumes had an immense value when they appeared, bringing a much-needed organization to the study of American literature, they seem less important today. Tyler is often too lenient in his criticism of poor writing, and sometimes excessive in his praise of merely good writing. Something of floridity in his style has dated these volumes, but students of American civilization will long continue to use them with profit.

No sooner were the first two volumes out of the way than Tyler prepared for their successors. In his diary on August 7, 1879, he wrote: ''Began work with reference to next volumes of American literature.'' Nearly a score of years, however, were to pass before they were published. The two volumes on *The Literary History of the American Revolution 1763-1783* [23] are Tyler's most valuable bequest to historians. In the preface he states with

[23] N. Y., 1897.

justifiable pride: "For the first time in a systematic and a fairly complete way, is set forth the inward history of our Revolution—the history of its ideas, its spiritual moods, its motives, its passions, even of its sportive caprices, and its whims as these uttered themselves at the time, whether consciously or not, in the various writings of the two parties of Americans who promoted or resisted that great movement." His plan was to let both parties "tell their own story freely in their own way, and without either of them being liable, at our hands, to posthumous outrage in the shape of partisan imputations on their sincerity, their magnanimity, their patriotism, or their courage." Lighter as well as soberer literary forms that shed illumination on the revolutionary era are included by Tyler—ballads, songs, and the like.

He describes the contents of these volumes by noting the characteristics that distinguish them from other works on this period. "Instead of fixing our eyes almost exclusively as is commonly done," Tyler writes, "upon statesmen and generals, upon party leaders, upon armies and navies, upon Congress, upon parliament, upon the ministerial agents of a brain-sick king, or even upon that brain-sick king himself," as the mainsprings of the Revolution, "we here for the most part turn our eyes away toward . . . mere penmen,—only essayists, pamphleteers, sermon writers, song writers, tale tellers, or satirists, the study of whose work, it is believed, may open to us a view of the more delicate and elusive, but not less profound or less real, forces which made that period so great and still so worthy of being truly understood by us."

The first volume of this book on the literature of the American Revolution examines the writings of the period from 1763 to 1776. After a brief enumeration of the different classes of writing in this period, the author proceeds to a careful study of the publications of noted political figures like John Adams, Daniel Dulany, and Jonathan Mayhew. Tyler brought to a larger public the story of the relationship between politics and religion in the prerevolutionary era—a relationship of which students have since become increasingly aware. The belle-tristic literature that belonged in the early literary tradition of America, and some examples that had a kinship with contemporary politics, also find space in this volume, particularly the work of Francis Hopkinson, Philip Freneau, and John Trumbull.

The volume gets back into its discussion of the purely political literature with an analysis of the writings that stimulated and were caused by "The Rekindling of the Great Dispute, 1766-1769." John Dickinson's *Letters from a Farmer in Pennsylvania* is described as constituting "upon the whole, the most brilliant event in the literary history of the Revolution." When Tyler is halfway through his volume he turns to a study of the literature of the Loyalists, in the course of which he pens remarks which dispel some hardy misconceptions about that unpopular group. He denies that the Tories were "a party of mere negation and obstruction," and points out that they "had positive political ideas, as well as precise measures in creative statesmanship." Secondly, writes Tyler, it is erroneous to think of the Tories as "opposed either to any reform in the relations of the colonists with the mother country, or to the extension of human rights and liberties here or elsewhere." Lastly, in a tone that puts to shame an outdated provincialism in our historical writing, Tyler says that it is an "error to represent the Tories of our Revolution as composed of Americans lacking in love for their native country, or in zeal for its liberty, or in willingness to labor, or fight, or even to die, for what they conceived to be its interests." The outstanding Loyalists, Jonathan Boucher, Joseph Galloway, and Daniel Leonard, author of *Massachusettensis,* receive extended consideration at the hands of Tyler. A discussion of Thomas Paine's *Common Sense,* the debate of the public over the suggestion of independence, and the Declaration of Independence, itself, conclude this volume.

"The chief aim of the first volume [is] to trace the development of political discontent . . . from about the year 1763 until the year when that discontent culminated in the resolve for American Independence." "The chief aim of the second volume," writes Tyler, "[is] to trace the development of the Revolutionary struggle under the altered conditions produced by this change in its object and its character, and to go on with the tale until the year when American Independence was formally acknowledged by the British government." A good part of this volume contains the literature—poetry and prose—of Loyalists, as well as the satirical writings directed against them by Freneau and Hopkinson. This second volume continues the study of "pulpit champions" of the Revolution, and also finds space for some literature that reflected the few eddies escaping the main stream of politics—the *Journal* of the Quaker John Woolman and the work of Crèvecoeur. With a study of Franklin's writings that relate to the Revolution, and an examination of the work of contemporary historians, Tyler brings his great work to a close.

Nothing better has ever been done in America in the composition of literary history, despite some defects of omission. For example, there is nothing on the relationship of letters to the economic background; more space might have been given to Southern writers. He neglected to include in his *Literary History of the American Revolution* some living writers in England who were of American birth or who had resided in America, notably George Chalmers. Tyler also failed to consider sufficiently the place of the newspaper in the American Revolution, but the judgment of Paul Leicester Ford on these two volumes, written more than thirty years ago, that they were "far and away the best treatment of the literature of those years of turmoil," still remains true. All later writers on early American literary history have had their labors considerably lightened because Moses Coit Tyler lived before them. In his younger days he had written that he intended to cover the whole of American literary history in three or four volumes. Four volumes brought him only to the writers in the era of the Revolution, but it is better for us that he treated them in detail instead of skimming over them lightly in order to adhere to his original program. Ghosts of buried controversialists encounter their ancient adversaries in the lively pages of Tyler, and whatever of immortality has been granted to them came through the enthusiastic research of the historian. A splendid standard of historical scholarship was not the least part of the heritage Tyler left for posterity.[24]

Vernon L. Parrington

In 1927 two volumes of a proposed three-volume work on *Main Currents in American Thought* were published by Vernon Louis Parrington, professor of English in the University of Washington. Before then his name had been known to a comparatively few students of literature who had read his lesser contribution, *The Connecticut Wits*,[25] but when Parrington died in 1929 his name was known to a large group of enthusiastic readers. His untimely end came while he was in the midst of his third volume, but despite the fact that most of that volume was left only in sketch form, his publishers paid Parrington the tribute of presenting it to the public even in its incompleted state.

[24] For Tyler's diary, see J. T. Austen, *M. C. Tyler* (N. Y., 1911) and Jones, *Moses Coit Tyler*.   [25] N. Y., 1926.

It was Parrington's wish to relate the literature of a people to its whole civilization; to do so meant the selection of material on other than belletristic grounds. Through the influence of Taine's *Histoire de la littérature,* and the work of a colleague, J. Allen Smith, who wrote on the economic basis of politics, Parrington was stimulated to examine American literature along similar lines.[26] He "envisaged American literature as American thought"; "economic forces imprint their mark upon political, social, and religious institutions; literature expresses the result in its thought content." He disclaimed any desire "to evaluate reputations or weigh literary merits, but rather to understand what our fathers thought, and why they wrote as they did."

In the foreword to his work Parrington indicates that his point of view is "liberal rather than conservative, Jeffersonian rather than Federalistic." Realist that he was, he confesses that in his search he had found what "he went forth to find, as others have discovered what they were seeking." Through the personalities of Roger Williams, Franklin, and Jefferson, Parrington traces the line of liberalism in colonial America. "The first," he writes, "transported to the new world the plentiful liberalisms of a great movement and a great century"; Franklin "gathered up the sum of native liberalisms that had emerged spontaneously from a decentralized society"; Jefferson "strengthened these native liberalisms with borrowings from the late seventeenth-century natural-rights school and from French romantic theory engrafting them upon the vigorous American stock." Against these individuals whose liberalism lay near to Parrington's heart, he places "the complementary figures of John Cotton, Jonathan Edwards, and Alexander Hamilton, men whose grandiose dreams envisaged dif-

[26] See Parrington's introduction to Smith's *The Growth and Decadence of Constitutional Government* (N. Y., 1930).

ferent ends for America and who followed different paths.''

The first volume, *The Colonial Mind 1620-1800*, closes with the political victory of Jefferson, who, in Parrington's interpretation, represents back-country agrarianism. The early part of the volume discusses the New England theocracy and Roger Williams's rebellion against it: ''He lived and dreamed in a future he was not to see, impatient to bring to men a heaven they were unready for.'' With a reference to the Mathers, Increase and Cotton, and to John Wise, the liberal, Parrington places ''the twilight of the oligarchy'' before 1720. Thence through the middle of the century was ''the creative springtime of democratic America—plebeian years that sowed what after times were to reap.'' ''The psychology of democratic individualism'' that was fashioned in these years (partly because of numerous small landholdings and also as an effect of the frontier) was, says Parrington, the ''determining influence'' in shaping ''the creative outlines of our history.'' Jonathan Edwards did not belong in that tradition; ''the greatest mind of New England had become an anachronism in a world that bred Benjamin Franklin.''

After the making of the American mind came its awakening in the Revolutionary era: ''The liberalism that before had been vaguely instructive quickly became eager and militant,'' and ''out of this primary revolution were to come other revolutions, social and economic, made possible by the new republican freedom.'' In Parrington's judgment ''the most important consequence of the Revolution was the striking down of this mounting aristocratic spirit that was making rapid headway with the increase of wealth.'' The passing of the Loyalists left the middle class ''free to create a civilization after its own ideals.'' It did so through the agency of the centralized state, which began to check ''the long movement of decentralization''—''the most revolutionary changes in three hundred years of American experience.'' Parrington's material on the Revolution owes a good deal to the works of Arthur M. Schlesinger and Claude H. Van Tyne, and particularly to Tyler's *Literary History of the American Revolution.*

The last part of Volume I, ''Liberalism and the Constitution,'' narrates the victory of the Federalists, under Hamilton's leadership, over the agrarian democracy. But shortly, because of the influence of French Revolutionary ideas, opposition ''to the aristocratic arrogance of Federalism, and disgust at its coercive measures,'' mounted quickly. The organizer and director of that discontent was Jefferson, who ''far more completely than any other of his generation . . . embodied the idealisms of the great revolution.'' The Hartford Wits and the group represented by Philip Freneau are examined mainly in the light of their political affiliations. Undoubtedly Parrington's own liberal sympathies helped determine the judgment that Freneau, Joel Barlow, and Hugh Henry Brackenridge represented the ''best intelligence then being devoted to literature in America.'' With Jefferson's victory, writes Parrington, ''the first democratic battle had been won at the polls.'' Although ''the new liberalism was in the saddle'' it had a precarious seat because the forces of capitalism and industrialism ''were already at work preparing a different pattern of life for America . . . wholly unlike that of the simpler agrarianism with its domestic economy, which Jefferson represents. A new romanticism of the middle class was eventually to shoulder aside the aspirations of gentleman and farmer alike, and refashion America after its own ideal.''

The theme of Parrington's second volume, *The Romantic Revolution in America 1800-1860,* is the growth of an acquisitive society whose pot of gold at the foot of the rainbow was more tempting than the hard-earned returns from the field of the colonial farmer. The philosophy of this middle-class society, expressed by Adam Smith, came into conflict with French Revolutionary equalitarianism, which had found a ready response in America in the Mississippi Valley at the close of the eighteenth century. In the South was developed "the conception of a Greek democracy," with slave labor, which rejected "alike French equalitarianism and English individualism." Because it took no account of the aspirations of the middle class, the latter destroyed the dream of the South, and "with the overthrow of the aristocratic principle in its final refuge the ground was cleared of the last vestiges of the eighteenth century."

Three books make up the volume: one on the Southern mind; another on the mind of the Middle East; and a third on the mind of New England. The absence of a treatment on the South in the first volume is somewhat compensated for in the second. The seed centers of Southern culture were Virginia and South Carolina; from the former came the intellectual offspring Kentucky and Tennessee, from the latter, Alabama and Mississippi. The intellectual leaders of these respective groups were Jefferson and Calhoun—the latter rejected equalitarian idealism and substituted for it economic realism. Through representative figures like the agrarian democrat, John Taylor, and John Marshall, Parrington traces a chart of the Virginia mind "with its liberalisms and conservatisms running at cross purposes." By the late 1820's Southern leadership had passed from Virginia to the more aggressive South Carolina. Rich praise is lavished upon William Gilmore Simms in the section on "Belles Lettres"; he was, thinks Parrington, "the most richly endowed of any son" South Carolina "ever gave birth to, . . . by far the most virile and interesting figure of the Old South."

In the mind of the Middle East, New York and Philadelphia, there was more of a diversity of thought than in the intellectual centers of New England or the South. By reason of its commercial pre-eminence New York succeeded to the leadership that Philadelphia had briefly enjoyed and gave to literature such men as Irving, Paulding, and Cooper. A friendliness, not so marked in his estimate of Irving, is apparent in Parrington's appraisal of Cooper: "The more intimately one comes to know him, the more one comes to respect his honest, manly nature that loved justice and decency more than popularity." New York's world of literature was greatly indebted to New England, writes Parrington, who sets up against Irving, Paulding, and Cooper, the contributions to idealism made by Bryant, Greeley, and Melville.

The New England renaissance of these years, whose stimulus to American life was of unusual strength, is, in Parrington's view, "the last flowering of a tree that was dying at the roots"; "it was the last and in certain respects the most brilliant of the several attempts to domesticate in America the romantic thought of revolutionary Europe; and with its passing, civilization in this western world fell into the hands of another breed of men to fashion as they saw fit."

In Emerson and Webster Parrington found the "diverse New England tendencies that derived from the Puritan and the Yankee; the idealistic and the practical; the ethical and the rationalistic; the intellectual revolutionary . . . and the soberly conservative. . . ." Webster "was a great man, built on a great pattern, who never achieved a great life." Along with Emerson, Thoreau and Theodore Parker best typify the ferment in the mind and heart of New England. A sense of kinship quickens the language of Parrington when he writes of them. Emerson was "a free soul . . . the flowering of two centuries of spiritual aspiration—Roger Williams and Jonathan Edwards come to more perfect fruition."

"In Thoreau the eighteenth century philosophy of individualism, the potent liberalisms let loose on the world by
Jean Jacques, came to fullest expression in New England.'' Parker was an unsparing critic of his contemporaries, and he was ''one of the greatest, if not the last,
of the excellent line of Puritan preachers.''

In his concluding sentences Parrington returns to a
familiar refrain: the defeat of slavery carried down as
well ''the old ideal of decentralized democracies, of individual liberty; and with the overthrow of the traditional principles in their last refuge, the nation hurried
forward along the path of an unquestioning and uncritical consolidation, that was to throw the coercive powers
of a centralizing state into the hands of the new industrialism''; this revolution engulfed ''the older romantic
America, its dignified literary ideals as well as its democratic political theory.'' But from the vague romanti-
cisms of these years was born at length ''a spirit of realistic criticism, seeking to evaluate the worth of this new
America'' and to evolve if possible new ways of life. The
expressions of this critical spirit were to be the theme
of a third volume.

In the unfinished last volume Parrington intended
to trace the decline of ''romantic optimism'' after 1860,
which resulted from three forces: ''The stratifying of
economics under the pressure of centralization; the rise
of a mechanistic science, and the emergence of a spirit
of skepticism which, under the pressure of industrialism,
the teachings of the physical sciences, and the lessons
of European intellectuals, is resulting in the questioning
of the ideal of democracy as it has been commonly held
hitherto, and the spread of a spirit of pessimism.'' America's intellectual history, thought Parrington, fell into
the three broad phases of Calvinistic pessimism, romantic optimism, and mechanistic pessimism. The pessimism
of our recent years was the reaction against the ideals

of the middle class under whose leadership America became industrialized in the second half of the nineteenth century. In that period "traditional agrarianism" was finally defeated. Although much of his material on this last period has the gloom of a Dreiserian darkness, Parrington never fails to strike the courageous note that is a tocsin to a drooping liberalism. No longer are the theologians, political philosophers, industrial masters, or bankers, "the spokesmen of this vibrant life of a continent, but the intellectuals, the dreamers, the critics, the historians, the men of letters, in short; and to them one may turn hopefully for a revelation of American life." To the end Parrington held out Jeffersonian democracy as a hopeful ideal.

There is thrilling writing in these volumes that call a wayward America back from the nightmare of a business civilization to the dream of an agrarian democracy. In Parrington's history there are serious omissions of facts, without which an observer cannot really understand the main currents of American thought, and there are also mistakes in judgment. For example, he was too harsh to the Puritans whose virtues he neglected while emphasizing their limitations. Historians complain that Parrington did not know enough history, while students of literature often disagree with his estimates of literary figures. And yet, after everything unfavorable is said, there remains an important body of achievement. Many students of American society have already used it as a point of departure for further research, and the stimulating quality of its fruitful generalizations will continue to inspire additional study. This study may also bear fruit of a kind different from that fancied by Parrington, but, whether in agreement or in disagreement with his main theses, no student of America should forego the joy of reading him.

A BIBLIOGRAPHICAL NOTE ON CULTURAL HISTORY

There is, as yet, no well-developed school of *kulturgeschichte* in America—no synthesis of the varied manifestations of our civilization. Studies of particular phases of culture have, however, appeared at various times, and a few of them are briefly noted here. Although Vernon L. Parrington concentrated on the relationship between literature and social development, his work and that of Charles A. Beard are perhaps the nearest we have to comprehensive histories of American civilization. In "A History of American Life" (see page 589), edited by Dixon Ryan Fox and Arthur Meier Schlesinger, are volumes dealing in detail with certain periods in American cultural progress. The *Cambridge History of American Literature,* which does not limit itself to belles-lettres, is valuable because of its broad approach to the subject (see page 591). Other books offering specialized treatments, more or less complete in literature but lacking fullness in other fields of American culture, have been published in large number, especially in the last few years.

Fred Lewis Pattee and Percy H. Boynton have written fairly comprehensive studies in an attempt to integrate literature with American social development. In 1915 Professor Pattee published a volume on American literature since 1870, and in 1930 he discussed the authors of a more recent day in *The New American Literature 1890-1930*. His latest work covers *The First Century of American Literature 1770-1870*.[27] For historians of American culture this is the most valuable of Professor Pattee's volumes. In it, to summarize the changing fashions of our writing, he makes use of a large mass

[27] N. Y., 1935.

of special studies in regional literature, periodicals, gift books and travel accounts. Compared with Parrington, Professor Pattee is conservative, and does not include as much social background. In the main he writes in the older tradition of the conventional literary historian represented by Barrett Wendell. Professor Boynton, in his *Literature and American Life,*[28] occupies something of a middle ground between Parrington and Professor Pattee. He relates literature more intimately to social development than does the latter, but he stresses the purely literary aspects more than does Parrington.

Interpretations of the American spirit, with rare charm and especial literary brilliance, have been made by Lewis Mumford in *The Golden Day* [29] and Van Wyck Brooks in the *Flowering of New England.*[30] The first is an enthusiastic study of the literary renaissance before the Civil War, the second is a more comprehensive picture of these years, skillfully interweaving the various threads of New England's colorful life to make a rich tapestry. Mr. Brooks, the foremost literary critic of the liberal school founded by Randolph Bourne, has a deep knowledge of the sources of American culture. He might have given more attention to the faults created by the new industrialism, thus clarifying the critical writings of such an individual as Theodore Parker.

Van Wyck Brooks describes the impact of European ideas on American culture, a phase of our history that has been given inadequate attention (except when incidental to histories of immigration into the United States). Orie W. Long, in his *Literary Pioneers,*[31] treats of the individuals who familiarized themselves in Germany with Goethe and other literary giants of the day, and brought back to America a love of fine literature which went far toward making possible the later flower-

[28] Boston, 1936.
[29] N. Y., 1926.
[30] Boston, 1936.
[31] Cambridge, 1935.

ing. A hundred years before it had been Addison, Pope, and Swift who had mainly shaped American literary tastes. These Anglo-American literary relations have been presented in a good study by Elizabeth C. Cook, *Literary Influences in Colonial Newspapers 1704-1750*.[32] A wide variety of materials on colonial culture, integrated with the growth of American nationality, is found in a volume by Michael Kraus, *Intercolonial Aspects of American Culture on the Eve of the Revolution*.[33] Thomas G. Wright's *Literary Culture in Early New England 1670-1730* [34] is a work of careful and broad scholarship which has had an important effect in bringing about a reinterpretation of the first century of American life. A number of special studies have been made of Franco-American intellectual relations by Gilbert Chinard and Bernard Faÿ, and the subject has been treated comprehensively by Howard Mumford Jones in *America and French Culture 1750-1848*.[35] This, which is the first of two volumes (the second to cover the American reaction to French literature), narrates in great detail French influences on American manners, art, religion, philosophy, and education. It is the most thorough work of its kind and not until more research along similar lines has been published can a comprehensive history of American culture be written.

New England's history, in its cultural as well as political phases, has received more attention than any other section of the country. The Middle West, however, has also had its literary historians who have celebrated her contribution to the national culture. William H. Venable in his *Beginnings of Literary Culture in the Ohio Valley* [36] included miscellaneous matter of use to later writers. Ralph L. Rusk went over similar ground but with

[32] N. Y., 1912.
[33] N. Y., 1928.
[34] New Haven, 1920.

[35] Chapel Hill, 1927.
[36] Cincinnati, 1891.

much deeper knowledge and greater inclusiveness in *The Literature of the Middle Western Frontier*.[37] Professor Rusk's work is rather formal and lacks the unifying interpretation found in Dorothy A. Dondore's *The Prairie and the Making of Middle America*,[38] or in Lucy L. Hazard's volume, which, however, applies the Turner thesis too rigidly in *The Frontier in American Literature*.[39] Constance Rourke's studies, especially *American Humor*,[40] are splendid portrayals of the relation between the social setting and the evolution of distinct culture expressions. Henry L. Mencken's *The American Language* [41] is invaluable for students of culture in America.

Related studies have been made of the newspaper and periodical press, but satisfactory comprehensive treatments are lacking. Isaiah Thomas's old *History of Printing in America* [42] will probably continue to be a standard authority for the earlier period. Frederic Hudson's *Journalism in the United States from 1690 to 1872* [43] still has useful materials, and the subject as a whole has been treated in summary fashion in James M. Lee's *History of American Journalism*,[44] and Willard G. Bleyer's *Main Currents in the History of American Journalism*.[45] For a fuller knowledge the student must consult more restricted studies, one of the best of which is Lawrence C. Wroth's *A History of Printing in Colonial Maryland*.[46] Douglas C. McMurtrie is now engaged on a large-scale history of printing in the United States and has published one volume on the Middle and South Atlantic States. Two good surveys of magazines in the earlier periods have appeared in recent years by Lyon N. Richardson and Frank L. Mott (the latter is of especial value), and the whole subject has been treated, rather

[37] 2 vols., N. Y., 1925.
[38] Cedar Rapids, 1926.
[39] N. Y., 1927.
[40] N. Y., 1931.
[41] N. Y., 1936 edn.

[42] 2 vols., Worcester, 1810.
[43] N. Y., 1873.
[44] Boston, 1923 rev. edn.
[45] Boston, 1927.
[46] Baltimore, 1922.

inadequately, by Algernon Tassin in *The Magazine in America*.[47] A deep insight into American culture may be gained from studies of several books that have had a mass appeal—the New England primer, whose history has been written by Paul L. Ford; the McGuffey readers, whose historian is Harvey C. Minnich; and the dime novel, whose significance has recently been appreciated in a delightful volume by Edmund Pearson.[48] The millions of copies of Noah Webster's books were of great importance in molding a common culture, and their creator has received the attention of two biographers within a year.[49]

The schools in which these volumes were read have had their historians too, such as Ellwood P. Cubberley, author of *Public Education in the United States*,[50] but the general histories must be supplemented by more thorough works covering portions of the field, like Walter H. Small's *Early New England Schools*,[51] Elmer E. Brown's *The Making of our Middle Schools*,[52] or the various contributions of Robert F. Seybolt. Higher education also needs a thoroughgoing survey. Charles F. Thwing's *A History of Higher Education in America*[53] and *History of Education in the United States Since the Civil War*[54] are not full enough, and the student must add to their stores by consulting particular college and university histories, notably Harvard's by Professor Morison (see pages 532 ff.), and Virginia's by Philip A. Bruce, as well

[47] N. Y., 1916. See also Lyon N. Richardson, *A History of American Magazines 1741-1789* (N. Y., 1931), and Frank L. Mott, *The History of American Magazines 1741-1850* (N. Y., 1930).

[48] Edmund Pearson, *Dime Novels* (Boston, 1929); Paul L. Ford, *The New England Primer* (N. Y., 1897); and Harvey C. Minnich, *William Holmes McGuffey and His Readers* (N. Y., 1936).

[49] Harry R. Warfel, *Noah Webster* (N. Y., 1936); Ervin Shoemaker, *Noah Webster* (N. Y., 1936). The latter concentrates on Webster as a pioneer of learning.

[50] Boston, 1934 edn.   [53] N. Y., 1906.

[51] Boston, 1914.   [54] Boston, 1910.

[52] N. Y., 1903.

as biographies of Eliot, Gilman, White, Angell, and other academic leaders. The history of women's education in the United States has been supplied by Thomas Woody, one of the most learned students of educational history in America. A splendid study of the interrelations between education and American society was made by Merle Curti in *The Social Ideas of American Educators.*[55]

Professor Curti is interested especially in American intellectual history. He has written the history of the peace movement in America—*Peace or War: The American Struggle, 1636-1936* [56]—and has published a volume on Elihu Burritt, who was connected with many humanitarian movements in the nineteenth century. These crusades often enlisted the aid of the clergy, but no complete study of the influence of the clergy in American history has been written. There are rather formal works on the history of religion, such as the older ones of Henry K. Carroll, Leonard W. Bacon, or recent, more satisfactory histories by Henry K. Rowe and William W. Sweet. More volumes are needed like Alice M. Baldwin's *The New England Clergy and the American Revolution* [57] and Edward F. Humphrey's *Nationalism and Religion in America 1774-1789.*[58] A more general work of much value is by Auguste Jorns, *The Quakers as Pioneers in Social Work.*[59]

Women have been especially active in humanitarian movements as in other phases of American life, but no comprehensive study of their very important role is available. Elizabeth A. Dexter's *Colonial Women of Affairs* [60] and Edith Abbott's *Women in Industry* [61] are restricted in subject matter. Mary S. Benson's work on *Women in Eighteenth Century America* [62] has a more

[55] N. Y., 1935.
[56] N. Y., 1936.
[57] Durham, 1928.
[58] Boston, 1924.

[59] N. Y., 1931.
[60] Boston, 1924.
[61] N. Y., 1910.
[62] N. Y., 1935.

general interest. The student must also consult the monumental work by Elizabeth C. Stanton, Susan B. Anthony, and others on *The History of Woman Suffrage* [63] which contains matter dealing with the whole subject of women's rights. Several of the volumes by Alice Morse Earle on the colonial period, although dealing in general with manners and customs, do tell much of the influence of women. The only fairly complete treatment of family mores, though far from adequate, is that by Arthur W. Calhoun, *Social History of the American Family*.[64] The main forces directing the evolution of family institutions in the United States, he says, are "the ascendancy of the bourgeois class, the dominance of a virgin continent and the industrial revolution." [65] George E. Howard's *A History of Matrimonial Institutions* [66] includes materials on the American family.

All observers have noted the dominant role that women have played in America as patrons of the arts, but the interconnection between societal evolution and the development of the arts has only very recently been treated in the volumes by Suzanne La Follette and Lewis Mumford.[67] Histories of a more conventional type deal specifically with architecture (in which Fiske Kimball has done some of the best work), painting, sculpture, and music, where the special studies of Oscar G. Sonneck are invaluable in supplementing the general surveys of Louis C. Elson and John T. Howard. Percy Scholes's volume is an important reinterpretation of the Puritan attitude toward music. One of the earliest works, and still useful, is William Dunlap's *History of the Rise and Progress of the Arts of Design in the United States*.[68] The theater

[63] 6 vols., Rochester, 1881-1922. [65] III, 332.
[64] 3 vols., Cleveland, 1917-1919. [66] 3 vols., Chicago, 1904.
[67] Suzanne La Follette, *Art in America* (N. Y., 1929); Lewis Mumford, *Sticks and Stones* (N. Y., 1924).
[68] 1834; rev. edn., 1918, ed. by F. W. Bayley and C. E. Goodspeed.

has good historians in George O. Seilhamer and Arthur H. Quinn, but the greatest contribution to the history of the American stage are the volumes by George C. D. Odell. An important phase of the culture of any people is its sports, and Americans have long realized their significance in the national life. An interesting history of the subject is that by John A. Krout, *Annals of American Sport.*[69]

The whole question of American culture, particularly the arts, is intimately bound up with the subject of immigration. But the historians of various immigrant groups are likely to exaggerate the influence of their own nationals, and their books must often be received with caution. Albert B. Faust, however, has written a good study of *The German Element in the United States.*[70] The best work in the field has been done for Scandinavian migrants, but even this is not entirely satisfactory. The old-world background has been studied for an understanding of the circumstances that lay behind the migration, and the interplay between the transplanted Scandinavians and those who stayed at home is often made clear. It is with this approach that the future student will be able to work out the interconnection between American and European economic and cultural developments and thus attain more nearly to a true history of the modern Western world. George M. Stephenson has made a good survey of the immigrant movement as a whole in *A History of American Immigration.*[71]

Whatever the conflicting claims made by various stocks to their share in building a national culture, there can be no dispute over responsibility for American legal customs. They are basically English, although the common law of England has undergone mutations in the American environment. This subject has long lain in too

[69] New Haven, 1929.   [71] Boston, 1926.
[70] 2 vols., Boston, 1909.

much obscurity because of the inaccessible nature of the materials, many of which are still in manuscript. A vigorous effort is now being made to lay the foundations for a satisfactory history of American law, and three volumes of *American Legal Records,* dealing with the pre-revolutionary period (each containing a valuable monographic essay) have recently been published. Earlier publications of useful materials are *Two Centuries' Growth of American Law* [72] and *Select Essays in Anglo-American Legal History.*[73] Some of the best work in the field is being done by Richard B. Morris, author of *Studies in the History of American Law.*[74] A number of volumes have been written on the courts and the legal profession. The outstanding works of this nature are those by Charles Warren, whose *History of the American Bar* [75] reveals great erudition.

Studies of the law and the legal profession have been rivaled in number by those dealing with medicine and its practitioners. The most comprehensive work has been done by Francis D. Packard, *History of Medicine in the United States,*[76] but the studies of prominent individuals and of individual states must be consulted to fill out the narrative. Doctors in the early days were often versatile scientists, especially in botany, and Howard A. Kelly has written a portion of their history in *Some American Medical Botanists.*[77] John W. Harshberger treats of one of the most important groups in *Botanists of Philadelphia and their Work.*[78]

There is no satisfactory history of science in America, but there are materials for one. Edward S. Dana and others have written *A Century of Science in America.*[79] Biology has found a historian in Robert T. Young; geol-

---

[72] Yale University, *Bicentennial Publications* (N. Y., 1901).
[73] 3 vols., Boston, 1907.
[74] N. Y., 1930.
[75] Cambridge, 1911.
[76] 2 vols., N. Y., 1931.

[77] N. Y., 1929.
[78] Phila., 1899.
[79] New Haven, 1918.

ogy in George P. Merrill; chemistry in Edgar F. Smith; and mathematics in a volume by David E. Smith and Jekuthiel Ginsburg. The several studies by George B. Goode and Frederick E. Brasch are especially valuable for the student of science in America. Not until more studies are made of the impact of European scientific ideas on America can anything of a comprehensive nature be written.[80]

The development of American philosophical thought has been told by I. Woodbridge Riley; his work for the early period, however, has been superseded by more recent publications. Herbert W. Schneider has written more understandingly of *The Puritan Mind* [81] and the subject has been sketched as a whole in Harvey Gates Townsend's *Philosophical Ideas in the United States.*[82] To lay a more solid basis for an understanding of American philosophical thought one must also consult the volumes on transcendentalism in New England, especially Frothingham's work; the biography of William James by Ralph Barton Perry; the papers of Charles S. Peirce (edited by Morris R. Cohen); and the several studies that have been made of John Dewey and George Santayana.[83]

Many subjects of fundamental importance to the historian of American culture are treated in the monographs comprising *Recent Social Trends in the United States,* whose more valuable materials and conclusions have been brought together in a summary study bearing the same

[80] R. T. Young, *Biology in America* (Boston, 1922); G. P. Merrill, *The First One Hundred Years of American Geology* (New Haven, 1924); E. F. Smith, *Chemistry in America* (N. Y., 1914); D. E. Smith and J. Ginsburg, *A History of Mathematics in America before 1900* (Chicago, 1934).

[81] N. Y., 1930.

[82] N. Y., 1934.

[83] I. Woodbridge Riley, *American Philosophy, the Early Schools* (N. Y., 1907); Riley, *American Thought* (rev. edn., 1923); Octavius B. Frothingham, *Transcendentalism in New England* (N. Y., 1876); Harold C. Goddard, *Studies in New England Transcendentalism* (N. Y., 1908).

title.[84] The two volumes on *Recent Economic Changes in the United States* [85] are also of much use. It is a safe prophecy that the number of books on American cultural history will be greatly multiplied by the students of this generation.

[84] N. Y., 1934.
[85] N. Y., 1929.

XV

THE FRONTIER AND SECTIONAL HISTORIANS

Historians have written works of major importance dealing with sections of the United States, and frequently in so doing they have cast new light on the history of the country as a whole. The vastness of the country, with its distinctive geographical divisions equal in size (and in economic significance as well) to entire European nations, has made it necessary for careful writers to spend perhaps the better part of a lifetime mastering the material pertaining to one section. Histories relating to New England alone have a tradition reaching back to the colonial period; in the South the histories that were written dealt mainly with single States. George Tucker and Lyman Draper were interested in the history of the West, but in their day that region was still in the making; not until the West was well settled did students arise to survey its history comprehensively, and as a result of the efforts of Frederick J. Turner and his co-workers our national history has been recast. In recent years there has been a great emphasis on cultural regionalism, in part an attempt to pick up the broken thread of a tradition once full of vitality, and in part a revulsion against a too-nebulous national pattern. In fiction, painting, music, and architecture, the renaissance of regionalism has resulted in outstanding contributions to the composite national culture. The writing of history, too, has been stimulated in this invigorating atmosphere.

THE WEST

Reuben Gold Thwaites

One of those who made possible the writing of a fuller history of the region beyond the Appalachians was Reuben Gold Thwaites, who had gone west to Wisconsin from Massachusetts as a youth. His training as a newspaper man helped him in later editorial work, and in 1876 he began his publications in history. Less than a decade later Thwaites was associated with the Wisconsin Historical Society, and as editor of its publications he made them a model for other societies. In an appreciative memorial address (1914) Turner pointed out that Thwaites was more interested in the records of individual achievement than he was in the history of institutions, of industrial development, or of laws and government.

The productivity of Thwaites was tremendous: in a period of some twenty-five years he wrote fifteen books, edited and published over a hundred and sixty volumes, besides writing articles and making addresses. His historical writing was, on occasion, good, but of far greater value was his work as editor. He understood, perhaps, wherein lay his superior accomplishments, for in one instance he wrote: "An editor of historical sources cannot with propriety comment upon the character or the motives of the actors in the drama outlined upon his pages; sufficient that . . . he presents materials from which philosophical historians may construct their edifices.''[1] His weak critical ability marred his writing as well as his editing, but the numerous volumes issued under his name made it possible for others to study many phases of western history. His most important edited publications are the *Jesuit Relations,* the *Original Journals of Lewis and Clark,*[2] and the reprints of *Early Western Travels 1748-1846.*[3]

The Jesuit Relations and Allied Documents is a monumental series of seventy-three volumes, which were published in the five years following 1896. Most of these documents were either rare printings or were still in manuscript. Thwaites had great admiration for the Jesuit missionaries, whose work he termed ''one of the most thrilling chapters in human history.'' Some of the explorers, notably Champlain, left narratives, but the Jesuits provided most of the information that remains concerning the frontiers of New France in the seventeenth century. From annual reports (1632-1673) made by missionaries, which eventually reached France, a series of volumes was issued under the title *The Jesuit Relations.* They have proved to be as useful to geographers and anthropologists as to historians, and their value is enhanced by an excellent index. The series begins with the earliest conversion of Indians in New France, in 1610, and in the course of the many volumes that follow practically the whole story of Jesuit activity in Canada and Louisiana is unfolded.

Because of Thwaites's labors documents and rare books which had been in the possession of a few individuals or libraries were now made available to a wide number of students, and his volumes gave a definite impetus to the study and writing of Western history. The

[1] Preface to Vol. LXXII, *Jesuit Relations.*
[2] 8 vols., N. Y., 1904-1905.
[3] 32 vols., Cleveland, 1904-1907.

Early Western Travels, collected in one vast publication, observes Turner, "present a picture of the irresistible tide of American settlement flowing into the wilderness, of societies forming in the forests, of cities evolving almost under our gaze as we see them through the eyes of these travelers in successive years." The student is thankful to Thwaites for preserving this and other pictures of American history.[4]

THEODORE ROOSEVELT

It is not surprising that Theodore Roosevelt, who was one of the men most influential in promoting an expansionist sentiment in the United States in the latter years of the nineteenth century, should have become interested in the early westward movement. Roosevelt had lived on the far western frontier for some time before writing his volumes on the pioneers. "The men who have shared in the fast-vanishing frontier life of the present," he wrote in his preface to *The Winning of the West,* "feel a peculiar sympathy with the already long-vanished frontier life of the past."

Roosevelt's interest in history was aroused very early. As an undergraduate, he says in his autobiography, "I was already writing one or two chapters of a book I afterwards published on the Naval War of 1812." This subject he found far more to his liking than the topics assigned to him by his professors at Harvard. He also remarked that at the time he wrote this volume in the early 1880's "the navy had reached its nadir." Roosevelt was always interested in history as literature, but sometimes he thought of it as propaganda. His methods would not always be considered orthodox by the pro-

[4] F. J. Turner, *Reuben Gold Thwaites, Memorial Address* (1914); C. W. Alvord on Thwaites in Miss. Valley Hist. Assn. *Proc.,* Vol. VII (1913-1914).

fessional guild today as, for example, on the occasion
when he wrote to Henry Cabot Lodge (half in jest, perhaps): "I have pretty nearly finished Benton [a biography in the "American Statesmen" series] mainly
evolving him from my inner consciousness." [5]

To his friend, Lodge, Roosevelt wrote in August,
1888: "I continue greatly absorbed in my new work [*The
Winning of the West*], but it goes very slowly; I am only
half way through the first volume. I shall try my best
not to hurry it, nor make it scamp work." Four months
earlier Parkman had granted Roosevelt's request that he
be allowed to dedicate this work to him. Parkman's volumes, said Roosevelt, "must be models for all historical
treatment of the founding of new communities and the
growth of the frontier here in the wilderness."

In accordance with his promise to his publishers,
Roosevelt had the first two volumes ready in 1889. Volume I treats of the settlement of the lands "From the
Alleghanies to the Mississippi" in the seven years before
the Declaration of Independence; the second volume discusses the progress of settlement during the Revolution.
Roosevelt first sketches in the groups who contended for
the possession of this territory: the English-speaking
peoples, the French, and the various tribes of Indians.
He has the frontiersman's view of the Indians, whose
cunning, stealth "and merciless cruelty" made them "the
tigers of the human race." But the historian is also critical of many of the whites who committed "deeds of the
foulest and most wanton aggression." Although most of
his work is concerned with the spectacular events of territorial expansion, some of his chapters are very interesting to the historian who would observe the backwoodsmen in their more peaceful moments. The Americans
had gained a firm foothold in Kentucky by 1775, he
writes, for "cabins had been built and clearings made;

[5] June 7, 1886.

there were women and children in the wooden forts, cattle grazed on the range, and two or three hundred acres of corn had been sown and reaped.'' Some three hundred men in Kentucky were ''surrounded by an overwhelming number of foes'' with whom a ''death struggle'' impended. Roosevelt, however, is at his best in descriptions of frontier fighting, and his full-blooded narrative is like a far-off echo of wilderness warfare.

By 1783, with the coming of peace, a large immigrant tide flowed into Kentucky. ''The days of the first game hunters and Indian fighters were over'' and the herds of buffalo in this region were nearly gone. Churches, schools, mills, stores, race tracks, and markets told of the planting of a new civilization. In Tennessee, also, a new civilization was in the making, but Roosevelt pays scant attention to the frontier of the Southwest. The backwoodsmen were spread now almost to the Mississippi, and they had increased to some twenty-five thousand. ''Beyond the Alleghanies,'' writes Roosevelt, ''the Revolution was fundamentally a struggle between England, bent on restricting the growth of the English race, and the Americans, triumphantly determined to acquire the right to conquer the continent.''

The third volume of the history was published in 1894, with the subtitle, ''The Founding of the Trans-Alleghany Commonwealths 1784-1790.'' During these years, says Roosevelt, ''the rifle-bearing freemen who founded their little republics on the western waters gradually solved the question of combining personal liberty with national union.'' Separatist movements were nullified, and by 1790 the commonwealths beyond the Alleghanies ''had become parts of the Federal Union.'' A good opening chapter is on ''The Inrush of Settlers 1784-1787,'' with special reference to Kentucky. Not for long, though, does Roosevelt leave off telling of the Indian Wars, which continued to ravage the frontier in the years following the end of the Revolution. Although much of what he writes here is interesting to a historian, about it clings the air of the sensational Sunday newspaper supplement.

In the section on the struggle between the Spaniards and the Americans for the navigation of the Mississippi, Roosevelt betrays his strong chauvinism. He convicts the Spaniards of "systematic and deliberate duplicity and treachery" in opposing "their stalwart and masterful foes." The spirit of the Elizabethan buccaneers blusters through some of these pages and through the later remarks on the "Ethics of Territorial Conquest." Here is the Bismarckian philosophy of "blood and iron" and "the end justifies the means." Turner's essay on "The Significance of the Frontier in American History" was quickly seized upon by Roosevelt and incorporated in this third volume. Roosevelt differentiates the settlement of the Northwest from that of the Southwest by stating that the former resulted from the "principle of collective national action," whereas in the latter "the spirit of intense individualism" was given free rein. A chapter on the Southwest territory is an inadequate treatment of this part of the frontier to which he pays insufficient attention throughout his work.

In late December, 1895, Roosevelt wrote to Lodge, "The 4th volume of my *Winning of the West* is done." Publication followed within a few months. It covers the period beginning with the wars against the Northwestern Indians, who had defeated St. Clair, and closes with the acquisition and exploration of the territory secured through the Louisiana Purchase. The graphic pages on the rout of St. Clair's army are followed by the story of Mad Anthony Wayne's victory over the Indians. In his chapter "Tennessee Becomes a State 1791-1796" the author includes some important items on land speculation, a subject then generally neglected by historians.

"The Men of the Western Waters, 1798-1802" contains Roosevelt's best pages on economic and social history. "The pioneers stood for an extreme Americanism, in social, political, and religious matters alike," concludes Roosevelt. "The trend of American thought was toward them, not away from them. More than ever before, the Westerners were able to make their demands felt at home, and to make their force felt in the event of a struggle with a foreign power."

Louisiana was not won by a statesman or by a group of statesmen, but by the "great westward thrust of the settler folk, a thrust which was delivered blindly, but which no rival race could parry, until it was stopped by the ocean itself." This section and the pages that follow on Burr's conspiracy and the explorations of the Far West depend very heavily on Henry Adams.

Turner, one of the best qualified of Roosevelt's reviewers, said that these volumes "rescued a whole movement in American development from the hands of unskilful annalists." Many sources, including those in manuscript hitherto unused, were drawn upon by Roosevelt. His emphasis on American controversies with England and Spain relating to the frontier is of value for a fuller understanding of the "truly national history of the United States—a work that remains to be accomplished," added Turner. The dramatic and the picturesque, rather than the institutional, usually interested Roosevelt, and it is because of that very fact that his work has much to offer the general reader. The special student who looks for more careful research, especially in the materials of foreign countries bearing on the questions arising from the settlement of the Mississippi Valley, will prefer to consult the volumes of Samuel F. Bemis, Arthur P. Whitaker, Verner W. Crane, and others.

Just before the annual meeting of the American Historical Association in 1912, Roosevelt wrote to Lodge in his characteristic manner: "I am to deliver a beastly lecture—'History as Literature.' " (It was the presidential address.) None of the members of the Association, he added, "believe that history is literature. I have spent much care on the lecture, and as far as I know it won't even be printed anywhere."

It is a matter for congratulation, perhaps, that American historians have not followed Roosevelt uncritically. It is, of course, preferable that history be well written, but if that means the insertion of obiter dicta in the Roosevelt fashion (for example, writing of America in the 1790's, and pausing to make unrelated remarks advocating preparedness in the 1890's), then let such literature be called not history but pamphleteering.[6]

FREDERICK J. TURNER

When Frederick Jackson Turner was growing to manhood, historical interests in the United States for the most part were still centered in a few communities close to the Atlantic coast. It is true that in some of the younger academic institutions like Michigan and Cornell, in the Historical Society in Wisconsin, and along the Pacific coast as a result of Hubert Howe Bancroft's enthusiasm, historical studies were promoted and work of good quality was being produced. Even when historians did enlarge their narratives to survey more of the country than the Atlantic coast, they were wont to pass over these Western sections hurriedly or else to write of them with but little understanding of their relationship to the areas eastward; for the most part it was a kind of enlarged New England which was then described.

[6] For letters between Roosevelt and Lodge quoted above, see *Selections from the Correspondence of Henry Cabot Lodge and Theodore Roosevelt 1884-1918* (2 vols., N. Y., 1925), Vol. I; August 12, 1888; December 23, 1895; December 26, 1912.

A few students, however, watching the West of the mid-nineteenth century in the process of growing, were aware, not always clearly perhaps, of the place of the frontier in American development.[7] Godkin, editor of *The Nation,* McMaster, and James Bryce understood the meaning of the frontier. Bryce, in his chapter on "The Temper of the West" in *The American Commonwealth,* speaks of the West as "the most American part of America; that is to say, the part where those features which distinguish America from Europe come out in the strongest relief. What Europe is to Asia, what England is to the rest of Europe, what America is to England, that the Western States and Territories are to the Atlantic States, the heat and pressure and hurry of life always growing as we follow the path of the sun." [8] Not until Turner began writing, however, was a clearly formulated expression of the place of the frontier in American life presented to students of American history. Woodrow Wilson, with his flair for the popularization of knowledge, presented to the general public the Turnerian thesis in *The Forum,* calling his article "The Proper Perspective of American History." [9]

Turner was born in a region that was not yet out of the frontier stage of development, where traditions of an earlier day were still of sufficient reality to have escaped romantic treatment. His ancestors, he recalls, moved at least once every generation. In an autobiographical note he tells us that he hunted and fished among Indian neighbors who came to town "to buy paints and trinkets and sell furs." "Is it strange that I saw the frontier as a real thing and experienced its changes?" On his mother's side he was descended from preachers. "Is it strange that I

[7] H. C. Nixon, "Precursors of Turner in the Interpretation of the American Frontier," *South Atlantic Quarterly* (January, 1929).

[8] 1888 edn., II, 681.

[9] 1895, Vol. XIX.

preached of the frontier?'' he remarked with a smile.[10] His father was a journalist and politician, and was interested in local history.

Frederick Jackson Turner was born in Portage, Wisconsin, 1861, studied at the University of Wisconsin, and then went on to Johns Hopkins, where he took his Ph.D. in 1890. At Wisconsin he studied European institutional history with William F. Allen. As an undergraduate he had access to the famous Draper collection of manuscripts on the West. It was at Wisconsin, where Turner was a member of the faculty until 1910, that he did his most effective teaching. When Carl Becker, then a freshman, saw Turner in 1893 he was a young professor, so zestful and buoyant that he lifted the students to new realms of the intellectual life. From no other man, said Professor Becker, did he ''ever get in quite the same measure that sense of watching a first-class mind at work on its own account, and not merely rehearsing for the benefit of others; the most delightful sense in the world of sitting there waiting for ideas to be born; expectantly waiting for secret meanings, convenient explanatory hypotheses to be discovered, lurking as like as not under the dullest mass of drab facts ever seen.'' [11] As a teacher he was not given to passing on to his students final judgments, and he was equally reluctant to do so in his writing. Born with a really intellectual curiosity, he had a mind that was ever alert, fresh, and independent, and that sought its own answer to the many problems that face a historian.

Dissatisfied with the overemphasis of Herbert Baxter Adams's ''germ theory of politics,'' which traced American political institutions back to primitive German

[10] Letter to Constance Lindsay Skinner, March 15, 1922, in *Wisc. Mag. of Hist.* (1935), pp. 91-103.

[11] ''Frederick Jackson Turner,'' in H. W. Odum, ed., *American Masters of Social Science,* pp. 281-282.

custom, he sought an explanation in terms of American environment. Thus Turner donned the garb of the sociologist in his earliest published work on *The Fur Trade in Wisconsin*. Here he posed the question which in one way or another he tried to answer ever afterward. "The exploitation of the Indian is generally dismissed," he observed, "with the convenient explanatory phrase, 'the march of civilization.'" And then came his troubling question: "But how did it march?" Confining his researches to America to illustrate this social process (although Adams had said that American institutions had already been sufficiently studied), Turner foreshadowed his own later approach when he wrote of the effects of the trading post upon the white man: "In every country the exploitation of the wild beasts, and of the raw-products generally, causes the entry of the disintegrating and transforming influences of a higher civilization." [12] And in studying American civilization Turner was particularly interested in finding out what gave it the particular stamp that served to differentiate it from an older European civilization.

The West appealed to him as a factor in the creation of American life. While Rhodes and Von Holst were immersed in the slavery struggle, and other historians— Roosevelt, Winsor, and Thwaites—were attracted to the epic period of the West, Turner was "trying to see it as a whole . . . on its institutional, social, economic and political side." He saw "that there was a persistent persuasive influence in American life which did not get its full attention from those who thought in terms of North and South, as well as from those who approached the West as fighting ground, or ground for exploration history." He was less interested in the West as a region in itself

[12] "The Character and Influence of the Indian Trade in Wisconsin," Johns Hopkins University "Studies," IX, 74-75.

than as an illustration of the process of American development.[13]

In 1892 the important ideas of the frontier thesis were presented in a paper, "The Problems of American History," which appeared in a student publication. The next year at Chicago, at the annual meeting of the American Historical Association, an essay, "The Significance of the Frontier in American History," was read before the assembled scholars. In his opening sentences Turner referred to the closing of the frontier and then added: "Up to our own day American history has been in a large degree the history of the colonization of the Great West. The existence of an area of free land, its continuous recession, and the advance of American settlement westward, explain American development."[14] Because of contact with each new frontier in its movement westward American social development was in constant process of being reborn, and it was this "continuous touch with the simplicity of primitive society" which furnished "the forces dominating American character." "The true point of view in the history of this nation is not the Atlantic Coast," said the professor from Wisconsin, "it is the Great West."[15]

In the process of transforming the wilderness, the pioneer is at first barbarized, but slowly he and the wilderness are changed, and in that change a new personality is created which is distinctly American. The advance of the frontier, says Turner, "has meant a steady movement away from the influence of Europe, a steady growth of independence on American lines. And to study this advance, the men who grew up under these conditions, and the political, economic, and social results of it,

[13] Letter to C. L. Skinner.
[14] Essays reprinted in *The Frontier in American History*, p. 1.
[15] *Ibid.*, pp. 2-3.

is to study the really American part of our history."[16] Unlike the Atlantic seaboard, where the population was predominantly English, the frontier was a region where immigrants became "Americanized, liberated, and fused into a mixed race English in neither nationality nor characteristics.[17] It was the frontier with its vast public domain that conditioned "the growth of nationalism and the evolution of American political institutions,"[18] but most importantly the frontier profoundly affected the growth of individualism and democracy.[19] Frontier life determined the type of religious organization built up in the United States and also had a profound effect in shaping intellectual characteristics—the inventive mind, often coarse and strong, with a comprehensive grasp of material things, and exhibiting an unquiet, nervous energy. Turner restates this concept in the preface to the volume of essays on the frontier: "The larger part of what has been distinctive and valuable in America's contribution to the history of the human spirit has been due to this nation's peculiar experience in extending its type of frontier into new regions; and in creating peaceful societies with new ideals in the successive vast and differing geographic provinces which together make up the United States." The disappearance of the frontier in 1890 marked the closing of the first period of American history.[20]

With the passing of the frontier came a gradual approach to social uniformity in the United States, and as Turner watched this change he endeavored to comprehend the play of forces in the country. To understand the contemporary scene he sought light in the past; and in several essays he expounded the idea that the United

[16] P. 4.
[17] P. 23.
[18] P. 24.

[19] P. 30.
[20] P. 38.

States was a federation of sections.[21] In a manuscript found among his papers after his death in 1932, Turner explains how he led up to his last studies: "Looking back over my work as a university teacher, which ends this year," he wrote in 1924, "I find that the central interest of my study has been that of . . . maps of population advance—not as a student of a region, but of a process. From cave man to the occupation of a planet. Study of American advance required examination of the geographic, economic, social, diplomatic advances of the frontier," in all of which Turner engaged. It led him also "to examination of the sectional aspects of the advance into new geographic areas, which compelled [him] to study conditions in the various Atlantic Coast regions leading to migration, and into the effects of the newer regions upon these older ones, and to study the special geographical problems into which the various zones of advance brought new societies—the interaction of the various migrating stocks, each in its particular geographic province, adjusting to new social types, and the resulting play of sectional forces in American politics as the old and the new sections found in Congress and in party the need of adjustment or the impulse to conflict. As a result," said Turner, he had "been led to a study of the various sections of the United States, both internally and in their mutual relations with each other and the federal government." [22] He was interested, too, in the way frontier forces acted upon foreign relations, and his studies in American diplomacy indicated the value of this approach.

Turner notes again and again the analogy between American sections and the nations of Europe; America, he believes, should be thought of in continental and not

[21] See collected essays in *The Significance of Sections in American History.*
[22] *Op. cit.,* Introduction, pp. iii-iv.

alone in national terms. But unlike European countries, which must compose their clashing interests peacefully by conferences or violently by war, the sections of the United States may compose theirs by parliamentary procedure. In a series of maps Turner is able to show the tendency of several sections to vote consistently in national elections over a long period of years. He is certain that sectionalism is not likely to disappear. Rather he believes that Congressional legislation will continue to "be shaped by compromises and combinations, which will in effect be treaties between rival sections, and the real federal aspect of our government will lie, not in the relation of state and nation, but in the relation of section and nation." Turner is careful to note that neither physical geography nor economic interests are the only factors in sectionalism; the inherited habits of thought of the various stocks are likewise of great importance. Although he does not look forward to the disappearance of sections, Turner sounds the danger of each region's insisting on its particular interests and ideals "without sympathetic comprehension of the ideals, the interests and the rights of other sections." "We must shape our national action," he says, "to the fact of a vast and varied Union of unlike sections."

Over a period of forty years Turner continued to study his great theme and to publish essays and monographs which served to illustrate his ideas. Once, by dint of persistent editorial persuasion, he was inveigled into writing a volume, the *Rise of the New West 1819-1829,* for the "American Nation" series (1906). The rise of the new West, says the author, "was the most significant fact in American history in the years immediately following the War of 1812." [23] Chapters on the "Social and Economic Development of the West" and "Western Commerce and Ideals" are of exceptional value, and in the

[23] P. 67.

latter Turner refers to the strongly national and democratic character of the West. "By the march of the westerners away from their native states to the public domain
of the nation, and by their organization as territories
of the United States, they lost that state particularism
which distinguished many of the old commonwealths of
the coast." "It was a self-confident section, believing in
its right to share in government, and troubled by no
doubts of its capacity to rule." [24]

Turner's writing did not often have the form of
a continuous narrative. The fact of the matter is that he
rarely concerned himself with history in the conventional
sense of a narrative of events chronologically arranged.
As one of his best-known students, Carl Becker, expresses it, Turner's writing "is all essentially descriptive, explicative, expository." [25] Because his writing was
of such a character, students of history waited in vain for
the comprehensive work that was never written. The illuminating generalizations that Turner worked out compressed much material in few pages. In his last years
after his retirement from Harvard (he had taught there
from 1910 to 1924), Turner was a research associate at
the Huntington Library in California, and while there he
brought almost to completion *The United States, 1830-
1850: The Nation and Its Sections*. The continual discovery of new material, as well as Turner's ill-health,
had postponed completion of the book.[26] This volume in
its incomplete form was published posthumously in 1935.

Not long after he had published his volume in the
"American Nation" series (1906) Turner became very
much interested in the period from 1830 to 1850. He
thought this score of years offered "the best opportunity

[24] Pp. 109-110.
[25] Odum, *op. cit.*, p. 313.
[26] Max Farrand, "F. J. Turner at the Huntington Library," Huntington
Library *Bulletin* (February, 1933), No. 3.

for a new work'' and he said that the West in this period needed special study, ''which as yet it hasn't received.'' ''But I find it very hard to write,'' he told Professor Becker, ''and suspect that I need to break for the wilderness and freshen up—rather than tie myself to the chair.'' [27]

A large portion of the volume, and in many ways the most satisfying, are the earlier chapters describing the various sections of the country. Although Turner's bias was always in favor of the West, he constantly refers to the great influence that native and transplanted New Englanders, as well as New Yorkers, had in the life of this period. The generalizations that enriched his other writings are found scattered in this volume also, and more than before Turner inclines to an interpretation in terms of the class struggle. In speaking of the New York Locofoco party, for example, he says that ''the movement was a landmark in the rise of organised demands of the common people for the control of government in the interests of their own economic and spiritual welfare. It presaged a succession of later movements (strongest in the western sections to which New England and New York sent settlers) that included the organisation of Anti-Monopolists, Grangers, Populists, and the whole group of later progressive parties.'' [28] In a discussion of the Bank and the failure to renew its charter, Turner says: ''The severance of official connection between the national government and the capitalist was one of the most important steps in American history. Thenceforth the industrial interests were obliged to act by underground methods and by the lobby.'' [29] In his usual unconventional manner Turner brings forth little-used facts— such as the need for planting corn before the virgin soil

[27] Preface, p. v.
[28] P. 125.
[29] P. 407.

could produce wheat—to explain the condition of life in the North Central States.

This period appeared to Turner as one of fundamental importance in the history of the country, for the very character of its population was then changing because of increased immigration, and in its economic, political, and intellectual life it was striking out in new directions. "Between 1830 and 1850," he writes, "there was . . . a cycle of change in American ideals and in the composition of the people." [30]

The thrill of the search for the meaning of American life was ever in the heart of Turner, and there is a warm pride that runs through much of his writing—the pride of frontier birth. The deeds of "The Children of the Pioneers" (one of his essays in *Sections in American History*) are recorded with a consciousness of the injustice of the aspersions on the character of the early settlers.[31] In after years he was more and more troubled by the question of the reconciliation and application to civilization in the twentieth century of frontier ideals of individualism and democracy.[32] But the exuberance and vitality of his writing and teaching in the main reflect a natural optimism. In his presidential address to the American Historical Association in 1910, Turner called upon his colleagues to see "in American society, with its vast spaces, its sections equal to European nations, its geographic influences, its brief period of development, its variety of nationalities and races, its extraordinary industrial growth under the conditions of freedom, its institutions, culture, ideals, social psychology, and even its religions forming and changing almost under [their] eyes, one of the richest fields ever offered for the pre-

[30] Pp. 579-580.
[31] See also "The Problem of the West," *Atlantic Monthly* (September, 1896), reprinted in *The Frontier in American History*, p. 214.
[32] *The Frontier in American History*, p. 203.

liminary recognition and study of the forces that operate and interplay in the making of society.'' [33]

In the process of developing his frontier thesis Turner more than once halted to ask himself, and his friends as well, whether he had overemphasized it. Scarcely any well-formulated criticism was directed at the thesis, although Channing at Harvard voiced his skepticism of its value. More recently vigorous statements have been made against the Turner doctrine. In an article on ''American Democracy and the Frontier'' [34] Benjamin F. Wright of Harvard presents one phase of the opposition case. The obvious shortcoming of the frontier interpretation of national development is its disregard of the fact that the growth of American democracy is part of the progress of Western civilization as a whole. ''The proper point of departure for the discussion of the rise of democracy in the United States,'' says Wright in his counterblast, ''is not the American west but the European background.'' The religions—Brownism, Puritanism, Quakerism, and Presbyterianism—brought over by most of the colonists had ''relatively decentralized and democratic forms of organization.'' A comparison with French and Spanish colonists shows that colonists everywhere brought to the new world institutions with which they were familiar in the old. It is therefore incorrect to ascribe to frontier conditions a primary influence in determining the type of the institutions planted there. ''The customs and ideas brought by the settlers from an older civilization,'' says Wright, ''are of vastly more importance in shaping the history of the new lands.'' It must be remembered also that the years after Jackson's election coincided with the period of revolt and unrest everywhere in the Western world, and the agitation for social and political change in Amer-

[33] Reprinted in *The Frontier in American History*, p. 334.
[34] *Yale Review* (Winter, 1931).

ica was related to similar movements in Europe. It is the machine age civilization that is more responsible than the disappearance of the frontier for the emphasis on social rather than individualist democracy. And, as in other respects, Europe has gone through these developments earlier than America, which follows in its wake. Other students have recently observed that the closing of the frontier line in 1890 meant little, for a large acreage still lay open for settlement. More damaging testimony is that the lands which presumably were the safety valve for the discontented of the East rarely came into their hands. Speculators and railroads generally got them first. Another point is that the frontier areas were settled by people living on adjoining lands—that is, farmers—and not those who were dissatisfied in urban communities. Sometimes, instead of going West, the unemployed went out of the country entirely to seek a livelihood.

Despite the valuable correctives that have been made of it, the Turner thesis has not been completely demolished by any means. Europeans corresponding in faith and circumstances to those living in America were often different in temperament; they differed in concepts of equalitarianism and, above all, were usually poles apart in hopefulness. The frontiersman was generally a democrat in action before the existence of the fact was translated into a political franchise. There was a lift of the spirit (after the first heartbreaking toil was over) that impressed the European visitor deeply. Even if Turner did exaggerate the role of the frontier in the promotion of democracy, his general thesis that the movement westward profoundly affected the course of American history and greatly influenced the formation of traits of the national character, is valid. Students in the various fields of literature, economics, political science, history, and sociology have accepted its validity, and while sometimes, in their ardent discipleship, they have pushed to extremes the thesis of the master, they have nevertheless producd fruitful works. The seminal teaching and writing of Turner resulted in a rich growth, and the school of frontier historians has flourished like the green bay tree.[35]

Clarence W. Alvord

Among the many students who sought to reinterpret American history with the Turner thesis as a key, none did better work than Clarence W. Alvord. Early in his career he established his claim to scholarly notice by his discovery of the records of the old French settlements in Illinois. He edited the *Kaskaskia Records 1778-1790* (1909) and, with Clarence E. Carter, also published *The New Regime 1765-1767* (1916). With Lee Bidgood, Alvord issued an important publication on *The First Explorations of the Transalleghany Region by the Virginians 1650-1674* (1912), which was dedicated to Turner. This was the first attempt to tell the story of the discovery of this region by the Virginians, whose achievements had been unknown to Parkman and Winsor. Under Alvord's editorship fourteen volumes of the Illinois Historical *Collections* appeared; he was the editor of one of the best state histories ever written—the *Centennial History of Illinois*—of which he wrote the first volume. In addition to his other interests he was very active in making the Mississippi Valley Historical Association of first-rate importance to scholarship.

Alvord's most noteworthy piece of historical composition is *The Mississippi Valley in British Politics.*[36]

[35] See articles by Murray Kane in *Miss. Valley Hist. Rev.* (September, 1936); Paul W. Gates and Fred Shannon in *Amer. Hist. Rev.* (July, 1936); and Carter Goodrich and Sol Davidson, "The Wage Earner in the Westward Movement," *Pol. Sci. Quart.* (June, 1935; March, 1936); also essays edited by Dixon Ryan Fox, *Sources of Culture in the Middle West* (N. Y., 1934).

[36] 2 vols., Cleveland, 1917.

Its subtitle describes its contents: "A study of the Trade, Land Speculation and Experiments in Imperialism Culminating in the American Revolution." The author informs the reader that in his pages the conventional narrative of the events leading up to the Revolution is not to be found. "Whenever the British ministers soberly and seriously discussed the American problem," says Alvord, "the vital phase to them was not the disturbances of . . . Boston and New York, but the development of that vast transmontane region that was acquired in 1763 by the Treaty of Paris." [37] Although his point of observation lay on the Western prairies, his work, says Alvord, is not a history of the West. Rather his eyes were fixed on the British ministry "in the hope of discovering the obscure development of a western policy"; for he thought it impossible to fathom the British-American policy unless contemporary British politics were thoroughly understood. The problems of Indians, land companies, fur traders, the rights of the various colonies in the West, imperial interests—all these had to be dealt with and Alvord describes the attempts made to solve them.

Although he made mistakes in his description of British politics,[38] Alvord's general interpretation did much to narrate more accurately the real scope of conflicting interests in the Revolutionary era. Some of his material is especially good, as one might have expected from a historian who had spent years poring over the frontier documents; in particular might be mentioned "The Beginning of Western Speculation." [39] At the close of this period, writes Alvord, "British muddling in the West was doomed. By 1774 the colonists of the eastern

[37] I, 13.
[38] See L. B. Namier, *England in the Age of the American Revolution* (London, 1930).
[39] I, Chap. III.

seacoast . . . were already preparing to assert themselves. Thus there culminated at the same time two series of events, one eastern and one western, which had for years run parallel, so closely interwoven that any attempt to understand the one without a knowledge of the other must inevitably fail. If historians would interpret rightly the causes of the American Revolution and the birth of the new nation,'' he concludes, ''they must not let their vision be circumscribed by the sequence of events in the East.'' [40] In his anxiety to redress the balance of emphasis Alvord minimizes English public interest in the region of the Atlantic seaboard. Publications of all sorts, especially newspapers and magazines, reflect that interest which he underestimated, but once having made this qualification on his work, it will be granted that Alvord's volumes mark an important development in the historiography of the American Revolution. [41]

HERBERT E. BOLTON

The way to the frontier has not always been from East to West; in the very earliest days of our history it was from South to North. In the study of New Spain's contribution to American history no one has done more important work than Herbert Eugene Bolton. Beginning with the exploration of Mexican archives he has enlarged the field of investigation to include materials of the homeland in Spain to round out his story of the Spanish Borderlands in North America. Going beyond his preceptors, McMaster and Turner, Professor Bolton has proclaimed the epic of a greater America in which the essential unity of American history, North and South, has been stressed; his is literally a history of the Americas, not merely the story of the expansion of the thirteen

[40] II, 250.
[41] Solon J. Buck, "Clarence Walworth Alvord, Historian," *Miss. Valley Hist. Rev.,* XV, 309 ff.

colonies into a nation. His researches in anthropology, cartography, and history have taken him all over the lands once part of Spain's empire in North America. His publications include *The Spanish Borderlands, An Outpost of Empire*,[42] *Rim of Christendom: A biography of Father Kino*,[43] and volumes of edited writings. A student of Professor Bolton, Lawrence Kinnaird, thus expresses the spirit of the school which has its center in California: "Many of the best-known students of the American frontier have failed to see that the proximity of Spanish territory to the United States had any bearing upon their subjects. Documents of vital importance to the understanding of American expansion have remained unused in Spanish and Mexican archives while old-school historians, apparently oblivious of their existence, have attempted to write and rewrite early United States history."

In a textbook, *The Colonization of North America 1492-1783*,[44] written with Thomas M. Marshall, Professor Bolton gives the key to his point of view. More emphasis is placed on non-English colonies and on those English colonies which were not among the original thirteen. "By following the larger story of European expansion it becomes plain that there was an Anglo-Spanish and a Franco-Spanish, as well as a Franco-English struggle for the continent, not to mention the ambitions and efforts of Dutch, Swedes, Russians, and Danes." Professor Bolton has stimulated many students to follow paths he has trod himself, and the historian who would gain more than an Anglo-American viewpoint on our history must read the works of this teacher and his disciples.[45]

[42] Berkeley, 1930.   [43] N. Y., 1936.   [44] N. Y., 1920.

[45] See *New Spain and the Anglo-American West: Historical contributions presented to Herbert Eugene Bolton* (2 vols., Los Angeles, 1932); also Professor Bolton's presidential address before the American Historical Association, "The Epic of Greater America," *Amer. Hist. Rev.*, Vol. XXXVIII.

Other Historians of the West

The number of students at work on the history of the Mississippi Valley and on regions farther west has increased greatly since the early days of George P. Garrison at Texas and of Turner at Wisconsin. The vigor of the *Mississippi Valley Historical Review* is a reflection of the vitality of students of this area whose contributions are of great importance to American historiography.

The movement westward of the older Eastern stock is the subject of Lois Kimball Mathews's *Expansion of New England 1620-1865.*[46] It is more than the mere transplanting of peoples that she describes, for they brought with them their culture pattern, which implanted a distinctive Puritan character on the regions of the Middle West. The territory settled by these migrant New Englanders in the early years is described by Beverly W. Bond in *The Civilization of the Old Northwest: A Study of Political, Social and Economic Development 1788-1812.*[47] Professor Bond, in his anxiety to stress the "distinctive" aspects of civilization in this area, does not take into sufficient account its ties with other parts of the United States—for example, with the South. A study by Henry C. Hubbart of a later period, *The Older Middle West, 1840-1880: Its Social, Economic, and Political Life and Sectional Tendencies before, during, and after the Civil War,*[48] is especially good on the Southern influence in these States. Professor Hubbart's volume, however, fails to treat adequately a subject fundamental to an understanding of life in this region—the changes associated with the growth of capitalism in the Middle West. The discontent produced by economic factors which per-

[46] Boston, 1909.
[47] N. Y., 1934.
[48] N. Y., 1936.

plexed the farmers, and which they sought to control, is the theme of a splendid volume by Solon J. Buck, the *Granger Movement.*[49] Fred E. Haynes likewise treats this subject in his *Third Party Movements since the Civil War*[50] and its latest historian is John D. Hicks, author of *The Populist Revolt: A History of the Farmers' Alliance and the People's Party.*[51] The farmer, says Professor Hicks, was waging "a long and perhaps a losing struggle . . . to save agricultural America from the devouring jaws of industrial America."

Of the modern historians who have carefully studied frontiers to the South and Southwest no one is more scholarly than Verner W. Crane, who has written of *The Southern Frontier 1670-1732.*[52] It is the Indian trade that furnishes the clue to the conflicts in this area, as in the Northwestern frontier in this period. Professor Crane minimizes the significance of Spain in affecting developments in this frontier, but other historians have stressed Spanish-American relations. In addition to the volumes of Professor Bolton and his students, Arthur P. Whitaker has made important contributions to this field with *The Spanish-American Frontier 1783-1795*[53] and *The Mississippi Question 1795-1803: A Study in Trade, Politics, and Diplomacy.*[54] The complexities of the acquisition of Louisiana, which have troubled many students, are greatly clarified by Professor Whitaker. To unravel the tangle of American relations with foreign powers, including Spain, has been the main enterprise of Samuel F. Bemis, the leading student of our diplomatic history. Beginning with *Jay's Treaty,*[55] he has published other studies which were the basis for his comprehensive *A Diplomatic History of the United States.*[56]

[49] Cambridge, 1913.
[50] Iowa City, 1916.
[51] Minneapolis, 1931.
[52] Durham, 1928.

[53] Boston, 1927.
[54] N. Y., 1934.
[55] N. Y., 1924.
[56] N. Y., 1936.

A volume of the first importance was published in 1931 by Walter P. Webb on *The Great Plains*. With distinct literary skill and imaginative research he constructs a narrative that explains how the environment determined the character of the white civilization that finally triumphed over the native red man. The Colt revolver, barbed wire, and the windmill were the tools that helped in the conquest, and in the process, "American institutions and cultural complexes that came from a humid and timbered region" were fundamentally altered.[57]

The regions farther westward have had innumerable chroniclers of particular episodes, but there are few good general accounts. Katharine Coman wrote one, *Economic Beginnings of the Far West*,[58] which contains a large body of useful materials, and William J. Ghent, a careful student, has given us *The Early Far West; 1540-1850*.[59] Joseph Schafer, an excellent scholar, wrote a *History of the Pacific Northwest* a number of years ago,[60] and the same subject has been presented in the light of more recent research by George W. Fuller.[61] For an important part of their study all historians of this region are dependent upon H. M. Chittenden's *The American Fur Trade of the Far West*.[62] Frederic L. Paxson, one of the closest students of the West, in his volume on *The Last American Frontier*,[63] deals with the period following that covered by William J. Ghent. A synthesis of the many materials embracing the whole field of the frontier is to be found in Professor Paxson's *History of the American Frontier 1763-1893*.[64] It is a rather conventional narrative of the older type and does not deal adequately with the effect of the frontier in creating the kind of civilization that ultimately developed in the newer

[57] Preface.
[58] 2 vols., N. Y., 1912.
[61] *A History of the Pacific Northwest* (N. Y., 1931).
[62] 3 vols., N. Y., 1902.
[63] N. Y., 1910.
[59] N. Y., 1931.
[60] N. Y., 1905.
[64] Boston, 1924.

regions. One aspect of that civilization, and an important one, is covered in a painstaking study on *Manifest Destiny* by Albert K. Weinberg.[65] This study of the expansionist philosophy and its effects on American history belongs with the volumes of Julius W. Pratt, *The Expansionists of 1812*,[66] which emphasizes a neglected factor in that struggle, and his *Expansionists of 1898*,[67] which ascribes much of the strength of this movement to the activities of Alfred T. Mahan, Theodore Roosevelt, and Henry Cabot Lodge.

NEW ENGLAND

From the days when Increase and Cotton Mather urged the writing of a history of New England, a number of writers have essayed the task. Nearly all writers of New England history have construed their subject in such a manner that they have dealt almost exclusively with Massachusetts, devoting comparatively little space to her neighbors. Charles Francis Adams wrote expressly on Massachusetts, but James Truslow Adams gave more attention than others have done to the Bay Colony's neighbors. William B. Weeden, a contemporary of Charles Francis Adams, was a successful manufacturer before he became a historian. He was keenly aware of the social problems created by the Industrial Revolution, and though he had something of the Christian Socialist outlook of the 1880's, he was in the main a strong economic individualist.[68] In 1890 he published his *Economic and Social History of New England 1670-1789*,[69] which was one of the first attempts to do for a section what McMaster was then doing for the nation as a whole. He consulted sources rarely used then by scholars, and his

[65] Baltimore, 1935.
[66] N. Y., 1921.
[67] Baltimore, 1936.

[68] See his *The Social Law of Labor* (1882).
[69] 2 vols., Boston, 1890.

chapters on money, lands, agriculture, fisheries, commerce, prices, manners, and so on, include materials that are still useful to the student. When he touches on political matters, such as the Navigation Acts, he gives an outmoded interpretation, but his volumes on the whole remain among the best of their type.

Writers on New England have gone through cycles of pietism and of pitiless criticism. In her early days her glories were presented untarnished by Cotton Mather and others. Then with the growth of skepticism came a more detached view of ancestors in the works of Hutchinson and Belknap. The filial piety of Palfrey expressed again the devotional spirit of Mather. A sharp reaction against the ancestor worship of Palfrey was revealed by Brooks Adams, Charles Francis Adams, and James Truslow Adams. The latter, in particular, in his anxiety to redress the balance, has erred seriously in his estimate of the Puritans. A sounder interpretation of the civilization of early New England has only recently been advanced in the several volumes of Samuel Eliot Morison, who heads the "revisionist" school whose organ is the *New England Quarterly*.[70]

CHARLES FRANCIS ADAMS

America's royal family, the Adams', made regal gifts to their native land in public service, in scholarship, and in the creation of a critical tradition. A prince of the blood was Charles Francis, son of the father with a like name who served his country brilliantly as minister to England during the Civil War. While his brother Henry was acting as secretary to their father in London, Charles Francis joined the Union Army, feeling that it

[70] Some stimulating remarks are found in Charles M. Andrews, "Historic Doubts Regarding Early Massachusetts History," Col. Soc. Mass. *Transactions*, Vol. XXVIII (1935).

was necessary that at least one member of the family offer deeds as well as words in behalf of his country. "For years our family has talked of slavery and of the South, and been most prominent in the contest of words," he wrote to his father, "and now that it has come to blows does it become us to stand aloof from the conflict?" [71]

Unlike Henry, Charles Francis entered rather vigorously into the currents of American political and business life; for a long time his historical interests were not much more than an avocation. But in the twenty-five years that followed his retirement from association with the Union Pacific Railroad in 1890, he delivered many addresses on history and published several works, including *The Life of Richard Henry Dana*,[72] *The Three Episodes of Massachusetts History*,[73] a critical appraisal of New England historians in *Massachusetts: Its Historians and History*,[74] and a volume of *Studies: Military and Diplomatic*.[75]

In his autobiography Charles Francis Adams tells us of two epoch-marking events in his life: one was the discovery of a book, the other was an invitation to deliver an address. The former occurred when he was in England in his thirtieth year, in 1865. "I one day chanced upon a copy of John Stuart Mill's essay on Auguste Comte," he writes. "That essay of Mill's revolutionized in a single morning my whole attitude. I emerged from the theological stage, in which I had been nurtured, and passed into the scientific. I had up to that time never even heard of Darwin. . . ." It was the invitation to deliver an address some eight years later that had the effect of fixing more certainly the direction of Adams's intellectual life. He was asked by the citizens of the town

[71] W. C. Ford, ed., *A Cycle of Adams Letters*, I, 10.
[72] 2 vols., Boston, 1890.   [74] Boston, 1893.
[73] 2 vols., Boston, 1892.   [75] Boston, 1911.

of Weymouth to deliver a historical address on the two hundred and fiftieth anniversary of its settlement, and out of so small a beginning he was led for forty years thereafter "through pastures green and pleasant places."

Of the harvests he reaped, none, perhaps, has been of greater value than the sheaf of papers gathered together in *The Three Episodes of Massachusetts History* which had been privately printed in 1883 as *Episodes in New England History*. The author said that his work, narrowly considered, was a history of the town of Quincy, but in reality it is the story of a people passing through three episodes of Massachusetts history. These episodes are the settlement of Boston Bay at Weymouth in 1623, the Antinomian controversy, and a study of church and town government. Seventy years before Adams published his history, his great-grandfather, John Adams, had written to Jefferson about his own reading: "Controversies between Calvinists and Arminians, Trinitarians and Unitarians, Deists and Christians, Atheists and both, have attracted my attention. . . . The history of this little village of Quincy, if it were worth recording, would explain to you how this happened." [76] The great-grandson decided that its history was worth recording.

The first episode is enlivened by the appearance of Thomas Morton, whose enigmatic personality, so un-Puritan in its characteristics, attracted Adams. His examination of the treatment of Anne Hutchinson in the Antinomian controversy led him to write that her "so-called trial was, in fact, no trial at all, but a mockery of justice rather,—a bare-faced inquisitorial proceeding." An Adams of the fourth generation was not likely to look at provincial events narrowly. The Antinomian controversy, writes the historian, was much more than a

[76] Wilstach, *Correspondence of John Adams and Thomas Jefferson,* p. 68; July 18, 1813.

religious dispute: "It was the first of the many New England quickenings in the direction of social, intellectual and political development—New England's earliest protest against formulas."[77] The Adams' were not accustomed to mince words when their minds were made up. Charles Francis Adams could not drop this subject without some caustic references to New England historians who had sought to palliate, or even to justify, their ancestors' actions. "In the treatment of doubtful historical points," he says,[78] "there are few things which need to be more carefully guarded against than patriotism or filial piety." On a later page,[79] he returns to the attack on the filiopietistic historians by writing that "the earlier times in New England were not pleasant times in which to live; the earlier generations were not pleasant generations to live with."

In his third episode, which is probably the most interesting to the present-day reader, Adams gives us the history of the mores of Quincy's people. He observes that "the American unit is to be sought" in the towns and their records. "The political philosopher can there study the slow development of a system as it grew from the germ up." There are chapters on "Population and Wealth," "Social Life," "Town Meetings"; one on "Intemperance and Immorality" still remains among the best treatments of this subject although it is somewhat of a pioneer effort.

In the opinion of Osgood, the work of Adams was "the most original and suggestive town history ever written in this country." It has certainly set a high standard for local history, and, for Massachusetts history in particular, it set a precedent of criticism that James Truslow Adams and others remembered when they began to write on New England. Charles Francis

[77] I, 367.   [79] II, 802.
[78] II, 561.

Adams had a quiet satisfaction contemplating in retrospect his *Three Episodes.* "It may not be great, and certainly has not nor will it obtain a recognized place in
general literature," he said, "but locally, it is a classic."
Posterity is not likely to quarrel with his own judgment
of his book.[80]

JAMES TRUSLOW ADAMS

It is a well-rooted tradition in our letters that non-
academicians are responsible for some of our finest historical writings. That tradition has thinned since Henry
Charles Lea, Francis Parkman, and others wrote their
notable volumes, but in our day it has been reinforced
by the work of James Truslow Adams. He has shown no
regret over a lack of academic experience. Indeed, he has
put himself on record "that too long an academic training and career is rather a detriment than a benefit to a
historian and that it should at least be supplemented by
some years of an active career in affairs among men." [81]
Turning from a business career more than twenty years
ago, he has brought out a succession of volumes which
have made it possible once again for a historian to live
by his writing. For himself he has fulfilled the ambition
of Macaulay—that his volumes should replace the latest
novel on the drawing-room table. No name is better
known than his today among the public that reads history
in America.

If we assume the *Epic of America* [82] to be the oak,
the acorn was, perhaps, the *Memorials of Old Bridgehampton,*[83] or the *History of the Town of Southampton.*[84]
From these small beginnings, Mr. Adams enlarged his

[80] See C. F. Adams, *Autobiography* (Boston, 1916).
[81] "Is History Science?" in *The Tempo of Modern Life* (N. Y., 1931),
p. 205.
[82] Boston, 1931.   [84] Bridgehampton, 1918.
[83] Bridgehampton, 1916.

sphere of activity to include all of New England (the be-
getter of his Long Island town) in a trilogy that runs
from the earliest settlements to approximately the year
1850. Then taking as his next theme a New England family, the Adams', whose record is part of the nation's heritage, the historian was definitely in the area of national
history, and thus the *Epic of America* appears as a natural evolution.

James Truslow Adams came into prominence among
the historical guildsmen with his *The Founding of New
England* (1921). It was acclaimed by Samuel Eliot Morison as the "best short history of early New England
that has appeared for a generation," but Professor
Morison and others questioned the justice of Mr.
Adams's severe criticism of Puritan religious intolerance. It seems to have been generally overlooked that
only three years before, in his history of Southampton,
the author had been very sympathetic to the Puritans:
"We should not sneer, as historians have some times
done," he wrote, "at those who came to secure religious
freedom and in turn denied it to some extent in others." [85]
He went on with a further defense: "Those engaged in
the work of laying the foundations of a new civil and religious polity should not be blamed for refusing to pas-
sively watch others sap those very foundations which
they were attempting to build up at the expense of so
much they had held dear. Nor was their attitude either
hypocritical or disingenuous." (This is amusing in the
light of James Truslow Adams's later criticism of
Samuel E. Morison's *Builders of the Bay Colony,* which
uses the same argument.) The work of the earliest settlers, writes Mr. Adams, "was stern and their theology
as well, but their lives, like ours, were filled with the
satisfaction of honest work and with the sweetness of

[85] P. 105.

love for their wives, tenderness for their children, and the joys of friendship.''

For some unknown reason, when he came to write on the New England Puritans, in 1921, he did not see their sweetness and tenderness, nor their joys. Rather he concentrated on their shortcomings, feeling perhaps the necessity of overcoming the influence of the filiopietistic school of historians as typified by Palfrey. (As already noted, Charles Francis Adams, a generation earlier, had listed the sins of the Puritan fathers.) Apart from this particular bias of James Truslow Adams and the fact that his volume is almost exclusively a political history, *The Founding of New England* does merit high praise. It makes excellent use of the work of Osgood, Beer, and Professor Andrews in presenting the colonies as cogs in an imperial machine; a chapter on ''The Theory of Empire'' is especially good in this respect. What Fiske, in his *Beginnings of New England,* called ''The Tyranny of Andros,'' Mr. Adams calls ''An Experiment in Administration.'' He emphasizes the economic factors behind the mass migration in the 1630's, but very recently some historians have reverted to the contention of earlier students that the movement was rather more the result of a religious impulse. Mr. Adams examines, also, the workings of the theocracy, and tells us that ''the domestic struggle against the tyranny exercised by the more bigoted members of the theocratic party was of greater importance in the history of liberty than the more dramatic contest with the mother country.'' His iconoclasm is refreshing, even if his brand of orthodoxy sets up a new idolatry—anti-Puritanism.[86]

The second volume in the series is *Revolutionary New England 1690-1776,* published in 1923. In the earlier part of this volume, the historian traces the beginnings

[86] In opposition see C. K. Shipton, "A Plea for Puritanism," *Amer. Hist. Rev.,* XL, 460.

of colonial grievances, the gradual development of revolutionary sentiment and the rise of a radical party. From 1713 to about 1750, he says, "we can see at work forces tending to develop democratic ideals in certain elements of the community, and foreshadowing the alignments and parties of a later time." The ten years preceding 1750, he thinks were "marked by an intense quickening of thought and action," and because of the significance of the changes following the Great Awakening (the religious revival), the chapter describing these events and their effects is called "The Great Divide." The historian studies the internal struggle for political and economic power between the mercantile aristocracy and the lower classes in the colonies and notes the growth in self-consciousness of these same lower classes. The modern attitude toward the Loyalists is given full expression in *Revolutionary New England,* in which the Revolution is referred to as a "Civil War." There is much more social and intellectual history in this volume than in its predecessor. Possibly in these two volumes Mr. Adams exaggerates the isolation of New England from the rest of the colonies. It is the opinion of Leonard W. Labaree, whose *Royal Government in America* emphasizes many features of the history of this period more lightly touched by Mr. Adams, that the latter's volume does not adequately explain the revolutionary movement.

The last of the trilogy is *New England in the Republic 1776-1850,* brought out in 1926. Its main theme, the author tells us, "may be considered to be the continued struggle of the common man to realize the doctrines of the Revolution in the life of the community." In his early chapters he examines the life of the people during the Revolution and the effects of the war upon their economic and moral life. In his analysis of the governmental structure, and unrest after the war, he gives a sympathetic review of Shays' Rebellion. In the conflict over the adoption of the Federal Constitution, the historian is especially interested in the struggle between the conservative element and the opposition, which was anxious to preserve and extend the liberal doctrines preached in 1776. In keeping with studies like those of Charles A. Beard, Mr. Adams maintains that, having achieved their object in gaining their independence from England, the conservative leaders in America strove to prevent the revolutionary movement from going further and thus altering the essential structure of American society. But once begun, the process of revolution is not easily stayed; the mass of the people had come to expect radical changes, "and for many decades after 1783," says Mr. Adams, "this struggle between these two groups constitutes the main interest of our history." He observes the struggle as it reveals itself in its various aspects—in business, politics, education, relations between capital and labor, religion, and in the debate over slavery. There is a delineation of the life of each successive period down to what he calls "the great outburst of humanitarianism and reform between 1830 and 1850." A subordinate subject is the gradual growth of sectionalism and its decline when the ties of union proved stronger. After 1850, Mr. Adams writes, nationalist forces "swept the New England states into the swift movement of what had by then become a genuinely national life."

This third volume has much more on social and intellectual history than the first two; there is little on military events because these belong in the realm of national affairs. The hostility to the Puritans is somewhat diminished in this study, and in his closing lines, Mr. Adams does mild penance: "We thus end the story as we began, with the leaders of the New England people wrestling with a transcendent moral problem [in 1850 it was slavery]. . . . Perhaps, at times, in a reaction against the old point of view which regarded all Puritans and all Revolutionary soldiers and agitators as saints and patriots, we may have been tempted to stress the shadows rather than the lights.'' [87] But the Puritans have not lacked defenders, and Samuel E. Morison, Kenneth B. Murdock, and Lawrence S. Mayo have given us views of the early New Englanders which endow them with something of that sweet humanity conspicuously absent in the pages of James Truslow Adams.

''A small part of the public, God bless it, does want to know something about the past of our race,'' writes Mr. Adams,[88] ''but it wants to be able to stay awake while it reads.'' In *The Epic of America* and *The March of Democracy,* Mr. Adams has kept hundreds of thousands of readers awake while they read in smoothly flowing prose and quoted poetry an interpretation of our past that has made use of the latest historical research. Perhaps these works teach little to the members of the historical guild, although they have undoubtedly stimulated some to more artistic composition. From this vantage point it appears that whatever of permanence resides in the books of James Truslow Adams is to be found in his three volumes on New England.

SAMUEL ELIOT MORISON

The tradition of New England historical scholarship is the strongest in American literature, and its present representatives are worthy heirs. The foremost of them is Samuel Eliot Morison, who combines the exact scholarship of his master, Edward Channing, with the literary skill of Henry Adams. Professor Morison, in his reexamination of the earlier years of New England, has thrown much new light on a familiar subject.

[87] P. 423.
[88] *The Tempo of Modern Life,* p. 212.

He began with a study of Harrison Gray Otis,[89] a distinguished Federalist who lived on long after his party had died. Professor Morison then wrote on a subject fancied by many New England historians—*The Maritime History of Massachusetts 1783-1860*.[90] The contents are much broader than the title would indicate, for in the period before the Civil War a large fraction of American commerce was handled by ships from Massachusetts, thus the volume covers more than a provincial area; in fact, like the ships that sailed from New England's ports, it covers the world. And for the lover of the sea (as well as for the student of history) there is real tang in the words, now gusty, now swinging, that describe the days of New England's glory.

After this volume Professor Morison turned back to the years of the founders and in his *Builders of the Bay Colony*[91] wrote about the characters of the first generation who interested him most—men and a woman (Anne Bradstreet) who typified the varied aspects of the first fifty years of Massachusetts. Professor Morison tells us that his "attitude toward seventeenth-century puritanism has passed through scorn and boredom to a warm interest and respect." In the sketches that make up this volume, the historian has pictured for us a people too rarely endowed, by other writers, with a broad humanity and aesthetic interests. The Puritans who emerge from his pages are real individuals whose characteristics belie the stereotype fashioned by superficial historians and cartoonists.

Professor Morison comes out strongly for the thesis that the motive for the Puritan migration was religious and not economic. He has pushed this view too far, perhaps, for while the leaders may have been thus largely motivated, the evidence is not convincing with respect

[89] 2 vols., Boston, 1913.   [91] Boston, 1930.
[90] Boston, 1921.

to the mass of their followers. He has crossed lances with James Truslow Adams on the subject of Puritan intolerance, arguing that the original inhabitants had the right to exclude any from their settlement whose presence might have endangered it. This position, practically condoning intolerance, is at variance with Professor Morison's liberalism on most other subjects.

Another volume, *The Puritan Pronaos,*[92] studies in seventeenth-century intellectual history, again reveals the historian's great knowledge of the Puritan mind. As in the earlier volume on the *Builders,* Professor Morison shows the awareness of the Puritan to the world of his own day, and the clergy in particular are credited with being not merely the religious leaders of the community, but the political and intellectual guides as well. Professor Morison modifies or discards many time-worn traditions about "reactionary clergy" who were drags on the progress of New England. Unlike other students who have maintained that New England led a life apart from Europe, he shows how closely in many ways intellectual activity in the new world paralleled that in the old.

The work on which he is now engaged, the tercentenary history of Harvard, is of the first importance for an understanding of the development of American education. Three volumes have already appeared,[93] carrying the story to the beginning of the eighteenth century.[94] The first, *The Founding of Harvard College* (1935), gives in detail the European background and the first fifteen years of the College. Emmanuel College, Cambridge, for example, exerted great influence in the creation of Harvard. The broad purposes of the charter providing for a general education are properly emphasized by Profes-

[92] N. Y., 1936.

[93] The second and third are called "Two Parts."

[94] He has edited a volume on the period since President Eliot's administration: *The Development of Harvard University, 1869-1929.*

sor Morison, in contrast to those who have so often pointed to the narrowly ecclesiastical objectives of Harvard's training.

The growth of the college in the seventeenth century is the theme of Volumes II and III. The sacrifices of the Puritans to make of their school a worthy institution and the returns it gave to the community in intellectual and spiritual guidance are made clear by the historian, justly proud of his alma mater. A splendid composite "portrait" of the Harvard alumni concludes the third volume. With the completion of this work Harvard will have a history matched by none in America (and perhaps none in Europe), and at the same time a contribution of the first order will have been made to the intellectual history of America.

THE SOUTH

Historical studies received a marked impetus in the North and Middle West soon after the Civil War but they lagged in the South. Problems far more pressing than the study and writing of history occupied the Southern States in the period of Reconstruction, but the publication of many war memoirs maintained the continuity with an earlier tradition of historical writing. Gayarré was still alive and influential among historical students, and one or two of the historical societies showed some signs of vigor. At the bar of history, the only tribunal available to the South, Southerners pleaded their cause. The Southern Historical Society, founded in 1869, had for its main purpose the preservation of materials bearing on the Civil War. It published a journal, beginning in 1876, called the *Southern Historical Society Papers,* which brought to light many documents. At a later time, 1896, the Southern History Association, with wider interests than the older society, was formed. It was the new university, Johns Hopkins, that provided a more vitalizing force. As late as 1890, however, there was no great activity of a historical nature in the South.[95] But at this very time young men were publishing their first studies, or finishing their graduate work, which enabled them to take high rank among America's scholars. It must also be remembered that students in other parts of the country were occasionally being drawn to Southern topics, even though Southerners at home might be negligent of them.

Herbert Baxter Adams and others were aware of the value of research in Southern history. A writer in *The Nation*,[96] for instance, pointed out that the history of the local institutions of the South remained to be written: "It is a good field of investigation for the rising generation of students in that section of the country," he concluded. William A. Dunning, not long after, was to begin the teaching that created an excellent body of scholars devoted to Southern history, while William E. Dodd and John Spencer Bassett performed similar services. Woodrow Wilson was studying his native region with an eye that looked askance at the conventional Northern aproach to Southern history.[97] William G. Brown, cut off too early in his career, published a suggestive reinterpretation in *The Lower South in American History*.[98]

PHILIP A. BRUCE

One of the most prolific of the Southern historical writers and one of the most important was Philip Alexander Bruce. In 1896 Bruce brought out an exceedingly

[95] W. P. Trent, "Historical Studies in the South," *Papers,* Amer. Hist. Assn. (October, 1890), pp. 57-65.

[96] May 26, 1881.

[97] See his *Division and Reunion* (1893), especially pp. 106 ff.

[98] N. Y., 1902.

valuable *Economic History of Virginia in the Seventeenth Century,*[99] in which he made use of hitherto unexplored manuscript collections. His was the first attempt, he tells us, "to describe the purely economic condition of the Virginia people in detail," and his volumes are filled with meticulous descriptions of manufactures and of the conditions of agriculture and labor. Bruce, of course, was too good a historian to accept the cavalier tradition of Virginia history, but he does say: "There are many evidences that a large number of the immigrants were sprung from English families of substance"; [100] and in another connection he states that "the moral influence of the large plantation was . . . extraordinary." [101] Throughout Bruce's work the reader senses his nostalgia for the spacious days of the old landed aristocracy. A very good summary is to be found in his concluding pages.

In 1907 Bruce issued another Virginia study, *Social Life of Virginia in the Seventeenth Century,* which is an inquiry into the origin of the planter aristocracy and a description of the manners and diversions of the people. Leaving aside slaves, he says, the population of Virginia was socially a duplication of the smaller rural communities in England, although the physical surroundings of the new world had made for some modifications. In 1929 Bruce paid tribute to the great Virginians in *The Virginia Plutarch* [102] and he took the opportunity to claim for them the homage that is rightfully theirs. The first volume deals with the characters of the colonial and revolutionary eras, among whom the historian and correspondent, William Byrd, receives high praise; the second volume is on the national era.

In opposition to Bruce, Thomas J. Wertenbaker min-

99 2 vols., N. Y.

100 II, 246.

101 II, 568.

102 2 vols., Chapel Hill, 1929.

imizes the influence of the aristocracy in Virginia's early
history. In his volume, *Planters of Colonial Virginia,*[103]
Professor Wertenbaker finds that the colony was filled
with comparatively small farms "owned and worked by
a sturdy class of English farmers." [104] These white yeo-
men were the most important element in the life of early
Virginia until the greater spread of slavery in the eighteenth century transformed the colony "from a land of
hard-working independent peasants, to a land of slaves
and slave holders."

ALEXANDER BROWN

At the time that Bruce was initiating his investigations into Virginia's early history Alexander Brown was
unearthing the sources of her history and publishing
them in important volumes. In 1890 Brown published
The Genesis of the United States . . . ,[105] covering the
years from 1605 to 1616, "the period of the first foundation." He continued the *Genesis,* with some changes of
opinions on men and events, in *The First Republic in
America* [106] and criticized severely the writings of John
Smith. Brown wrote about the enemies of the Virginia
Company almost as though they were his personal opponents. His thesis is that James I frustrated the growth
of democracy in Virginia and thus began the long history of royal tyranny that ended with George III.[107]
Alexander Brown's ability lay in collecting, not in interpreting.

[103] Princeton, 1922.
[104] P. 59.
[105] 2 vols., Boston.
[106] Boston, 1898.
[107] For a good analysis of Brown's work see W. F. Craven, *Dissolution
of the Virginia Company,* pp. 12-21.

Edward McCrady

Interesting as the history of colonial Virginia has been to the modern student, equally rich in charm and incident is the history of colonial South Carolina. Edward McCrady, a lawyer by profession and historian by avocation, wrote a four-volume *History of South Carolina* (1897-1902), which covers her story from the founding to the close of the Revolutionary War. The first volume is on the period of the proprietary government to 1719, and the second narrates the colony's history as a royal province to the time of the Revolution. Several chapters captioned "1765-1775" give an excellent picture of the professions and the economic and social life at the outbreak of the Revolution. Although treating rather fully social conditions in the eighteenth century, McCrady does not consider the interaction between social and political events. He also fails to make clear South Carolina's position in relation to the rest of the empire. The remaining two volumes cover the war period, and so well does McCrady carry out his task that his work is recognized as one of the finest state histories ever written.

William A. Dunning

William Archibald Dunning, who was a very sympathetic student of Southern history, was one of the many products of John W. Burgess's classes in Columbia University. It was through the influence of an intelligent father that Dunning was first drawn to the problems of Reconstruction. The maiden effort of the young Ph.D. in 1885 was *The Constitution of the United States in Civil War and Reconstruction 1860-1867,* in which he showed an independence of judgment that remained always a distinctive characteristic. When writing of the

plans of Thaddeus Stevens and others for the confisca-
tion of Southern property, Dunning said that "all such
propositions were the passionate fancies of fanatics
more extreme than the Southern fire-eaters who had pre-
cipitated the war." In his closing lines he states his thesis—that in the revolution which had occurred "the written Constitution had been pronounced finished. It had
held the fragments of the nation together till they should
be welded inseparably in the white heat of war, but it had
not itself escaped the blaze."

This concern with constitutional and institutional
history, so marked a feature of Dunning's interests, is
further manifested in his *Essays on the Civil War and
Reconstruction*,[108] which is a collection of previously
printed papers. Unlike some recent students who see in
the Reconstruction Acts evidences of powerful Northern
economic forces, Dunning writes that their chief end was
"purely political." [109] He has high regard for the political and administrative capacity shown in the Reconstruction of the Southern States, judging it to be "one of the
most remarkable achievements in the history of government"; his condemnation of the purpose of Reconstruction is equally straightforward. In his essay on the impeachment and trial of President Johnson, Dunning
writes: "The single vote by which Andrew Johnson escaped conviction marks the narrow margin by which the
presidential element in our system escaped destruction."

At Columbia Dunning had built up a whole school
of scholars devoting themselves to Southern history, and
to him was assigned the volume in the "American Nation" series covering the years immediately following
the Civil War. *Reconstruction: Political and Economic
1865-1877* instantly took its place as the foremost treatment of those troubled years. Instead of fixing his at-

[108] N. Y., 1897.
[109] P. 138.

tention exclusively on the South during Reconstruction, as so many before him had done, the historian looked at "the period as a step in the progress of the American nation." Because the social, economic, and political forces that "wrought positively for progress are to be found in the record, not of the vanquished, but of the victorious section," it is the North that attracts Dunning's chief attention. "In this record," he says, "there is less that is spectacular, less that is pathetic, and more that seems inexcusably sordid than in the record of the South." He does not draw the picture of those years in all white or all black as so many others have done, but he does try to make the reader understand more clearly the motives of the Southerners in undoing the plans of Reconstruction.

As might have been expected from Dunning's earlier studies, a valuable characteristic of his volume is the account of important court decisions relating to Reconstruction. A chapter on "The Nadir of National Disgrace 1875-1876," describing the corruption of the period, ends with a reference to the enthusiasm evoked by the Philadelphia Centennial, and gives him an opportunity to display something of his noted wit. "The occasion," he says, "depressing as it was to those who felt most keenly the incongruities of things, served a very useful purpose in diverting the great masses who wished to be diverted from the evidence that the venerated institutions of the fathers had not produced precisely what the fathers would have desired."

In 1914 a number of Dunning's former pupils inscribed to him a volume of *Studies in Southern History and Politics*. Some of the authors of this testimonial, which is a fitting commentary on Dunning's influence in the promotion of study of the South, are among the leading students of this section: Ulrich B. Phillips, Charles W. Ramsdell, J. G. de Roulhac Hamilton, William K.

Boyd, and Holland Thompson. The writings of his many students of Reconstruction in the several States supplemented Dunning's own investigations, but the "Old Chief," as this stimulating lecturer was affectionately called, did more than anyone else to rewrite the history of the years following the Civil War. "He was the first," says Professor Hamilton, "to make scientific and scholarly investigation of the period of Reconstruction." His reputation as a historian was no less than his fame as a student of political science; from 1913 to 1922, when he died, he was the Francis Lieber Professor of History and Political Philosophy at Columbia. His three volumes on the history of political theories, from ancient times to Herbert Spencer, cover, more completely than does any other work, this vast field. In this branch of investigation, as well as in history, Dunning developed a group of students who paid him a similar tribute with a volume on political theories in recent times. The more intensive specialization of our own day is not likely to favor again such distinguished versatility.

ULRICH B. PHILLIPS

Some of the most significant of the contributions made to the history of the South are those of Ulrich B. Phillips. He spent his teaching years at several institutions, and he was at Yale when he died in 1933. In 1902 he published his *Georgia and State Rights,* which owed its inspiration, in part at least, to Turner. He originally intended to study the effect of nullification upon Georgia politics, but his work expanded to become a complete survey of the State's history before the Civil War. Phillips was a native of the cotton belt, and in picturing the region he was anxious to correct current historical misconceptions concerning it. "The contrast between the extremes of wealth and poverty in the South," he says, "has been exaggerated." "The social system was by no means rigid in the cotton belt." [110] Other works followed in due course: *The History of Transportation in the Eastern Cotton Belt* (1908) and *The Life of Robert Toombs* (1913). He edited two volumes on the *Plantation and Frontier 1649-1863* in the "Documentary History of American Industrial Society," to which he prefixed valuable introductions. These volumes contain little-known materials on the South at work; his attempt, says Phillips, is to give a "reasonably full view of Southern industrial society." [111] He was also the author of *American Negro Slavery* (1918), and published articles on various phases of politics and economics besides contributing to the co-operative history, "The South in the Building of the Nation." In more recent years he was co-editor of *Florida Plantation Records* (1927), but the most important publication of his last days was his *Life and Labor in the Old South*,[112] perhaps the best book yet published on the South as a whole.

This volume was the result of his own familiarity with conditions in the South and the distillation of minute knowledge gained from old records of which he possessed a valuable collection. He once had written: "A sympathetic understanding of plantation conditions was my inevitable heritage from my family and from my neighbors, white and black"; [113] and throughout his work his warm attachment to his native soil is in evidence. Sometimes the reader may feel that Phillips presents a little too favorably the position of the Negro under the slave system, but he was not guilty of willful distortion of the facts as were many Northern writers on the South. (Frederic Bancroft's *Slave-Trading in the Old South* [114]

[110] P. 107.
[111] I, 94.
[112] Boston, 1929.
[113] *Plantation and Frontier 1649-1863*, I, 103.
[114] Baltimore, 1931.

gives a more somber picture than does Phillips.) Although he was only fifty-six when he died, the work Phillips did in his comparatively short career bulks large in the revision of the history of the South that this generation of scholars has been making.[115]

William E. Dodd

Another scholar and teacher who has contributed much in this field of research is William E. Dodd. Although he has published few volumes, through them and through various articles and addresses he has educated his numerous readers and students to a better understanding of the old South. He is a man of wide interests, examining the characteristics of political leadership in his *Statesmen of the Old South* [116] as well as in other biographies, and ranging at length over *The Cotton Kingdom* in a compact little volume that contains enough ideas for a shelfful of books. A volume, *Expansion and Conflict*,[117] anticipated other writers in pointing to the economic causes which operated to bring on the Civil War.[118]

Professor Dodd long ago had as clear an understanding of the necessity for research in Southern history as any student in the field. In an article [119] on ''Profitable Fields of Investigation in American History 1815-1860'' he suggested political, economic, and biographical studies, a study of the Illinois Central Railroad, a survey of the attitude of the churches to slavery, and so on. Taking to task McMaster and Henry Adams for confining their histories to a restricted area, Professor Dodd said that a

---

[115] See Fred Landon and E. E. Edwards, "A Bibliography of the Writings of Prof. U. B. Phillips," *Agricultural History* (October, 1934).

[116] N. Y., 1911.

[117] Boston, 1915.

[118] Cf. pp. 277, 290, 328.

[119] *Amer. Hist. Rev.* (1913), Vol. XVIII; a number of these studies have since been undertaken and published.

comprehensive work would include the debtor regions, West and South. Contrary to conventional impression, the abolitionists, said he, "were in no sense one of the great forces which shaped the national destiny"; [120] they would have brought about a Northern secession had it not been for stronger economic and social forces opposing them. Powerful economic groups fought for mastery in the period from 1815 to 1860, and for a time the plantation owners dominated, but toward the end Northern industrialists, the protagonists of nationalism, were victorious—a nationalism that protected its economic interests. Throughout his work in scholarship and in public life (he was named ambassador to Germany in 1933) Professor Dodd is the disciple of Jefferson.

OTHER HISTORIANS OF THE SOUTH

Another Jeffersonian with less scholarship but a more dynamic style is Claude G. Bowers—journalist, orator, historian, and ambassador to Spain since 1933. In three volumes he has given us a Democratic interpretation of important periods of our history. The first to appear was *The Party Battles of the Jackson Period* [121] which, in the main, glorifies Jackson and Benton. Bowers then turned back to write *Jefferson and Hamilton: The Struggle for Democracy in America,*[122] which reveals the depth of his devotion to the great Virginian. In his next work *The Tragic Era: The Revolution after Lincoln,*[123] Bowers follows the lead of Dunning and his students, and with a luxurious phraseology that scholars rarely permit themselves, he severely indicts the Radical Republicans whose policy ruined the South. The whole approach of Bowers is through the conflicts of leading personalities who symbolize certain forces. His episodic treatment is a

[120] P. 536.
[121] Boston, 1922.

[122] Boston, 1925.
[123] Boston, 1929.

throwback to the narrative style of Prescott, with the significant difference that the latter had an essentially aristocratic view of history. Although Bowers does not present much that is new (he uses a large variety of printed sources) he does accent familiar episodes in a manner that gives them new vitality.

Within recent years Negroes have been producing valuable works on the history of their people. For some time they have published the *Journal of Negro History* under the editorship of Carter G. Woodson, who has also written volumes on Negro education and labor. One of the best Negro students has been W. E. Burghardt Du Bois, who published a volume on the *Suppression of the Slave Trade* (1896). A short time ago he brought out a volume on *Black Reconstruction,* which advanced the thesis that the former slaves were well on the way to creating a better society in the period after the Civil War, but were defeated by reactionary forces. In fact, there was a democratic movement in the North as well as in the South which was crushed by the combination of reactionary elements in both sections. Dr. Du Bois, rightly noting that historians have generally emphasized the evils of the Reconstruction period and have thus missed the constructive achievements of these years, vigorously redresses the balance. He claims that because leading radicals— Thaddeus Stevens and Sumner especially—were genuinely interested in the welfare of the colored people white historians have vilified them and purposely distorted history.

The interest that was awakened in Southern history at the end of the last century has developed at an accelerated rate. Economic interpretations have clarified large portions of Southern history. Avery O. Craven's *Soil Exhaustion as a Factor in the Agricultural History of Virginia and Maryland, 1606-1860* [124] is a work of prime

[124] Urbana, 1926.

importance. Robert R. Russel's *Economic Aspects of Southern Sectionalism, 1840-1861*,[125] and John G. Van Deusen's *Economic Bases of Disunion in South Carolina*,[126] detail the interrelations between politics, agriculture, and finance. Thomas P. Abernethy's *From Frontier to Plantation in Tennessee: A Study in Frontier Democracy*,[127] is an iconoclastic work of genuine originality. Additional studies of the States in war and Reconstruction have been made, and through the emphasis of such factors as States' rights and opposition to conscription, as well as the shortage of salt, among the causes for the failure of the Confederacy, the story of these tragic years has been further clarified. New viewpoints on the plantation legend have been asserted, and the rehabilitation of Andrew Johnson has been a feature of recent historical literature. A splendid synthesis of the new studies is found in James G. Randall's *The Civil War and Reconstruction*.[128] In no field of study is there greater vitality today than in the history of the South, and her own universities are contributing largely to its vigorous growth.[129]

[125] Urbana, 1923.

[126] N. Y., 1928.

[127] Chapel Hill, 1932.

[128] Boston, 1937. See also Frank L. Owsley, *State Rights in the Confederacy* (Chicago, 1925); Albert B. Moore, *Conscription and Conflict in the Confederacy* (N. Y., 1924); Ella Lonn, *Salt as a Factor in the Confederacy* (N. Y., 1934); Francis P. Gaines, *The Southern Plantation: A Study in the Development and the Accuracy of a Tradition* (N. Y., 1924); George F. Milton, *The Age of Hate: Andrew Johnson and the Radicals* (N. Y., 1930); Howard K. Beale, *The Critical Year: A Study of Andrew Johnson and Reconstruction* (N. Y., 1930); James G. Randall, *Constitutional Problems under Lincoln* (N. Y., 1926); F. B. Simkins and R. H. Woody, *South Carolina during Reconstruction* (Chapel Hill, 1932).

[129] See W. H. Stephenson, "The South Lives in History," *The Historical Outlook* (April, 1932).

XVI

BIOGRAPHY

Biographies have always comprised a large part of the literary output in America. In colonial days many of them were sketches of the lives of eminent clergymen, and in the early national period eulogistic prose celebrated the deeds of Revolutionary leaders. New Englanders, Bancroft once observed, were a documentary people, and the diaries and autobiographies they left swelled the volume of this material. New Englanders, removed to other regions, retained the practice of keeping a personal record, and their descendants have followed the tradition. The mind of a typical, intelligent Puritan is disclosed in the diary of Samuel Sewall; the more cosmopolitan eighteenth-century spirit is fully revealed in Franklin's autobiography.

All during the nineteenth century biographies came in great number from the presses, and the current periodicals likewise fed this interest in distinctive personalities. Nathan Sargent, a Whig (later Republican) journalist, famous as "Oliver Oldschool," wrote his memories of *Public Men and Events 1817-1853.*[1] His letters

[1] 2 vols., Phila., 1875.

from Washington, with witty descriptions of Congressional proceedings, were widely published in Northern newspapers before the Civil War. A contemporary from Virginia, Henry A. Wise, left a narrative, *Seven Decades of the Union*,[2] which purported to cover the years 1790 to 1860, but it was mainly concerned with personalities of the Jacksonian period. Wise was a prominent figure in Virginia politics (he served as governor from 1855 to 1859), and his close association with John Tyler was reflected in his eulogistic treatment of the President.

Of first importance in biographical literature in the middle of the century are the works of James Parton. His first significant biography was *The Life and Times of Aaron Burr*,[3] which went far to rehabilitate the duelist whose memory had been execrated since the tragic death of Hamilton. The constructive aspects of Burr's career receive their due recognition from Parton, who tells us that he had examined closely the documents and literature bearing on his subject. In 1860 he brought out his *Life of Andrew Jackson*,[4] which is his finest achievement. In his next work, *The Life and Times of Benjamin Franklin*,[5] he reinforced the picture that Sparks had drawn of a versatile man, famed equally as a philosopher and statesman. Parton, always a Democrat in his sympathies, was drawn to Thomas Jefferson, whom he warmly presented in a biography published in 1874. Contrary to popular impression, Parton was not an uncritical worshiper of American democracy. He rather favored an aristocracy of intellect with democratic sympathies, which explains his natural attachment for Jefferson. In concluding his biography of Jackson, Parton remarks that, notwithstanding the good that Jackson had done, the elevation of the general "to power was a mistake on the

[2] Phila., 1872.
[3] N. Y., 1858.

[4] 3 vols., N. Y.
[5] 2 vols., N. Y., 1864.

part of the people of the United States. The good which he effected has not continued, while the evil which he began remains, has grown more formidable . . . with regard to the corruptions and inefficiency of the government." In Parton's judgment, Jackson was a fighting man and "little more." [6] Better lives of these subjects have been written since his day by students with more material at their disposal, but for a long time the popular conceptions of these departed figures were shaped by Parton's volumes.

The era of the Civil War contributed a number of biographical and autobiographical volumes of the leading figures of these years. That the reading public consumed a vast quantity of such material is attested by the fact that one publishing house alone made over a million dollars from the publication of Civil War books.[7] Grant's *Memoirs,* the most important of this type of publication, and the reminiscences of his contemporaries, John Sherman and James G. Blaine, help us to understand the political history of the postwar decades. Grant's *Memoirs* [8] were written for the most part by Adam Badeau; John Sherman's *Recollections* [9] might well have benefited from such ghost writing. For a better understanding of many of the events of this period Edward L. Pierce gave us a *Memoir and Letters of Charles Sumner* in four volumes (1877-1893). This vast amorphous collection was the source of later studies of Sumner. Some years later, the man who was the martyred hero in the crusade for abolition was commemorated in Oswald Garrison Villard's *John Brown.*[10] The author's inheritance of the antislavery tradition made him a sympathetic student of

[6] III, 694-695.
[7] R. U. Johnson, *Remembered Yesterdays,* p. 190.
[8] 2 vols., N. Y., 1886.
[9] N. Y., 1895.
[10] Boston, 1910.

the abolitionist who had been alternately execrated and ecstatically praised.

Eighteenth-century figures still attracted the biographer, who frequently embalmed his subject in a monumental work running to two or three volumes of the conventional "life and times" pattern. Generally designed to indicate how much the subject of the biography had influenced the times, these works usually failed to show how the milieu had affected their hero. Usually, too, in order to present him most favorably, the biographer "wrote down" the colleagues of his subject. In these biographies there was rarely any attempt artistically to re-create the personality. We get no understanding of the inner man, at times uncertain of himself; whatever character analysis we do get is too often immature. The volumes that these biographers have given us have much of value to the historian, but as contributions to the art of biography they are negligible.

One of the best of these works, though incomplete, is William C. Rives's *Life and Times of James Madison*,[11] in three volumes. It is of the school of Marshall's earlier multivolumed *Washington,* in which the "life" seems to be overwhelmed by the "times." Another of the same genre is *The Life and Public Services of Samuel Adams*,[12] by William V. Wells. Adams's efforts in behalf of the Revolution are given adequate recognition here, particularly his contributions to the technique of revolution in the Committees of Correspondence. *Patrick Henry: Life, Correspondence, and Speeches*,[13] by William W. Henry, glowingly commemorates another Revolutionary figure, although as biography Moses Coit Tyler's shorter work is to be preferred.

More skilled in its construction, and better written

[11] Boston, 1859-1868.
[12] 3 vols., Boston, 1865.
[13] 3 vols., N. Y., 1891.

than most of these books, is *The Life of Albert Gallatin* by Henry Adams. The biography is in one volume (1879), while the papers of the Secretary of the Treasury fill three additional volumes. Although Adams included much of the "times" in his narrative, his artistic sense enabled him to keep in the foreground the character of Gallatin, whose career and personality strongly attracted the biographer. Thomas Paine, a more rabid Republican than Gallatin, finally secured his just deserts at the hands of Moncure D. Conway, in 1892.[14] Not until this publication appeared did a later generation become better acquainted with the work Paine had done in the Revolutionary era in behalf of America. His inspiriting journalism had been largely ignored because of the nineteenth-century reaction against his religious and social heterodoxy. "The filthy little atheist," so contemned by Theodore Roosevelt, was rehabilitated by Conway as the man who fired with a religious fervor the revolutionary zeal of Americans.

Figures of lesser prominence were also memorialized in careful biographies. Among the more valuable of these works is Charles J. Stillé's *Life and Times of John Dickinson*,[15] which reminded a forgetful people of Dickinson's writings in behalf of rebellious America in the 1760's, especially the *Pennsylvania Farmer*. Two other useful studies of this Revolutionary generation are by Kate M. Rowland: *The Life of George Mason*[16] and the *Life of Charles Carroll of Carrollton*.[17] Mason's work in drawing up the Virginia Bill of Rights, the model for later documents, is brought to the attention of the reader, and in the other biography the Catholic signer of the Declaration is presented as a warm and tolerant human being who lived long enough to celebrate the building of America's first railway.

[14] *The Life of Thomas Paine.*
[15] Phila., 1891.
[16] 2 vols., N. Y., 1892.
[17] 2 vols., N. Y., 1898.

With the firmer establishment of biography as a literary form, authors more consciously shaped their narratives to dramatize the lives and to analyze the causes and
nature of their development. Selected incidents in the
lives of individuals were chosen as indices of growth or
decay, and the biographer sought to penetrate the inner-
most recesses of his subject's soul. Sometimes these psychological expeditions were successful, more often they
were stumblings in the dark. In a few instances, where
the materials were plentiful and the talent at hand adequate to use them, we have had contributions of the first
importance to the art of biography without too much
thinning of the historical background. Such have been
Albert J. Beveridge's *Marshall* and *Lincoln,* Allan
Nevins's *Cleveland* and *Hamilton Fish,* and Douglas S.
Freeman's *Lee.*

A product of mature scholarship and ripe understanding is John Spencer Bassett's *Life of Andrew Jackson.*[18] Bassett's familiarity with the period as a historian
gives to this work an authenticity that more lightly
freighted biographies lack. He used a great mass of Jackson's papers [19] that had not been seen by earlier biographers, and from this source shed new light on his public and private career. A leader of a later generation and
on the other side of the political fence, Mark Hanna, is
the subject of an excellent biography by Herbert Croly
(1912). Croly was one of the most stimulating writers
among the liberal school of the era before the World
War, and though opposed to Hanna's way of life, he
wrote a realistic study of the American Warwick.

A favorite with biographers for many years has been
Franklin. Two authors have done very well with him in
recent years: William Cabell Bruce in *Benjamin Frank-*

[18] 2 vols., N. Y., 1911.
[19] These have since been edited by Bassett and J. Franklin Jameson.

lin, Self-Revealed [20] and Bernard Faÿ in *Franklin, The Apostle of Modern Times.*[21] A skillful arrangement of Franklin's writings makes Bruce's work something of a continuation of the autobiography, but Bruce did not forego the function of a critical biographer. Faÿ's volume is a clever dissection of Franklin's intellectual growth and shows him evolving from provincialism to a cosmopolitanism that had no superior in the eighteenth century. Bruce also published a life of John Randolph of Roanoke, in 1922,[22] which made that eccentric a little more understandable.

The most popular American subject has been Abraham Lincoln, and his elusive personality continues to attract the biographer. The conflicting legends that grew up about him even before his death made the task of the biographer who essayed the truth a difficult one indeed. The law partner of Lincoln, William H. Herndon, early began collecting material on his friend's life. In collaboration with Jesse W. Weik, in 1889, he brought out *Abraham Lincoln: The True Story of a Great Life.*[23] Herndon had said that Lincoln's fame would not suffer from the truth and that therefore he would tell an unvarnished story, much of which had unfolded itself before his own eyes. The material on Lincoln as a lawyer and a husband is an original contribution of great value, but that part of Herndon's biography on Lincoln as President is of minor importance.

While Herndon was gathering material on the life of Lincoln, others were also engaged in the same task. Two former secretaries of the President, John G. Nicolay and John Hay, who had lived in the White House, wrote, from the fullness of their love for Lincoln, their tribute. Hay had once told Herndon that Lincoln was the greatest

[20] 2 vols., N. Y., 1917.
[21] Boston, 1929.

[22] 2 vols., N. Y.
[23] 3 vols., Chicago.

character since Christ, and thus we may readily understand the adoration of the biographer. Hay had kept a
diary which in sprightly, clever language told many of
the secrets of the war years. The work of the two secretaries, which came out in 1890, after first appearing in
part in magazine form, was called *Abraham Lincoln, a
History*.[24] Hay told Charles Francis Adams that he and
Nicolay had not "set down a single fact from our personal recollection, nor in the course of those ten volumes
did we quote one word of Lincoln of which we had not a
written memorandum made at the time."[25] The work is
of especial value to the historian for its record of the impact of the war on the White House and its revelation of
many events behind the scenes in the capital.

A work of the keenest insight is Nathaniel W.
Stephenson's *Lincoln*.[26] Stephenson had already published a masterly essay on Lincoln in the *Cambridge History of American Literature,* which analyzed the development of his mind and literary style. The biography emphasizes particularly the mental growth of Lincoln in the
later years of his life, and opens new paths for the ana-
lytical biographer. It treats, too, of the war years, which
had been poorly handled, when at all, by earlier biographers. Stephenson tries to explain those periods of in-
decision in Lincoln's life which alternately marked his
development up to the last phase, in 1862, when he
emerged in his full greatness. Stephenson's volume is one
of the best biographies published in America, written, as
it is, with literary distinction and a sure understanding
of history.

Lincoln might have had his greatest biographer in
Beveridge had the author lived to complete his task. For-

[24] 10 vols., N. Y.
[25] Tyler Dennett, *John Hay,* p. 137.
[26] Indianapolis, 1922.

tunately for us we have at least a part of this work in addition to the finished achievement of his *John Marshall*.

ALBERT J. BEVERIDGE

The name of Albert J. Beveridge stands high in the history of American political life, but it is probable that his firmer reputation will rest on the activities of his later years when he turned biographer. It was while engaged in legal studies in the office of ex-Senator Joseph E. McDonald, in Indianapolis, that Beveridge first became acquainted with the quality of John Marshall's thought. On learning that no satisfactory biography had been written of the Chief Justice, Beveridge decided that some day he would write one. But long years of intense activity in politics were to intervene—years in which he was among the standard bearers of the Progressive movement.

Even in the midst of the exciting days that preceded the birth of the Progressive party, Beveridge had begun serious work on his biography, and he was in fear that politics would distract him from the work. "Confidentially," he wrote to a friend in 1914, "I am in terror that our party will nominate me for Senator. . . . It must not be done. It would mean the absolute and final end of my book—two years of desperately hard work thrown away; and the one real ambition of my life—the writing of a Life of Chief Justice Marshall—completely defeated.[27] Literary pursuits were to engross him more and more, even during the hectic war years, and at the end of the war he was still hard at work on his Marshall. In 1921 a movement was started to put Beveridge back in the Senate, but he hesitated to accept the nomination, because his plans for a Lincoln biography had been formulated. His defeat in the elections of the next year left him free

[27] Claude G. Bowers, *Beveridge and the Progressive Era* (Boston, 1932), p. 449.

to devote himself with customary ardor to the work that he had designed as his masterpiece.

In originally planning the *Marshall,* Beveridge thought of a one-volume work that might appear serially in magazine form. In a letter to his friend, Robert Underwood Johnson, editor of the *Century Magazine,* Beveridge referred to Oliver's treatment of Alexander Hamilton as the model for a similar study of Marshall. "During the last decade," said Beveridge, "the powers of the Nation have been in the public mind much more than they have ever been in our history, excepting only during the Civil War." "For this reason, Marshall's work is coming more and more under public consideration and the public is more and more interested in him every day." [28] Beveridge's proposal for a rather popular biography of Marshall met with little enthusiasm in the *Century* office, and during the next four years politics usurped most of his time. Not until the summer of 1913 did he begin writing the life of Marshall. His conception of the work gradually developed to dimensions that no hurried biography could satisfy. Finally he arrived at the point where he believed (like Marshall himself, writing his biography of Washington) that the life of a public man is but a part of the nation's history which he had helped to create, and therefore must be fitted into the history of that nation. With such a plan in mind the original one-volume biography appeared ludicrously inadequate, and Beveridge soon found himself allotting two volumes to the period before Marshall's Supreme Court service. Two volumes more would be needed for a history and analysis of the great decisions.

In 1917 the first two volumes appeared and, two years later, the remainder of the *Marshall* was published. The counsel of leading students of American history—

[28] *Ibid.,* p. 546; July 10, 1908.

Channing, Jameson, W. C. Ford, Beard, Dodd, and others —had helped Beveridge in his research, as did that of Justice Holmes. Thus when the volumes appeared they bore the stamp of authoritative scholarship. The range of learning is wide and deep and the style has unusual vigor, although at times the work is overwritten. Viscount Haldane wrote appreciatively to Beveridge: "How he [Marshall] developed that Constitution into what was essential for the growth of a very great nation, you have made appear before us. In your hands, the task of Marshall, as well as his solution, grows as a living growth." [29] The book was hailed as one of the greatest biographies in the language, and the Pulitzer Prize and other awards were given to the author. Only one serious blemish mars the work, and that is Beveridge's anti-Jeffersonian bias. Of the Federalist school, he championed a strong central government and disliked Jefferson personally. Critical readers of his manuscript tried to dissuade Beveridge from so harsh a treatment of Jefferson, but he was adamant. Several years later, however, Beveridge finally admitted that if he were to rewrite his *Marshall* he would be less certain in his criticisms of Jefferson.

Volume I of the biography of the Chief Justice, *Frontiersman, Soldier, Lawmaker 1755-1788,* tells of his earlier years, and Beveridge states that Marshall's service in the Revolutionary Army was the "fountain head" of his national thinking,[30] which was further strengthened by his term in the Virginia legislature. In the hundred pages or so devoted to a discussion of the debate on the Federal Constitution, Beveridge points out that Marshall in these arguments stated the elements of most of his "immortal Nationalist opinions." [31] This volume, although it contains a chapter of unnecessary length on the "Life of the People: Community Isolation," was

[29] *Ibid.,* p. 560.
[30] P. 147.
[31] P. 454.

written with perhaps more spirit and interest than the others. It is very dramatic, and, in his pages on the constitutional debate in Virginia, Beveridge makes an important contribution to history as well as to the biography of Marshall. In the second volume, which continues the narrative to 1800, Beveridge speaks of Marshall's political life, and on various occasions the biographer notes the relationship between the thought of Hamilton and Marshall. "Upon Hamilton's constitutional doctrine," says Beveridge, "John Marshall was to place the seal of finality"; and in a note the author writes that "the student of Marshall cannot devote too much attention to Hamilton's great state papers.[32] The chapters on Marshall's part in the X Y Z affair are excellent, and they show how his experiences abroad fortified his American nationalism.

When writing of Marshall's decisions in the third volume (1800-1815), *Conflict and Construction,* Beveridge's emphasis is as much upon their quality as acts of statesmanship as it is upon their character as judicial verdicts. They were "nothing less than state papers and of the first rank," is the judgment of Beveridge. In order to understand the opinions in relation to contemporary events, the biographer found it necessary to include much history. The final volume, 1815-1835, was subtitled "The Building of the Nation," and in speaking of the effects of the Dartmouth College decision Beveridge observes the creation of corporations and the alignment of powerful business interests on the side of nationalism.[33] The opponents of Marshall's nationalism—for example, Spencer Roane of Virginia—are treated with scant respect.[34] In several instances the biographer notes the similarity between the nationalist views of Marshall and Lincoln,[35] and in the decision of *Cohens* v. *Va.* the Chief Justice

32 P. 77 and note 1.　　34 P. 358.
33 IV, 276 ff.　　35 P. 293 and note 3.

blazed "the way for Abraham Lincoln." [36] In describing
Marshall's character, appearance, and intellect, Beveridge wrote that "we must imagine a person very much
like Abraham Lincoln." [37] Thus we can see how inevitable
was the choice of the author's next subject—the later exponent of nationalism.

Plans for another biography were now rapidly being
formulated. For a brief time a life of Taney, Marshall's
successor, was under consideration, but Lincoln had already captured the imagination of Beveridge. To Felix
Frankfurter of Harvard, who had urged a biography of
Taney, Beveridge replied: "All the time I was writing
'Marshall' there was in the back of my head the idea
that the work ought to be continued, but built up around
a character which in itself, is attractive. Up to this time
it seems to me that there was only one such personage—
Abraham Lincoln,—of course." [38] A few months earlier he
had indicated his intention of doing the *Lincoln* in exactly
the manner in which he had done the *Marshall,* and it was
to be likewise a further interpretation of the development
of American nationalism. With great energy Beveridge
turned to the *Lincoln,* and very shortly he made disconcerting discoveries—that people were unwilling to give
him access to papers, and that there was a mythical and
a real Lincoln. Writing to Edward Channing, he said,
after a few months' research: "It is already fairly clear
that the Lincoln of youth, early and middle manhood
showed few signs of the Lincoln of the second inau-
gural." [39]

The more he dug into the material for the *Lincoln*
the greater did his problems become. He was soon convinced that no thoroughgoing biography had yet been
written, and it did not take him long to arrive at the conclusion that the *Lincoln* was far more difficult than the

[36] P. 353.
[37] Pp. 91-92.

[38] Bowers, p. 561; July 11, 1921.
[39] *Ibid.,* p. 565.

Marshall. At first he had intended to pass lightly over the years before Lincoln entered politics; then he found he had to lay a firmer foundation for the later years than existing biographies could give him. But the decision to go minutely into Lincoln's early years disappointed Channing, who was fearful lest Beveridge might not reach the period of Lincoln's later political life. "Lincoln needs someone schooled in affairs and the wiles of politicians to penetrate under his mask and under their masks and tell the truth," said Channing, adding, "You are the man to do it." [40] To Channing's proposal that he do the later career of Lincoln first, Beveridge returned a negative reply. In the vast amount of research that went into the biography, Beveridge learned things about his subject that made him sorry he had undertaken it. He had not the spirit that loved "debunking," but facing the facts as he found them, he could only conclude that Lincoln's legislative career in Illinois was shifty and opportunistic. To his friend, Worthington C. Ford, Beveridge expressed his disappointment: "I wish to the Lord he could have gone straight forward about something or other. Of all uncertain, halting and hesitating conduct, his takes the prize." [41] When he finally came to write the biography, Beveridge said that Lincoln possessed in earlier years "the characteristics of the national politician, a type of which he was to become, excepting only Jefferson, the supreme example." [42]

In the search for the real Lincoln, Beveridge rehabilitated Douglas, who was the object of much defamation by Lincoln worshipers. "It becomes clearer and clearer to me," said Beveridge to Channing, "that the literary Lincolnites had almost a hijacker conspiracy against Douglas—and against any other man of power who for

[40] *Ibid.*, p. 567.   [42] *Abraham Lincoln,* I, 118.
[41] *Ibid.*, p. 569; January 28, 1925.

any cause happened to run counter to their hero; and especially is this true of Douglas.'' [43] The more he studied the material the firmer grew Beveridge's conviction that Douglas was a great man. All of Beveridge's inherited traditions of the virtue of the abolitionists, the slave power's influence in the overthrow of the Missouri Compromise, and other incidents told from the Northern point of view, were rudely jolted. Most of the teachings of his youth on these subjects, concluded Beveridge, were ''bunk'' and were born out of political propaganda. But it was a sorrowful task for Beveridge to write the pages that tore to shreds the fabricated history of his childhood. Steadily he plodded through legislative journals, newspapers, manuscripts, judicial decisions, and other material, until a Lincoln hitherto unknown gradually emerged. For a moment the lure of politics attracted Beveridge again in 1926, when he was proposed for Senator from Indiana. The distraction was only momentary, however, for Beveridge replied to the invitation to run for office: ''I must choose either between the Senate or the 'Lincoln,' and of course I cannot drop the book.'' [44] He did not drop the book, rather he worked at high speed to push to completion his researches on Lincoln's prepresidential years. The next year, however, with the first two volumes nearly ready for publication, Beveridge died. In 1928 these volumes on *Abraham Lincoln, 1809-1858* appeared, under the editorial supervision of Worthington C. Ford.

With infinite care Beveridge had picked his way through the tangled trail of Lincolniana, and his two volumes were longer than they needed to be because of his anxiety to present all the conflicting evidence. The biographer, however, had worked a clearing in the half light, and arrived at his conclusions though with re-

[43] Bowers, p. 571; May 21, 1925.
[44] *Ibid.*, p. 581; to Judge U. Z. Wiley, February 2, 1926.

luctance. "With that strange mingling of caution, secretiveness and craft, which so confounded his opponents and puzzled his supporters in after years," says Beveridge, referring to the Lincoln of 1828-1830, the latter "kept to himself his changed or changing conviction and his purposes." [45] After all his research, Beveridge thought that perhaps no one ever understood Lincoln, "or ever will understand him." [46] At least two decades had passed "before Lincoln showed much, if any, concern about slavery. Never the apostle of a cause, he was to become the perfect interpreter of public thought and feeling and so the instrument of events." [47] Continuing on a later page the thought expressed in this last sentence, Beveridge again speaks of Lincoln, who "by instinct as well as mind . . . understood and responded to the sinuosities, twists and contradictions through which a democracy expresses itself." [48]

The second volume of the *Lincoln* opens with a chapter on "Seeds of War: Abolition Attack and Southern Defence." Herndon, Lincoln's younger law partner, was an abolitionist, and this fact, says Beveridge, "is of the greatest possible moment in the development of Lincoln's opinions, and of the origin of memorable language spoken by him." [49] As for Lincoln himself, few people in the North were more familiar with Southern thought and feeling than he, "nor did any Northern man who was opposed to slavery on principle have a more comprehending sympathy with the Southern people in their racial situation." [50] In tracing the genealogy of Lincoln's ideas, Beveridge notes that in the address at Springfield, 1854, were "all the ideas, or the germs of them, that Lincoln expressed thereafter and up to the time he wrote the

[45] I, 99.
[46] I, 538.
[47] I, 107.

[48] I, 464.
[49] II, 19.
[50] II, 32.

Emancipation Proclamation.'' [51] Thus Beveridge traces the slow, halting development of Lincoln's mind up through the memorable debates with Douglas in 1858. This part of the work had been planned to end with Lincoln's inauguration, 1861, and only with the sudden cessation of the biography was it fully revealed to the world of scholarship how great a loss was caused by Beveridge's death. The Lincoln of the war years would probably have been a noble monument in the hands of Beveridge, who anxiously looked forward to the re-creation of that glorious figure. But that Lincoln still awaits an artist the equal of Beveridge.

Many years elapsed after Irving's life of Washington appeared before another hardy author attempted a large-scale study. In our day Rupert Hughes is making the effort, and to date has published three volumes of his *George Washington*. The first is *The Human Being & the Hero 1732-1762*, the second *The Rebel & the Patriot 1762-1777*, and the third *The Savior of the States, 1777-1781*. Each of the volumes is followed by an afterword in which the author explains his approach and justifies his iconoclasm. What he has tried to do, says Mr. Hughes, ''is to restore an old masterpiece by mopping off the daubs and accretions and letting the original colors shine forth in their variety and brilliance, shadow and radiance.'' [52] He intended to let Washington tell his own story ''as fully as possible in his own words.'' [53] Unlike many earlier biographers, he wished to be scrupulously fair in dealing with Washington's opponents, who had often been vilified by the General's panegyrists. Historians were generally familiar with much of the material presented by Mr. Hughes, but to the average reader it came as something of a shock perhaps to learn of Washington's tempera-

[51] II, 244.
[52] II, 607.

[53] I, 491.

mental outbursts and of his hearty dislike of many of his fellow Americans. In his desire to humanize Washington, Mr. Hughes has on occasion romanticized history and thus drawn upon his head the ire of the critical scholar.[54]

Among the biographers of high standing that are writing today is Claude M. Fuess, whose *Life of Caleb Cushing*[55] helped make clearer the role of this ''scholar-statesman.'' Cushing was an unpopular but courageous man whose diplomatic counsel to the government was of high value. Dr. Fuess is also the author of a scholarly biography of Daniel Webster;[56] more recently his interest was drawn to the career of *Carl Schurz, Reformer*.[57] The evolution of the young radical to the mature man fighting in behalf of liberal principles is sketched with sympathy and an understanding of the historical background.

Gilbert Chinard, a leading student of Franco-American intellectual relations, has written judicious interpretations of *Thomas Jefferson, the Apostle of Americanism*[58] and *Honest John Adams*.[59] Professor Chinard is thoroughly familiar with the unprinted materials on Jefferson and from them and the printed sources (many of which he has himself edited) he has written an enthusiastic study of the American who, in European eyes, best typified his country's ideals. The volume on John Adams is a more restrained bit of writing and is less of a contribution than that on Jefferson. Professor Chinard is temperamentally more interested in the Jefferson mentality than in the Adams mind, and therefore the work on the Virginian has more vitality. In *John Jay, Defender of*

[54] See N. W. Stephenson, "The Romantics and George Washington," *Amer. Hist. Rev.* (January, 1934).

[55] 2 vols., N. Y., 1923.

[56] 2 vols., Boston, 1930.

[57] N. Y., 1932.

[58] Boston, 1929.

[59] Boston, 1933.

Liberty,[60] Frank Monaghan restores a neglected founding father to the position of eminence granted him by his own contemporaries. Jay was a very distinguished contributor to the welfare of the early Republic, and in this excellent biography his contributions are justly assessed.

Figures from the colonial past have attracted comparatively few biographers in recent years. Two of the best works are Kenneth B. Murdock's *Increase Mather, the foremost American Puritan*[61] and *Johnson of the Mohawks: a Biography of Sir William Johnson*[62] by Arthur Pound and Richard E. Day. In a stimulating reinterpretation Professor Murdock frees Mather from many of the aspersions aimed at him by unfriendly critics and shows him to be one of the progressive intellects of his generation. Sir William Johnson's romantic career is more interesting to read about, and the authors give to their volume a lightness of touch that is in keeping with the unconventionality of their subject.

The equally romantic figure of Sam Houston is presented in a racily written narrative, *The Raven,*[63] by Marquis James. The character of Houston is shown developing under the stress and strain of Tennessee politics and frontier conflict until he becomes one of the dominant personalities of his generation. In its entirety Mr. James's work is beautifully formed. Houston's defeated rival for the presidency of the new republic of Texas was Stephen F. Austin, the founder of the American colony in the Southwest. Eugene C. Barker, the leading student of this area, has written a scholarly biography of Austin, whose statesmanship made possible the establishment and continuance of the new community.[64] Houston, unlike many other Southern leaders, was opposed to se-

[60] N. Y., 1935.
[61] Cambridge, 1925.
[62] N. Y., 1930.
[63] Indianapolis, 1929.
[64] *The Life of Stephen F. Austin, Founder of Texas, 1793-1836* (Dallas, 1925).

cession. The growth of the secessionist spirit in the mind
of a versatile Virginian is clearly pictured in *Edmund
Ruffin*,[65] a biography by Avery Craven. A distinguished
reformer, interested particularly in better agricultural
methods, Ruffin's character is representative of the increasing number of individuals who were clamoring for
Southern independence. Another reformer of a different
stripe, a militant abolitionist and champion of social and
intellectual progress, is brilliantly presented in Henry
Steele Commager's *Theodore Parker*.[66] No American was
more aware of the spirit of his time, and he blasted away
at obscurantism and conservatism.

The place of many political leaders has been re-
assessed in numerous biographies in recent years, notably in a series edited by Allan Nevins. One of the best
biographies that has been written by an American is
Henry F. Pringle's *Theodore Roosevelt*.[67] Mr. Pringle
strips Roosevelt of much of the glamour with which he
had been invested by uncritical biographers. Roosevelt's
contemporaries loom up much larger than they appeared
when the blustering President held the center of the
stage. One of those contemporaries, John Hay, has been
rehabilitated in a volume written by Tyler Dennett.[68]
Dr. Dennett shows the important part played by Hay in
the shaping of foreign policy at the turn of the century
and credits him with much that has hitherto been at-
tributed to Roosevelt. In David S. Muzzey's thorough
and unbiased biography of James G. Blaine, *The Plumed
Knight*, the idol of an earlier generation struts before
the reader once more, but the tarnish that his reputation
suffered in life will not wear off in death.

[65] N. Y., 1932.
[66] Boston, 1936.
[67] N. Y., 1931.
[68] *John Hay* (N. Y., 1933).

ALLAN NEVINS

Allan Nevins is one of the most productive historians and biographers in the United States. By editing the diaries of John Quincy Adams, Philip Hone, and President Polk, he has made accessible to a larger audience publications that were difficult to secure. He has also written on the American States during the Revolution, but more recently he has shown special interest in the period since the Civil War. He has written a life of *Fremont, the West's Greatest Adventurer*,[69] which attempts to hold the balance between the excessive praise and detraction of earlier biographers. Professor Nevins includes as much of the account of the period of expansion as is relevant to the career of the pathfinder. In this, as in his other biographies, the author consulted original authorities wherever possible; his use of unpublished sources has enabled him to shed new light on the careers of his subjects, and also to place a number of events in a broader setting. For example, in his *Grover Cleveland: A Study in Courage*,[70] we are given a new understanding of the President's relationship to the Pullman strike and his part in the Venezuela affair.

The theme of Cleveland's courage is constantly kept before the reader, who is reminded that the President's greatness lay "in typical rather than unusual qualities. He had no endowments that thousands of men do not have. He possessed honesty, courage, firmness, independence, and common sense. But he possessed them in a degree that others did not." [71] Cleveland will live in history, says Professor Nevins, "as a strong man, a man of character." In a period of low morality in business and public affairs, Cleveland's rugged honesty and firm attach-

[69] 2 vols., N. Y., 1928.   [71] P. 4.
[70] N. Y., 1932.

ment to his principles invigorated the American people:
"His breach with Tammany caught the public imagination as nothing else could. The groping moral forces that
were slowly gathering strength below the surface, and
were ready to break forth in a powerful movement, demanded a moral hero; and the spectacle of the stolid,
stubborn Cleveland smiting Tammany without thought of
the consequences appealed to it." [72] In his *Abram S.
Hewitt, with Some Account of Peter Cooper* [73] Professor
Nevins again shows how, by a judicious use of private
papers, familiar events may be placed in new perspectives. Among the episodes which are reinterpreted in this
volume is the election of 1876.

Cleveland was one of the outstanding figures in the
period after the Civil War. Of a stature equally impos-
ing was Grant's Secretary of State, Hamilton Fish, who
stands fully revealed in one of Professor Nevins's finest
biographies. Making skillful use of Fish's lengthy diary,
which was kept during the eight years that the Secretary
held office, Professor Nevins has been able to clarify
many events of Grant's administration hitherto incom-
pletely known. It was the great task of Fish to prevent
Grant from being embroiled in foreign complications
over Cuba and Santo Domingo and to restrain Charles
Sumner from wrecking the diplomatic negotiations between the United States and Great Britain. In the second
administration Fish moved among a gang of intriguers
who had the President almost completely under their
control. More than once the Secretary sought release
from office, but it was fortunate that he was not permitted to resign. "Again and again he saved the government from misfortune, once or twice even from disaster."
Hamilton Fish redeemed the character of public servants,
who generally sank in these years to the lowest levels of

[72] P. 126.
[73] N. Y., 1935.

behavior. In each of his biographies Allan Nevins is interested not only in the development of his subject's personality and career; the evolution of the individual is depicted against a broad canvas of contemporary history.

Recently a number of biographers have been attracted by captains of industry, and while many of their productions are slight, some are of real value to historians. One of the best is Kenneth W. Porter's *John Jacob Astor, Business Man*.[74] Issued as the first in a projected series in the "Harvard Studies in Business History," Dr. Porter's work necessarily emphasizes Astor's career in business. Many hitherto unused sources were consulted by the author, and to the student of the West as well as to the economic historian generally, these volumes have proved to be of great value. Another study of a leading industrial figure is that by Burton J. Hendrick, *The Life of Andrew Carnegie*.[75] This contains more personal material than Dr. Porter's *Astor* and is especially good on Carnegie's influence in international politics. It is a very sympathetic presentation of the Scotch-American, whose actions in the Homestead strike of 1892 are defended by the biographer. The economic historian will learn much about the development of the steel industry from Hendrick's pages. A knowledge of how the Middle West grew to be a great farming and industrial center will be enriched by a reading of William T. Hutchinson's *Cyrus Hall McCormick*.[76] This work is of value, also, to the student of politics, for McCormick was an important factor among the Douglas Democrats.

[74] 2 vols., Cambridge, 1931.   [76] 2 vols., N. Y., 1930, 1935.
[75] 2 vols., N. Y., 1932.

Douglas S. Freeman

In 1934 Douglas S. Freeman brought out the first two volumes of his long-awaited biography of Robert E. Lee, and the final two volumes came soon after. Many years of devotion to his task lay behind the biographer, who tells us that he was "privileged to live, as it were, for more than a decade in the company of a great gentleman." "What he seemed, he was—a wholly human gentleman, the essential elements of whose positive character were two and only two, simplicity and spirituality." [77] Mr. Freeman unearthed a vast fund of material dealing with Lee's strategy and he adopted the unusual device of allowing the reader no more knowledge than Lee possessed at the time of any particular battle or campaign. The first volume takes Lee through his schooling at West Point, on through his brilliant services in the Mexican War and then to his soul-searching days in 1861, when he threw in his lot with his beloved State. "His mind was for the Union; his instinct was for his State, Virginia"; "He looked on Virginia much as he did on his family. He did not then or thereafter stop to reason out the nature of this feeling, which was instinctive." [78] He felt sure where his duty lay and after the tragic years of war had passed he still maintained that "if it all were to be done over again, I should act in precisely the same manner." [79] Mr. Freeman dwells on the unfolding of Lee's personality in these years and emphasizes particularly the value of his training in Mexico. "Twenty months of service in Mexico had been ended when Lee saw the castle and the towers of Vera Cruz fade from view, never again to be seen by him. They were probably the twenty most useful months of his training as a soldier. Their effect on him can be seen during nearly the

[77] IV, 494.   [79] I, 447.
[78] I, 416.

whole of the War between the States. The lessons he learned on the road to Mexico City he applied in much of his strategy. Warnings he read in that campaign he never forgot.'' [80]

The second volume takes Lee through the battle of Chancellorsville which ''was undoubtedly the most remarkable victory he ever achieved,'' [81] and leaves him at the high tide of his military fortunes. But the shadow cast by Stonewall Jackson's death is already before his path and one gets the impression that Lee is engaged in a hopeless cause. Especially is this so after Gettysburg, the description of which is a literary masterpiece. The third volume carries on the narrative to the winter of 1864 with Grant still holding on and pressing hard on Lee's diminishing forces. But the men who served under him never faltered in their intense devotion to him: ''He came in their minds not only to represent their cause, but to incarnate it and to idealize it. Proud as was the name of the Army of Northern Virginia, they almost ceased to say that they belonged to that host and spoke of themselves as serving in Lee's army. And by that more personal name, with all the tribute to Lee that it implied, they usually styled the army in familiar conversation till it had become only the glamorous memory of their waning years.'' [82]

The fourth volume is the climax of this moving biography. In the chapter, ''The Ninth of April,'' Mr. Freeman describes the surrender and the reaction of Lee's men to the news: ''Some blasphemed and some babbled, but all who could do so crowded to say farewell to Lee. Catching hold of his hands, they looked up at him and cried the more. They touched his uniform or his bridle rein, if they could not grasp his hand, and if they could not reach him, they smoothed Traveller's flank or patted

[80] I, 294.
[81] III, 3.
[82] III, 239.

his neck. And in a confused roar, half-sob, half-acclama-
tion, they voiced their love for him, their faith in him,
their goodbye to him as their commander." [83] The chapter, "The Sword of Robert E. Lee," is a recapitulation
of the general's military exploits and an excellent analysis of the factors that made for his success as a soldier.

With the war at an end Lee determined to do all in
his power to set the South an example of reconciliation,
and he impressed upon all who spoke and wrote to him
the necessity of reforging a new society. When a correspondent wrote to him about abandoning the country, he
replied that he preferred "to struggle for its restoration
and share its fate, rather than give up all as lost. [Vir-
ginia] has need for all of her sons, and can ill afford to
spare you," he said to Matthew F. Maury.[84] Lee's acceptance of the presidency of Washington College [85] at
a low salary was a stimulus to the men of the South to
adjust themselves to altered conditions. He kept counsel-
ing them that in time injustices would be remedied and
his correspondence had a note of optimism that was
heartening to the discouraged. "More than any other
American, General Lee kept the tragedy of the war from
being a continuing national calamity." [86] One is ready to
believe that the most heroic years of Lee's life were the
five that remained to him after the war. His social vision
at this time marked him as one with unusual foresight
who merited the veneration with which he was followed
in peace as well as in war. It is hard to believe that we
shall ever need another biography of Lee, for Douglas S.
Freeman's work has no superior in the whole range of
American biographical literature.

The most important work in the subject of biography
as a whole is, of course, the *Dictionary of American*

[83] IV, 145.   [85] Later Washington and Lee.
[84] IV, 196, note 18.   [86] IV, 484.

Biography.[87] Scholars have long desired an American counterpart of Great Britain's *Dictionary of National Biography,* but it is only recently, with the publication of the *D.A.B.,* that this wish has been realized. Under the editorial direction of Allen Johnson and later of Dumas Malone, many hundreds of contributors have written the thousands of biographies of the greater and lesser men and women who have shared variously in the making of American civilization.[88] Athletes, Indian chiefs, statesmen, scientists, writers, businessmen, reformers, soldiers, scholars, *et al.,* are the subjects who are treated in these twenty volumes. Many names half-forgotten or almost wholly lost have been rescued, and the reader may now discover easily the facts that were often difficult to unearth. The *Dictionary* will prove a stimulus to further research in the lives of some of these figures, and has already proved a great boon to historical scholars. The best of these sketches are well written, and, having made use of the latest findings of scholarship, they are the most authoritative interpretations of eminent lives available. Naturally no work of such monumental proportions can escape serious criticism. A number of names have been omitted which might better have been included, and some of the sketches seem to have been done by individuals who were unfamiliar with their subjects. More space should have been allotted to labor leaders and to social dissenters in general. But with its weaknesses, the *Dictionary* is far and away the best in America and compares favorably with its European prototypes. It is the latest and one of the best products of co-operative historical scholarship ever published in the United States.[89]

[87] 20 vols., N. Y., 1928-1936.

[88] There are 13,633 biographies written by 2,243 contributors.

[89] Edward H. O'Neill, *A History of American Biography: 1800-1935* (Phila., 1935), will be found helpful.

XVII

CO-OPERATIVE HISTORIES

HUBERT HOWE BANCROFT

Co-operative historical writing was first suggested in the colonial period, and in the early part of the nineteenth century several series of biographies by a number of writers, issued under a single editor, were published. Of the many co-operative works of a historical nature that were projected, few, however, materialized. Not until the second half of the century did publications of this character begin to multiply. One of the first of these, in time and importance, was Hubert Howe Bancroft's history of the Pacific coast.

Bancroft was of New England ancestry, but, like so many others of this migrant stock, he was born in Ohio. Early in life he worked for a bookseller, and in 1858 he founded his own publishing and mercantile firm in San Francisco, whither he had moved. It was at about this time, the garrulous Bancroft tells us in his *Retrospection*,[1] that he began to bring together all the books in his stock on California. He extended his field gradually to

[1] See chapter, "Evolution of a Library."

include the western half of North America from Alaska to Panama, including Mexico and Central America. He collected every scrap of material he could on this territory, made trips everywhere, employing copyists for years to build up the collections, taking down the stories of surviving old pioneers, and buying libraries in Europe and America. After a decade of such extensive and intensive collecting—he gathered some 60,000 volumes in all—Bancroft set to work to write the history of the Coast.[2] Because his training had been exclusively for business, Bancroft remarks, he could apply only business methods to the task of historical composition. "I became satisfied," he said, "that in no other way could anything have been made out of the situation."[3] About a dozen writers worked in Bancroft's library under his managerial direction, and the assignment of credit for the composition of the various volumes is not always an easy matter. Bancroft's own contributions as writer make up some four volumes of the history.[4]

It was Bancroft's original intention to start with Central America, inasmuch as the first of the continental discoveries were made there. But because the natives who occupied the territory before the discoveries played so large a part in the early story of the whole region, he had to give much space to them. Thus there appeared, in 1875, the first of the long series of volumes, *The Native Races of the Pacific States of North America* (five volumes), which anthropologists still find useful. Then over a period of fifteen years came others—*Central America* (three volumes), followed by the *History of Mexico* (six volumes) with a separate publication in two volumes re-

[2] Bancroft, *Works,* Vol. XXXIX, *Literary Industries,* "From Bibliopolist to Bibliophile," p. 197.
[3] *Retrospection,* "Methods of Writing History," p. 328.
[4] W. A. Morris, "The Origin and Authorship of the Bancroft Pacific States Publications; A History of a History," *Oregon Hist. Soc. Quart.,* IV, 287 ff.

served for the *History of the North Mexican States and Texas;* then came the *History of California* (seven volumes), *Arizona and New Mexico* (one volume), the *Northwest Coast* (two volumes), *Oregon* (two volumes), *Washington, Idaho, and Montana* (one volume), *British Columbia* (one volume), *Alaska* (one volume), *Utah* (one volume), *Nevada, Wyoming and Colorado* (one volume). The history *proper* thus embraces twenty-eight volumes. To the reader who wonders at the need for such bulk, Bancroft retorts that his great trouble was how to condense without injuring the work.[5] Subsequent volumes on *Popular Tribunals* and miscellaneous essays, six in number and largely written by himself, nearly complete the catalogue of this group of publications appearing under Bancroft's name; later in life (he died in 1918) he published additional works.

The stamp of the factory system of production that marks Bancroft's work should not make the student insensitive to his real achievement. In the first place he did amass a great collection of material (it eventually went to the University of California at Berkeley), and he also had a vision of a broad historical approach, rarely realized then or since. In an essay on "History Writing,"[6] Bancroft remarks that great men deserve their place in history, but not in the foreground. He urged historians to see how nations originate and develop, to study ecclesiastical as well as civil government, family relationships, "the affinities and antagonisms of class, occupation, and every species of social phenomena," including labor, industry, the arts, the intellect— "in short the progress of man's domination over nature." Perhaps in self-defense Bancroft went on to say that a writer of history need be no genius—"indeed, genius is ordinarily too erratic for faithful plodding"—

[5] Vol. XXXIX, *Literary Industries,* p. 753.
[6] XXXVIII, 84-85.

but he must have good judgment, common sense, broad experience, and a wide range of knowledge.[7] Bancroft did render a great service to historical literature, and his histories, although marred by flaws, are generally dependable.

Bancroft's enterprise was only one of a number of significant co-operative works undertaken in the last quarter of the nineteenth century. Justin Winsor's great "Narrative and Critical History" was pushed to completion in the 1880's, and a series of volumes on the separate "American Commonwealths," edited by Horace E. Scudder, was also published at that time. While some of the volumes of the latter series are poor, others are noteworthy, especially George P. Garrison's *Texas,* and Josiah Royce's *California,* which benefited from Bancroft's collection of materials. Royce, who was professor of philosophy at Harvard, subtitled his volume "A Study of American Character," and in the course of his work punctured many of the bubbles of tradition blown up by earlier chroniclers.

JUSTIN WINSOR

The ferment in historical circles in the two decades following the Civil War indicated that the time was ripe for a synthesis of the materials on American history. Justin Winsor, who had ably edited *The Memorial History of Boston,* a co-operative publication in four volumes, appeared to be a logical choice as editor of a more ambitious work on the entire field of American history. In Channing's judgment, Winsor, at the time of his death in 1897, was the foremost student of American history. Many historians, including Henry Adams, leaned for support upon the capable Winsor. Between 1884 and 1889 the "Narrative and Critical History of America," under

[7] P. 103.

Winsor's editorship, was published in eight volumes, to which thirty-nine writers contributed. The Massachusetts Historical Society was especially active in bringing the work to completion.

The first five volumes contain a history of North and South America to the eighteenth century; Volumes VI and VII are on the *United States of North America, 1763-1850;* the last volume continues with *The Later History of British, Spanish, and Portuguese America.*

Volume I, *Aboriginal America,* reflects the particular interest that students of the mid-nineteenth century had in earliest America. It is a notable characteristic, indicating perhaps an absence of provincialism, that Winsor did not think of America as exclusively the region comprising the United States. In the second volume, *Spanish Explorations and Settlements in America from the fifteenth to the seventeenth century,* Winsor, whose specialty was geography and the early discoveries, gave full rein to his interest. He was rather unfriendly to Columbus, in whose character Winsor discerned "some of the attributes of the small and mean." Edward Channing, then a young historian teaching at Harvard, contributed a chapter on "The Companions of Columbus." Charles Deane, one of the most learned students of early American history, wrote two chapters in Volume III, *English Explorations and Settlements in North America 1497-1689.* Among the contributors to the fourth volume, *French Explorations and Settlements in North America and those of the Portuguese, Dutch, and Swedes,* was John Gilmary Shea, whose studies in American Catholicism qualified him to write authoritatively on the Jesuits. The editor, whose interest in the Mississippi Valley led him in after years to publish several volumes on this section, wrote on Joliet, Marquette, Hennepin, and La Hontan.

An especially bulky volume in this massive series is the fifth, *The English and French in North America 1689-1763*. The lengthiest chapters are the editor's on New England and on "The Struggle for the Great Valleys of North America." In an age of moral certainties Winsor could write with assurance: "The baleful influence of the Mathers . . . conduced to commit the unwary Phips to instituting a court, which disgraced itself by the judicial murders attending the witchcraft frenzy. . . ." Winsor, it may be added, was in heavy debt to Parkman for his treatment of the Anglo-French conflict.

Volume VI, Part I on the United States, is devoted wholly to the American Revolution, with two-thirds of the space on the military and naval aspects of the struggle. "The Revolution Impending," a chapter by Mellen Chamberlain, was a great advance over Bancroft's treatment of the causes of the Revolution, for it laid particular stress on the Navigation Acts. Volume VII, Part II, on the United States, has chapters on American diplomacy, "The History of Political Parties," by Alexander Johnston, and a chapter on the wars which took place during the years 1789-1850. The disinclination of nineteenth-century historians to treat recent history was notorious; the nearest Winsor's history got to mentioning the Civil War was the last line in an eighteen-page chapter on "The Constitution of the United States and its History," by George T. Curtis. These volumes on the United States are perhaps the poorest of the eight. The modern student can get no clearer picture of some of the differences between recent viewpoints on American history, and those of fifty years ago, than by comparing Channing's third, fourth, and fifth volumes with Winsor's sixth and seventh.

With chapters on Canada and Spain in America— one of them written by the English authority on Spanish colonial history, Clements R. Markham—the narrative of Winsor's eighth volume is brought to a close. Then, in an appendix, the editor brings together some of the notes of his vast collection on the sources in manuscript of American history, with particular reference to the Revolution. There is added, too, a list of printed authorities upon the history of the United States.

The reader of today hesitates to acquaint himself with the forbidding volumes of the "Narrative and Critical History." The writing of Winsor himself bears the mark of hasty composition and decidedly lacks grace. Although the work, at the time of publication in the 1880's, indicated the approach of scholars to their own history, it was not representative of the interests of the younger group of historians. They pointed to the preponderance of material on the period of discovery and exploration, and noted also that the narrative did not extend beyond 1850. In "the editor's final statement" Winsor said that, "when he undertook this History," his purpose was "to add a distinctly critical treatment to the combined authorship." He disclaimed any intention of offering "a model for the general writing of history, based on a co-operative and critical method. There is no substitute for the individuality of an historian," he remarked. Winsor suggested that one great value of works of this nature was to make accessible to students a summary of scattered material and to furnish them with a guide to the sources. Each chapter is accompanied by editorial notes and a critical essay on bibliography. To judge by the mere mass of the notes one might say that it was these that were accompanied by the narrative chapters. As a matter of fact, it is the notes that still earn Winsor's volumes a place on the student's shelf. They unearthed a great treasure for historians fifty years ago and they are still the open sesame for many subjects on American history. Winsor, said Channing in gratitude, "made the scientific study of American history possible by making available the rich mines of material." [8]

Another series of importance was that entitled "American Statesmen," edited by John T. Morse, in thirty-nine volumes (the fortieth was the index). In a reminiscent mood, Morse tells us that a reading of Morley's English "Men of Letters" series suggested a like work for American statesmen. Morse had a difficult time before he finally succeeded in interesting a publisher. The principle he adopted was to select those subjects whose careers might furnish the reader with a view of the development of the country. Morse himself wrote five of the biographies, including those of John Adams and John Quincy Adams, while Moses Coit Tyler did a splendid piece of work on Patrick Henry. Sometimes editorial arrangements went astray; Carl Schurz, for example, angered Morse by turning in two volumes instead of one on Henry Clay, but the editor learned to like Schurz's work and his judgment was vindicated by the approbation that has ever since favored this biography. Henry Cabot Lodge took an active interest in the series and asked that Theodore Roosevelt, who needed the money, be permitted to do Gouverneur Morris; the request was granted although such a volume was not originally contemplated. Morse had difficulty in getting Charles Francis Adams to do the biography of his father, minister to England, but the son finally agreed, and the volume was very well received. In fact the series in general was both a scholarly and a commercial success. [9]

At the turn of the century many of the younger scholars, dissatisfied with the existing state of historical writing and feeling the need for a work that would summarize the latest findings, were brought together to produce the "American Nation" series.

[8] Edward Channing on "Justin Winsor," in *Amer. Hist. Rev.*, Vol. III.
[9] J. T. Morse in Mass. Hist. Soc. *Proc.*, LXIV, 370-388.

The "American Nation" Series

"The American Nation, A History," a series edited by Albert Bushnell Hart, represents the work of the first generation of trained American scholarship. The previous generation that had co-operated to produce Winsor's "Narrative and Critical History of America" was a mixture of the old and the new; predominant among them were skilled amateurs, to whom history was an avocation. In 1898, Professor Hart, writing on "The Historical Opportunity in America," said that a fundamental need was a "proper general history of the United States," which he thought that a co-operative work might possibly fill.[10]

The twenty-seven volumes of the "American Nation" series were published between 1904 and 1908; a volume on the most recent period appeared some years afterward. The editor introduced the series by remarking that no one would deny "that a new history of the United States is needed, extending from the discovery down to the present time." "No such comprehensive work by a competent writer is now in existence," Professor Hart added. Restricted fields, treated chronologically, had been handled by individual authors. "Meantime there is a rapid increase of published sources and of serviceable monographs based on material hitherto unused. On the one side there is a necessity for an intelligent summarizing of the present knowledge of American history by trained specialists; on the other hand there is need of a complete work, written in untechnical style, which shall serve for the instruction and the entertainment of the general reader." The co-operative method was the only one that could meet the problems involved. Although several European historical enterprises had employed

[10] *Amer. Hist. Rev.* (October, 1898), p. 13.

the division of labor, "this is the first attempt to carry out that system on a large scale for the whole of the United States," the editor asserted.

The historian was to tell what had been done, and also what had been planned by the leaders in public life. Thus the work was intended to describe the personalities "who have stood forth as leaders and seers; not simply the founders of commonwealths or the statesmen of the republic, but also the great divines, the inspiring writers, and the captains of industry." These volumes were to be something more than political or constitutional history; they must include, said the editor, "the social life of the people, their religion, their literature, and their schools . . . their economic life, occupations, labor systems, and organizations of capital." Wars and diplomacy were also to be treated by the historians, whose volumes were to be written from original sources. A bibliographical essay was appended to each volume.

The series is divided into five groups: the first, "foundations of the nation," includes five volumes that carry the story to about the end of the seventeenth century; group two, "transformation into a nation," begins with *Provincial America,* by Evarts B. Greene, and concludes with *The Confederation and the Constitution,* by Andrew C. McLaughlin, which is Volume X; the next group, the "development of the nation," reaches down through *Jacksonian Democracy,* by William MacDonald, and includes the excellent *Rise of the New West,* by Frederick J. Turner. These earlier volumes, on the whole, present a continuous narrative, well proportioned, and are, as a group, superior to the later ones. Group four, "trial of nationality," is disproportionately devoted to the Civil War, although it contains a very good volume by George P. Garrison. The last group, on "national expansion," is scarcely adequate to meet its promise, although it does include the valuable *Reconstruction, Political and Economic,* by William A. Dunning.

Volume I, by Edward P. Cheyney, is titled *European Background of American History.* At the time of its publication many readers were probably surprised to read in the author's preface that "the history of America is a branch of that of Europe." Professor Cheyney presented much fresh material in his volume; perhaps one of the most important of his chapters is that on "The System of Chartered Commercial Companies (1550-1700)." *Spain in America,* by Edward G. Bourne, one of the finest books in the series, naturally deals more with Latin America than with Anglo-America. This volume follows consecutively that of Professor Cheyney, and one would expect to find in it such chapters as "Spanish Emigration to America (1500-1600)," and "The Transmission of European Culture (1493-1821)." *Colonial Self-Government 1652-1689,* by Charles M. Andrews, deals with the separate colonies, and also represents the author's own findings on the Navigation Acts and the problem of imperial administration. Many of the ideas presented in this volume were novel to historians and general readers alike in the first years of the twentieth century. Two closing chapters insufficiently explore the "Social and Religious Life in the Colonies 1652-1689," and "Commercial and Economic Conditions in the Colonies (1652-1689)," although this last, when it was written, was very good.

Before Professor Greene wrote his volume, the period from 1689 to 1740 was known as "the forgotten half century." The historians Bancroft and Hildreth had not treated this later period with as much detail as the earlier years, so that not even a general background was available for the student of the first half of the eighteenth century. "Scholars generally agree that the subject matter of this volume has never been adequately treated as a whole,'' wrote the author. The interest of this period, he rightly asserts, ''lies rather in the aggregate of small transactions, constituting what are called general tendencies, which gradually and obscurely prepare the way for the more striking but not necessarily more important periods of decisive conflict and revolution.'' Two outstanding features characterized the history of these years: the first was a great expansion in the area of settlement, and in industry and commerce; the second was ''the interaction of imperial and provincial interests.'' There is more of social history in this volume than in most of the others in the series.

The passage of time, with new perspectives and additional materials, has made more obsolete those volumes on the Revolution than those on some of the earlier periods. Claude H. Van Tyne, who wrote *The American Revolution,* turned to this subject again in later years and published two excellent volumes embodying the latest research. Van Tyne made use of newly discovered materials on the revolutionary era, of which he had an unrivaled knowledge. Andrew C. McLaughlin did a valuable service in pointing out that the Confederation ''was more creditable to the men of that time than posterity has been willing to allow . . . from its mistakes the framers of the Constitution learned wisdom.'' In the author's eyes his chapters on ''Proposals to alter the Articles of Confederation'' and ''The Law and the Land'' are the most important in his book. This is but one of the volumes on constitutional history that Professor McLaughlin has published as a result of many years of close study. He recently summarized his studies in *A Constitutional History of the United States.*[11]

John S. Bassett's volume on *The Federalist System* describes the successful establishment of the new gov-

[11] N. Y., 1935.

ernment, the organization of the Republican party, and the difficult problems faced by the young Republic in adhering to neutrality in the era of the French Revolution. The question of antislavery is also discussed for its bearing on the growth of sectionalism. Bassett quite fairly credits the Federalists with a great achievement in launching the new nation. Edward Channing's *The Jeffersonian System* had the benefit of the prior publication of Henry Adams's work, but, of course, independent research went into its composition. A useful volume on the mid-nineteenth-century period is George P. Garrison's *Westward Extension*. It is the West beyond the Mississippi that he describes, the causes for its settlement and the development of sectionalism. Garrison was one of the comparatively few Western scholars of this period whose researches had made important contributions to American historical knowledge. The standard of Dunning's *Reconstruction* was not maintained in the books on the Civil War nor in the remaining volumes.

For its services in co-ordinating the contributions of many different authors and in presenting the latest results of American scholarship, the series received then, and still receives, the gratitude of students. A work of this magnitude, however, was expected to contain not only the summing up of the results of one period of research but also a forecast of the period to come. This it failed to do. In the main the work follows conventional lines of political history in chronological sequence with a chapter or two of "social" history thrown in as a sort of concession to the younger element in historical circles. When Hart called for a general history in 1898, he had pointed out that one of the most serious failings in scholarship was an insufficient knowledge of social history. The volumes he edited, however, did not go far to remedy that omission. In general, the facts were there, but little attempt at interpretation was made. And yet the "American Nation'' was unquestionably a stimulus to historical writing, for it showed the many gaps that needed to be filled. It also improved the writing of those textbooks whose authors found in Professor Hart's series short cuts to knowledge.

OTHER CO-OPERATIVE WORKS

Contemporaneous with the better-known ''American Nation'' series was ''The History of North America,'' [12] edited by Guy Carleton Lee and Francis N. Thorpe. Some of the volumes deserve more consideration than they have been given, particularly William B. Munro's *Canada and British North America* (Vol. XI) and Philip A. Bruce's *The Rise of the New South* (Vol. XVII). In its sections on the United States this series sought to give more space to the South, assigning, for example, a whole volume to the Civil War from a Southern standpoint (Vol. XIV).

A co-operative work more specifically the expression of Southern consciousness, and a reflection of the widening interest in its history, was ''The South in the Building of the Nation.'' [13] Although there are no footnotes, a bibliography is appended to each chapter; the scholarship of some of the writers insures the high quality of their contributions. Philip A. Bruce wrote on Virginia, Bernard C. Steiner on Maryland, William K. Boyd and J. G. de Roulhac Hamilton on North Carolina, Ulrich B. Phillips on Georgia and Walter L. Fleming on Alabama. The writers looked upon the South as something of a distinct political and economic unit, ''with an interrelated and separate history.'' The eleven States that organized the Confederacy, the border States of Kentucky, Maryland, and Missouri, and the State of West Virginia

[12] 20 vols., 1903-1907.
[13] 12 vols. and index vol., 1909; XI and XII are volumes of biography.

fall within the scope of the history, whose justification is that "no true history of the South has been written."

The fourth volume is on the South as a whole, and Part IV, "The South in Federal Politics," is a valuable contribution. Volume V, economic history from 1607 to 1865, was the first comprehensive attempt to compile information on economic development in the South since De Bow's work in 1852. This fifth volume and the sixth, on economic history from 1865 to 1909, were largely breaking new ground in research. In the former volume, John H. Latané wrote a useful section on "The Economic Causes of the Civil War," which redirected attention too long focused on the constitutional and moral aspects of the struggle. The series was broad enough to include volumes on the intellectual life of the South and one, the tenth, on its social life; the latter refers not only to the upper classes but to other groups as well, native and immigrant. Students wishing quick access to material on the South might still use these volumes with profit.

A series of interest to the scholar and the layman alike was edited by Allen Johnson under the title of "The Chronicles of America." Published in fifty small volumes and modeled on the chronicles of old England, which had presented her history in dramatic form, this series was expected to do a similar service for America. Although its main appeal was to the layman, a number of the volumes in the series contain the concentrated essence of much special research and continue to be useful to the student. The first group of ten volumes includes two by Charles M. Andrews (his *Colonial Folkways* is notable), while in the next group, covering the Revolutionary period, are the thoughtful *Eve of the Revolution,* by Carl Becker, and Max Farrand's *Fathers of the Constitution.* Dr. Farrand's vast erudition in this field makes him well qualified to write this volume. The next group of volumes purports to carry the history of the country to the Civil

War. One of the most important contributions is William E. Dodd's *Cotton Kingdom;* others of especial value are those by Nathaniel W. Stephenson. A group of volumes attempts to deal with social and economic history apart from politics (e.g., John Moody's two on business and railroads), and other volumes contain the history of the United States since the Civil War. To the latter group valuable contributions were made by Holland Thompson, who wrote *The New South,* and Solon J. Buck, who told of the Populist movement in *The Agrarian Crusade.* A volume on Canada and another on Hispanic America, by William R. Shepherd, complete the series. Although well written generally, the series as a whole gives the reader a rather disjointed view of American history, as chronicles usually do when there is no relationship among the facts chronicled. In some respects several of the volumes are more useful to the student than to the lay reader because their generalizations are based on knowledge assumed to be in the reader's possession.

"THE HISTORY OF AMERICAN LIFE" SERIES

The importance of including more of a people's activities than politics and war in a historical narrative was granted long since, and individual and co-operative histories had frequently adopted this principle. A vigorous proponent of the "new history," as a record of the culture of a people, was Edward Eggleston, who had already attained fame as the author of *The Hoosier Schoolmaster*. He had been interested in historical fiction and it was an easy transition for him to study and write history for its own sake. He planned a series of volumes to constitute a history of American life—the sources of its ideas and habits and the course of their development. "It will be a work," he said, "designed to answer the questions 'How?' and 'Whence?' and 'Why?'" Unfortunately Eggleston lived to finish only two volumes, *The Beginners of a Nation* (1896) and *The Transit of Civilization* (1901), which covered less than half of the seventeenth century. Because his work is incomplete, Eggleston's volumes are not as well known as they should be. They are informative and are better written than most books on American history. Eggleston, opposed as he was to "drum and trumpet" history, had a strong influence on the younger generation of scholars, who saw in his volumes an excellent example of social history written with charm and coherence.[14]

It remained however for "The History of American Life," under the editorship of Dixon Ryan Fox and Arthur Meier Schlesinger, to swing over wholly to the position that politics might be almost entirely neglected in a narrative. A series of twelve volumes was projected, of which ten have been published thus far; illustrations and bibliographies are important features of this publication. Herbert I. Priestley wrote *The Coming of the White Man 1492-1848,* making special reference to the French and Spanish settlements, and noting the existence of a rich Spanish culture long before the English colonies were established. In the last two chapters the Dutch and Swedes are included, and Professor Priestley gives a very sensible estimate of the Dutch heritage in American life. Thomas J. Wertenbaker, in the next volume, writes on *The First Americans,* which covers the seventeenth century to about 1690, at which point James Truslow Adams continues the social history of the colonies to about 1760 in a volume on *Provincial Society.* After a gap of two unpublished volumes, Carl Russell Fish's *The Rise of the Common Man* continues the story of the

[14] See his presidential address before the American Historical Association, "The New History," *Ann. Rep.* of the Amer. Hist. Assn. for the year 1900, Vol. I.

development of American civilization. Arthur C. Cole's *The Irrepressible Conflict* then carries the narrative through the Civil War. The two succeeding volumes, by Allan Nevins on *The Emergence of Modern America* and Arthur M. Schlesinger on *The Rise of the City 1878-1898,* cover the period of economic and social reconstruction and expansion; a volume by Ida Tarbell, *The Nationalizing of Business 1878-1898,* deals specifically with economic development. Harold U. Faulkner's *The Quest for Social Justice* is filled with the successes and failures of the liberal movement (1898-1914) and the abandonment of *laissez faire,* while Preston W. Slosson's *The Great Crusade and After 1914-1928* continues the narrative to the time of publication. The war and postwar years with their exhilaration and their disillusionment are the theme of this volume, which contains many of the facts but which is weak in interpretation.

In truth the weakness of most of the volumes is a lack of comment on what the facts mean; around some of these volumes clings the atmosphere of a catalogue. The historian may not be sure what the facts mean, but he is not absolved from some attempt at interpretation. Although it would have been possible to write each one of these volumes with a different set of facts, the ones selected do give a picture of what was happening in the life of American society. The whole question of the proper scope of social history is filled with controversial elements, and the problem of relative emphasis on the materials involved is not easy of solution.

Co-operative histories on specialized fields have proved of great value to the general historian. One of this type, the "American Church History" series, edited by Philip Schaff and others, has long been in use. It was published in thirteen volumes (1893-1901) of which the first, Henry K. Carroll's *The Religious Forces of the United States,* covers all religions. Two of the best volumes in the series are Williston Walker's on the Congregational Church and Edward T. Corwin's on the Dutch Reformed Church.[15]

Another useful specialized work is the "American Secretaries of State," in ten volumes under the editorship of Samuel Flagg Bemis. Several of these biographies (which are usually favorable to their subjects) are generally included in one volume: for example, the last contains the lives of Bryan, Lansing, Colby, and Hughes. The earlier volumes on the whole are much better than the later ones, for the materials are more abundant and it is possible to be more definite in describing the events and policies connected with the names of the older secretaries of state. H. Barrett Learned's biography of William L. Marcy is one of the best in the series. Despite the value of such a publication it is obvious that its usefulness would have been much enhanced had the biographers included a study of the interrelationship of diplomacy with public opinion. As the biographies now stand they have too much the appearance of pictures of men in isolated offices divorced from the everyday world.

One of the works of greatest value to the general historian is the *Cambridge History of American Literature*.[16] It was modeled on the English publication, and it was the intention of the editors to make it "a survey of the life of the American people as expressed in their writings rather than a history of belles-lettres alone." Travels, oratory, memoirs, philosophy, newspapers, histories (the last well summarized by John Spencer Bassett) are all included as departments of literature. The final volume includes chapters on economists, scholars, book publishing, non-English writing done in America, and a lengthy bibliography covering the whole work. The fact that these volumes, edited by professors of literature

[15] The latter also includes other groups.
[16] 4 vols., N. Y., 1917-1921.

—William P. Trent, John Erskine, Stuart P. Sherman, and Carl Van Doren—have been widely used by historians is one illustration of the process by which scholars have been erasing boundary lines of departmentalized knowledge.

Under the auspices of the Carnegie Institution of Washington, several works of an extremely valuable character to the economic historian have appeared. They have covered industry, agriculture, and transportation, and while they are not for the general reader, the historian has benefited greatly from their accumulation of facts and from their bibliographies. Emory R. Johnson and his collaborators are responsible for the *History of Domestic and Foreign Commerce of the United States.*[17] The first volume contains the data on American commerce to 1789, although the section on internal commerce runs on to a later date. In the second volume is to be found a treatment of American fisheries, as well as a discussion of government aid and commercial policy. The *History of Manufactures in the United States,* prepared by Victor S. Clark, is in two volumes, divided at 1860. A tremendous amount of research went into this publication, which follows the topical method. The first volume is smoother, but the second volume contains interpretive chapters and summary conclusions which add to the value of this work. The *History of Transportation in the United States before 1860* was compiled by Balthasar H. Meyer, Caroline E. MacGill, and others. Agriculture in the North and South has been accorded separate treatment in the *History of Agriculture in the Northern United States, 1620-1860* (1925) by Percy W. Bidwell and John I. Falconer, and in *The History of Southern Agriculture to 1860,*[18] by Lewis C. Gray and Esther K. Thompson. The work on Southern agriculture is one of

[17] 2 vols., 1915.
[18] 2 vols., 1933.

the finest collections of economic materials available to the historian. Part VII, "Geographical Expansion and Regional Development," is of particular significance for the student of the middle period.

The *History of Labour in the United States,* recently completed in four volumes, is the standard work in its field. It is written by a group of scholars, trained for the most part by John R. Commons at the University of Wisconsin. Professor Commons has been engaged for many years in securing more liberal labor conditions, not only in Wisconsin but elsewhere in the United States. The two volumes published in 1918 carry the narrative to the 1890's; the two published in 1935 conclude with the inauguration of the New Deal.

The basis of the first two volumes had been laid in the publication of the "Documentary History of American Industrial Society" edited by Professor Commons.[19] The latter contained valuable introductions to the documentary materials, but a comprehensive narrative on American labor was lacking until 1918. The story of labor before the Civil War is not so well done as the later period; more abundant materials and the greater intensity of research expended upon them accounts for this unevenness.

The third volume contains a good section on "Working Conditions" by Don D. Lescohier, and a contribution of great value on "Labor Legislation" by Elizabeth Brandeis. The fourth volume, *Labor Movements,* by Selig Perlman and Philip Taft, picks up the story of organized labor's development since the late 1890's. Professor Commons, in his editorial introduction, points to the differences between the two periods covered by the earlier and later volumes. In the former, he says, "we dealt with a period of employer capitalism, where the employer and the wage-earner were rather closely connected in the

[19] 10 vols., 1910.

same localities. But this [latter] is a period when the owners of industry are absentee stock and bond holders.'' The long tale of conflict between capital and labor justifies the conclusion that ''American labor history has been principally a fighting history.'' [20]

A vast amount of material has been brought together in these volumes but it is not always well integrated, a failing common in books of combined authorship. The point of view consistently maintained is the editor's— an emphasis on American experimentalism in the adjustment to new conditions, with a distinct aversion to doctrinaire positions. American labor, so runs the argument, should get what it can when it can and not wait for its improvement upon the creation of some Utopia.

Conclusion

That each generation views the story of an earlier day in its own image is a truism long accepted. Among a people with intense conviction of direct relationship with God a testament of deeds done for the Lord's service was history. When the nation became proudly conscious of its unique place in the system of world governments and of its growing strength, a record of deeds done for the country's good became history—political history. In the interpretation of the past the historian was usually swayed by his party convictions, so that our political histories generally may be divided into two schools, Jeffersonian or Hamiltonian.

The personal flavor communicated to his writing by an individual such as Bancroft, for example, became less acceptable in an age preferring an author's anonymity achieved by means of a façade of ''scientific,'' ''objective,'' scholarship. And because modern science demands

[20] IV, 623.

organization, and historical scholars claimed—or at least sought—scientific standing, they organized, founding associations, journals, and the like, for the accumulation and dissemination of data on which scientific generalizations were to rest. The artist was a lost individual in a group of collective artisans who became entombed in their own labyrinth. The worship of foreign scholarship that returned Americans practiced made many of them oblivious to the continuity of a sound tradition in native historical scholarship which reached back to the eighteenth century. Important as was the contribution to teaching and writing made by the European-trained men of the 1870's and 1880's, they depreciated earlier American scholarship, thus obscuring its genuine value.

It should be remembered that the early historian had to depend mainly on his own ingenuity in gathering materials, and the quality of his achievement was measured by his personal resources, both intellectual and material. When the circle of students of history grew larger a historian might levy upon his fellows for aid to scholarship, but, on the whole, his remained a pioneer effort. With the accumulation of wealth came the opportunity to gather libraries of great value; only a Bancroft had at his command riches that today in public collections are accessible to the humblest student. But the tradition of individual enterprise in history was paralleled by an equally early tradition of public support, as the grants of Massachusetts to Hubbard, and New Hampshire to Belknap, indicate. The greater resources of the national government in the early nineteenth century were drawn upon in aiding Sparks and Peter Force, and in our own time a Federal archivist has been appointed.

The emphasis once given to political democracy was later shifted to social and industrial democracy and the wider vistas opened to the historian enlarged the scope of his research. But his problems, too, were thereby multiplied. It was a comparatively easy thing to keep a narrative of political and military history moving in a chronological sequence with dramatic moments interspersed here and there. It was not so easy to depict within a narrow range of time a steady movement of all the events, manners, customs, ideas, and the like, which are embraced in the data called social history. Civilization thus depicted appeared static, whereas the historian's premise demanded dynamism. Moreover, he was convinced of a progressive movement, for the eighteenth-century idea of progress has permeated the whole of historical writing. But how make a moving narrative from events that seem to stand still or which, by accepted standards, are even retrogressive? Faced with this dilemma the historian resorts to description, crowding as much data together as his conscience and publisher will allow, to reproduce the character of the period in which he is interested. Interpretation is condescendingly left to the "philosophic" historian, who is generally credited with knowing more philosophy than history.

A surfeit of merely descriptive material, however, often leads to intellectual indigestion and not to wisdom, and the reader is now asking that the historian cease merely to photograph, but to try also to penetrate beneath the surface of past events, to find, if possible, a meaning in them. Even when "scientific" historians were protesting most strongly their objectivity, the reader could detect a line of interpretation. The difficulties inherent in finding clues that spell meanings in past events are granted, but the task laid on the historian is inescapable. From the vantage point of a world already troubled enough and groping to understand its present status, the view of the past is likely to be uncertain, perhaps chaotic, but the historian is once again called upon to read the past as a guide post to the future.

INDEX